BENEDICT DE SPINOZA

ON THE IMPROVEMENT OF THE UNDERSTANDING

THE ETHICS

CORRESPONDENCE

Translated from the Latin
With an Introduction by

R. H. M. ELWES

DOVER PUBLICATIONS, INC.
NEW YORK

Published in Canada by General Publishing Company, Ltd., 30 Lesmill Road, Don Mills, Toronto, Ontario.

Published in the United Kingdom by Constable and Company, Ltd.

This Dover edition, first published in 1955 under the title *Works of Spinoza,* Volume II, is an unabridged and unaltered republication of the Bohn Library edition originally published by George Bell and Sons in 1883.

International Standard Book Number: 0-486-20250-X
Library of Congress Catalog Card Number: 55-2221

Manufactured in the United States of America
Dover Publications, Inc., 31 East 2nd Street
Mineola, N.Y. 11501

CONTENTS

ON THE IMPROVEMENT OF THE UNDERSTANDING

THE ETHICS

CORRESPONDENCE

ON THE IMPROVEMENT OF THE UNDERSTANDING.

AFTER experience had taught me that all the usual surroundings of social life are vain and futile; seeing that none of the objects of my fears contained in themselves anything either good or bad, except in so far as the mind is affected by them, I finally resolved to inquire whether there might be some real good having power to communicate itself, which would affect the mind singly, to the exclusion of all else: whether, in fact, there might be anything of which the discovery and attainment would enable me to enjoy continuous, supreme, and unending happiness. I say "I *finally* resolved," for at first sight it seemed unwise willingly to lose hold on what was sure for the sake of something then uncertain. I could see the benefits which are acquired through fame and riches, and that I should be obliged to abandon the quest of such objects, if I seriously devoted myself to the search for something different and new. I perceived that if true happiness chanced to be placed in the former I should necessarily miss it; while if, on the other hand, it were not so placed, and I gave them my whole attention, I should equally fail.

I therefore debated whether it would not be possible to arrive at the new principle, or at any rate at a certainty concerning its existence, without changing the conduct and usual plan of my life; with this end in view I made many efforts, but in vain. For the ordinary surroundings of life which are esteemed by men (as their actions testify) to be the highest good, may be classed under the three heads—Riches, Fame, and the Pleasures of Sense: with these three the mind is so absorbed that it has little power to reflect on any different good. By sensual pleasure the mind is enthralled to the extent of quiescence, as if the supreme good were actually attained, so that it is quite incapable of thinking of any other object; when such pleasure has been gratified it is followed by extreme melancholy, whereby the mind, though not enthralled, is disturbed and dulled.

The pursuit of honours and riches is likewise very absorbing, especially if such objects be sought simply for their own sake[1],inasmuch as they are then supposed to constitute the highest good. In the case of fame the mind is still more absorbed, for fame is conceived as always good for its own sake, and as the ultimate end to which all actions are directed. Further, the attainment of riches and fame is not followed as in the case of sensual pleasures by repentance, but, the more we acquire, the greater is our delight, and, consequently, the more are we incited to increase both the one and the other; on the other hand, if our hopes happen to be frustrated we are plunged into the deepest sadness. Fame has the further drawback that it compels its votaries to order their lives according to the opinions of their fellow-men, shunning what they usually shun, and seeking what they usually seek.

When I saw that all these ordinary objects of desire would be obstacles in the way of a search for something different and new—nay, that they were so opposed thereto, that either they or it would have to be abandoned, I was forced to inquire which would prove the most useful to me: for, as I say, I seemed to be willingly losing hold on a sure good for the sake of something uncertain. However, after I had reflected on the matter, I came in the first place to the conclusion that by abandoning the ordinary objects of pursuit, and betaking myself to a new quest, I should be leaving a good, uncertain by reason of its own nature, as may be gathered from what has been said, for the sake of a good not uncertain in its nature (for I sought for a fixed good), but only in the possibility of its attainment.

Further reflection convinced me, that if I could really get to the root of the matter I should be leaving certain evils for a certain good. I thus perceived that I was in a state of great peril, and I compelled myself to seek with all my

[1] See NOTE, p. 41.

strength for a remedy, however uncertain it might be; as a sick man struggling with a deadly disease, when he sees that death will surely be upon him unless a remedy be found, is compelled to seek such a remedy with all his strength, inasmuch as his whole hope lies therein. All the objects pursued by the multitude not only bring no remedy that tends to preserve our being, but even act as hindrances, causing the death not seldom of those who possess them, and always of those who are possessed by them.[1] There are many examples of men who have suffered persecution even to death for the sake of their riches, and of men who in pursuit of wealth have exposed themselves to so many dangers, that they have paid away their life as a penalty for their folly. Examples are no less numerous of men, who have endured the utmost wretchedness for the sake of gaining or preserving their reputation. Lastly, there are innumerable cases of men, who have hastened their death through over-indulgence in sensual pleasure. All these evils seem to have arisen from the fact, that happiness or unhappiness is made wholly to depend on the quality of the object which we love. When a thing is not loved, no quarrels will arise concerning it—no sadness will be felt if it perishes—no envy if it is possessed by another—no fear, no hatred, in short no disturbances of the mind. All these arise from the love of what is perishable, such as the objects already mentioned. But love towards a thing eternal and infinite feeds the mind wholly with joy, and is itself unmingled with any sadness, wherefore it is greatly to be desired and sought for with all our strength. Yet it was not at random that I used the words, "If I could go to the root of the matter," for, though what I have urged was perfectly clear to my mind, I could not forthwith lay aside all love of riches, sensual enjoyment, and fame. One thing was evident, namely, that while my mind was employed with these thoughts it turned away from its former objects of desire, and seriously considered the search for a new principle; this state of things was a great comfort to me, for I perceived that the evils were not such as to resist all remedies. Although these intervals were at first rare, and

[1] These considerations should be set forth more precisely.

of very short duration, yet afterwards, as the true good became more and more discernible to me, they became more frequent and more lasting; especially after I had recognized that the acquisition of wealth, sensual pleasure, or fame, is only a hindrance, so long as they are sought as ends not as means; if they be sought as means, they will be under restraint, and, far from being hindrances, will further not a little the end for which they are sought, as I will show in due time.

I will here only briefly state what I mean by true good, and also what is the nature of the highest good. In order that this may be rightly understood, we must bear in mind that the terms good and evil are only applied relatively, so that the same thing may be called both good and bad, according to the relations in view, in the same way as it may be called perfect or imperfect. Nothing regarded in its own nature can be called perfect or imperfect; especially when we are aware that all things which come to pass, come to pass according to the eternal order and fixed laws of nature. However, human weakness cannot attain to this order in its own thoughts, but meanwhile man conceives a human character much more stable than his own, and sees that there is no reason why he should not himself acquire such a character. Thus he is led to seek for means which will bring him to this pitch of perfection, and calls everything which will serve as such means a true good. The chief good is that he should arrive, together with other individuals if possible, at the possession of the aforesaid character. What that character is we shall show in due time, namely, that it is the knowledge of the union existing between the mind and the whole of nature.[1] This, then, is the end for which I strive, to attain to such a character myself, and to endeavour that many should attain to it with me. In other words, it is part of my happiness to lend a helping hand, that many others may understand even as I do, so that their understanding and desire may entirely agree with my own. In order to bring this about, it is necessary to understand as much of nature as will enable us to attain to the aforesaid character, and also to form a

[1] These matters are explained more at length elsewhere.

social order such as is most conducive to the attainment of this character by the greatest number with the least difficulty and danger. We must seek the assistance of Moral Philosophy[1] and the Theory of Education; further, as health is no insignificant means for attaining our end, we must also include the whole science of Medicine, and, as many difficult things are by contrivance rendered easy, and we can in this way gain much time and convenience, the science of Mechanics must in no way be despised. But, before all things, a means must be devised for improving the understanding and purifying it, as far as may be at the outset, so that it may apprehend things without error, and in the best possible way.

Thus it is apparent to everyone that I wish to direct all sciences to one end and aim,[2] so that we may attain to the supreme human perfection which we have named; and, therefore, whatsoever in the sciences does not serve to promote our object will have to be rejected as useless. To sum up the matter in a word, all our actions and thoughts must be directed to this one end. Yet, as it is necessary that while we are endeavouring to attain our purpose, and bring the understanding into the right path, we should carry on our life, we are compelled first of all to lay down certain rules of life as provisionally good, to wit the following:—

I. To speak in a manner intelligible to the multitude, and to comply with every general custom that does not hinder the attainment of our purpose. For we can gain from the multitude no small advantages, provided that we strive to accommodate ourselves to its understanding as far as possible: moreover, we shall in this way gain a friendly audience for the reception of the truth.

II. To indulge ourselves with pleasures only in so far as they are necessary for preserving health.

III. Lastly, to endeavour to obtain only sufficient money or other commodities to enable us to preserve our life and health, and to follow such general customs as are consistent with our purpose.

[1] N.B. I do no more here than enumerate the sciences necessary for our purpose; I lay no stress on their order.

[2] There is for the sciences but one end, to which they should all be directed.

Having laid down these preliminary rules, I will betake myself to the first and most important task, namely, the amendment of the understanding, and the rendering it capable of understanding things in the manner necessary for attaining our end.

In order to bring this about, the natural order demands that I should here recapitulate all the modes of perception, which I have hitherto employed for affirming or denying anything with certainty, so that I may choose the best, and at the same time begin to know my own powers and the nature which I wish to perfect.

Reflection shows that all modes of perception or knowledge may be reduced to four:—

I. Perception arising from hearsay or from some sign which everyone may name as he pleases.

II. Perception arising from mere experience—that is, from experience not yet classified by the intellect, and only so called because the given event has happened to take place, and we have no contradictory fact to set against it, so that it therefore remains unassailed in our mind.

III. Perception arising when the essence of one thing is inferred from another thing, but not adequately; this comes[1] when from some effect we gather its cause, or when it is inferred from some general proposition that some property is always present.

IV. Lastly, there is the perception arising when a thing is perceived solely through its essence, or through the knowledge of its proximate cause.

All these kinds of perception I will illustrate by examples. By hearsay I know the day of my birth, my parentage, and other matters about which I have never felt any doubt. By mere experience I know that I shall die, for this I can affirm from having seen that others like myself have died, though all did not live for the same period, or die by the same dis-

[1] In this case we do not understand anything of the cause from the consideration of it in the effect. This is sufficiently evident from the fact that the cause is only spoken of in very general terms, such as—there exists then something; there exists then some power, &c.; or from the fact that we only express it in a negative manner—it is not this or that, &c. In the second case something is ascribed to the cause because of the effect, as we shall show in an example, but only a property, never the essence.

ease: I know by mere experience that oil has the property of feeding fire, and water of extinguishing it. In the same way I know that a dog is a barking animal, man a rational animal, and in fact nearly all the practical knowledge of life.

We deduce one thing from another as follows: when we clearly perceive that we feel a certain body and no other, we thence clearly infer that the mind is united to the body,[1] and that their union is the cause of the given sensation; but we cannot thence absolutely understand the nature of the sensation and the union.[2] Or, after I have become acquainted with the nature of vision, and know that it has the property of making one and the same thing appear smaller when far off than when near, I can infer that the sun is larger than it appears, and can draw other conclusions of the same kind.

Lastly, a thing may be perceived solely through its essence; when, from the fact of knowing something, I know what it is to know that thing, or when, from knowing the essence of the mind, I know that it is united to the body. By the same kind of knowledge we know that two and three make five, or that two lines each parallel to a third, are parallel to one another, &c. The things which I have been able to know by this kind of knowledge are as yet very few.

In order that the whole matter may be put in a clearer light, I will make use of a single illustration as follows. Three numbers are given—it is required to find a fourth, which shall be to the third as the second is to the first.

[1] From this example may be clearly seen what I have just drawn attention to. For through this union we understand nothing beyond the sensation, the effect, to wit, from which we inferred the cause of which we understand nothing.

[2] A conclusion of this sort, though it be certain, is yet not to be relied on without great caution; for unless we are exceedingly careful we shall forthwith fall into error. When things are conceived thus abstractedly, and not through their true essence, they are apt to be confused by the imagination. For that which is in itself one, men imagine to be multiplex. To those things which are conceived abstractedly, apart, and confusedly, terms are applied which are apt to become wrested from their strict meaning, and bestowed on things more familiar; whence it results that these latter are imagined in the same way as the former to which the terms were originally given.

Tradesmen will at once tell us that they know what is required to find the fourth number, for they have not yet forgotten the rule which was given to them arbitrarily without proof by their masters; others construct a universal axiom from their experience with simple numbers, where the fourth number is self-evident, as in the case of 2, 4, 3, 6; here it is evident that if the second number be multiplied by the third, and the product divided by the first, the quotient is 6; when they see that by this process the number is produced which they knew beforehand to be the proportional, they infer that the process always holds good for finding a fourth number proportional. Mathematicians, however, know by the proof of the nineteenth proposition of the seventh book of Euclid, what numbers are proportionals, namely, from the nature and property of proportion it follows that the product of the first and fourth will be equal to the product of the second and third: still they do not see the adequate proportionality of the given numbers, or, if they do see it, they see it not by virtue of Euclid's proposition, but intuitively, without going through any process.

In order that from these modes of perception the best may be selected, it is well that we should briefly enumerate the means necessary for attaining our end.

I. To have an exact knowledge of our nature which we desire to perfect, and to know as much as is needful of nature in general.

II. To collect in this way the differences, the agreements, and the oppositions of things.

III. To learn thus exactly how far they can or cannot be modified.

IV. To compare this result with the nature and power of man. We shall thus discern the highest degree of perfection to which man is capable of attaining. We shall then be in a position to see which mode of perception we ought to choose.

As to the first mode, it is evident that from hearsay our knowledge must always be uncertain, and, moreover, can give us no insight into the essence of a thing, as is manifest in our illustration; now one can only arrive at knowledge of a thing through knowledge of its essence, as will hereafter appear. We may, therefore, clearly conclude that the certainty arising from hearsay cannot be scientific in its character. For simple hearsay cannot affect anyone whose understanding does not, so to speak, meet it half way.

The second mode of perception[1] cannot be said to give us the idea of the proportion of which we are in search. Moreover its results are very uncertain and indefinite, for we shall never discover anything in natural phenomena by its means, except accidental properties, which are never clearly understood, unless the essence of the things in question be known first. Wherefore this mode also must be rejected.

Of the third mode of perception we may say in a manner that it gives us the idea of the thing sought, and that it enables us to draw conclusions without risk of error; yet it is not by itself sufficient to put us in possession of the perfection we aim at.

The fourth mode alone apprehends the adequate essence of a thing without danger of error. This mode, therefore, must be the one which we chiefly employ. How, then, should we avail ourselves of it so as to gain the fourth kind of knowledge with the least delay concerning things previously unknown? I will proceed to explain.

Now that we know what kind of knowledge is necessary for us, we must indicate the way and the method whereby we may gain the said knowledge concerning the things needful to be known. In order to accomplish this, we must first take care not to commit ourselves to a search, going back to infinity—that is, in order to discover the best method for finding out the truth, there is no need of another method to discover such method; nor of a third method for discovering the second, and so on to infinity. By such proceedings, we should never arrive at the knowledge of the truth, or, indeed, at any knowledge at all. The matter stands on the same footing as the making of material tools, which might be argued about in a similar way. For, in order to work iron, a hammer is needed, and the hammer cannot be forthcoming unless it has been made;

[1] I shall here treat a little more in detail of experience, and shall examine the method adopted by the Empirics, and by recent philosophers.

but, in order to make it, there was need of another hammer and other tools, and so on to infinity. We might thus vainly endeavour to prove that men have no power of working iron. But as men at first made use of the instruments supplied by nature to accomplish very easy pieces of workmanship, laboriously and imperfectly, and then, when these were finished, wrought other things more difficult with less labour and greater perfection; and so gradually mounted from the simplest operations to the making of tools, and from the making of tools to the making of more complex tools, and fresh feats of workmanship, till they arrived at making, with small expenditure of labour, the vast number of complicated mechanisms which they now possess. So, in like manner, the intellect, by its native strength,[1] makes for itself intellectual instruments, whereby it acquires strength for performing other intellectual operations,[2] and from these operations gets again fresh instruments, or the power of pushing its investigations further, and thus gradually proceeds till it reaches the summit of wisdom.

That this is the path pursued by the understanding may be readily seen, when we understand the nature of the method for finding out the truth, and of the natural instruments so necessary for the construction of more complex instruments, and for the progress of investigation. I thus proceed with my demonstration.

A true idea[3] (for we possess a true idea) is something different from its correlate (*ideatum*); thus a circle is different from the idea of a circle. The idea of a circle is not something having a circumference and a centre, as a circle has; nor is the idea of a body that body itself. Now, as it is something different from its correlate, it is capable of being understood through itself; in other words, the idea, in so far as its actual essence (*essentia formalis*) is concerned, may be the subject of another subjective essence

[1] By native strength, I mean that not bestowed on us by external causes, as I shall afterwards explain in my philosophy.

[2] I here term them operations: I shall explain their nature in my philosophy.

[3] I shall take care not only to demonstrate what I have just advanced, but also that we have hitherto proceeded rightly, and other things needful to be known.

(*essentia objectiva*).[1] And, again, this second subjective essence will, regarded in itself, be something real, and capable of being understood; and so on, indefinitely. For instance, the man Peter is something real; the true idea of Peter is the reality of Peter represented subjectively, and is in itself something real, and quite distinct from the actual Peter. Now, as this true idea of Peter is in itself something real, and has its own individual existence, it will also be capable of being understood—that is, of being the subject of another idea, which will contain by representation (*objective*) all that the idea of Peter contains actually (*formaliter*). And, again, this idea of the idea of Peter has its own individuality, which may become the subject of yet another idea; and so on, indefinitely. This everyone may make trial of for himself, by reflecting that he knows what Peter is, and also knows that he knows, and further knows that he knows that he knows, &c. Hence it is plain that, in order to understand the actual Peter, it is not necessary first to understand the idea of Peter, and still less the idea of the idea of Peter. This is the same as saying that, in order to know, there is no need to know that we know, much less to know that we know that we know. This is no more necessary than to know the nature of a circle before knowing the nature of a triangle.[2] But, with these ideas, the contrary is the case: for, in order to know that I know, I must first know. Hence it is clear that certainty is nothing else than the subjective essence of a thing: in other words, the mode in which we perceive an actual reality is certainty. Further, it is also evident that, for the certitude of truth, no further sign is necessary beyond the possession of a true idea: for, as I have shown, it is not necessary to know that we know that we know. Hence, again, it is clear that no one can know the nature of the highest certainty, unless he possesses an adequate idea, or the subjective essence of a thing: for certainty is identical with such

[1] In modern language, " the idea may become the subject of another representation." *Objectivus* generally corresponds to the modern " subjective," *formalis* to the modern " objective."—[Tr.]

[2] Observe that we are not here inquiring how this first subjective essence is innate in us. This belongs to an investigation into nature, where all these matters are amply explained, and it is shown that without ideas neither affirmation, nor negation, nor volition are possible.

subjective essence. Thus, as the truth needs no sign—it being sufficient to possess the subjective essence of things, or, in other words, the ideas of them, in order that all doubts may be removed—it follows that the true method does not consist in seeking for the signs of truth after the acquisition of the idea, but that the true method teaches us the order in which we should seek for truth itself,[1] or the subjective essences of things, or ideas, for all these expressions are synonymous. Again, method must necessarily be concerned with reasoning or understanding—I mean, method is not identical with reasoning in the search for causes, still less is it the comprehension of the causes of things: it is the discernment of a true idea, by distinguishing it from other perceptions, and by investigating its nature, in order that we may thus know our power of understanding, and may so train our mind that it may, by a given standard, comprehend whatsoever is intelligible, by laying down certain rules as aids, and by avoiding useless mental exertion.

Whence we may gather that method is nothing else than reflective knowledge, or the idea of an idea; and that as there can be no idea of an idea—unless an idea exists previously,—there can be no method without a pre-existent idea. Therefore, that will be a good method which shows us how the mind should be directed, according to the standard of the given true idea.

Again, seeing that the ratio existing between two ideas is the same as the ratio between the actual realities corresponding to those ideas, it follows that the reflective knowledge which has for its object the most perfect being is more excellent than reflective knowledge concerning other objects—in other words, that method will be most perfect which affords the standard of the given idea of the most perfect being whereby we may direct our mind. We thus easily understand how, in proportion as it acquires new ideas, the mind simultaneously acquires fresh instruments for pursuing its inquiries further. For we may gather from what has been said, that a true idea must necessarily first of all exist in us as a natural instrument; and that

[1] The nature of mental search is explained in my philosophy.

when this idea is apprehended by the mind, it enables us to understand the difference existing between itself and all other perceptions. In this, one part of the method consists.

Now it is clear that the mind apprehends itself better in proportion as it understands a greater number of natural objects; it follows, therefore, that this portion of the method will be more perfect in proportion as the mind attains to the comprehension of a greater number of objects, and that it will be absolutely perfect when the mind gains a knowledge of the absolutely perfect being, or becomes conscious thereof. Again, the more things the mind knows, the better does it understand its own strength and the order of nature; by increased self-knowledge, it can direct itself more easily, and lay down rules for its own guidance; and, by increased knowledge of nature, it can more easily avoid what is useless.

And this is the sum total of method, as we have already stated. We may add that the idea in the world of thought is in the same case as its correlate in the world of reality. If, therefore, there be anything in nature which is without connection[1] with any other thing, and if we assign to it a subjective essence, which would in every way correspond to the objective reality, the subjective essence would have no connection with any other ideas—in other words, we could not draw any conclusion with regard to it. On the other hand, those things which are connected with others—as all things that exist in nature—will be understood by the mind, and their subjective essences will maintain the same mutual relations as their objective realities—that is to say, we shall infer from these ideas other ideas, which will in turn be connected with others, and thus our instruments for proceeding with our investigation will increase. This is what we were endeavouring to prove. Further, from what has just been said—namely, that an idea must, in all respects, correspond to its correlate in the world of reality,—it is evident that, in order to reproduce in every respect the faithful image of nature, our mind must deduce all its ideas from the idea which represents

[1] To be connected with other things is to be produced by them, or to produce them.

the origin and source of the whole of nature, so that it may itself become the source of other ideas.

It may, perhaps, provoke astonishment that, after having said that the good method is that which teaches us to direct our mind according to the standard of the given true idea, we should prove our point by reasoning, which would seem to indicate that it is not self-evident. We may, therefore, be questioned as to the validity of our reasoning. If our reasoning be sound, we must take as a starting-point a true idea. Now, to be certain that our starting-point is really a true idea, we need a proof. This first course of reasoning must be supported by a second, the second by a third, and so on to infinity. To this I make answer that, if by some happy chance anyone had adopted this method in his investigations of nature—that is, if he had acquired new ideas in the proper order, according to the standard of the original true idea, he would never have doubted of the truth of his knowledge,[1] inasmuch as truth, as we have shown, makes itself manifest, and all things would flow, as it were, spontaneously towards him. But as this never, or rarely, happens, I have been forced so to arrange my proceedings, that we may acquire by reflection and forethought what we cannot acquire by chance, and that it may at the same time appear that, for proving the truth, and for valid reasoning, we need no other means than the truth and valid reasoning themselves: for by valid reasoning I have established valid reasoning, and, in like measure, I seek still to establish it. Moreover, this is the order of thinking adopted by men in their inward meditations. The reasons for its rare employment in investigations of nature are to be found in current misconceptions, whereof we shall examine the causes hereafter in our philosophy. Moreover, it demands, as we shall show, a keen and accurate discernment. Lastly, it is hindered by the conditions of human life, which are, as we have already pointed out, extremely changeable. There are also other obstacles, which we will not here inquire into.

If anyone asks why I have not at the starting-point set forth all the truths of nature in their due order, inasmuch

[1] In the same way as we have here no doubt of the truth of our knowledge

as truth is self-evident, I reply by warning him not to reject as false any paradoxes he may find here, but to take the trouble to reflect on the chain of reasoning by which they are supported; he will then be no longer in doubt that we have attained to the truth. This is why I have begun as above.

If there yet remains some sceptic, who doubts of our primary truth, and of all deductions we make, taking such truth as our standard, he must either be arguing in bad faith, or we must confess that there are men in complete mental blindness, either innate or due to misconceptions—that is, to some external influence.

Such persons are not conscious of themselves. If they affirm or doubt anything, they know not that they affirm or doubt: they say that they know nothing, and they say that they are ignorant of the very fact of their knowing nothing. Even this they do not affirm absolutely, they are afraid of confessing that they exist, so long as they know nothing; in fact, they ought to remain dumb, for fear of haply supposing something which should smack of truth. Lastly, with such persons, one should not speak of sciences: for, in what relates to life and conduct, they are compelled by necessity to suppose that they exist, and seek their own advantage, and often affirm and deny, even with an oath. If they deny, grant, or gainsay, they know not that they deny, grant, or gainsay, so that they ought to be regarded as automata, utterly devoid of intelligence.

Let us now return to our proposition. Up to the present, we have, first, defined the end to which we desire to direct all our thoughts; secondly, we have determined the mode of perception best adapted to aid us in attaining our perfection; thirdly, we have discovered the way which our mind should take, in order to make a good beginning—namely, that it should use every true idea as a standard in pursuing its inquiries according to fixed rules. Now, in order that it may thus proceed, our method must furnish us, first, with a means of distinguishing a true idea from all other perceptions, and enabling the mind to avoid the latter; secondly, with rules for perceiving unknown things according to the standard of the true idea; thirdly, with an order which enables us to avoid useless labour.

When we became acquainted with this method, we saw that, fourthly, it would be perfect when we had attained to the idea of the absolutely perfect Being. This is an observation which should be made at the outset, in order that we may arrive at the knowledge of such a being more quickly.

Let us then make a beginning with the first part of the method, which is, as we have said, to distinguish and separate the true idea from other perceptions, and to keep the mind from confusing with true ideas those which are false, fictitious, and doubtful. I intend to dwell on this point at length, partly to keep a distinction so necessary before the reader's mind, and also because there are some who doubt of true ideas, through not having attended to the distinction between a true perception and all others. Such persons are like men who, while they are awake, doubt not that they are awake, but afterwards in a dream, as often happens, thinking that they are surely awake, and then finding that they were in error, become doubtful even of being awake. This state of mind arises through neglect of the distinction between sleeping and waking.

Meanwhile, I give warning that I shall not here give the essence of every perception, and explain it through its proximate cause. Such work lies in the province of philosophy. I shall confine myself to what concerns method—that is, to the character of fictitious, false, and doubtful perception, and the means of freeing ourselves therefrom. Let us then first inquire into the nature of a fictitious idea.

Every perception has for its object either a thing considered as existing, or solely the essence of a thing. Now "fiction" is chiefly occupied with things considered as existing. I will, therefore, consider these first—I mean cases where only the existence of an object is feigned, and the thing thus feigned is understood, or assumed to be understood. For instance, I feign that Peter, whom I know to have gone home, is gone to see me,[1] or something of that kind. With what is such an idea concerned? It is con-

[1] See below the note on hypotheses, whereof we have a clear understanding; the fiction consists in saying that such hypotheses exist in heavenly bodies.

cerned with things possible, and not with things necessary or impossible. I call a thing *impossible* when its existence would imply a contradiction; *necessary*, when its non-existence would imply a contradiction; *possible*, when neither its existence nor its non-existence imply a contradiction, but when the necessity or impossibility of its nature depends on causes unknown to us, while we feign that it exists. If the necessity or impossibility of its existence depending on external causes were known to us, we could not form any fictitious hypothesis about it; whence it follows that if there be a God, or omniscient Being, such an one cannot form fictitious hypotheses. For, as regards ourselves, when I know that I exist, I cannot hypothesize that I exist or do not exist,[1] any more than I can hypothesize an elephant that can go through the eye of a needle; nor when I know the nature of God, can I hypothesize that He exists or does not exist.[2] The same thing must be said of the Chimæra, whereof the nature implies a contradiction. From these considerations, it is plain, as I have already stated, that fiction cannot be concerned with eternal truths.[3]

But before proceeding further, I must remark, in passing, that the difference between the essence of one thing and the essence of another thing is the same as that which exists between the reality or existence of one thing and the reality or existence of another; therefore, if we wished to conceive the existence, for example, of Adam, simply by means of existence in general, it would be the same as if, in order to conceive his existence, we went back to the nature of being, so as to define Adam as a being. Thus, the more existence is conceived generally, the more is it conceived

[1] As a thing, when once it is understood, manifests itself, we have need only of an example without further proof. In the same way the contrary has only to be presented to our minds to be recognized as false, as will forthwith appear when we come to discuss fiction concerning essences.

[2] Observe, that although many assert that they doubt whether God exists, they have nought but his name in their minds, or else some fiction which they call God: this fiction is not in harmony with God's real nature, as we will duly show.

[3] I shall presently show that no fiction can concern eternal truths. By an eternal truth, I mean that which being positive could never become negative. Thus it is a primary and eternal truth that *God exists*, but it is not an eternal truth that *Adam thinks*. That the *Chimæra does not exist* is an eternal truth, that *Adam does not think* is not so.

confusedly, and the more easily can it be ascribed to a given object. Contrariwise, the more it is conceived particularly, the more is it understood clearly, and the less liable is it to be ascribed, through negligence of Nature's order, to anything save its proper object. This is worthy of remark.

We now proceed to consider those cases which are commonly called fictions, though we clearly understand that the thing is not as we imagine it. For instance, I know that the earth is round, but nothing prevents my telling people that it is a hemisphere, and that it is like a half apple carved in relief on a dish; or, that the sun moves round the earth, and so on. However, examination will show us that there is nothing here inconsistent with what has been said, provided we first admit that we may have made mistakes, and be now conscious of them; and, further, that we can hypothesize, or at least suppose, that others are under the same mistake as ourselves, or can, like us, fall under it. We can. I repeat, thus hypothesize so long as we see no impossibility. Thus, when I tell anyone that the earth is not round, &c., I merely recall the error which I perhaps made myself, or which I might have fallen into, and afterwards I hypothesize that the person to whom I tell it, is still, or may still fall under the same mistake. This I say, I can feign so long as I do not perceive any impossibility or necessity; if I truly understood either one or the other I should not be able to feign, and I should be reduced to saying that I had made the attempt.

It remains for us to consider hypotheses made in problems, which sometimes involve impossibilities. For instance, when we say—let us assume that this burning candle is not burning, or, let us assume that it burns in some imaginary space, or where there are no physical objects. Such assumptions are freely made, though the last is clearly seen to be impossible. But, though this be so, there is no fiction in the case. For, in the first case, I have merely recalled to memory another candle[1] not burning, or

[1] Afterwards, when we come to speak of fiction that is concerned with essences, it will be evident that fiction never creates or furnishes the mind with anything new; only such things as are already in the

conceived the candle before me as without a flame, and then I understand as applying to the latter, leaving its flame out of the question, all that I think of the former. In the second case, I have merely to abstract my thoughts from the objects surrounding the candle, for the mind to devote itself to the contemplation of the candle singly looked at in itself only; I can then draw the conclusion that the candle contains in itself no cause for its own destruction, so that if there were no physical objects the candle, and even the flame, would remain unchangeable, and so on. Thus there is here no fiction, but true and bare assertions.[1]

Let us now pass on to the fictions concerned with essences only, or with some reality or existence simultaneously. Of these we must specially observe that in proportion as the mind's understanding is smaller, and its experience multiplex, so will its power of coining fictions be larger, whereas as its understanding increases, its capacity for entertaining fictitious ideas becomes less. For instance, in the same way as we are unable, while we are thinking, to feign that we are thinking or not thinking, so, also, when we know the nature of body we cannot imagine an infinite fly; or, when we know the nature of the soul,[2] we cannot imagine it as square, though anything may be expressed verbally. But, as we said above, the less men know of nature the

brain or imagination are recalled to the memory, when the attention is directed to them confusedly and all at once. For instance, we have remembrance of spoken words and of a tree; when the mind directs itself to them confusedly, it forms the notion of a tree speaking. The same may be said of existence, especially when it is conceived quite generally as entity; it is then readily applied to all things occurring together in the memory. This is specially worthy of remark.

[1] We must understand as much in the case of hypotheses put forward to explain certain movements accompanying celestial phenomena; but from these, when applied to the celestial motions, we may draw conclusions as to the nature of the heavens, whereas this last may be quite different, especially as many other causes are conceivable which would account for such motions.

[2] It often happens that a man recalls to mind this word soul, and forms at the same time some corporeal image: as the two representations are simultaneous, he easily thinks that he imagines and feigns a corporeal soul: thus confusing the name with the thing itself. I here beg that my readers will not be in a hurry to refute this proposition; they will, I hope, have no mind to do so, if they pay close attention to the examples given and to what follows.

more easily can they coin fictitious ideas, such as trees speaking, men instantly changed into stones, or into fountains, ghosts appearing in mirrors, something issuing from nothing, even gods changed into beasts and men, and infinite other absurdities of the same kind.

Some persons think, perhaps, that fiction is limited by fiction, and not by understanding; in other words, after I have formed some fictitious idea, and have affirmed of my own free will that it exists under a certain form in nature, I am thereby precluded from thinking of it under any other form. For instance, when I have feigned (to repeat their argument) that the nature of body is of a certain kind, and have of my own free will desired to convince myself that it actually exists under this form, I am no longer able to hypothesize that a fly, for example, is infinite; so, when I have hypothesized the essence of the soul, I am not able to think of it as square, &c. But these arguments demand further inquiry. First, their upholders must either grant or deny that we can understand anything. If they grant it, then necessarily the same must be said of understanding, as is said of fiction. If they deny it, let us, who know that we do know something, see what they mean. They assert that the soul can be conscious of, and perceive in a variety of ways, not itself nor things which exist, but only things which are neither in itself nor anywhere else, in other words, that the soul can, by its unaided power, create sensations or ideas unconnected with things. In fact, they regard the soul as a sort of god. Further, they assert that we or our soul have such freedom that we can constrain ourselves, or our soul, or even our soul's freedom. For, after it has formed a fictitious idea, and has given its assent thereto, it cannot think or feign it in any other manner, but is constrained by the first fictitious idea to keep all its other thoughts in harmony therewith. Our opponents are thus driven to admit, in support of their fiction, the absurdities which I have just enumerated; and which are not worthy of rational refutation.[1]

[1] Though I seem to deduce this from experience, some may deny its cogency because I have given no formal proof. I therefore append the following for those who may desire it. As there can be nothing in nature contrary to nature's laws, since all things come to pass by fixed

While leaving such persons in their error, we will take care to derive from our argument with them a truth serviceable for our purpose, namely, that the mind, in paying attention to a thing hypothetical or false, so as to meditate upon it and understand it, and derive the proper conclusions in due order therefrom, will readily discover its falsity; and if the thing hypothetical be in its nature true, and the mind pays attention to it, so as to understand it, and deduce the truths which are derivable from it, the mind will proceed with an uninterrupted series of apt conclusions; in the same way as it would at once discover (as we showed just now) the absurdity of a false hypothesis, and of the conclusions drawn from it.

We need, therefore, be in no fear of forming hypotheses, so long as we have a clear and distinct perception of what is involved. For, if we were to assert, haply, that men are suddenly turned into beasts, the statement would be extremely general, so general that there would be no conception, that is, no idea or connection of subject and predicate, in our mind. If there were such a conception we should at the same time be aware of the means and the causes whereby the event took place. Moreover, we pay no attention to the nature of the subject and the predicate. Now, if the first idea be not fictitious, and if all the other ideas be deduced therefrom, our hurry to form fictitious ideas will gradually subside. Further, as a fictitious idea cannot be clear and distinct, but is necessarily confused, and as all confusion arises from the fact that the mind has only partial knowledge of a thing either simple or complex, and does not distinguish between the known and the unknown, and, again, that it directs its attention promiscuously to all parts of an object at once without making distinctions, it follows, *first*, that if the idea be of something very simple, it must necessarily be clear and distinct. For a very simple object cannot be known in part, it must either be known altogether or not at all. *Secondly*, it follows that if a complex object be divided by thought into a number of

laws, so that each thing must irrefragably produce its own proper effect, it follows that the soul, as soon as it possesses the true conception of a thing, proceeds to reproduce in thought that thing's effects. See below, where I speak of the false idea.

simple component parts, and if each part be regarded separately, all confusion will disappear. *Thirdly*, it follows that fiction cannot be simple, but is made up of the blending of several confused ideas of diverse objects or actions existent in nature, or rather is composed of attention[1] directed to all such ideas at once, and unaccompanied by any mental assent.

Now a fiction that was simple would be clear and distinct, and therefore true, also a fiction composed only of distinct ideas would be clear and distinct, and therefore true. For instance, when we know the nature of the circle and the square, it is impossible for us to blend together these two figures, and to hypothesize a square circle, any more than a square soul, or things of that kind. Let us shortly come to our conclusion, and again repeat that we need have no fear of confusing with true ideas that which is only a fiction. As for the first sort of fiction of which we have already spoken, when a thing is clearly conceived, we saw that if the existence of that thing is in itself an eternal truth, fiction can have no part in it; but if the existence of the thing conceived be not an eternal truth, we have only to be careful that such existence be compared to the thing's essence, and to consider the order of nature. As for the second sort of fiction, which we stated to be the result of simultaneously directing the attention, without the assent of the intellect, to different confused ideas representing different things and actions existing in nature, we have seen that an absolutely simple thing cannot be feigned, but must be understood, and that a complex thing is in the same case if we regard separately the simple parts whereof it is composed; we shall not even be able to hypothesize any untrue action concerning such objects, for we shall be obliged to consider at the same time the causes and the manner of such action.

These matters being thus understood, let us pass on to

[1] Observe that fiction regarded in itself, only differs from dreams in that in the latter we do not perceive the external causes which we perceive through the senses while awake. It has hence been inferred that represensations occurring in sleep have no connection with objects external to us. We shall presently see that error is the dreaming of a waking man: if it reaches a certain pitch it becomes delirium.

consider the false idea, observing the objects with which it is concerned, and the means of guarding ourselves from falling into false perceptions. Neither of these tasks will present much difficulty, after our inquiry concerning fictitious ideas. The false idea only differs from the fictitious idea in the fact of implying a mental assent—that is, as we have already remarked, while the representations are occurring, there are no causes present to us, wherefrom, as in fiction, we can conclude that such representations do not arise from external objects: in fact, it is much the same as dreaming with our eyes open, or while awake. Thus, a false idea is concerned with, or (to speak more correctly) attributable to, the existence of a thing whereof the essence is known, or the essence itself, in the same way as a fictitious idea. If attributable to the existence of the thing, it is corrected in the same way as a fictitious idea under similar circumstances. If attributable to the essence, it is likewise corrected in the same way as a fictitious idea. For if the nature of the thing known implies necessary existence, we cannot possibly be in error with regard to its existence; but if the nature of the thing be not an eternal truth, like its essence, but contrariwise the necessity or impossibility of its existence depends on external causes, then we must follow the same course as we adopted in the case of fiction, for it is corrected in the same manner. As for false ideas concerned with essences, or even with actions, such perceptions are necessarily always confused, being compounded of different confused perceptions of things existing in nature, as, for instance, when men are persuaded that deities are present in woods, in statues, in brute beasts, and the like; that there are bodies which, by their composition alone, give rise to intellect; that corpses reason, walk about, and speak; that God is deceived, and so on. But ideas which are clear and distinct can never be false: for ideas of things clearly and distinctly conceived are either very simple themselves, or are compounded from very simple ideas—that is, are deduced therefrom. The impossibility of a very simple idea being false is evident to everyone who understands the nature of truth or understanding and of falsehood.

As regards that which constitutes the reality of truth, it

is certain that a true idea is distinguished from a false one, not so much by its extrinsic object as by its intrinsic nature. If an architect conceives a building properly constructed, though such a building may never have existed, and may never exist, nevertheless the idea is true; and the idea remains the same, whether it be put into execution or not. On the other hand, if anyone asserts, for instance, that Peter exists, without knowing whether Peter really exists or not, the assertion, as far as its asserter is concerned, is false, or not true, even though Peter actually does exist. The assertion that Peter exists is true only with regard to him who knows for certain that Peter does exist. Whence it follows that there is in ideas something real, whereby the true are distinguished from the false. This reality must be inquired into, if we are to find the best standard of truth (we have said that we ought to determine our thoughts by the given standard of a true idea, and that method is reflective knowledge), and to know the properties of our understanding. Neither must we say that the difference between true and false arises from the fact, that true knowledge consists in knowing things through their primary causes, wherein it is totally different from false knowledge, as I have just explained it: for thought is said to be true, if it involves subjectively the essence of any principle which has no cause, and is known through itself and in itself. Wherefore the reality (*forma*) of true thought must exist in the thought itself, without reference to other thoughts; it does not acknowledge the object as its cause, but must depend on the actual power and nature of the understanding. For, if we suppose that the understanding has perceived some new entity which has never existed, as some conceive the understanding of God before He created things (a perception which certainly could not arise from any object), and has legitimately deduced other thoughts from the said perception, all such thoughts would be true, without being determined by any external object; they would depend solely on the power and nature of the understanding. Thus, that which constitutes the reality of a true thought must be sought in the thought itself, and deduced from the nature of the understanding. In order to pursue our investigation, let us confront ourselves with some *true* idea, whose object we know for certain to be dependent on our power of thinking, and to have nothing corresponding to it in nature. With an idea of this kind before us, we shall, as appears from what has just been said, be more easily able to carry on the research we have in view. For instance, in order to form the conception of a sphere, I invent a cause at my pleasure—namely, a semicircle revolving round its centre, and thus producing a sphere. This is indisputably a true idea; and, although we know that no sphere in nature has ever actually been so formed, the perception remains true, and is the easiest manner of conceiving a sphere. We must observe that this perception asserts the rotation of a semicircle—which assertion would be false, if it were not associated with the conception of a sphere, or of a cause determining a motion of the kind, or absolutely, if the assertion were isolated. The mind would then only tend to the affirmation of the sole motion of a semicircle, which is not contained in the conception of a semicircle, and does not arise from the conception of any cause capable of producing such motion.

Thus *falsity* consists only in this, that something is affirmed of a thing, which is not contained in the conception we have formed of that thing, as motion or rest of a semicircle. Whence it follows that simple ideas cannot be other than *true—e.g.* the simple idea of a semicircle, of motion, of rest, of quantity, &c.

Whatsoever affirmation such ideas contain is equal to the concept formed, and does not extend further. Wherefore we may form as many simple ideas as we please, without any fear of error. It only remains for us to inquire by what power our mind can form true ideas, and how far such power extends. It is certain that such power cannot extend itself infinitely. For when we affirm somewhat of a thing, which is not contained in the concept we have formed of that thing, such an affirmation shows a defect of our perception, or that we have formed fragmentary or mutilated ideas. Thus we have seen that the motion of a semicircle is false when it is isolated in the mind, but true when it is associated with the concept of a sphere, or of some cause determining such a motion. But if it be the nature of a thinking being, as seems, *primâ facie*, to be the case, to form true or adequate thoughts, it is plain that inadequate ideas arise in us only because we are parts of a thinking being, whose thoughts—some in their entirety, others in fragments only—constitute our mind.

But there is another point to be considered, which was not worth raising in the case of fiction, but which gives rise to complete deception—namely, that certain things presented to the imagination also exist in the understanding—in other words, are conceived clearly and distinctly. Hence, so long as we do not separate that which is distinct from that which is confused, certainty, or the true idea, becomes mixed with indistinct ideas. For instance, certain Stoics heard, perhaps, the term "soul," and also that the soul is immortal, yet imagined it only confusedly; they imagined, also, and understood that very subtle bodies penetrate all others, and are penetrated by none. By combining these ideas, and being at the same time certain of the truth of the axiom, they forthwith became convinced that the mind consists of very subtle bodies; that these very subtle bodies cannot be divided, &c. But we are freed from mistakes of this kind, so long as we endeavour to examine all our perceptions by the standard of the given true idea. We must take care, as has been said, to separate such perceptions from all those which arise from hearsay or unclassified experience.

Moreover, such mistakes arise from things being conceived too much in the abstract; for it is sufficiently self-evident that what I conceive as in its true object I cannot apply to anything else. Lastly, they arise from a want of understanding of the primary elements of nature as a whole; whence we proceed without due order, and confound nature with abstract rules, which, although they be true enough in their sphere, yet, when misapplied, confound themselves, and pervert the order of nature. However, if we proceed with as little abstraction as possible, and begin from primary elements—that is, from the source and origin of nature, as far back as we can reach,—we need not fear any deceptions of this kind. As far as the knowledge of the origin of nature is concerned, there is no danger of our confounding it with abstractions. For when a thing is conceived in the abstract, as are all universal notions, the said universal notions are always more extensive in the mind than the number of individuals forming their contents really existing in nature.

Again, there are many things in nature, the difference between which is so slight as to be hardly perceptible to the understanding; so that it may readily happen that such things are confounded together, if they be conceived abstractedly. But since the first principle of nature cannot (as we shall see hereafter) be conceived abstractedly or universally, and cannot extend further in the understanding than it does in reality, and has no likeness to mutable things, no confusion need be feared in respect to the idea of it, provided (as before shown) that we possess a standard of truth. This is, in fact, a being single[1] and infinite; in other words, it is the sum total of being,[2] beyond which there is no being found.

Thus far we have treated of the false idea. We have now to investigate the doubtful idea—that is, to inquire what can cause us to doubt, and how doubt may be removed. I speak of real doubt existing in the mind, not of such doubt as we see exemplified when a man says that he doubts, though his mind does not really hesitate. The cure of the latter does not fall within the province of method, it belongs rather to inquiries concerning obstinacy and its cure. Real doubt is never produced in the mind by the thing doubted of. In other words, if there were only one idea in the mind, whether that idea were true or false, there would be no doubt or certainty present, only a certain sensation. For an idea is in itself nothing else than a certain sensation; but doubt will arise through another idea, not clear and distinct enough for us to be able to draw any certain conclusion with regard to the matter under consideration; that is, the idea which causes

[1] These are not attributes of God displaying His essence, as I will show in my philosophy.

[2] This has been shown already. For if such a being did not exist it would never be produced: therefore the mind would be able to understand more than nature could furnish; and this has been shown above to be false.

us to doubt is not clear and distinct. To take an example. Supposing that a man has never reflected, taught by experience, or by any other means, that our senses sometimes deceive us, he will never doubt whether the sun be greater or less than it appears. Thus rustics are generally astonished when they hear that the sun is much larger than the earth. But from reflection on the deceitfulness of the senses[1] doubt arises, and if, after doubting, we acquire a true knowledge of the senses, and how things at a distance are represented through their instrumentality, doubt is again removed. Hence we cannot cast doubt on true ideas by the supposition that there is a deceitful Deity, who leads us astray even in what is most certain. We can only hold such an hypothesis so long as we have no clear and distinct idea—in other words, until we reflect on the knowledge which we have of the first principle of all things, and find that which teaches us that God is not a deceiver, and until we know this with the same certainty as we know from reflecting on the nature of a triangle that its three angles are equal to two right angles. But if we have a knowledge of God equal to that which we have of a triangle, all doubt is removed. In the same way as we can arrive at the said knowledge of a triangle, though not absolutely sure that there is not not some arch-deceiver leading us astray, so can we come to a like knowledge of God under the like condition, and when we have attained to it, it is sufficient, as I said before, to remove every doubt which we can possess concerning clear and distinct ideas. Thus, if a man proceeded with our investigations in due order, inquiring first into those things which should first be inquired into, never passing over a link in the chain of association, and with knowledge how to define his questions before seeking to answer them, he will never have any ideas save such as are very certain, or, in other words, clear and distinct; for doubt is only a suspension of the spirit concerning some affirmation or negation which it would pronounce upon unhesitatingly if it were not in ignorance of something, without which the knowledge of the matter in hand must needs be imperfect. We may,

[1] That is, it is known that the senses sometimes deceive us. But it is only known confusedly, for it is not known how they deceive us.

therefore, conclude that doubt always proceeds from want of due order in investigation.

These are the points I promised to discuss in this first part of my treatise on method. However, in order not to omit anything which can conduce to the knowledge of the understanding and its faculties, I will add a few words on the subject of memory and forgetfulness.

The point most worthy of attention is, that memory is strengthened both with and without the aid of the understanding. For the more intelligible a thing is, the more easily is it remembered, and the less intelligible it is, the more easily do we forget it. For instance, a number of unconnected words is much more difficult to remember than the same number in the form of a narration. The memory is also strengthened without the aid of the understanding by means of the power wherewith the imagination or the sense called common is affected by some particular physical object. I say *particular*, for the imagination is only affected by particular objects. If we read, for instance, a single romantic comedy, we shall remember it very well, so long as we do not read many others of the same kind, for it will reign alone in the memory. If, however, we read several others of the same kind, we shall think of them altogether, and easily confuse one with another. I say, also, *physical*. For the imagination is only affected by physical objects. As, then, the memory is strengthened both with and without the aid of the understanding, we may conclude that it is different from the understanding, and that in the latter considered in itself there is neither memory nor forgetfulness. What, then, is memory? It is nothing else than the actual sensation of impressions on the brain, accompanied with the thought of a definite duration of the sensation.[1] This is also shown by reminiscence. For then we think of the sensation, but without the notion of continuous duration;

[1] If the duration be indefinite, the recollection is imperfect; this everyone seems to have learnt from nature. For we often ask, to strengthen our belief in something we hear of, when and where it happened; though ideas themselves have their own duration in the mind, yet, as we are wont to determine duration by the aid of some measure of motion which, again, takes place by aid of the imagination, we preserve no memory connected with pure intellect.

thus the idea of that sensation is not the actual duration of the sensation or actual memory. Whether ideas are or are not subject to corruption will be seen in my philosophy. If this seems too absurd to anyone, it will be sufficient for our purpose, if he reflect on the fact that a thing is more easily remembered in proportion to its singularity, as appears from the example of the comedy just cited. Further, a thing is remembered more easily in proportion to its intelligibility; therefore we cannot help remembering that which is extremely singular and sufficiently intelligible.

Thus, then, we have distinguished between a true idea and other perceptions, and shown that ideas fictitious, false, and the rest, originate in the imagination—that is, in certain sensations fortuitous (so to speak) and disconnected, arising not from the power of the mind, but from external causes, according as the body, sleeping or waking, receives various motions.

But one may take any view one likes of the imagination so long as one acknowledges that it is different from the understanding, and that the soul is passive with regard to it. The view taken is immaterial, if we know that the imagination is something indefinite, with regard to which the soul is passive, and that we can by some means or other free ourselves therefrom with the help of the understanding. Let no one then be astonished that before proving the existence of body, and other necessary things, I speak of imagination of body, and of its composition. The view taken is, I repeat, immaterial, so long as we know that imagination is something indefinite, &c. As regards a true idea, we have shown that it is simple or compounded of simple ideas; that it shows how and why something is or has been made; and that its subjective effects in the soul correspond to the actual reality of its object. This conclusion is identical with the saying of the ancients, that true science proceeds from cause to effect; though the ancients, so far as I know, never formed the conception put forward here that the soul acts according to fixed laws, and is as it were an immaterial automaton. Hence, as far as is possible at the outset, we have acquired a knowledge of our understanding, and such a standard of a true idea that we need no longer fear confounding truth with falsehood and fiction. Neither shall we wonder why we understand some things which in nowise fall within the scope of the imagination, while other things are in the imagination but wholly opposed to the understanding, or others, again, which agree therewith. We now know that the operations, whereby the effects of imagination are produced, take place under other laws quite different from the laws of the understanding, and that the mind is entirely passive with regard to them. Whence we may also see how easily men may fall into grave errors through not distinguishing accurately between the imagination and the understanding; such as believing that extension must be localized, that it must be finite, that its parts are really distinct one from the other, that it is the primary and single foundation of all things, that it occupies more space at one time than at another, and other similar doctrines, all entirely opposed to truth, as we shall duly show.

Again, since words are a part of the imagination—that is, since we form many conceptions in accordance with confused arrangements of words in the memory, dependent on particular bodily conditions,—there is no doubt that words may, equally with the imagination, be the cause of many and great errors, unless we keep strictly on our guard. Moreover, words are formed according to popular fancy and intelligence, and are, therefore, signs of things as existing in the imagination, not as existing in the understanding. This is evident from the fact that to all such things as exist only in the understanding, not in the imagination, negative names are often given, such as incorporeal, infinite, &c. So, also, many conceptions really affirmative are expressed negatively, and *vice versâ,* such as uncreate, independent, infinite, immortal, &c., inasmuch as their contraries are much more easily imagined, and, therefore, occurred first to men, and usurped positive names. Many things we affirm and deny, because the nature of words allows us to do so, though the nature of things does not. While we remain unaware of this fact, we may easily mistake falsehood for truth.

Let us also beware of another great cause of confusion, which prevents the understanding from reflecting on itself. Sometimes, while making no distinction between the imagination and the intellect, we think that what we more readily imagine is clearer to us; and also we think that what we imagine we understand. Thus, we put first that which should be last: the true order of progression is reversed, and no legitimate conclusion is drawn.

Now, in order at length to pass on to the second part of this method,[1] I shall first set forth the object aimed at, and next the means for its attainment. The object aimed at is the acquisition of clear and distinct ideas, such as are produced by the pure intellect, and not by chance physical motions. In order that all ideas may be reduced to unity, we shall endeavour so to associate and arrange them that our mind may, as far as possible, reflect subjectively the reality of nature, both as a whole and as parts.

As for the first point, it is necessary (as we have said) for our purpose that everything should be conceived, either *solely through its essence,* or *through its proximate cause.* If the thing be self-existent, or, as is commonly said, the cause of itself, it must be understood through its essence only; if it be not self-existent, but requires a cause for its existence, it must be understood through its proximate cause. For, in reality, the knowledge of an effect is nothing else than the acquisition of more perfect knowledge of its cause.[2] Therefore, we may never, while we are concerned with inquiries into actual things, draw any conclusion from abstractions; we shall be extremely careful not to confound that which is only in the understanding with that which is in the thing itself. The best basis for drawing a conclusion will be either some particular affirmative essence, or a true and legitimate definition. For the understanding cannot descend from universal axioms by themselves to particular things, since axioms are of infinite extent, and do not determine the understanding to contemplate one particular thing more than another. Thus the true method

[1] The chief rule of this part is, as appears from the first part, to review all the ideas coming to us through pure intellect, so as to distinguish them from such as we imagine: the distinction will be shown through the properties of each, namely, of the imagination and of the understanding.

[2] Observe that it is hereby manifest that we cannot understand anything of nature without at the same time increasing our knowledge of the first cause, or God.

of discovery is to form thoughts from some given definition. This process will be the more fruitful and easy in proportion as the thing given be better defined. Wherefore, the cardinal point of all this second part of method consists in the knowledge of the conditions of good definition, and the means of finding them. I will first treat of the conditions of definition.

A definition, if it is to be called perfect, must explain the inmost essence of a thing, and must take care not to substitute for this any of its properties. In order to illustrate my meaning, without taking an example which would seem to show a desire to expose other people's errors, I will choose the case of something abstract, the definition of which is of little moment. Such is a circle. If a circle be defined as a figure, such that all straight lines drawn from the centre to the circumference are equal, every one can see that such a definition does not in the least explain the essence of a circle, but solely one of its properties. Though, as I have said, this is of no importance in the case of figures and other abstractions, it is of great importance in the case of physical beings and realities: for the properties of things are not understood so long as their essences are unknown. If the latter be passed over, there is necessarily a perversion of the succession of ideas which should reflect the succession of nature, and we go far astray from our object.

In order to be free from this fault, the following rules should be observed in definition:—

I. If the thing in question be created, the definition must (as we have said) comprehend the proximate cause. For instance, a circle should, according to this rule, be defined as follows: the figure described by any line whereof one end is fixed and the other free. This definition clearly comprehends the proximate cause.

II. A conception or definition of a thing should be such that all the properties of that thing, in so far as it is considered by itself, and not in conjunction with other things, can be deduced from it, as may be seen in the definition given of a circle: for from that it clearly follows that all straight lines drawn from the centre to the circumference are equal. That this is a necessary characteristic of a definition is so clear to anyone, who reflects on the matter, that there is no need to spend time in proving it, or in showing that, owing to this second condition, every definition should be affirmative. I speak of intellectual affirmation, giving little thought to verbal affirmations which, owing to the poverty of language, must sometimes, perhaps, be expressed negatively, though the idea contained is affirmative.

The rules for the definition of an uncreated thing are as follows:—

I. The exclusion of all idea of cause—that is, the thing must not need explanation by anything outside itself.

II. When the definition of the thing has been given, there must be no room for doubt as to whether the thing exists or not.

III. It must contain, as far as the mind is concerned, no substantives which could be put into an adjectival form; in other words, the object defined must not be explained through abstractions.

IV. Lastly, though this is not absolutely necessary, it should be possible to deduce from the definition all the properties of the thing defined.

All these rules become obvious to anyone giving strict attention to the matter.

I have also stated that the best basis for drawing a conclusion is a particular affirmative essence. The more specialized the idea is, the more is it distinct, and therefore clear. Wherefore a knowledge of particular things should be sought for as diligently as possible.

As regards the order of our perceptions, and the manner in which they should be arranged and united, it is necessary that, as soon as is possible and rational, we should inquire whether there be any being (and, if so, what being), that is the cause of all things, so that its essence, represented in thought, may be the cause of all our ideas, and then our mind will to the utmost possible extent reflect nature. For it will possess, subjectively, nature's essence, order, and union. Thus we can see that it is before all things necessary for us to deduce all our ideas from physical things—that is, from real entities, proceeding, as far as may be, according to the series of causes, from one real entity to another real entity, never passing to universals and abstractions, either for the purpose of deducing some real entity from them, or deducing them from some real entity. Either of these processes interrupts the true progress of the understanding. But it must be observed that, by the series of causes and real entities, I do not here mean the series of particular and mutable things, but only the series of fixed and eternal things. It would be impossible for human infirmity to follow up the series of particular mutable things, both on account of their multitude, surpassing all calculation, and on account of the infinitely diverse circumstances surrounding one and the same thing, any one of which may be the cause for its existence or non-existence. Indeed, their existence has no connection with their essence, or (as we have said already) is not an eternal truth. Neither is there any need that we should understand their series, for the essences of particular mutable things are not to be gathered from their series or order of existence, which would furnish us with nothing beyond their extrinsic denominations, their relations, or, at most, their circumstances, all of which are very different from their inmost essence. This inmost essence must be sought solely from fixed and eternal things, and from the laws, inscribed (so to speak) in those things as in their true codes, according to which all particular things take place and are arranged; nay, these mutable particular things depend so intimately and essentially (so to phrase it) upon the fixed things, that they cannot either be or be conceived without them.

Whence these fixed and eternal things, though they are themselves particular, will nevertheless, owing to their presence and power everywhere, be to us as universals, or genera of definitions of particular mutable things, and as the proximate causes of all things.

But, though this be so, there seems to be no small difficulty in arriving at the knowledge of these particular things, for to conceive them all at once would far surpass the powers of the human understanding. The arrangement whereby one thing is understood before another, as we have stated, should not be sought from their series of existence, nor from eternal things. For the latter are all by nature simultaneous. Other aids are therefore needed besides those employed for understanding eternal things and their laws; however, this is not the place to recount such aids, nor is there any need to do so, until we have acquired a sufficient knowledge of eternal things and their infallible laws, and until the nature of our senses has become plain to us.

Before betaking ourselves to seek knowledge of particular things, it will be seasonable to speak of such aids, as all tend to teach us the mode of employing our senses, and to make certain experiments under fixed rules and arrangement which may suffice to determine the object of our inquiry, so that we may therefrom infer what laws of eternal things it has been produced under, and may gain an insight into its inmost nature, as I will duly show. Here, to return to my purpose, I will only endeavour to set forth what seems necessary for enabling us to attain to knowledge of eternal things, and to define them under the conditions laid down above.

With this end, we must bear in mind what has already been stated, namely, that when the mind devotes itself to any thought, so as to examine it, and to deduce therefrom in due order all the legitimate conclusions possible, any falsehood which may lurk in the thought will be detected; but if the thought be true, the mind will readily proceed without interruption to deduce truths from it. This, I say, is necessary for our purpose, for our thoughts may be brought to a close by the absence of a foundation. If, therefore, we wish to investigate the first thing of all, it will be necessary to supply some foundation which may direct our thoughts thither. Further, since method is reflective knowledge, the foundation which must direct our thoughts can be nothing else than the knowledge of that which constitutes the reality of truth, and the knowledge of the understanding, its properties, and powers. When this has been acquired we shall possess a foundation wherefrom we can deduce our thoughts, and a path whereby the intellect, according to its capacity, may attain the knowledge of eternal things, allowance being made for the extent of the intellectual powers.

If, as I stated in the first part, it belongs to the nature of thought to form true ideas, we must here inquire what is meant by the faculties and power of the understanding.

The chief part of our method is to understand as well as possible the powers of the intellect, and its nature; we are, therefore, compelled (by the considerations advanced in the second part of the method) necessarily to draw these conclusions from the definition itself of thought and understanding. But, so far, we have not got any rules for finding definitions, and, as we cannot set forth such rules without a previous knowledge of nature, that is without a definition of the understanding and its power, it follows either that the definition of the understanding must be clear in itself, or that we can understand nothing. Nevertheless this definition is not absolutely clear in itself; however, since its properties, like all things that we possess through the understanding, cannot be known clearly and distinctly, unless its nature be known previously, the definition of the understanding makes itself manifest, if we pay attention to its properties, which we know clearly and distinctly. Let us, then, enumerate here the properties of the understanding, let us examine them, and begin by discussing the instruments for research which we find innate in us.

The properties of the understanding which I have chiefly remarked, and which I clearly understand, are the following:—

I. It involves certainty—in other words, it knows that a thing exists in reality as it is reflected subjectively.

II. That it perceives certain things, or forms some ideas absolutely, some ideas from others. Thus it forms the idea of quantity absolutely, without reference to any other thoughts; but ideas of motion it only forms after taking into consideration the idea of quantity.

III. Those ideas which the understanding forms absolutely express infinity; determinate ideas are derived from other ideas. Thus in the idea of quantity, perceived by means of a cause, the quantity is determined, as when a body is perceived to be formed by the motion of a plane, a plane by the motion of a line, or, again, a line by the motion of a point. All these are perceptions which do not serve towards understanding quantity, but only towards determining it. This is proved by the fact that we conceive them as formed as it were by motion, yet this motion is not perceived unless the quantity be perceived also; we can even prolong the motion so as to form an infinite line, which we certainly could not do unless we had an idea of infinite quantity.

IV. The understanding forms positive ideas before forming negative ideas.

V. It perceives things not so much under the condition of duration as under a certain form of eternity, and in an infinite number; or rather in perceiving things it does not consider either their number or duration, whereas, in imagining them, it perceives them in a determinate number, duration, and quantity.

VI. The ideas which we form as clear and distinct, seem so to follow from the sole necessity of our nature, that they appear to depend absolutely on our sole power; with confused ideas the contrary is the case. They are often formed against our will.

VII. The mind can determine in many ways the ideas of things, which the understanding forms from other ideas: thus, for instance, in order to define the plane of an ellipse, it supposes a point adhering to a cord to be moved round two centres, or, again, it conceives an infinity of points, always in the same fixed relation to a given straight line, or a cone cut in an oblique plane, so that the angle of inclination is greater than the angle of the vertex of the cone, or in an infinity of other ways.

VIII. The more ideas express perfection of any object, the more perfect are they themselves; for we do not admire the architect who has planned a chapel so much as the architect who has planned a splendid temple.

I do not stop to consider the rest of what is referred to thought, such as love, joy, &c. They are nothing to our present purpose, and cannot even be conceived unless the understanding be perceived previously. When perception is removed, all these go with it.

False and fictitious ideas have nothing positive about them (as we have abundantly shown), which causes them to be called false or fictitious; they are only considered as such through the defectiveness of knowledge. Therefore, false and fictitious ideas as such can teach us nothing concerning the essence of thought; this must be sought from the positive properties just enumerated; in other words, we must lay down some common basis from which these properties necessarily follow, so that when this is given, the properties are necessarily given also, and when it is removed, they too vanish with it.

* * * * * *

The rest of the treatise is wanting.

NOTE, page 4.

The pursuit of honours and riches is likewise very absorbing, especially if such objects be sought simply for their own sake. This might be explained more at large and more clearly: I mean, by distinguishing riches according as they are pursued for their own sake, or in furtherance of fame, or sensual pleasure, or the advancement of science and art. But this subject is reserved to its own place, for it is not here proper to investigate the matter more accurately.

THE ETHICS.

[*ETHICA ORDINE GEOMETRICO DEMONSTRATA.*]

THE ETHICS.

PART I. CONCERNING GOD.

Definitions.

I.

BY that which is *self-caused,* I mean that of which the essence involves existence, or that of which the nature is only conceivable as existent.

II. A thing is called *finite after its kind,* when it can be limited by another thing of the same nature; for instance, a body is called finite because we always conceive another greater body. So, also, a thought is limited by another thought, but a body is not limited by thought, nor a thought by body.

III. By *substance,* I mean that which is in itself, and is conceived through itself: in other words, that of which a conception can be formed independently of any other conception.

IV. By *attribute,* I mean that which the intellect perceives as constituting the essence of substance.

V. By *mode,* I mean the modifications[1] of substance, or that which exists in, and is conceived through, something other than itself.

VI. By *God,* I mean a being absolutely infinite—that is, a substance consisting in infinite attributes, of which each expresses eternal and infinite essentiality.

Explanation.—I say absolutely infinite, not infinite after its kind: for, of a thing infinite only after its kind, infinite attributes may be denied; but that which is absolutely infinite,

[1] "*Affectiones.*"

contains in its essence whatever expresses reality, and involves no negation.

VII. That thing is called free, which exists solely by the necessity of its own nature, and of which the action is determined by itself alone. On the other hand, that thing is necessary, or rather constrained, which is determined by something external to itself to a fixed and definite method of existence or action.

VIII. By *eternity*, I mean existence itself, in so far as it is conceived necessarily to follow solely from the definition of that which is eternal.

Explanation.—Existence of this kind is conceived as an eternal truth, like the essence of a thing, and, therefore, cannot be explained by means of continuance or time, though continuance may be conceived without a beginning or end.

Axioms.

I. Everything which exists, exists either in itself or in something else.

II. That which cannot be conceived through anything else must be conceived through itself.

III. From a given definite cause an effect necessarily follows; and, on the other hand, if no definite cause be granted, it is impossible that an effect can follow.

IV. The knowledge of an effect depends on and involves the knowledge of a cause.

V. Things which have nothing in common cannot be understood, the one by means of the other; the conception of one does not involve the conception of the other.

VI. A true idea must correspond with its ideate or object.

VII. If a thing can be conceived as non-existing, its essence does not involve existence.

Propositions.

Prop. I. *Substance is by nature prior to its modifications.*

Proof.—This is clear from Deff. iii. and v.

Prop. II. *Two substances, whose attributes are different, have nothing in common.*

Proof.—Also evident from Def. iii. For each must exist in itself, and be conceived through itself; in other words, the conception of one does not imply the conception of the other.

PROP. III. *Things which have nothing in common cannot be one the cause of the other.*

Proof.—If they have nothing in common, it follows that one cannot be apprehended by means of the other (Ax. v.), and, therefore, one cannot be the cause of the other (Ax. iv.). *Q.E.D.*

PROP. IV. *Two or more distinct things are distinguished one from the other, either by the difference of the attributes of the substances, or by the difference of their modifications.*

Proof.—Everything which exists, exists either in itself or in something else (Ax. i.),—that is (by Deff. iii. and v.), nothing is granted in addition to the understanding, except substance and its modifications. Nothing is, therefore, given besides the understanding, by which several things may be distinguished one from the other, except the substances, or, in other words (see Ax. iv.), their attributes and modifications. *Q.E.D.*

PROP. V. *There cannot exist in the universe two or more substances having the same nature or attribute.*

Proof.—If several distinct substances be granted, they must be distinguished one from the other, either by the difference of their attributes, or by the difference of their modifications (Prop. iv.). If only by the difference of their attributes, it will be granted that there cannot be more than one with an identical attribute. If by the difference of their modifications—as substance is naturally prior to its modifications (Prop. i.),—it follows that setting the modifications aside, and considering substance in itself, that is truly, (Deff. iii. and vi.), there cannot be conceived one substance different from another,—that is (by Prop. iv.), there cannot be granted several substances, but one substance only. *Q.E.D.*

PROP. VI. *One substance cannot be produced by another substance.*

Proof.—It is impossible that there should be in the universe two substances with an identical attribute, *i.e.* which have anything common to them both (Prop. ii.), and, therefore (Prop. iii.), one cannot be the cause of another, neither can one be produced by the other. *Q.E.D.*

Corollary.—Hence it follows that a substance cannot be produced by anything external to itself. For in the universe nothing is granted, save substances and their modifications (as appears from Ax. i. and Deff. iii. and v.). Now (by the last Prop.) substance cannot be produced by another substance, therefore it cannot be produced by anything external to itself. *Q.E.D.* This is shown still more readily by the absurdity of the contradictory. For, if substance be produced by an external cause, the knowledge of it would depend on the knowledge of its cause (Ax. iv.), and (by Def. iii.) it would itself not be substance.

PROP. VII. *Existence belongs to the nature of substance.*

Proof.—Substance cannot be produced by anything external (Corollary, Prop. vi.), it must, therefore, be its own cause—that is, its essence necessarily involves existence, or existence belongs to its nature.

PROP. VIII. *Every substance is necessarily infinite.*

Proof.—There can only be one substance with an identical attribute, and existence follows from its nature (Prop. vii.); its nature, therefore, involves existence, either as finite or infinite. It does not exist as finite, for (by Def. ii.) it would then be limited by something else of the same kind, which would also necessarily exist (Prop. vii.); and there would be two substances with an identical attribute, which is absurd (Prop. v.). It therefore exists as infinite. *Q.E.D.*

Note I.—As finite existence involves a partial negation, and infinite existence is the absolute affirmation of the given nature, it follows (solely from Prop. vii.) that every substance is necessarily infinite.

Note II.—No doubt it will be difficult for those who think about things loosely, and have not been accustomed to know them by their primary causes, to comprehend the demonstration of Prop. vii.: for such persons make no distinction between the modifications of substances and the substances themselves, and are ignorant of the manner in which things are produced; hence they attribute to substances the beginning which they observe in natural objects. Those who are ignorant of true causes, make complete confusion—think that trees might talk just as well as men—that men might be formed from stones as well as from seed; and imagine that any form might be changed into any other. So, also, those who confuse the two natures, divine and human, readily attribute human passions to the deity, especially so long as they do not know how passions originate in the mind. But, if people would consider the nature of substance, they would have no doubt about the truth of Prop. vii. In fact, this proposition would be a universal axiom, and accounted a truism. For, by substance, would be understood that which is in itself, and is conceived through itself—that is, something of which the conception requires not the conception of anything else; whereas modifications exist in something external to themselves, and a conception of them is formed by means of a conception of the thing in which they exist. Therefore, we may have true ideas of non-existent modifications; for, although they may have no *actual* existence apart from the conceiving intellect, yet their essence is so involved in something external to themselves that they may through it be conceived. Whereas the only truth substances can have, external to the intellect, must consist in their existence, because they are conceived through themselves. Therefore, for a person to say that he has a clear and distinct—that is, a true—idea of a substance, but that he is not sure whether such substance exists, would be the same as if he said that he had a true idea, but was not sure whether or no it was false (a little consideration will make this plain); or if anyone affirmed that substance is created, it would be the same as saying that a false idea was true—in short, the height of absurdity. It must, then, necessarily be admitted that the existence of substance as its essence is an eternal truth. And we can hence conclude by another process of reasoning—that there is but one such substance. I think that this may profitably be done at once; and, in order to proceed regularly with the demonstration, we must premise:—

1. The true definition of a thing neither involves nor expresses anything beyond the nature of the thing defined. From this it follows that—

2. No definition implies or expresses a certain number of

individuals, inasmuch as it expresses nothing beyond the nature of the thing defined. For instance, the definition of a triangle expresses nothing beyond the actual nature of a triangle: it does not imply any fixed number of triangles.

3. There is necessarily for each individual existent thing a cause why it should exist.

4. This cause of existence must either be contained in the nature and definition of the thing defined, or must be postulated apart from such definition.

It therefore follows that, if a given number of individual things exist in nature, there must be some cause for the existence of exactly that number, neither more nor less. For example, if twenty men exist in the universe (for simplicity's sake, I will suppose them existing simultaneously, and to have had no predecessors), and we want to account for the existence of these twenty men, it will not be enough to show the cause of human existence in general; we must also show why there are exactly twenty men, neither more nor less: for a cause must be assigned for the existence of each individual. Now this cause cannot be contained in the actual nature of man, for the true definition of man does not involve any consideration of the number twenty. Consequently, the cause for the existence of these twenty men, and, consequently, of each of them, must necessarily be sought externally to each individual. Hence we may lay down the absolute rule, that everything which may consist of several individuals must have an external cause. And, as it has been shown already that existence appertains to the nature of substance, existence must necessarily be included in its definition; and from its definition alone existence must be deducible. But from its definition (as we have shown, Notes ii., iii.), we cannot infer the existence of several substances; therefore it follows that there is only one substance of the same nature. *Q.E.D.*

PROP. IX. *The more reality or being a thing has the greater the number of its attributes* (Def. iv.).

PROP. X. *Each particular attribute of the one substance must be conceived through itself.*

Proof.—An attribute is that which the intellect perceives of substance, as constituting its essence (Def. iv.).

and, therefore, must be conceived through itself (Def. iii.). *Q.E.D.*

Note.—It is thus evident that, though two attributes are, in fact, conceived as distinct—that is, one without the help of the other—yet we cannot, therefore, conclude that they constitute two entities, or two different substances. For it is the nature of substance that each of its attributes is conceived through itself, inasmuch as all the attributes it has have always existed simultaneously in it, and none could be produced by any other; but each expresses the reality or being of substance. It is, then, far from an absurdity to ascribe several attributes to one substance: for nothing in nature is more clear than that each and every entity must be conceived under some attribute, and that its reality or being is in proportion to the number of its attributes expressing necessity or eternity and infinity. Consequently it is abundantly clear, that an absolutely infinite being must necessarily be defined as consisting in infinite attributes, each of which expresses a certain eternal and infinite essence.

If anyone now ask, by what sign shall he be able to distinguish different substances, let him read the following propositions, which show that there is but one substance in the universe, and that it is absolutely infinite, wherefore such a sign would be sought for in vain.

PROP. XI. *God, or substance, consisting of infinite attributes, of which each expresses eternal and infinite essentiality, necessarily exists.*

Proof.—If this be denied, conceive, if possible, that God does not exist: then his essence does not involve existence. But this (by Prop. vii.) is absurd. Therefore God necessarily exists.

Another proof.—Of everything whatsoever a cause or reason must be assigned, either for its existence, or for its non-existence—*e.g.* if a triangle exist, a reason or cause must be granted for its existence; if, on the contrary, it does not exist, a cause must also be granted, which prevents it from existing, or annuls its existence. This reason or cause must either be contained in the nature of the thing in question, or be external to it. For instance, the reason for the non-existence of a square circle is indicated in its nature, namely, because it would involve a contradiction. On the other hand, the existence of substance follows also solely from its nature, inasmuch as its nature involves existence. (See Prop. vii.)

But the reason for the existence of a triangle or a circle does not follow from the nature of those figures, but from the order of universal nature in extension. From the latter it must follow, either that a triangle necessarily exists, or that it is impossible that it should exist. So much is self-evident. It follows therefrom that a thing necessarily exists, if no cause or reason be granted which prevents its existence.

If, then, no cause or reason can be given, which prevents the existence of God, or which destroys his existence, we must certainly conclude that he necessarily does exist. If such a reason or cause should be given, it must either be drawn from the very nature of God, or be external to him —that is, drawn from another substance of another nature. For if it were of the same nature, God, by that very fact, would be admitted to exist. But substance of another nature could have nothing in common with God (by Prop. ii.), and therefore would be unable either to cause or to destroy his existence.

As, then, a reason or cause which would annul the divine existence cannot be drawn from anything external to the divine nature, such cause must perforce, if God does not exist, be drawn from God's own nature, which would involve a contradiction. To make such an affirmation about a being absolutely infinite and supremely perfect, is absurd; therefore, neither in the nature of God, nor externally to his nature, can a cause or reason be assigned which would annul his existence. Therefore, God necessarily exists. *Q.E.D.*

Another proof.—The potentiality of non-existence is a negation of power, and contrariwise the potentiality of existence is a power, as is obvious. If, then, that which necessarily exists is nothing but finite beings, such finite beings are more powerful than a being absolutely infinite, which is obviously absurd; therefore, either nothing exists, or else a being absolutely infinite necessarily exists also. Now we exist either in ourselves, or in something else which necessarily exists (see Axiom i. and Prop. vii.). Therefore a being absolutely infinite—in other words, God (Def. vi.)—necessarily exists. *Q.E.D.*

Note.—In this last proof, I have purposely shown God's existence *à posteriori*, so that the proof might be more easily followed, not because, from the same premises, God's existence does not follow *à priori*. For, as the potentiality of existence is a power, it follows that, in proportion as reality increases in the nature of a thing, so also will it increase its strength for existence. Therefore a being absolutely infinite, such as God, has from himself an absolutely infinite power of existence, and hence he does absolutely exist. Perhaps there will be many who will be unable to see the force of this proof, inasmuch as they are accustomed only to consider those things which flow from external causes. Of such things, they see that those which quickly come to pass—that is, quickly come into existence—quickly also disappear; whereas they regard as more difficult of accomplishment—that is, not so easily brought into existence—those things which they conceive as more complicated.

However, to do away with this misconception, I need not here show the measure of truth in the proverb, "What comes quickly, goes quickly," nor discuss whether, from the point of view of universal nature, all things are equally easy, or otherwise: I need only remark, that I am not here speaking of things, which come to pass through causes external to themselves, but only of substances which (by Prop. vi.) cannot be produced by any external cause. Things which are produced by external causes, whether they consist of many parts or few, owe whatsoever perfection or reality they possess solely to the efficacy of their external cause, and therefore their existence arises solely from the perfection of their external cause, not from their own Contrariwise, whatsoever perfection is possessed by substance is due to no external cause; wherefore the existence of substance must arise solely from its own nature, which is nothing else but its essence. Thus, the perfection of a thing does not annul its existence, but, on the contrary, asserts it. Imperfection, on the other hand, does annul it; therefore we cannot be more certain of the existence of anything, than of the existence of a being absolutely infinite or perfect—that is, of God. For inasmuch as his essence excludes all imperfection, and involves absolute perfection, all cause for doubt concerning his existence is done away, and the utmost certainty on the question is given. This, I think, will be evident to every moderately attentive reader.

PROP. XII. *No attribute of substance can be conceived from which it would follow that substance can be divided.*

Proof.—The parts into which substance as thus conceived would be divided, either will retain the nature of substance, or they will not. If the former, then (by Prop. viii.) each part will necessarily be infinite, and (by Prop. vi.) self-caused, and (by Prop. v.) will perforce consist of a different attribute, so that, in that case, several substances could be formed out of one substance, which (by Prop. vi.) is absurd. Moreover, the parts (by Prop. ii.) would have nothing in common with their whole, and the whole (by Def. iv. and Prop. x.) could both exist and be conceived without its parts, which everyone will admit to be absurd. If we adopt the second alternative—namely, that the parts will not retain the nature of substance—then, if the whole substance were divided into equal parts, it would lose the nature of substance, and would cease to exist, which (by Prop. vii.) is absurd.

PROP. XIII. *Substance absolutely infinite is indivisible.*

Proof.—If it could be divided, the parts into which it was divided would either retain the nature of absolutely infinite substance, or they would not. If the former, we should have several substances of the same nature, which (by Prop. v.) is absurd. If the latter, then (by Prop. vii.) substance absolutely infinite could cease to exist, which (by Prop. xi.) is also absurd.

Corollary.—It follows, that no substance, and consequently no extended substance, in so far as it is substance, is divisible.

Note.—The indivisibility of substance may be more easily understood as follows. The nature of substance can only be conceived as infinite, and by a part of substance, nothing else can be understood than finite substance, which (by Prop. viii.) involves a manifest contradiction.

PROP. XIV. *Besides God no substance can be granted or conceived.*

Proof.—As God is a being absolutely infinite, of whom

no attribute that expresses the essence of substance can be denied (by Def. vi.), and he necessarily exists (by Prop. xi.); if any substance besides God were granted, it would have to be explained by some attribute of God, and thus two substances with the same attribute would exist, which (by Prop. v.) is absurd; therefore, besides God no substance can be granted, or, consequently, be conceived. If it could be conceived, it would necessarily have to be conceived as existent; but this (by the first part of this proof) is absurd. Therefore, besides God no substance can be granted or conceived. *Q.E.D.*

Corollary I.—Clearly, therefore: 1. God is one, that is (by Def. vi.) only one substance can be granted in the universe, and that substance is absolutely infinite, as we have already indicated (in the note to Prop. x.).

Corollary II.—It follows: 2. That extension and thought are either attributes of God or (by Ax. i.) accidents (*affectiones*) of the attributes of God.

PROP. XV. ***Whatsoever is, is in God, and without God nothing can be, or be conceived.***

Proof.—Besides God, no substance is granted or can be conceived (by Prop. xiv.), that is (by Def. iii.) nothing which is in itself and is conceived through itself. But modes (by Def. v.) can neither be, nor be conceived without substance; wherefore they can only be in the divine nature, and can only through it be conceived. But substances and modes form the sum total of existence (by Ax. i.), therefore, without God nothing can be, or be conceived. *Q.E.D.*

Note.—Some assert that God, like a man, consists of body and mind, and is susceptible of passions. How far such persons have strayed from the truth is sufficiently evident from what has been said. But these I pass over. For all who have in anywise reflected on the divine nature deny that God has a body. Of this they find excellent proof in the fact that we understand by body a definite quantity, so long, so broad, so deep, bounded by a certain shape, and it is the height of absurdity to predicate such a thing of God, a being absolutely infinite. But meanwhile by the other reasons with which they try to prove their point, they show that they think corporeal or extended substance wholly apart from the divine nature, and say it was created by God. Wherefrom the divine nature can have been created, they are wholly ignorant; thus they clearly show, that they do not know the meaning of their own words. I myself have proved sufficiently clearly, at any rate in my own judgment (Coroll. Prop. vi., and Note 2, Prop. viii.), that no substance can be produced or created by anything other than itself. Further, I showed (in Prop. xiv.), that besides God no substance can be granted or conceived. Hence we drew the conclusion that extended substance is one of the infinite attributes of God. However, in order to explain more fully, I will refute the arguments of my adversaries, which all start from the following points:—

Extended substance, in so far as it is substance, consists, as they think, in parts, wherefore they deny that it can be infinite, or, consequently, that it can appertain to God. This they illustrate with many examples, of which I will take one or two. If extended substance, they say, is infinite, let it be conceived to be divided into two parts; each part will then be either finite or infinite. If the former, then infinite substance is composed of two finite parts, which is absurd. If the latter, then one infinite will be twice as large as another infinite, which is also absurd.

Further, if an infinite line be measured out in foot lengths, it will consist of an infinite number of such parts; it would equally consist of an infinite number of parts, if each part measured only an inch: therefore, one infinity would be twelve times as great as the other.

Lastly, if from a single point there be conceived to be drawn two diverging lines which at first are at a definite distance apart, but are produced to infinity, it is certain that the distance between the two lines will be continually increased, until at length it changes from definite to indefinable. As these absurdities follow, it is said, from considering quantity as infinite, the conclusion is drawn, that extended substance must necessarily be finite, and, consequently, cannot appertain to the nature of God.

The second argument is also drawn from God's supreme perfection. God, it is said, inasmuch as he is a supremely perfect being, cannot be passive; but extended substance, in so far as it is divisible, is passive. It follows, therefore, that extended substance does not appertain to the essence of God.

Such are the arguments I find on the subject in writers, who by them try to prove that extended substance is unworthy of the divine nature, and cannot possibly appertain thereto. However, I think an attentive reader will see that I have already answered their propositions; for all their arguments are founded on the hypothesis that extended substance is composed of parts, and such a hypothesis I have shown (Prop. xii., and Coroll. Prop. xiii.) to be absurd. Moreover, anyone who reflects will see that all these absurdities (if absurdities they be, which I am not now discussing), from which it is sought to extract the conclusion that extended substance is finite, do not at all follow from the notion of an infinite quantity, but merely from the notion that an infinite quantity is measurable, and composed of finite parts: therefore, the only fair conclusion to be drawn is that infinite quantity is not measurable, and cannot be composed of finite parts. This is exactly what we have already proved (in Prop. xii.). Wherefore the weapon which they aimed at us has in reality recoiled upon themselves. If, from this absurdity of theirs, they persist in drawing the conclusion that extended substance must be finite, they will in good sooth be acting like a man who asserts that circles have the properties of squares, and, finding himself thereby landed in absurdities, proceeds to deny that circles have any centre, from which all lines drawn to the circumference are equal. For, taking extended substance, which can only be conceived as infinite, one, and indivisible (Props. viii., v., xii.) they assert, in order to prove that it is finite, that it is composed of finite parts, and that it can be multiplied and divided.

So, also, others, after asserting that a line is composed of points, can produce many arguments to prove that a line cannot be infinitely divided. Assuredly it is not less absurd to assert that extended substance is made up of bodies or parts, than it would be to assert that a solid is made up of surfaces, a surface of lines, and a line of points. This must be admitted by all who know clear reason to be infallible, and most of all by those who deny the possibility of a vacuum. For if extended substance could be so divided that its parts were really separate, why should not one part admit of being destroyed, the others remaining joined together as before? And why should all be so fitted into one another as to leave no vacuum? Surely in the case of things, which are really distinct one from the other, one can exist without the other, and can remain in its original condition. As, then, there does not exist a vacuum in nature (of which anon), but all parts are bound to come together to prevent it, it follows from this also that the parts cannot be really distinguished, and that extended substance in so far as it is substance cannot be divided.

If anyone asks me the further question, Why are we naturally so prone to divide quantity? I answer, that quantity is conceived by us in two ways; in the abstract and superficially, as we imagine it; or as substance, as we conceive it solely by the intellect. If, then, we regard quantity as it is represented in our imagination, which we often and more easily do, we shall find that it is finite, divisible, and compounded of parts; but if we regard it as it is represented in our intellect, and conceive it as substance, which it is very difficult to do, we shall then, as I have sufficiently proved, find that it is infinite, one, and indivisible. This will be plain enough to all, who make a distinction between the intellect and the imagination, especially if it be remembered, that matter is everywhere the same, that its parts are not distinguishable, except in so far as we conceive matter as diversely modified, whence its parts are distinguished, not really, but modally. For instance, water, in so far as it is water, we conceive to be divided, and its parts to be separated one from the other; but not in so far as it is extended substance; from this point of view it is neither separated nor divisible. Further, water, in so far as it is water, is produced and corrupted; but, in so far as it is substance, it is neither produced nor corrupted.

I think I have now answered the second argument; it is, in fact, founded on the same assumption as the first—namely, that matter, in so far as it is substance, is divisible, and composed of parts. Even if it were so, I do not know why it should be considered unworthy of the divine nature, inasmuch as besides God (by Prop. xiv.) no substance can be granted, wherefrom it could receive its modifications. All things, I repeat, are in God, and all things which come to pass, come to pass solely through the laws of the infinite nature of God, and follow (as I will shortly show) from the necessity of his essence. Wherefore it can in nowise be said, that God is passive in respect to anything other than himself, or that extended substance is unworthy of the Divine nature, even if it be supposed divisible, so long as it is granted to be infinite and eternal. But enough of this for the present.

PROP. XVI. *From the necessity of the divine nature must follow an infinite number of things in infinite ways—that is, all things which can fall within the sphere of infinite intellect.*

Proof.—This proposition will be clear to everyone, who remembers that from the given definition of any thing the intellect infers several properties, which really necessarily follow therefrom (that is, from the actual essence of the thing defined); and it infers more properties in proportion as the definition of the thing expresses more reality, that is, in proportion as the essence of the thing defined involves more reality. Now, as the divine nature has absolutely infinite attributes (by Def. vi.), of which each expresses infinite essence after its kind, it follows that from the necessity of its nature an infinite number of things (that is, everything which can fall within the sphere of an infinite intellect) must necessarily follow. *Q.E.D.*

Corollary I.—Hence it follows, that God is the efficient cause of all that can fall within the sphere of an infinite intellect.

Corollary II.—It also follows that God is a cause in himself, and not through an accident of his nature.

Corollary III.—It follows, thirdly, that God is the absolutely first cause.

PROP. XVII. *God acts solely by the laws of his own nature, and is not constrained by anyone.*

Proof.—We have just shown (in Prop. xvi.), that solely from the necessity of the divine nature, or, what is the same thing, solely from the laws of his nature, an infinite number of things absolutely follow in an infinite number of ways; and we proved (in Prop. xv.), that without God nothing can be nor be conceived; but that all things are in God. Wherefore nothing can exist outside himself, whereby he can be conditioned or constrained to act. Wherefore God acts solely by the laws of his own nature, and is not constrained by anyone. *Q.E.D.*

Corollary I.—It follows: 1. That there can be no cause which, either extrinsically or intrinsically, besides the perfection of his own nature, moves God to act.

Corollary II.—It follows: 2. That God is the sole free cause. For God alone exists by the sole necessity of his nature (by Prop. xi. and Prop. xiv., Coroll. i.), and acts by the sole necessity of his nature, wherefore God is (by Def. vii.) the sole free cause. *Q.E.D.*

Note.—Others think that God is a free cause, because he can, as they think, bring it about, that those things which we have said follow from his nature—that is, which are in his power, should not come to pass, or should not be produced by him. But this is the same as if they said, that God could bring it about, that it should not follow from the nature of a triangle, that its three interior angles should not be equal to two right angles; or that from a given cause no effect should follow, which is absurd.

Moreover, I will show below, without the aid of this proposition, that neither intellect nor will appertain to God's nature. I know that there are many who think that they can show, that supreme intellect and free will do appertain to God's nature; for they say they know of nothing more perfect, which they can attribute to God, than that which is the highest perfection in ourselves. Further, although they conceive God as actually supremely intelligent, they yet do not believe, that he can bring into existence everything which he actually understands, for they think that they would thus destroy God's power. If, they contend, God had created everything which is in his intellect, he would not be able to create anything more, and this, they think, would clash with God's omnipotence; therefore, they prefer to assert that God is indifferent to all things, and that he creates nothing except that which he has decided, by some absolute exercise of will, to create. However, I think I have shown sufficiently clearly (by Prop. xvi.), that from God's supreme power, or infinite nature, an infinite number of things—that is, all things have necessarily flowed forth in an infinite number of ways, or always follow from the same necessity; in the same way as from the nature of a triangle it follows from eternity and for eternity, that its three interior angles are equal to two right angles. Wherefore the omnipotence of God has been displayed from all eternity, and will for all eternity remain in the same state of activity. This manner of treating the question attributes to God an omnipotence, in my opinion, far more perfect. For, otherwise, we are compelled to confess that God understands an infinite number of creatable things, which he will never be able to create, for, if he created all that he understands, he would, according to this showing, exhaust his omnipotence, and render himself imperfect. Wherefore, in order to establish that God is perfect, we should be reduced to establishing at the same time, that he cannot bring to pass everything over which his power extends; this seems to be a hypothesis most absurd, and most repugnant to God's omnipotence.

Further (to say a word here concerning the intellect and the will which we attribute to God), if intellect and will appertain to the eternal essence of God, we must take these words in some significations quite different from those they usually bear. For intellect and will, which should constitute the essence of God, would perforce be as far apart as the poles from the human intellect and will, in fact, would have nothing in common with them but the name; there would be about as much correspondence between the two as there is between the Dog, the heavenly constellation, and a dog, an animal that barks. This I will prove as follows. If intellect belongs to the divine nature, it cannot be in nature, as ours is generally thought to be, posterior to, or simultaneous with the things understood, inasmuch as God is prior to all things by reason of his causality (Prop. xvi., Coroll. i.). On the contrary, the truth and formal essence of things is as it is, because it exists by representation as such in the intellect of God. Wherefore the intellect of God, in so far as it is conceived to constitute God's essence, is, in reality, the cause of things, both of their essence and of their existence. This seems to have been recognized by those who have asserted, that God's intellect, God's will, and God's power, are one and the same. As, therefore, God's intellect is the sole cause of things, namely, both of their essence and existence, it must necessarily differ from them in respect to its essence, and in respect to its existence. For a cause differs from a thing it causes, precisely in the quality which the latter gains from the former.

For example, a man is the cause of another man's existence, but not of his essence (for the latter is an eternal truth), and, therefore, the two men may be entirely similar in essence, but must be different in existence; and hence if the existence of one of them cease, the existence of the other will not necessarily cease also; but if the essence of one could be destroyed, and be made false, the essence of the other would be destroyed also. Wherefore, a thing which is the cause both of the essence and of the existence of a given effect, must differ from such effect both in respect to its essence, and also in respect to its existence. Now the intellect of God is the cause of both the essence and the existence of our intellect; therefore, the intellect of God in so far as it is conceived to constitute the divine essence, differs from our intellect both in respect to essence and in respect to existence, nor can it in anywise agree therewith save in name, as we said before. The reasoning would be identical in the case of the will, as anyone can easily see.

Prop. XVIII. *God is the indwelling and not the transient cause of all things.*

Proof.—All things which are, are in God, and must be conceived through God (by Prop. xv.), therefore (by Prop. xvi., Coroll. i.) God is the cause of those things which are in him. This is our first point. Further, besides God there can be no substance (by Prop. xiv.), that is nothing in itself external to God. This is our second point. God, therefore, is the indwelling and not the transient cause of all things. *Q.E.D.*

Prop. XIX. *God, and all the attributes of God, are eternal.*

Proof.—God (by Def. vi.) is substance, which (by Prop. xi.) necessarily exists, that is (by Prop. vii.) existence appertains to its nature, or (what is the same thing) follows from its definition; therefore, God is eternal (by Def. viii.). Further, by the attributes of God we must understand that which (by Def. iv.) expresses the essence of the divine substance—in other words, that which appertains to substance: that, I say, should be involved in the attributes of substance. Now eternity appertains to the nature of substance (as I have already shown in Prop. vii.); therefore, eternity must appertain to each of the attributes, and thus all are eternal. *Q.E.D.*

Note.—This proposition is also evident from the manner in which (in Prop. xi.) I demonstrated the existence of God; it is evident, I repeat, from that proof, that the existence of God, like his essence, is an eternal truth. Further (in Prop. xix. of my "Principles of the Cartesian Philosophy"), I have proved the eternity of God, in another manner, which I need not here repeat.

PROP. XX. *The existence of God and his essence are one and the same.*

Proof.—God (by the last Prop.) and all his attributes are eternal, that is (by Def. viii.) each of his attributes expresses existence. Therefore the same attributes of God which explain his eternal essence, explain at the same time his eternal existence—in other words, that which constitutes God's essence constitutes at the same time his existence. Wherefore God's existence and God's essence are one and the same. *Q.E.D.*

Coroll. I.—Hence it follows that God's existence, like His essence, is an eternal truth.

Coroll. II.—Secondly, it follows that God, and all the attributes of God, are unchangeable. For if they could be changed in respect to existence, they must also be able to be changed in respect to essence—that is, obviously, be changed from true to false, which is absurd.

PROP. XXI. *All things which follow from the absolute nature of any attribute of God must always exist and be infinite, or, in other words, are eternal and infinite through the said attribute.*

Proof.—Conceive, if it be possible (supposing the proposition to be denied), that something in some attribute of God can follow from the absolute nature of the said attribute, and that at the same time it is finite, and has a conditioned existence or duration; for instance, the idea of God expressed in the attribute thought. Now thought, in so far as it is supposed to be an attribute of God, is necessarily (by Prop. xi.) in its nature infinite. But, in so far as it possesses the idea of God, it is supposed finite. It cannot, however, be conceived as finite, unless it be limited by thought (by Def. ii.); but it is not limited by thought itself, in so far as it has constituted the idea of God (for so far it is supposed to be finite); therefore, it is limited by thought, in so far as it has not constituted the idea of God, which nevertheless (by Prop. xi.) must necessarily exist.

We have now granted, therefore, thought not constituting the idea of God, and, accordingly, the idea of God does not naturally follow from its nature in so far as it is absolute thought (for it is conceived as constituting, and also as not constituting, the idea of God), which is against our hypothesis. Wherefore, if the idea of God expressed in the attribute thought, or, indeed, anything else in any attribute of God (for we may take any example, as the proof is of universal application) follows from the necessity of the absolute nature of the said attribute, the said thing must necessarily be infinite, which was our first point.

Furthermore, a thing which thus follows from the necessity of the nature of any attribute cannot have a limited duration. For if it can, suppose a thing, which follows from the necessity of the nature of some attribute, to exist in some attribute of God, for instance, the idea of God expressed in the attribute thought, and let it be supposed at some time not to have existed, or to be about not to exist.

Now thought being an attribute of God, must necessarily exist unchanged (by Prop. xi., and Prop. xx., Coroll. ii.); and beyond the limits of the duration of the idea of God (supposing the latter at some time not to have existed, or not to be going to exist) thought would perforce have existed without the idea of God, which is contrary to our hypothesis, for we supposed that, thought being given, the idea of God necessarily flowed therefrom. Therefore the idea of God expressed in thought, or anything which necessarily follows from the absolute nature of some attribute of God, cannot have a limited duration, but through the said attribute is eternal, which is our second point. Bear in mind that the same proposition may be affirmed of anything, which in any attribute necessarily follows from God's absolute nature.

PROP. XXII. *Whatsoever follows from any attribute of God, in so far as it is modified by a modification, which exists necessarily and as infinite, through the said attribute, must also exist necessarily and as infinite.*

Proof.—The proof of this proposition is similar to that of the preceding one.

PROP. XXIII. *Every mode, which exists both necessarily and as infinite, must necessarily follow either from the absolute nature of some attribute of God, or from an attribute modified by a modification which exists necessarily, and as infinite.*

Proof.—A mode exists in something else, through which it must be conceived (Def. v.), that is (Prop. xv.), it exists solely in God, and solely through God can be conceived. If therefore a mode is conceived as necessarily existing and infinite, it must necessarily be inferred or perceived through some attribute of God, in so far as such attribute is conceived as expressing the infinity and necessity of existence, in other words (Def. viii.) eternity; that is, in so far as it is considered absolutely. A mode, therefore, which necessarily exists as infinite, must follow from the absolute nature of some attribute of God, either immediately (Prop. xxi.) or through the means of some modification, which follows from the absolute nature of the said attribute; that is (by Prop. xxii.), which exists necessarily and as infinite.

PROP. XXIV. *The essence of things produced by God does not involve existence.*

Proof.—This proposition is evident from Def. i. For that of which the nature (considered in itself) involves existence is self-caused, and exists by the sole necessity of its own nature.

Corollary.—Hence it follows that God is not only the cause of things coming into existence, but also of their continuing in existence, that is, in scholastic phraseology,

God is cause of the being of things (*essendi rerum*). For whether things exist, or do not exist, whenever we contemplate their essence, we see that it involves neither existence nor duration; consequently, it cannot be the cause of either the one or the other. God must be the sole cause, inasmuch as to him alone does existence appertain. (Prop. xiv. Coroll. i.) *Q.E.D.*

PROP. XXV. *God is the efficient cause not only of the existence of things, but also of their essence.*

Proof.—If this be denied, then God is not the cause of the essence of things; and therefore the essence of things can (by Ax. iv.) be conceived without God. This (by Prop. xv.) is absurd. Therefore, God is the cause of the essence of things. *Q.E.D.*

Note.—This proposition follows more clearly from Prop. xvi. For it is evident thereby that, given the divine nature, the essence of things must be inferred from it, no less than their existence—in a word, God must be called the cause of all things, in the same sense as he is called the cause of himself. This will be made still clearer by the following corollary.

Corollary.—Individual things are nothing but modifications of the attributes of God, or modes by which the attributes of God are expressed in a fixed and definite manner. The proof appears from Prop. xv. and Def. v.

PROP. XXVI. *A thing which is conditioned to act in a particular manner, has necessarily been thus conditioned by God; and that which has not been conditioned by God cannot condition itself to act.*

Proof.—That by which things are said to be conditioned to act in a particular manner is necessarily something positive (this is obvious); therefore both of its essence and of its existence God by the necessity of his nature is the efficient cause (Props. xxv. and xvi.); this is our first point. Our second point is plainly to be inferred therefrom. For if a thing, which has not been conditioned by God, could condition itself, the first part of our proof would be false, and this, as we have shown, is absurd.

PROP. XXVII. *A thing, which has been conditioned by God to act in a particular way, cannot render itself unconditioned.*

Proof.—This proposition is evident from the third axiom.

PROP. XXVIII.—*Every individual thing, or everything which is finite and has a conditioned existence, cannot exist or be conditioned to act, unless it be conditioned for existence and action by a cause other than itself, which also is finite, and has a conditioned existence; and likewise this cause cannot in its turn exist, or be conditioned to act, unless it be conditioned for existence and action by another cause, which also is finite, and has a conditioned existence, and so on to infinity.*

Proof.—Whatsoever is conditioned to exist and act, has been thus conditioned by God (by Prop. xxvi. and Prop. xxiv., Coroll.)

But that which is finite, and has a conditioned existence, cannot be produced by the absolute nature of any attribute of God; for whatsoever follows from the absolute nature of any attribute of God is infinite and eternal (by Prop. xxi.). It must, therefore, follow from some attribute of God, in so far as the said attribute is considered as in some way modified; for substance and modes make up the sum total of existence (by Ax. i. and Def. iii., v.), while modes are merely modifications of the attributes of God. But from God, or from any of his attributes, in so far as the latter is modified by a modification infinite and eternal, a conditioned thing cannot follow. Wherefore it must follow from, or be conditioned for, existence and action by God or one of his attributes, in so far as the latter are modified by some modification which is finite, and has a conditioned existence. This is our first point. Again, this cause or this modification (for the reason by which we established the first part of this proof) must in its turn be conditioned by another cause, which also is finite, and has a conditioned existence, and, again, this last by another (for the same reason); and so on (for the same reason) to infinity. *Q.E.D.*

Note.—As certain things must be produced immediately by God, namely those things which necessarily follow from his absolute nature, through the means of these primary attributes, which, nevertheless, can neither exist nor be conceived without God, it follows:—1. That God is absolutely the proximate cause of those things immediately produced by him. I say absolutely, not after his kind, as is usually stated. For the effects of God cannot either exist or be conceived without a cause (Prop. xv. and Prop.

xxiv., Coroll.). 2. That God cannot properly be styled the remote cause of individual things, except for the sake of distinguishing these from what he immediately produces, or rather from what follows from his absolute nature. For, by a remote cause, we understand a cause which is in no way conjoined to the effect. But all things which are, are in God, and so depend on God, that without him they can neither be nor be conceived.

PROP. XXIX. *Nothing in the universe is contingent, but all things are conditioned to exist and operate in a particular manner by the necessity of the divine nature.*

Proof.—Whatsoever is, is in God (Prop. xv.). But God cannot be called a thing contingent. For (by Prop. xi.) he exists necessarily, and not contingently. Further, the modes of the divine nature follow therefrom necessarily, and not contingently (Prop. xvi.); and they thus follow, whether we consider the divine nature absolutely, or whether we consider it as in any way conditioned to act (Prop. xxvii.). Further, God is not only the cause of these modes, in so far as they simply exist (by Prop. xxiv., Coroll.), but also in so far as they are considered as conditioned for operating in a particular manner (Prop. xxvi.). If they be not conditioned by God (Prop. xxvi.), it is impossible, and not contingent, that they should condition themselves; contrariwise, if they be conditioned by God, it is impossible, and not contingent, that they should render themselves unconditioned. Wherefore all things are conditioned by the necessity of the divine nature, not only to exist, but also to exist and operate in a particular manner, and there is nothing that is contingent. *Q.E.D.*

Note.—Before going any further, I wish here to explain, what we should understand by nature viewed as active (*natura naturans*), and nature viewed as passive (*natura naturata*). I say to explain, or rather call attention to it, for I think that, from what has been said, it is sufficiently clear, that by nature viewed as active we should understand that which is in itself, and is conceived through itself, or those attributes of substance, which express eternal and infinite essence, in other words (Prop. xiv., Coroll. i., and Prop. xvii., Coroll. ii.) God, in so far as he is considered as a free cause.

By nature viewed as passive I understand all that which follows from the necessity of the nature of God, or of any of the attributes of God, that is, all the modes of the attributes of God, in so far as they are considered as things which are in God, and which without God cannot exist or be conceived.

PROP. XXX. *Intellect, in function (actu) finite, or in function infinite, must comprehend the attributes of God and the modifications of God, and nothing else.*

Proof.—A true idea must agree with its object (Ax. vi.); in other words (obviously), that which is contained in the intellect in representation must necessarily be granted in nature. But in nature (by Prop. xiv., Coroll. i.) there is no substance save God, nor any modifications save those (Prop. xv.) which are in God, and cannot without God either be or be conceived. Therefore the intellect, in function finite, or in function infinite, must comprehend the attributes of God and the modifications of God, and nothing else. *Q.E.D.*

PROP. XXXI. *The intellect in function, whether finite or infinite, as will, desire, love, &c., should be referred to passive nature and not to active nature.*

Proof.—By the intellect we do not (obviously) mean absolute thought, but only a certain mode of thinking, differing from other modes, such as love, desire, &c., and therefore (Def. v.) requiring to be conceived through absolute thought. It must (by Prop. xv. and Def. vi.), through some attribute of God which expresses the eternal and infinite essence of thought, be so conceived, that without such attribute it could neither be nor be conceived. It must therefore be referred to nature passive rather than to nature active, as must also the other modes of thinking. *Q.E.D.*

Note.—I do not here, by speaking of intellect in function, admit that there is such a thing as intellect in potentiality: but, wishing to avoid all confusion, I desire to speak only of what is most clearly perceived by us, namely, of the very act of understanding, than which nothing is more clearly perceived. For we cannot perceive anything without adding to our knowledge of the act of understanding.

PROP. XXXII. *Will cannot be called a free cause, but only a necessary cause.*

Proof.—Will is only a particular mode of thinking, like intellect; therefore (by Prop. xxviii.) no volition can exist, nor be conditioned to act, unless it be conditioned by some cause other than itself, which cause is conditioned by a third cause, and so on to infinity. But if will be supposed infinite, it must also be conditioned to exist and act by God, not by virtue of his being substance absolutely infinite, but by virtue of his possessing an attribute which expresses the infinite and eternal essence of thought (by Prop. xxiii.). Thus, however it be conceived, whether as finite or infinite, it requires a cause by which it should be conditioned to exist and act. Thus (Def. vii.) it cannot be called a free cause, but only a necessary or constrained cause. *Q.E.D.*

Coroll. I.—Hence it follows, first, that God does not act according to freedom of the will.

Coroll. II.—It follows, secondly, that will and intellect stand in the same relation to the nature of God as do motion, and rest, and absolutely all natural phenomena, which must be conditioned by God (Prop. xxix.) to exist and act in a particular manner. For will, like the rest, stands in need of a cause, by which it is conditioned to exist and act in a particular manner. And although, when will or intellect be granted, an infinite number of results may follow, yet God cannot on that account be said to act from freedom of the will, any more than the infinite number of results from motion and rest would justify us in saying that motion and rest act by free will. Wherefore will no more appertains to God than does anything else in nature, but stands in the same relation to him as motion, rest, and the like, which we have shown to follow from the necessity of the divine nature, and to be conditioned by it to exist and act in a particular manner.

PROP. XXXIII. *Things could not have been brought into being by God in any manner or in any order different from that which has in fact obtained.*

Proof.—All things necessarily follow from the nature of God (Prop. xvi.), and by the nature of God are conditioned to exist and act in a particular way (Prop. xxix.). If things, therefore, could have been of a different nature, or have been conditioned to act in a different way, so that the order of nature would have been different, God's nature would also have been able to be different from what it now is; and therefore (by Prop. xi.) that different nature also would have perforce existed, and consequently there would have been able to be two or more Gods. This (by Prop. xiv., Coroll. i.) is absurd. Therefore things could not have been brought into being by God in any other manner, &c. *Q.E.D.*

Note I.—As I have thus shown, more clearly than the sun at noonday, that there is nothing to justify us in calling things contingent, I wish to explain briefly what meaning we shall attach to the word contingent; but I will first explain the words necessary and impossible.

A thing is called necessary either in respect to its essence or in respect to its cause; for the existence of a thing necessarily follows, either from its essence and definition, or from a given efficient cause. For similar reasons a thing is said to be impossible; namely, inasmuch as its essence or definition involves a contradiction, or because no external cause is granted, which is conditioned to produce such an effect; but a thing can in no respect be called contingent, save in relation to the imperfection of our knowledge.

A thing of which we do not know whether the essence does or does not involve a contradiction, or of which, knowing that it does not involve a contradiction, we are still in doubt concerning the existence, because the order of causes escapes us,—such a thing, I say, cannot appear to us either necessary or impossible. Wherefore we call it contingent or possible.

Note II.—It clearly follows from what we have said, that things have been brought into being by God in the highest perfection, inasmuch as they have necessarily followed from a most perfect nature. Nor does this prove any imperfection in God, for it has compelled us to affirm his perfection. From its contrary proposition, we should clearly gather (as I have just shown), that God is not supremely perfect, for if things had been brought into being in any other way, we should have to assign to God a nature different from that, which we are bound to attribute to him from the consideration of an absolutely perfect being.

I do not doubt, that many will scout this idea as absurd, and will refuse to give their minds up to contemplating it, simply because they are accustomed to assign to God a freedom very different from that which we (Def. vii.) have deduced. They assign to him, in short, absolute free will. However, I am also convinced that if such persons reflect on the matter, and duly weigh in their minds our series of propositions, they will reject such freedom as they now attribute to God, not only as nugatory, but also as a great impediment to organized knowledge. There is no need for me to repeat what I said in the note to Prop. xvii. But, for the sake of my opponents, I will show further, that although it be granted that will appertains to the essence of God, it nevertheless follows from his perfection, that things could not have been by him created other than they are, or in a different order; this is easily proved, if we reflect on what our opponents themselves concede, namely, that it depends solely on the decree and will of God, that each thing is what it is. If it were otherwise, God would not be the cause of all things. Further, that all the decrees of God have been ratified from all eternity by God himself. If it were otherwise, God would be convicted of imperfection or change. But in eternity there is no such thing as when, before, or after; hence it follows solely from the perfection of God, that God never can decree, or never could have decreed anything but what is; that God did not exist before his decrees, and would not exist without them. But, it is said, supposing that God had made a different universe, or had ordained other decrees from all eternity concerning nature and her order, we could not therefore conclude any imperfection in God. But persons who say this must admit that God can change his decrees. For if God had ordained any decrees concerning nature and her order, different from those which he has ordained—in other words, if he had willed and conceived something different concerning nature—he would perforce have had a different intellect from that which he has, and also a different will. But if it were allowable to assign to God a different intellect and a different will, without any change in his essence or his perfection, what would there be to prevent him changing the decrees which he has made concerning created things, and nevertheless remaining perfect? For his intellect and will concerning things created and their order are the same, in respect to his essence and perfection, however they be conceived.

Further, all the philosophers whom I have read admit that God's intellect is entirely actual, and not at all potential; as they also admit that God's intellect, and God's will, and God's essence are identical, it follows that, if God had had a different actual intellect and a different will, his essence would also have been different; and thus, as I concluded at first, if things had been brought into being by God in a different way from that which has obtained, God's intellect and will, that is (as is admitted) his essence would perforce have been different, which is absurd.

As these things could not have been brought into being by God in any but the actual way and order which has obtained; and as the truth of this proposition follows from the supreme perfection of God; we can have no sound reason for persuading ourselves to believe that God did not wish to create all the things which were in his intellect, and to create them in the same perfection as he had understood them.

But, it will be said, there is in things no perfection nor imperfection; that which is in them, and which causes them to be called perfect or imperfect, good or bad, depends solely on the will of God. If God had so willed, he might have brought it about that what is now perfection should be extreme imperfection, and *vice versâ*. What is such an assertion, but an open declaration that God, who necessarily understands that which he wishes, might bring it about by his will, that he should understand things differently from the way in which he does understand them? This (as we have just shown) is the height of absurdity. Wherefore, I may turn the argument against its employers, as follows:—All things depend on the power of God. In order that things should be different from what they are, God's will would necessarily have to be different. But God's will cannot be different (as we have just most clearly demonstrated) from God's perfection. Therefore neither can things be different. I confess, that the theory which subjects all things to the will of an indifferent deity, and asserts that they are all dependent on his fiat, is less far from the truth than the theory of those, who maintain that God acts in all things with a view of promoting what is good. For these latter persons seem to set up something beyond God, which does not depend on God, but which God in acting looks to as an exemplar, or which he aims at as a definite goal. This is only another name for subjecting God to the dominion of destiny, an utter absurdity in respect to God, whom we have shown to be the first and only free cause of the essence of all things and also of their existence. I need, therefore, spend no time in refuting such wild theories.

PROP. XXXIV. *God's power is identical with his essence.*

Proof.—From the sole necessity of the essence of God it follows that God is the cause of himself (Prop. xi.) and of all things (Prop. xvi. and Coroll.). Wherefore the power of God, by which he and all things are and act, is identical with his essence. *Q.E.D.*

PROP. XXXV. *Whatsoever we conceive to be in the power of God, necessarily exists.*

Proof.—Whatsoever is in God's power, must (by the last Prop.) be comprehended in his essence in such a manner, that it necessarily follows therefrom, and therefore necessarily exists. *Q.E.D.*

PROP. XXXVI. *There is no cause from whose nature some effect does not follow.*

Proof.—Whatsoever exists expresses God's nature or essence in a given conditioned manner (by Prop. xxv., Coroll.); that is (by Prop. xxxiv.), whatsoever exists, expresses in a given conditioned manner God's power, which is the cause of all things, therefore an effect must (by Prop. xvi.) necessarily follow. *Q.E.D.*

APPENDIX.—In the foregoing I have explained the nature and properties of God. I have shown that he necessarily exists, that he is one: that he is, and acts solely by the necessity of his own nature; that he is the free cause of all things, and how he is so; that all things are in God, and so depend on him, that without him they could neither exist nor be conceived; lastly, that all things are predetermined by God, not through his free will or absolute fiat, but from the very nature of God or infinite power. I have further, where occasion offered, taken care to remove the prejudices, which might impede the comprehension of my demonstrations. Yet there still remain misconceptions not a few, which might and may prove very grave hindrances to the understanding of the concatenation of things, as I have explained it above. I have therefore thought it worth while to bring these misconceptions before the bar of reason.

All such opinions spring from the notion commonly entertained, that all things in nature act as men themselves act, namely, with an end in view. It is accepted as certain, that God himself directs all things to a definite goal (for it is said that God made all things for man, and man that he might worship him). I will, therefore, consider this opinion, asking first, why it obtains general credence, and why all men are naturally so prone to adopt it? secondly, I will point out its falsity; and, lastly, I will show how it has given rise to prejudices about good and bad, right and wrong, praise and blame, order and confusion, beauty and ugliness, and the like. However, this is not the place to deduce these misconceptions from the nature of the human mind: it will be sufficient here, if I assume as a starting point, what ought to be universally admitted, namely, that all men are born ignorant of the causes of things, that all have the desire to seek for what is useful to them, and that they are conscious of such desire. Herefrom it follows, first, that men think themselves free inasmuch as they are conscious of their volitions and desires, and never even dream, in their ignorance, of the causes which have disposed them so to wish and desire. Secondly, that men do all things for an end, namely, for that which is useful to them, and which they seek. Thus it comes to pass that they only look for a knowledge of the final causes of events, and when these are learned, they are content, as having no cause for further doubt. If they cannot learn such causes from external sources, they are compelled to turn to considering themselves, and reflecting what end would have induced them personally to bring about the given event, and thus they necessarily judge other natures by their own. Further, as they find in themselves and outside themselves many means which assist them not a little in their search for what is useful, for instance, eyes for seeing, teeth for chewing, herbs and animals for yielding food, the sun for giving light, the sea for breeding fish, &c., they come to look on the whole of nature as a means for obtaining such conveniences. Now as they are aware, that they found these conveniences and did not make them, they think they have cause for believing, that some other being has made them for their use. As they look upon things as means, they cannot believe them to be self-created; but, judging from the means which they are accustomed to prepare for themselves, they are bound to believe in some ruler or rulers of the universe endowed with human freedom, who have arranged and adapted everything for human use. They are bound to estimate the nature of such rulers (having no information on the subject) in accordance with their own nature, and therefore they assert that the gods ordained everything for the use of man, in order to bind man to themselves and obtain from him the highest honour. Hence also it follows, that everyone thought out for himself, according to his abilities, a different way of worshipping God, so that God might love him more than his fellows, and direct the whole course of nature for the satisfaction of his blind cupidity and insatiable avarice. Thus the prejudice developed into superstition, and took deep root in the human mind; and for this reason everyone strove most zealously to understand and explain the final causes of things; but in their endeavour to show that nature does nothing in vain, *i.e.*, nothing which is useless to man, they only seem to have demonstrated that nature, the gods, and men are all mad together. Consider, I pray you, the result: among the many helps of nature they were bound to find some hindrances, such as storms, earthquakes, diseases, &c.: so they declared that such things happen, because the gods are angry at some wrong done them by men, or at some fault committed in their worship. Experience day by day protested and showed by infinite examples, that good and evil fortunes fall to the lot of pious and impious alike; still they would not abandon their inveterate prejudice, for it was more easy for them to class such contradictions among other unknown things of whose use they were ignorant, and thus to retain their actual and innate condition of ignorance, than to destroy the whole fabric of their reasoning and start afresh. They therefore laid down as an axiom, that God's judgments far transcend human understanding. Such a doctrine might well have sufficed to conceal the truth from the human race for all eternity, if mathematics had not furnished another standard of verity in considering solely the essence and properties of figures without regard to their final causes. There are other reasons (which I need not mention here) besides mathematics, which might have caused men's minds to be directed to these general prejudices, and have led them to the knowledge of the truth.

I have now sufficiently explained my first point. There is no need to show at length, that nature has no particular goal in view, and that final causes are mere human figments. This, I think, is already evident enough, both from the causes and foundations on which I have shown such prejudice to be based, and also from Prop. xvi., and the Corollary of Prop. xxxii., and, in fact, all those propositions in which I have shown, that everything in nature proceeds from a sort of necessity, and with the utmost perfection. However, I will add a few remarks, in order to overthrow this doctrine of a final cause utterly. That which is really a cause it considers as an effect, and *vice versâ*: it makes that which is by nature first to be last, and that which is highest and most perfect to be most imperfect. Passing over the questions of cause and priority as self-evident, it is plain from Props. xxi., xxii., xxiii. that that effect is most perfect which is produced immediately by God; the effect which requires for its production several intermediate causes is, in that respect, more imperfect. But if those things which were made immediately by God were made to enable him to attain his end, then the things which come after, for the sake of which the first were made, are necessarily the most excellent of all.

Further, this doctrine does away with the perfection of God: for, if God acts for an object, he necessarily desires something which he lacks. Certainly, theologians and metaphysicians draw a distinction between the object of want and the object of assimilation; still they confess that God made all things for the sake of himself, not for the sake of creation. They are unable to point to anything prior to creation, except God himself, as an object for which God should act, and are therefore driven to admit (as they clearly must), that God lacked those things for whose attainment he created means, and further that he desired them.

We must not omit to notice that the followers of this doctrine, anxious to display their talent in assigning final causes, have imported a new method of argument in proof of their theory—namely, a reduction, not to the impossible, but to ignorance; thus showing that they have no other method of exhibiting their doctrine. For example, if a stone falls from a roof on to someone's head, and kills him, they will demonstrate by their new method, that the stone fell in order to kill the man; for, if it had not by God's will fallen with that object, how could so many circumstances (and there are often many concurrent circumstances) have all happened together by chance? Perhaps you will answer that the event is due to the facts that the wind was blowing, and the man was walking that way. "But why," they will insist, "was the wind blowing, and why was the man at that very time walking that way?" If you again answer, that the wind had then sprung up because the sea had begun to be agitated the day before, the weather being previously calm, and that the man had been invited by a friend, they will again insist: "But why was the sea agitated, and why was the man invited at that time?" So they will pursue their questions from cause to cause, till at last you take refuge in the will of God—in other words, the sanctuary of ignorance. So, again, when they survey the frame of the human body, they are amazed; and being ignorant of the causes of so great a work of art, conclude that it has been fashioned, not mechanically, but by divine and supernatural skill, and has been so put together that one part shall not hurt another.

Hence anyone who seeks for the true causes of miracles, and strives to understand natural phenomena as an intelligent being, and not to gaze at them like a fool, is set down and denounced as an impious heretic by those, whom the masses adore as the interpreters of nature and the gods. Such persons know that, with the removal of ignorance, the wonder which forms their only available means for proving and preserving their authority would vanish also. But I now quit this subject, and pass on to my third point.

After men persuaded themselves, that everything which is created is created for their sake, they were bound to consider as the chief quality in everything that which is most useful to themselves, and to account those things the best of all which have the most beneficial effect on mankind. Further, they were bound to form abstract notions for the explanation of the nature of things, such as *goodness, badness, order, confusion, warmth, cold, beauty, deformity*, and so on; and from the belief that they are free agents arose the further notions *praise* and *blame, sin* and *merit*.

I will speak of these latter hereafter, when I treat of human nature; the former I will briefly explain here.

Everything which conduces to health and the worship of God they have called *good*, everything which hinders these objects they have styled *bad;* and inasmuch as those who do not understand the nature of things do not verify phenomena in any way, but merely imagine them after a fashion, and mistake their imagination for understanding, such persons firmly believe that there is an *order* in things, being really ignorant both of things and their own nature. When phenomena are of such a kind, that the impression they make on our senses requires little effort of imagination, and can consequently be easily remembered, we say that they are *well-ordered;* if the contrary, that they are *ill-ordered* or *confused*. Further, as things which are easily imagined are more pleasing to us, men prefer order to confusion—as though there were any order in nature, except in relation to our imagination—and say that God has created all things in order; thus, without knowing it, attributing imagination to God, unless, indeed, they would have it that God foresaw human imagination, and arranged everything, so that it should be most easily imagined. If this be their theory, they would not, perhaps, be daunted by the fact that we find an infinite number of phenomena, far surpassing our imagination, and very many others which confound its weakness. But enough has been said on this subject. The other abstract notions are nothing but modes of imagining, in which the imagination is differently affected.

though they are considered by the ignorant as the chief attributes of things, inasmuch as they believe that everything was created for the sake of themselves; and, according as they are affected by it, style it good or bad, healthy or rotten and corrupt. For instance, if the motion which objects we see communicate to our nerves be conducive to health, the objects causing it are styled *beautiful;* if a contrary motion be excited, they are styled *ugly.*

Things which are perceived through our sense of smell are styled fragrant or fetid; if through our taste, sweet or bitter, full-flavoured or insipid; if through our touch, hard or soft, rough or smooth, &c.

Whatsoever affects our ears is said to give rise to noise, sound, or harmony. In this last case, there are men lunatic enough to believe, that even God himself takes pleasure in harmony; and philosophers are not lacking who have persuaded themselves, that the motion of the heavenly bodies gives rise to harmony—all of which instances sufficiently show that everyone judges of things according to the state of his brain, or rather mistakes for things the forms of his imagination. We need no longer wonder that there have arisen all the controversies we have witnessed, and finally scepticism: for, although human bodies in many respects agree, yet in very many others they differ; so that what seems good to one seems bad to another; what seems well ordered to one seems confused to another; what is pleasing to one displeases another, and so on. I need not further enumerate, because this is not the place to treat the subject at length, and also because the fact is sufficiently well known. It is commonly said: "So many men, so many minds; everyone is wise in his own way; brains differ as completely as palates." All of which proverbs show, that men judge of things according to their mental disposition, and rather imagine than understand: for, if they understood phenomena, they would, as mathematics attest, be convinced, if not attracted, by what I have urged.

We have now perceived, that all the explanations commonly given of nature are mere modes of imagining, and do not indicate the true nature of anything, but only the constitution of the imagination; and, although they have names, as though they were entities, existing externally to the imagination, I call them entities imaginary rather than real; and, therefore, all arguments against us drawn from such abstractions are easily rebutted.

Many argue in this way. If all things follow from a necessity of the absolutely perfect nature of God, why are there so many imperfections in nature? such, for instance, as things corrupt to the point of putridity, loathsome deformity, confusion, evil, sin, &c. But these reasoners are, as I have said, easily confuted, for the perfection of things is to be reckoned only from their own nature and power; things are not more or less perfect, according as they delight or offend human senses, or according as they are serviceable or repugnant to mankind. To those who ask why God did not so create all men, that they should be governed only by reason, I give no answer but this: because matter was not lacking to him for the creation of every degree of perfection from highest to lowest; or, more strictly, because the laws of his nature are so vast, as to suffice for the production of everything conceivable by an infinite intelligence, as I have shown in Prop. xvi.

Such are the misconceptions I have undertaken to note; if there are any more of the same sort, everyone may easily dissipate them for himself with the aid of a little reflection.

PART II.

OF THE NATURE AND ORIGIN OF THE MIND.

Preface.

I NOW pass on to explaining the results, which must necessarily follow from the essence of God, or of the eternal and infinite being; not, indeed, all of them (for we proved in Part. i., Prop. xvi., that an infinite number must follow in an infinite number of ways), but only those which are able to lead us, as it were by the hand, to the knowledge of the human mind and its highest blessedness.

Definitions.

I. By *body* I mean a mode which expresses in a certain determinate manner the essence of God, in so far as he is considered as an extended thing. (See Pt. i., Prop. xxv. Coroll.)

II. I consider as belonging to the essence of a thing that, which being given, the thing is necessarily given also, and, which being removed, the thing is necessarily removed also; in other words, that without which the thing, and which itself without the thing, can neither be nor be conceived.

III. By *idea*, I mean the mental conception which is formed by the mind as a thinking thing.

Explanation.—I say *conception* rather than perception, because the word perception seems to imply that the mind is passive in respect to the object; whereas conception seems to express an activity of the mind.

IV. By *an adequate idea*, I mean an idea which, in so far as it is considered in itself, without relation to the object, has all the properties or intrinsic marks of a true idea.

Explanation.—I say *intrinsic*, in order to exclude that mark which is extrinsic, namely, the agreement between the idea and its object (*ideatum*).

V. *Duration* is the indefinite continuance of existing.

Explanation.—I say *indefinite*, becouse it cannot be determined through the existence itself of the existing thing, or by its efficient cause, which necessarily gives the existence of the thing, but does not take it away.

VI. *Reality* and *perfection* I use as synonymous terms.

VII. By *particular things*, I mean things which are finite and have a conditioned existence; but if several individual things concur in one action, so as to be all simultaneously the effect of one cause, I consider them all, so far, as one particular thing.

Axioms.

I. The essence of man does not involve necessary existence, that is, it may, in the order of nature, come to pass that this or that man does or does not exist.

II. Man thinks.

III. Modes of thinking, such as love, desire, or any other of the passions, do not take place, unless there be in the same individual an idea of the thing loved, desired, &c. But the idea can exist without the presence of any other mode of thinking.

IV. We perceive that a certain body is affected in many ways.

V. We feel and perceive no particular things, save bodies and modes of thought.

N.B. *The postulates are given after the conclusion of* Prop. xiii.

Propositions.

Prop. I. *Thought is an attribute of God, or God is a thinking thing.*

Proof.—Particular thoughts, or this or that thought, are modes which, in a certain conditioned manner, express the nature of God (Pt. i., Prop. xxv., Coroll.). God therefore possesses the attribute (Pt. i., Def. v.) of which the concept is involved in all particular thoughts, which latter are conceived thereby. Thought, therefore, is one of the infinite attributes of God, which express God's eternal and infinite essence (Pt. i., Def. vi.). In other words, God is a thinking thing. *Q.E.D.*

Note.—This proposition is also evident from the fact, that we are able to conceive an infinite thinking being. For, in proportion as a thinking being is conceived as thinking more thoughts, so is it conceived as containing more reality or perfection. Therefore a being, which can think an infinite number of things in an infinite number of ways, is, necessarily, in respect of thinking, infinite. As, therefore, from the consideration of thought alone we conceive an infinite being, thought is necessarily (Pt. i., Deff. iv. and vi.) one of the infinite attributes of God, as we w^re desirous of showing.

PROP. II. *Extension is an attribute of God, or God is an extended thing.*

Proof.—The proof of this proposition is similar to that of the last.

PROP. III. *In God there is necessarily the idea not only of his essence, but also of all things which necessarily follow from his essence.*

Proof.—God (by the first Prop. of this Part) can think an infinite number of things in infinite ways, or (what is the same thing, by Prop. xvi., Part i.) can form the idea of his essence, and of all things which necessarily follow therefrom. Now all that is in the power of God necessarily is. (Pt. i., Prop. xxxv.) Therefore, such an idea as we are considering necessarily is, and in God alone. *Q.E.D.* (Part i., Prop. xv.)

Note.—The multitude understand by the power of God the free will of God, and the right over all things that exist, which latter are accordingly generally considered as contingent. For it is said that God has the power to destroy all things, and to reduce them to nothing. Further, the power of God is very often likened to the power of kings. But this doctrine we have refuted (Pt. i., Prop. xxxii., Corolls. i. and ii.), and we have shown (Part i., Prop. xvi.) that God acts by the same necessity, as that by which he understands himself; in other words, as it follows from the necessity of the divine nature (as all admit), that God understands himself, so also does it follow by the same necessity, that God performs infinite acts in infinite ways. We further showed (Part i., Prop. xxxiv.), that God's power is identical with God's essence in action; therefore it is as impossible for us to conceive God as not acting, as to conceive him as non-existent. If we might pursue the subject further, I could point out, that the power which is commonly attributed to God is not only human (as showing that God is conceived by the multitude as a man, or in the likeness of a man), but involves a negation of power. However, I am unwilling to go over the same ground so often. I would only beg the reader again and again, to turn over frequently in his mind what I have said in Part i. from Prop. xvi. to the end. No one will be able to follow my meaning, unless he is scrupulously careful not to confound the power of God with the human power and right of kings.

PROP. IV. *The idea of God, from which an infinite number of things follow in infinite ways, can only be one.*

Proof.—Infinite intellect comprehends nothing save the attributes of God and his modifications (Part i., Prop. xxx.). Now God is one (Part i., Prop. xiv., Coroll.). Therefore the idea of God, wherefrom an infinite number of things follow in infinite ways, can only be one. *Q.E.D.*

PROP. V. *The actual being of ideas owns God as its cause, only in so far as he is considered as a thinking thing, not in so far as he is unfolded in any other attribute; that is, the ideas both of the attributes of God and of particular things do not own as their efficient cause their objects (ideata) or the things perceived, but God himself in so far as he is a thinking thing.*

Proof.—This proposition is evident from Prop. iii. of this Part. We there drew the conclusion, that God can form the idea of his essence, and of all things which follow necessarily therefrom, solely because he is a thinking thing, and not because he is the object of his own idea. Wherefore the actual being of ideas owns for cause God, in so far as he is a thinking thing. It may be differently proved as follows: the actual being of ideas is (obviously) a mode of thought, that is (Part i., Prop. xxv., Coroll.) a mode which expresses in a certain manner the nature of God, in so far as he is a thinking thing, and therefore (Part i., Prop. x.) involves the conception of no other attribute of God, and consequently (by Part i., Ax. iv.) is not the effect of any attribute save thought. Therefore the actual being of ideas owns God as its cause, in so far as he is considered as a thinking thing, &c. *Q.E.D.*

Prop. VI. *The modes of any given attribute are caused by God, in so far as he is considered through the attribute of which they are modes, and not in so far as he is considered through any other attribute.*

Proof.—Each attribute is conceived through itself, without any other (Part i., Prop. x.); wherefore the modes of each attribute involve the conception of that attribute, but not of any other. Thus (Part i., Ax. iv.) they are caused by God, only in so far as he is considered through the attribute whose modes they are, and not in so far as he is considered through any other. *Q.E.D.*

Corollary.—Hence the actual being of things, which are not modes of thought, does not follow from the divine nature, because that nature has prior knowledge of the things. Things represented in ideas follow, and are derived from their particular attribute, in the same manner, and with the same necessity as ideas follow (according to what we have shown) from the attribute of thought.

Prop. VII. *The order and connection of ideas is the same as the order and connection of things.*

Proof.—This proposition is evident from Part i., Ax. iv. For the idea of everything that is caused depends on a knowledge of the cause, whereof it is an effect.

Corollary.—Hence God's power of thinking is equal to his realized power of action—that is, whatsoever follows from the infinite nature of God in the world of extension (*formaliter*), follows without exception in the same order and connection from the idea of God in the world of thought (*objective*).

Note.—Before going any further, I wish to recall to mind what has been pointed out above—namely, that whatsoever can be perceived by the infinite intellect as constituting the essence of substance, belongs altogether only to one substance: consequently, substance thinking and substance extended are one and the same substance, comprehended now through one attribute, now through the other. So, also, a mode of extension and the idea of that mode are one and the same thing, though expressed in two ways. This truth seems to have been dimly recognized by those Jews who maintained that God, God's intellect, and the things understood by God are identical. For instance, a circle existing in nature, and the idea of a circle existing, which is also in God, are one and the same thing displayed through different attributes. Thus, whether we conceive nature under the attribute of extension, or under the attribute of thought, or under any other attribute, we shall find the same order, or one and the same chain of causes—that is, the same things following in either case.

I said that God is the cause of an idea—for instance, of the idea of a circle,—in so far as he is a thinking thing; and of a circle, in so far as he is an extended thing, simply because the actual being of the idea of a circle can only be perceived as a proximate cause through another mode of thinking, and that again through another, and so on to infinity; so that, so long as we consider things as modes of thinking, we must explain the order of the whole of nature, or the whole chain of causes, through the attribute of thought only. And, in so far as we consider things as modes of extension, we must explain the order of the whole of nature through the attribute of extension only; and so on, in the case of other attributes. Wherefore of things as they are in themselves God is really the cause, inasmuch as he consists of infinite attributes. I cannot for the present explain my meaning more clearly.

PROP. VIII. *The ideas of particular things, or of modes, that do not exist, must be comprehended in the infinite idea of God, in the same way as the formal essences of particular things or modes are contained in the attributes of God.*

Proof.—This proposition is evident from the last; it is understood more clearly from the preceding note.

Corollary.—Hence, so long as particular things do not exist, except in so far as they are comprehended in the attributes of God, their representations in thought or ideas do not exist, except in so far as the infinite idea of God exists; and when particular things are said to exist, not only in so far as they are involved in the attributes of God, but also in so far as they are said to continue, their ideas will also involve existence, through which they are said to continue.

Note.—If anyone desires an example to throw more light on this question, I shall, I fear, not be able to give him any, which adequately explains the thing of which I here speak, inasmuch as it is unique; however, I will endeavour to illustrate it as far as possible. The nature of a circle is such that if any number of straight lines intersect within it, the rectangles formed by their segments will be equal to one another; thus, infinite equal rectangles are contained in a circle. Yet none of these rectangles can be said to exist, except in so far as the circle exists; nor can the idea of any of these rectangles be said to exist, except in so far as they are comprehended in the idea of the circle. Let us grant that, from this infinite number of rectangles, two only exist. The ideas of these two not only exist, in so far as they are contained in the idea of the circle, but also as they involve the existence of those rectangles; wherefore they are distinguished from the remaining ideas of the remaining rectangles.

PROP. IX. *The idea of an individual thing actually existing is caused by God, not in so far as he is infinite, but in so far as he is considered as affected by another idea of a thing actually existing, of which he is the cause, in so far as he is affected by a third idea, and so on to infinity.*

Proof.—The idea of an individual thing actually existing is an individual mode of thinking, and is distinct from other modes (by the Corollary and Note to Prop. viii. of this part); thus (by Prop. vi. of this part) it is caused by God, in so far only as he is a thinking thing. But not (by Prop. xxviii. of Part i.) in so far as he is a thing thinking absolutely, only in so far as he is considered as affected by another mode of thinking; and he is the cause of this latter, as being affected by a third, and so on to infinity. Now, the order and connection of ideas is (by Prop. vii. of this book) the same as the order and connection of causes. Therefore of a given individual idea another individual idea, or God, in so far as he is considered as modified by that idea, is the cause; and of this second idea God is the cause, in so far as he is affected by another idea, and so on to infinity. *Q.E.D.*

Corollary.—Whatsoever takes place in the individual object of any idea, the knowledge thereof is in God, in so far only as he has the idea of the object.

Proof.—Whatsoever takes place in the object of any idea, its idea is in God (by Prop. iii. of this part), not in so far as he is infinite, but in so far as he is considered as affected by another idea of an individual thing (by the last Prop.); but (by Prop. vii. of this part) the order and connection of ideas is the same as the order and connection of things. The knowledge, therefore, of that which takes place in any individual object will be in God, in so far only as he has the idea of that object. *Q.E.D.*

PROP. X. *The being of substance does not appertain to the essence of man—in other words, substance does not constitute the actual being*[1] *of man.*

Proof.—The being of substance involves necessary existence (Part i., Prop. vii.). If, therefore, the being of substance appertains to the essence of man, substance being granted, man would necessarily be granted also (II. Def. ii.), and, consequently, man would necessarily exist, which is absurd (II. Ax. i.). Therefore, &c. *Q.E.D.*

Note.—This proposition may also be proved from I. v., in which it is shown that there cannot be two substances of the same nature; for as there may be many men, the being of substance is not that which constitutes the actual being of man. Again, the proposition is evident from the other properties of substance—namely, that substance is in its nature infinite, immutable, indivisible, &c., as anyone may see for himself.

Corollary.—Hence it follows, that the essence of man is constituted by certain modifications of the attributes of God. For (by the last Prop.) the being of substance does not belong to the essence of man. That essence therefore (by i. 15) is something which is in God, and which without God can neither be nor be conceived, whether it be a modification (i. 25 Coroll.), or a mode which expresses God's nature in a certain conditioned manner.

Note.—Everyone must surely admit, that nothing can be or be conceived without God. All men agree that God is the one and only cause of all things, both of their essence and of their existence; that is, God is not only the cause of things in respect to their being made (*secundum fieri*), but also in respect to their being (*secundum esse*).

At the same time many assert, that that, without which a thing cannot be nor be conceived, belongs to the essence of that thing; wherefore they believe that either the nature

1 "*Forma.*"

of God appertains to the essence of created things, or else that created things can be or be conceived without God; or else, as is more probably the case, they hold inconsistent doctrines. I think the cause for such confusion is mainly, that they do not keep to the proper order of philosophic thinking. The nature of God, which should be reflected on first, inasmuch as it is prior both in the order of knowledge and the order of nature, they have taken to be last in the order of knowledge, and have put into the first place what they call the objects of sensation; hence, while they are considering natural phenomena, they give no attention at all to the divine nature, and, when afterwards they apply their mind to the study of the divine nature, they are quite unable to bear in mind the first hypotheses, with which they have overlaid the knowledge of natural phenomena, inasmuch as such hypotheses are no help towards understanding the Divine nature. So that it is hardly to be wondered at, that these persons contradict themselves freely.

However, I pass over this point. My intention here was only to give a reason for not saying, that that, without which a thing cannot be or be conceived, belongs to the essence of that thing: individual things cannot be or be conceived without God, yet God does not appertain to their essence. I said that "I considered as belonging to the essence of a thing that, which being given, the thing is necessarily given also, and which being removed, the thing is necessarily removed also; or that without which the thing, and which itself without the thing can neither be nor be conceived." (II. Def. ii.)

PROP. XI. *The first element, which constitutes the actual being of the human mind, is the idea of some particular thing actually existing.*

Proof.—The essence of man (by the Coroll. of the last Prop.) is constituted by certain modes of the attributes of God, namely (by II. Ax. ii.), by the modes of thinking, of all which (by II. Ax. iii.) the idea is prior in nature, and, when the idea is given, the other modes (namely, those of which the idea is prior in nature) must be in the same individual (by the same Axiom). Therefore an idea is the first element constituting the human mind. But not the idea of a non-existent thing, for then (II. viii. Coroll.) the idea itself cannot be said to exist; it must therefore be the idea of something actually existing. But not of an infinite thing. For an infinite thing (I. xxi., xxii.), must always necessarily exist; this would (by II. Ax. i.) involve an absurdity. Therefore the first element, which constitutes the actual being of the human mind, is the idea of something actually existing. *Q.E.D.*

Corollary.—Hence it follows, that the human mind is part of the infinite intellect of God; thus when we say, that the human mind perceives this or that, we make the assertion, that God has this or that idea, not in so far as he is infinite, but in so far as he is displayed through the nature of the human mind, or in so far as he constitutes the essence of the human mind; and when we say that God has this or that idea, not only in so far as he constitutes the essence of the human mind, but also in so far as he, simultaneously with the human mind, has the further idea of another thing, we assert that the human mind perceives a thing in part or inadequately.

Note.—Here, I doubt not, readers will come to a stand, and will call to mind many things which will cause them to hesitate; I therefore beg them to accompany me slowly, step by step, and not to pronounce on my statements, till they have read to the end.

PROP. XII. *Whatsoever comes to pass in the object of the idea, which constitutes the human mind, must be perceived by the human mind, or there will necessarily be an idea in the human mind of the said occurrence. That is, if the object of the idea constituting the human mind be a body, nothing can take place in that body without being perceived by the mind.*

Proof.—Whatsoever comes to pass in the object of any idea, the knowledge thereof is necessarily in God (II. ix. Coroll.), in so far as he is considered as affected by the idea of the said object, that is (II. xi.), in so far as he constitutes the mind of anything. Therefore, whatsoever takes place in the object constituting the idea of the human mind, the knowledge thereof is necessarily in God, in so far as he constitutes the nature of the human mind; that is (by II. xi. Coroll.) the knowledge of the said thing will necessarily be in the mind, in other words the mind perceives it.

Note.—This proposition is also evident, and is more clearly to be understood from II. vii., which see.

PROP. XIII. *The object of the idea constituting the human mind is the body, in other words a certain mode of extension which actually exists, and nothing else.*

Proof.—If indeed the body were not the object of the human mind, the ideas of the modifications of the body would not be in God (II. ix. Coroll.) in virtue of his constituting our mind, but in virtue of his constituting the mind of something else; that is (II. xi. Coroll.) the ideas of the modifications of the body would not be in our mind: now (by II. Ax. iv.) we do possess the ideas of the modifications of the body. Therefore the object of the idea constituting the human mind is the body, and the body as it actually exists (II. xi.). Further, if there were any other object of the idea constituting the mind besides body, then, as nothing can exist from which some effect does not follow (I. xxxvi.) there would necessarily have to be in our mind an idea, which would be the effect of that other object (II. xi.); but (II. Ax. v.) there is no such idea. Wherefore the object of our mind is the body as it exists, and nothing else. *Q.E.D.*

Note.—We thus comprehend, not only that the human mind is united to the body, but also the nature of the union between mind and body. However, no one will be able to grasp this adequately or distinctly, unless he first has adequate knowledge of the nature of our body. The propositions we have advanced hitherto have been entirely general, applying not more to men than to other individual things, all of which, though in different degrees, are animated.[1] For of everything there is necessarily an idea in God, of which God is the cause, in the same way as there is an idea of the human body; thus whatever we have asserted of the idea of the human body must necessarily also be asserted of the idea of everything else. Still, on the other hand, we cannot deny that ideas, like objects, differ one from the other, one being more excellent than another and containing more reality, just as the object of one idea is more excellent than the object of another idea, and contains more reality.

Wherefore, in order to determine, wherein the human

[1] "*Animata.*"

mind differs from other things, and wherein it surpasses them, it is necessary for us to know the nature of its object, that is, of the human body. What this nature is, I am not able here to explain, nor is it necessary for the proof of what I advance, that I should do so. I will only say generally, that in proportion as any given body is more fitted than others for doing many actions or receiving many impressions at once, so also is the mind, of which it is the object, more fitted than others for forming many simultaneous perceptions; and the more the actions of one body depend on itself alone, and the fewer other bodies concur with it in action, the more fitted is the mind of which it is the object for distinct comprehension. We may thus recognize the superiority of one mind over others, and may further see the cause, why we have only a very confused knowledge of our body, and also many kindred questions, which I will, in the following propositions, deduce from what has been advanced. Wherefore I have thought it worth while to explain and prove more strictly my present statements. In order to do so, I must premise a few propositions concerning the nature of bodies.

Axiom I. All bodies are either in motion or at rest.

Axiom II. Every body is moved sometimes more slowly, sometimes more quickly.

Lemma I. *Bodies are distinguished from one another in respect of motion and rest, quickness and slowness, and not in respect of substance.*

Proof.—The first part of this proposition is, I take it, self-evident. That bodies are not distinguished in respect of substance, is plain both from I. v. and I. viii. It is brought out still more clearly from I. xv., note.

Lemma II. *All bodies agree in certain respects.*

Proof.—All bodies agree in the fact, that they involve the conception of one and the same attribute (II., Def. i.). Further, in the fact that they may be moved less or more quickly, and may be absolutely in motion or at rest.

Lemma III. *A body in motion or at rest must be determined to motion or rest by another body, which other body has been determined to motion or rest by a third body, and that third again by a fourth, and so on to infinity.*

Proof.—Bodies are individual things (II., Def. i.), which

(Lemma I.) are distinguished one from the other in respect to motion and rest; thus (I. xxviii.) each must necessarily be determined to motion or rest by another individual thing, namely (II. vi.), by another body, which other body is also (Ax. i.) in motion or at rest. And this body again can only have been set in motion or caused to rest by being determined by a third body to motion or rest. This third body again by a fourth, and so on to infinity. *Q.E.D.*

Corollary.—Hence it follows, that a body in motion keeps in motion, until it is determined to a state of rest by some other body; and a body at rest remains so, until it is determined to a state of motion by some other body. This is indeed self-evident. For when I suppose, for instance, that a given body, A, is at rest, and do not take into consideration other bodies in motion, I cannot affirm anything concerning the body A, except that it is at rest. If it afterwards comes to pass that A is in motion, this cannot have resulted from its having been at rest, for no other consequence could have been involved than its remaining at rest. If, on the other hand, A be given in motion, we shall, so long as we only consider A, be unable to affirm anything concerning it, except that it is in motion. If A is subsequently found to be at rest, this rest cannot be the result of A's previous motion, for such motion can only have led to continued motion; the state of rest therefore must have resulted from something, which was not in A, namely, from an external cause determining A to a state of rest.

Axiom I.—All modes, wherein one body is affected by another body, follow simultaneously from the nature of the body affected and the body affecting; so that one and the same body may be moved in different modes, according to the difference in the nature of the bodies moving it; on the other hand, different bodies may be moved in different modes by one and the same body.

Axiom II.—When a body in motion impinges on another body at rest, which it is unable to move, it recoils, in order to continue its motion, and the angle made by the line of motion in the recoil and the plane of the body at rest, whereon the moving body has impinged, will be equal to the angle formed by the line of motion of incidence and the same plane.

So far we have been speaking only of the most simple bodies, which are only distinguished one from the other by motion and rest, quickness and slowness. We now pass on to compound bodies.

Definition.—When any given bodies of the same or different magnitude are compelled by other bodies to remain in contact, or if they be moved at the same or different rates of speed, so that their mutual movements should preserve among themselves a certain fixed relation, we say that such bodies are in union, and that together they compose one body or individual, which is distinguished from other bodies by this fact of union.

Axiom III.—In proportion as the parts of an individual, or a compound body, are in contact over a greater or less superficies, they will with greater or less difficulty admit of being moved from their position; consequently the individual will, with greater or less difficulty, be brought to assume another form. Those bodies, whose parts are in contact over large superficies, are called *hard;* those, whose parts are in contact over small superficies, are called *soft;* those, whose parts are in motion among one another, are called *fluid.*

LEMMA IV. *If from a body or individual, compounded of several bodies, certain bodies be separated, and if, at the same time, an equal number of other bodies of the same nature take their place, the individual will preserve its nature as before, without any change in its actuality (forma).*

Proof.—Bodies (Lemma i.) are not distinguished in respect of substance: that which constitutes the actuality (*formam*) of an individual consists (by the last Def.) in a union of bodies; but this union, although there is a continual change of bodies, will (by our hypothesis) be maintained; the individual, therefore, will retain its nature as before, both in respect of substance and in respect of mode. *Q.E.D.*

LEMMA V. *If the parts composing an individual become greater or less, but in such proportion, that they all preserve the same mutual relations of motion and rest, the individual will still preserve its original nature, and its actuality will not be changed.*

Proof.—The same as for the last Lemma.

LEMMA VI. *If certain bodies composing an individual be compelled to change the motion, which they have in one direction, for motion in another direction, but in such a manner, that they be able to continue their motions and their mutual communication in the same relations as before, the individual will retain its own nature without any change of its actuality.*

Proof.—This proposition is self-evident, for the individual is supposed to retain all that, which, in its definition, we spoke of as its actual being.

LEMMA VII. *Furthermore, the individual thus composed preserves its nature, whether it be, as a whole, in motion or at rest, whether it be moved in this or that direction; so long as each part retains its motion, and preserves its communication with other parts as before.*

Proof.—This proposition is evident from the definition of an individual prefixed to Lemma iv.

Note.—We thus see, how a composite individual may be affected in many different ways, and preserve its nature notwithstanding. Thus far we have conceived an individual as composed of bodies only distinguished one from the other in respect of motion and rest, speed and slowness; that is, of bodies of the most simple character. If, however, we now conceive another individual composed of several individuals of diverse natures, we shall find that the number of ways in which it can be affected, without losing its nature, will be greatly multiplied. Each of its parts would consist of several bodies, and therefore (by Lemma vi.) each part would admit, without change to its nature, of quicker or slower motion, and would consequently be able to transmit its motions more quickly or more slowly to the remaining parts. If we further conceive a third kind of individuals composed of individuals of this second kind, we shall find that they may be affected in a still greater number of ways without changing their actuality. We may easily proceed thus to infinity, and conceive the whole of nature as one individual, whose parts, that is, all bodies, vary in infinite ways, without any change in the individual as a whole. I should feel bound to explain and demonstrate this point at more length, if I were writing a special treatise on body. But I have already said that such is not my object, I have only touched on the question, because it enables me to prove easily that which I have in view.

POSTULATES.

I. The human body is composed of a number of individual parts, of diverse nature, each one of which is in itself extremely complex.

II. Of the individual parts composing the human body some are fluid, some soft, some hard.

III. The individual parts composing the human body, and consequently the human body itself, are affected in a variety of ways by external bodies.

IV. The human body stands in need for its preservation of a number of other bodies, by which it is continually, so to speak, regenerated.

V. When the fluid part of the human body is determined by an external body to impinge often on another soft part, it changes the surface of the latter, and, as it were, leaves the impression thereupon of the external body which impels it.

VI. The human body can move external bodies, and arrange them in a variety of ways.

PROP. XIV. *The human mind is capable of perceiving a great number of things, and is so in proportion as its body is capable of receiving a great number of impressions.*

Proof.—The human body (by Post. iii. and vi.) is affected in very many ways by external bodies, and is capable in very many ways of affecting external bodies. But (II. xii.) the human mind must perceive all that takes place in the human body; the human mind is, therefore, capable of perceiving a great number of things, and is so in proportion, &c. *Q.E.D.*

PROP. XV. *The idea, which constitutes the actual being of the human mind, is not simple, but compounded of a great number of ideas.*

Proof.—The idea constituting the actual being of the human mind is the idea of the body (II. xiii.), which (Post. i.) is composed of a great number of complex individual parts. But there is necessarily in God the idea of each individual part whereof the body is composed (II. viii.

Coroll.); therefore (II. vii.), the idea of the human body is composed of these numerous ideas of its component parts. *Q.E.D.*

PROP. XVI. *The idea of every mode, in which the human body is affected by external bodies, must involve the nature of the human body, and also the nature of the external body.*

Proof.—All the modes, in which any given body is affected, follow from the nature of the body affected, and also from the nature of the affecting body (by Ax. i., after the Coroll. of Lemma iii.), wherefore their idea also necessarily (by I. Ax. iv.) involves the nature of both bodies; therefore, the idea of every mode, in which the human body is affected by external bodies, involves the nature of the human body and of the external body. *Q.E.D.*

Corollary I.—Hence it follows, first, that the human mind perceives the nature of a variety of bodies, together with the nature of its own.

Corollary II.—It follows, secondly, that the ideas, which we have of external bodies, indicate rather the constitution of our own body than the nature of external bodies. I have amply illustrated this in the Appendix to Part I.

PROP. XVII. *If the human body is affected in a manner which involves the nature of any external body, the human mind will regard the said external body as actually existing, or as present to itself, until the human body be affected in such a way, as to exclude the existence or the presence of the said external body.*

Proof.—This proposition is self-evident, for so long as the human body continues to be thus affected, so long will the human mind (II. xii.) regard this modification of the body—that is (by the last Prop.), it will have the idea of the mode as actually existing, and this idea involves the nature of the external body. In other words, it will have the idea which does not exclude, but postulates the existence or presence of the nature of the external body; therefore the mind (by II. xvi., Coroll. i.) will regard the external body as actually existing, until it is affected, &c. *Q.E.D.*

Corollary.—The mind is able to regard as present external bodies, by which the human body has once been affected, even though they be no longer in existence or present.

Proof.—When external bodies determine the fluid parts of the human body, so that they often impinge on the softer parts, they change the surface of the last named (Post. v.); hence (Ax. ii., after Coroll. of Lemma iii.) they are refracted therefrom in a different manner from that which they followed before such change; and, further, when afterwards they impinge on the new surfaces by their own spontaneous movement, they will be refracted in the same manner, as though they had been impelled towards those surfaces by external bodies; consequently, they will, while they continue to be thus refracted, affect the human body in the same manner, whereof the mind (II. xii.) will again take cognizance—that is (II. xvii.), the mind will again regard the external body as present, and will do so, as often as the fluid parts of the human body impinge on the aforesaid surfaces by their own spontaneous motion. Wherefore, although the external bodies, by which the human body has once been affected, be no longer in existence, the mind will nevertheless regard them as present, as often as this action of the body is repeated. *Q.E.D.*

Note.—We thus see how it comes about, as is often the case, that we regard as present things which are not. It is possible that the same result may be brought about by other causes; but I think it suffices for me here to have indicated one possible explanation, just as well as if I had pointed out the true cause. Indeed, I do not think I am very far from the truth, for all my assumptions are based on postulates, which rest, almost without exception, on experience, that cannot be controverted by those who have shown, as we have, that the human body, as we feel it, exists (Coroll. after II. xiii.). Furthermore (II. vii. Coroll., II. xvi. Coroll. ii.), we clearly understand what is the difference between the idea, say, of Peter, which constitutes the essence of Peter's mind, and the idea of the said Peter, which is in another man, say, Paul. The former directly answers to the essence of Peter's own body, and only implies existence so long as Peter exists; the latter indicates rather the disposition of Paul's body than the nature of Peter, and, therefore, while this disposition of Paul's body lasts, Paul's mind will regard Peter as present to itself, even though he no longer exists. Further, to retain the usual phraseology, the modifications of the human body, of which the ideas represent external bodies as present to us, we will call the images of things, though they do not recall the figure of things. When the mind regards bodies in this fashion, we say that it imagines. I will here draw attention to the fact, in order to indicate where error lies, that the imaginations of the mind, looked at in themselves, do not contain error. The mind does not err in the mere act of imagining, but only in so far as it is regarded as being without the idea, which excludes the existence of such things as it imagines to be present to it. If the mind, while imagining non-existent things as present to it, is at the same time conscious that they do not really exist, this power of imagination must be set down to the efficacy of its nature, and not to a fault, especially if this faculty of imagination depend solely on its own nature—that is (I. Def. vii.), if this faculty of imagination be free.

PROP. XVIII. *If the human body has once been affected by two or more bodies at the same time, when the mind afterwards imagines any of them, it will straightway remember the others also.*

Proof.—The mind (II. xvii. Coroll.) imagines any given body, because the human body is affected and disposed by the impressions from an external body, in the same manner as it is affected when certain of its parts are acted on by the said external body; but (by our hypothesis) the body was then so disposed, that the mind imagined two bodies at once; therefore, it will also in the second case imagine two bodies at once, and the mind, when it imagines one, will straightway remember the other. *Q.E.D.*

Note.—We now clearly see what *Memory* is. It is simply a certain association of ideas involving the nature of things outside the human body, which association arises in the mind according to the order and association of the modifications (*affectiones*) of the human body. I say, first, it is an association of those ideas only, which involve the nature of things outside the human body: not of ideas which answer to the nature of the said things: ideas of the modifications of the human body are, strictly speaking (II. xvi.), those which involve the nature both of the human body and of external bodies. I say, secondly, that this association arises according to the order and association of the modifications of the human body, in order to distinguish it from that association of ideas, which arises from the order of the intellect, whereby the mind perceives things through their primary causes, and which is in all men the same. And hence we can further clearly understand, why the mind from the thought of one thing, should straightway arrive at the thought of another thing, which has no similarity with the first; for instance, from the thought of the word *pomum* (an apple), a Roman would straightway arrive at the thought of the fruit apple, which has no similitude with the articulate sound in question, nor anything in common with it, except that the body of the man has often been affected by these two things; that is, that the man has often heard the word *pomum*, while he was looking at the fruit; similarly every man will go on from one thought to another, according as his habit has ordered the images of things in his body. For a soldier, for instance, when he sees the tracks of a horse in sand, will at once pass from the thought of a horse to the thought of a horseman, and thence to the thought of war, &c.; while a countryman will proceed from the thought of a horse to the thought of a plough, a field, &c. Thus every man will follow this or that train of thought, according as he has been in the habit of conjoining and associating the mental images of things in this or that manner.

PROP. XIX. *The human mind has no knowledge of the body, and does not know it to exist, save through the ideas of the modifications whereby the body is affected.*

Proof.—The human mind is the very idea or knowledge of the human body (II. xiii.), which (II. ix.) is in God, in so far as he is regarded as affected by another idea of a particular thing actually existing: or, inasmuch as (Post. iv.) the human body stands in need of very many bodies whereby it is, as it were, continually regenerated; and the order and connection of ideas is the same as the order and connection of causes (II. vii.); this idea will therefore be in God, in so far as he is regarded as affected by the ideas of very many particular things. Thus God has the idea of the human body, or knows the human body, in so far as he is affected by very many other ideas, and not in so far as he constitutes the nature of the human mind; that is (by II. xi. Coroll.), the human mind does not know the human body. But the ideas of the modifications of body are in God, in so far as he constitutes the nature of the human mind, or the human mind perceives those modifications (II. xii.), and consequently (II. xvi.) the human body itself, and as actually existing; therefore the mind perceives thus far only the human body. *Q.E.D.*

PROP. XX. *The idea or knowledge of the human mind is also in God, following in God in the same manner, and being referred to God in the same manner, as the idea or knowledge of the human body.*

Proof.—Thought is an attribute of God (II. i.); therefore (II. iii.) there must necessarily be in God the idea both of thought itself and of all its modifications, consequently also of the human mind (II. xi.). Further, this idea or knowledge of the mind does not follow from God, in so far as he is infinite, but in so far as he is affected by another idea of an individual thing (II. ix.). But (II. vii.) the order and connection of ideas is the same as the order and connection of causes; therefore this idea or knowledge of the mind is in God and is referred to God, in the same manner as the idea or knowledge of the body. *Q.E.D.*

PROP. XXI. *This idea of the mind is united to the mind in the same way as the mind is united to the body.*

Proof.—That the mind is united to the body we have shown from the fact, that the body is the object of the mind (II. xii. and xiii.); and so for the same reason the idea of the mind must be united with its object, that is, with the mind in the same manner as the mind is united to the body. *Q.E.D.*

Note.—This proposition is comprehended much more clearly from what we said in the note to II. vii. We there showed that the idea of body and body, that is, mind and body (II. xiii.), are one and the same individual conceived now under the attribute of thought, now under the attribute of extension; wherefore the idea of the mind and the mind itself are one and the same thing, which is conceived under one and the same attribute, namely, thought. The idea of the mind, I repeat, and the mind itself are in God by the same necessity and follow from him from the same power of thinking. Strictly speaking, the idea of the mind, that is, the idea of an idea, is nothing but the distinctive quality (*forma*) of the idea in so far as it is conceived as a mode of thought without reference to the object; if a man knows anything, he, by that very fact, knows that he knows it, and at the same time knows that he knows that he knows it, and so on to infinity. But I will treat of this hereafter.

PROP. XXII. *The human mind perceives not only the modifications of the body, but also the ideas of such modifications.*

Proof.—The ideas of the ideas of modifications follow in God in the same manner, and are referred to God in the same manner, as the ideas of the said modifications. This is proved in the same way as II. xx. But the ideas of the modifications of the body are in the human mind (II. xii.), that is, in God, in so far as he constitutes the essence of the human mind; therefore the ideas of these ideas will be in God, in so far as he has the knowledge or idea of the human mind, that is (II. xxi.), they will be in the human mind itself, which therefore perceives not only the modifications of the body, but also the ideas of such modifications. *Q.E.D.*

PROP. XXIII. *The mind does not know itself, except in so far as it perceives the ideas of the modifications of the body.*

Proof.—The idea or knowledge of the mind (II. xx.) follows in God in the same manner, and is referred to God in the same manner, as the idea or knowledge of the body. But since (II. xix.) the human mind does not know the human body itself, that is (II. xi. Coroll.), since the knowledge of the human body is not referred to God, in so far as he constitutes the nature of the human mind; therefore, neither is the knowledge of the mind referred to God, in so far as he constitutes the essence of the human mind; therefore (by the same Coroll. II. xi.), the human mind thus far has no knowledge of itself. Further the ideas of the modifications, whereby the body is affected, involve the nature of the human body itself (II. xvi.), that is (II. xiii.), they agree with the nature of the mind; wherefore the knowledge of these ideas necessarily involves knowledge of the mind; but (by the last Prop.) the knowledge of these ideas is in the human mind itself; wherefore the human mind thus far only has knowledge of itself. *Q.E.D.*

PROP. XXIV.—*The human mind does not involve an adequate knowledge of the parts composing the human body.*

Proof.—The parts composing the human body do not belong to the essence of that body, except in so far as they communicate their motions to one another in a certain fixed relation (Def. after Lemma iii), not in so far as they can be regarded as individuals without relation to the human body. The parts of the human body are highly complex individuals (Post. i.), whose parts (Lemma iv.) can be separated from the human body without in any way destroying the nature and distinctive quality of the latter, and they can communicate their motions (Ax. i., after Lemma iii.) to other bodies in another relation; therefore (II. iii.) the idea or knowledge of each part will be in God, inasmuch (II. ix.) as he is regarded as affected by another idea of a particular thing, which particular thing is prior in the order of nature to the aforesaid part (II. vii.). We may affirm the same thing of each part of each individual composing the human body; therefore, the knowledge of each part composing the human body is in God, in so far as he is affected by very many ideas of things, and not in so far as he has the idea of the human body only, in other words, the idea which constitutes the nature of the human mind (II. xiii.); therefore (II. xi. Coroll.), the human mind does not involve an adequate knowledge of the human body. *Q.E.D.*

PROP. XXV. *The idea of each modification of the human body does not involve an adequate knowledge of the external body.*

Proof.—We have shown that the idea of a modification of the human body involves the nature of an external body, in so far as that external body conditions the human body in a given manner. But, in so far as the external body is an individual, which has no reference to the human body, the knowledge or idea thereof is in God (II. ix.), in so far as God is regarded as affected by the idea of a further thing, which (II. vii.) is naturally prior to the said external body. Wherefore an adequate knowledge of the external body is not in God, in so far as he has the idea of the modification of the human body; in other words, the idea of the modification of the human body does not involve an adequate knowledge of the external body. *Q.E.D.*

PROP. XXVI. *The human mind does not perceive any external body as actually existing, except through the ideas of the modifications of its own body.*

Proof.—If the human body is in no way affected by a given external body, then (II. vii.) neither is the idea of the human body, in other words, the human mind, affected in any way by the idea of the existence of the said external body, nor does it any manner perceive its existence. But, in so far as the human body is affected in any way by a given external body, thus far (II. xvi. and Coroll.) it perceives that external body. *Q.E.D.*

Corollary.—In so far as the human mind imagines an external body, it has not an adequate knowledge thereof.

Proof.—When the human mind regards external bodies through the ideas of the modifications of its own body, we say that it imagines (see II. xvii. note); now the mind can only imagine external bodies as actually existing. Therefore (by II. xxv.), in so far as the mind imagines external bodies, it has not an adequate knowledge of them. *Q.E.D.*

PROP. XXVII. *The idea of each modification of the human body does not involve an adequate knowledge of the human body itself.*

Proof.—Every idea of a modification of the human body involves the nature of the human body, in so far as the human body is regarded as affected in a given manner (II. xvi.). But, inasmuch as the human body is an individual which may be affected in many other ways, the idea of the said modification, &c. *Q.E.D.*

PROP. XXVIII. *The ideas of the modifications of the human body, in so far as they have reference only to the human mind, are not clear and distinct, but confused.*

Proof.—The ideas of the modifications of the human body involve the nature both of the human body and of external bodies (II. xvi.); they must involve the nature not only of the human body but also of its parts; for the modifications are modes (Post. iii.), whereby the parts of the human body, and, consequently, the human body as a whole are affected. But (by II. xxiv., xxv.) the adequate knowledge of external bodies, as also of the parts composing the human body, is not in God, in so far as he is regarded as affected by the human mind, but in so far as he is regarded as affected by other ideas. These ideas of modifications, in so far as they are referred to the human mind alone, are as consequences without premisses, in other words, confused ideas. *Q.E.D.*

Note.—The idea which constitutes the nature of the human mind is, in the same manner, proved not to be, when considered in itself alone, clear and distinct; as also is the case with the idea of the human mind, and the ideas of the ideas of the modifications of the human body, in so far as they are referred to the mind only, as everyone may easily see.

PROP. XXIX. *The idea of the idea of each modification of the human body does not involve an adequate knowledge of the human mind.*

Proof.—The idea of a modification of the human body (II. xxvii.) does not involve an adequate knowledge of the said body, in other words, does not adequately express its nature; that is (II. xiii.) it does not agree with the nature of the mind adequately; therefore (I. Ax. vi.) the idea of this idea does not adequately express the nature of the human mind, or does not involve an adequate knowledge thereof.

Corollary.—Hence it follows that the human mind, when it perceives things after the common order of nature, has not an adequate but only a confused and fragmentary knowledge of itself, of its own body, and of external bodies. For the mind does not know itself, except in so far as it perceives the ideas of the modifications of body (II. xxiii.). It only perceives its own body (II. xix.) through the ideas of the modifications, and only perceives external bodies through the same means; thus, in so far as it has such ideas of modification, it has not an adequate knowledge of itself (II. xxix.), nor of its own body (II. xxvii.), nor of external bodies (II. xxv.), but only a fragmentary and confused knowledge thereof (II. xxviii. and note.) *Q.E.D.*

Note.—I say expressly, that the mind has not an adequate but only a confused knowledge of itself, its own body, and of external bodies, whenever it perceives things after the common order of nature; that is, whenever it is determined from without, namely, by the fortuitous play of circumstance, to regard this or that; not at such times as it is determined from within, that is, by the fact of regarding several things at once, to understand their points of agreement, difference, and contrast. Whenever it is determined in anywise from within, it regards things clearly and distinctly, as I will show below.

PROP. XXX. *We can only have a very inadequate knowledge of the duration of our body.*

Proof.—The duration of our body does not depend on its essence (II. Ax. i.), nor on the absolute nature of God (I. xxi.). But (I. xxviii.) it is conditioned to exist and operate by causes, which in their turn are conditioned to exist and operate in a fixed and definite relation by other causes, these last again being conditioned by others, and so on to infinity. The duration of our body therefore depends on the common order of nature, or the constitution of things. Now, however a thing may be constituted, the adequate knowledge of that thing is in God, in so far as he has the ideas of all things, and not in so far as he has the idea of the human body only. (II. ix. Coroll.) Wherefore the knowledge of the duration of our body is in God very inadequate, in so far as he is only regarded as constituting the nature of the human mind; that is (II. xi. Coroll.), this knowledge is very inadequate in our mind. *Q.E.D.*

PROP. XXXI. *We can only have a very inadequate knowledge of the duration of particular things external to ourselves.*

Proof.—Every particular thing, like the human body, must be conditioned by another particular thing to exist and operate in a fixed and definite relation; this other particular thing must likewise be conditioned by a third, and so on to infinity. (I. xxviii.) As we have shown in the foregoing proposition, from this common property of particular things, we have only a very inadequate knowledge of the duration of our body; we must draw a similar conclusion with regard to the duration of particular things, namely, that we can only have a very inadequate knowledge of the duration thereof. *Q.E.D.*

Corollary.—Hence it follows that all particular things are contingent and perishable. For we can have no adequate idea of their duration (by the last Prop.), and this is what we must understand by the contingency and perishableness of things. (I. xxxiii., Note i.) For (I. xxix.), except in this sense, nothing is contingent.

PROP. XXXII. *All ideas, in so far as they are referred to God, are true.*

Proof.—All ideas which are in God agree in every respect with their objects (II. vii. Coroll.), therefore (I. Ax. vi.) they are all true. *Q.E.D.*

PROP. XXXIII. *There is nothing positive in ideas, which causes them to be called false.*

Proof.—If this be denied, conceive, if possible, a positive mode of thinking, which should constitute the distinctive quality of falsehood. Such a mode of thinking cannot be in God (II. xxxii.); external to God it cannot be or be conceived (I. xv.). Therefore there is nothing positive in ideas which causes them to be called false. *Q.E.D.*

PROP. XXXIV. *Every idea, which in us is absolute or adequate and perfect, is true.*

Proof.—When we say that an idea in us is adequate and perfect, we say, in other words (II. xi. Coroll.), that the idea is adequate and perfect in God, in so far as he constitutes the essence of our mind; consequently (II. xxxii.), we say that such an idea is true. *Q.E.D.*

PROP. XXXV. *Falsity consists in the privation of knowledge, which inadequate, fragmentary, or confused ideas involve.*

Proof.—There is nothing positive in ideas, which causes them to be called false (II. xxxiii); but falsity cannot consist in simple privation (for minds, not bodies, are said to err and to be mistaken), neither can it consist in absolute ignorance, for ignorance and error are not identical; wherefore it consists in the privation of knowledge, which inadequate, fragmentary, or confused ideas involve. *Q.E.D.*

Note.—In the note to II. xvii. I explained how error consists in the privation of knowledge, but in order to throw more light on the subject I will give an example. For instance, men are mistaken in thinking themselves free; their opinion is made up of consciousness of their own actions, and ignorance of the causes by which they are conditioned. Their idea of freedom, therefore, is simply their ignorance of any cause for their actions. As for their saying that human actions depend on the will, this is a mere phrase without any idea to correspond thereto. What the will is, and how it moves the body, they none of them know; those who boast of such knowledge, and feign dwellings and habitations for the soul, are wont to provoke either laughter or disgust. So, again, when we look at the sun, we imagine that it is distant from us about two hundred feet; this error does not lie solely in this fancy, but in the fact that, while we thus imagine, we do not know the sun's true distance or the cause of the fancy. For although we afterwards learn, that the sun is distant from us more than six hundred of the earth's diameters, we none the less shall fancy it to be near; for we do not imagine the sun as near us, because we are ignorant of its true distance, but because the modification of our body involves the essence of the sun, in so far as our said body is affected thereby.

PROP. XXXVI. *Inadequate and confused ideas follow by the same necessity, as adequate or clear and distinct ideas.*

Proof.—All ideas are in God (I. xv.), and in so far as they are referred to God are true (II. xxxii.) and (II. vii. Coroll.) adequate; therefore there are no ideas confused or inadequate, except in respect to a particular mind (cf. II. xxiv. and xxviii.); therefore all ideas, whether adequate or inadequate, follow by the same necessity (II. vi.). *Q.E.D.*

PROP. XXXVII. *That which is common to all* (cf. *Lemma II. above*), *and which is equally in a part and in the whole, does not constitute the essence of any particular thing.*

Proof.—If this be denied, conceive, if possible, that it constitutes the essence of some particular thing; for instance, the essence of B. Then (II. Def. ii.) it cannot without B either exist or be conceived; but this is against our hypothesis. Therefore it does not appertain to B's essence, nor does it constitute the essence of any particular thing. *Q.E.D.*

PROP. XXXVIII. *Those things, which are common to all, and which are equally in a part and in the whole, cannot be conceived except adequately.*

Proof.—Let A be something, which is common to all bodies, and which is equally present in the part of any given body and in the whole. I say A cannot be conceived except adequately. For the idea thereof in God will necessarily be adequate (II. vii. Coroll.), both in so far as God has the idea of the human body, and also in so far as he has the idea of the modifications of the human body, which (II. xvi., xxv., xxvii.) involve in part the nature of the human body and the nature of external bodies; that is (II. xii., xiii.), the idea in God will necessarily be adequate, both in so far as he constitutes the human mind, and in so far as he has the ideas, which are in the human mind. Therefore the mind (II. xi. Coroll.) necessarily perceives A adequately, and has this adequate perception, both in so far as it perceives itself, and in so far as it perceives its own or any external body, nor can A be conceived in any other manner. *Q.E.D.*

Corollary.—Hence it follows that there are certain ideas or notions common to all men; for (by Lemma ii.) all bodies agree in certain respects, which (by the foregoing Prop.) must be adequately or clearly and distinctly perceived by all.

PROP. XXXIX. *That, which is common to and a property of the human body and such other bodies as are wont to affect the human body, and which is present equally in each part of either, or in the whole, will be represented by an adequate idea in the mind.*

Proof.—If A be that, which is common to and a property of the human body and external bodies, and equally present in the human body and in the said external bodies, in each part of each external body and in the whole, there will be an adequate idea of A in God (II. vii. Coroll.), both in so far as he has the idea of the human body, and in so far as he has the ideas of the given external bodies. Let it now be granted, that the human body is affected by an external body through that, which it has in common therewith, namely, A; the idea of this modification will involve the property A (II. xvi.), and therefore (II. vii. Coroll.) the idea of this modification, in so far as it involves the property A, will be adequate in God, in so far as God is affected by the idea of the human body; that is (II. xiii.), in so far as he constitutes the nature of the human mind; therefore (II. xi. Coroll.) this idea is also adequate in the human mind. *Q.E.D.*

Corollary.—Hence it follows that the mind is fitted to perceive adequately more things, in proportion as its body has more in common with other bodies.

PROP. XL. *Whatsoever ideas in the mind follow from ideas which are therein adequate, are also themselves adequate.*

Proof.—This proposition is self-evident. For when we say that an idea in the human mind follows from ideas which are therein adequate, we say, in other words (II. xi. Coroll.), that an idea is in the divine intellect, whereof God is the cause, not in so far as he is infinite, nor in so far as he is affected by the ideas of very many particular things, but only in so far as he constitutes the essence of the human mind.

Note I.—I have thus set forth the cause of those notions, which are common to all men, and which form the basis of our ratiocination. But there are other causes of certain axioms or notions, which it would be to the purpose to set forth by this method of ours; for it would thus appear what notions are more useful than others, and what notions have scarcely any use at all. Furthermore, we should see what notions are common to all men, and what notions are only clear and distinct to those who are unshackled by prejudice, and we should detect those which are ill-founded. Again we should discern whence the notions called *secondary* derived their origin, and consequently the axioms on which they are founded, and other points of interest connected with these questions. But I have decided to pass over the subject here, partly because I have set it aside for another treatise, partly because I am afraid of wearying the reader by too great prolixity. Nevertheless, in order not to omit anything necessary to be known, I will briefly set down the causes, whence are derived the terms styled *transcendental*, such as Being, Thing, Something. These terms arose from the fact, that the human body, being limited, is only capable of distinctly forming a certain number of images (what an image is I explained in II. xvii. note) within itself at the same time; if this number be exceeded, the images will begin to be confused; if this number of images, which the body is capable of forming distinctly within itself, be largely exceeded, all will become entirely confused one with another. This being so, it is evident (from II. Prop. xvii. Coroll. and xviii.) that the human mind can distinctly imagine as many things simultaneously, as its body can form images simultaneously. When the images become quite confused in the body, the mind also imagines all bodies confusedly without any distinction, and will comprehend them, as it were, under one attribute, namely, under the attribute of Being, Thing, &c. The same conclusion can be drawn from the fact that images are not always equally vivid, and from other analogous causes, which there is no need to explain here; for the purpose which we have in view it is sufficient for us to consider one only. All may be reduced to this, that these terms represent ideas in the highest degree confused. From similar causes arise those notions, which we call *general*, such as man, horse, dog, &c. They arise, to wit, from the fact that so many images, for instance, of men, are formed simultaneously in the human mind, that the powers of imagination break down, not indeed utterly, but to the extent of the mind losing count of small differences between individuals (*e.g.* colour, size, &c.) and their definite number, and only distinctly imagining that, in which all the individuals, in so far as the body is affected by them, agree; for that is the point, in which each of the said individuals chiefly affected the body; this the mind expresses by the name man, and this it predicates of an infinite number of particular individuals. For, as we have said, it is unable to imagine the definite number of individuals. We must, however, bear in mind, that these general notions are not formed by all men in the same way, but vary in each individual according as the point varies, whereby the body has been most often affected and which the mind most easily imagines or remembers. For instance, those who have most often regarded with admiration the stature of man, will by the name of man understand an animal of erect stature; those who have been accustomed to regard some other attribute, will form a different general image of man, for instance, that man is a laughing animal, a two-footed animal without feathers, a rational animal, and thus, in other cases, everyone will form general images of things according to the habit of his body.

It is thus not to be wondered at, that among philosophers, who seek to explain things in nature merely by the images formed of them, so many controversies should have arisen.

Note II.—From all that has been said above it is clear, that we, in many cases, perceive and form our general notions:—(1.) From particular things represented to our intellect fragmentarily, confusedly, and without order through our senses (II. xxix. Coroll.); I have settled to call such perceptions by the name of knowledge from the mere suggestions of experience.[1] (2.) From symbols, *e.g.*, from the fact of having read or heard certain words we remember things and form certain ideas concerning them, similar to those through which we imagine things (II. xviii. note). I shall call both these ways of regarding things *knowledge of the first kind, opinion,* or *imagination.* (3.) From the fact that we have notions common to all men, and adequate ideas of the properties of things (II. xxxviii. Coroll., xxxix. and Coroll. and xl.); this I call *reason* and *knowledge of the second kind.* Besides these two kinds of knowledge, there is, as I will hereafter show, a third kind of knowledge, which we will call intuition. This kind of knowledge proceeds from an adequate idea of the absolute essence of certain attributes of God to the adequate knowledge of the essence of things. I will illustrate all three kinds of knowledge by a single example. Three numbers are given for finding a fourth, which shall be to the third as the second is to the first. Tradesmen without hesitation multiply the second by the third, and divide the product by the first; either because they have not forgotten the rule which they received from a master without any proof, or because they have often made trial of it with simple numbers, or by virtue of the proof of the nineteenth proposition of the seventh book of Euclid, namely, in virtue of the general property of proportionals.

But with very simple numbers there is no need of this. For instance, one, two, three, being given, everyone can see that the fourth proportional is six; and this is much clearer, because we infer the fourth number from an in-

[1] A Baconian phrase. Nov. Org. Aph. 100. [Pollock, p. 126, *n.*]

tuitive grasping of the ratio, which the first bears to the second.

PROP. XLI. *Knowledge of the first kind is the only source of falsity, knowledge of the second and third kinds is necessarily true.*

Proof.—To knowledge of the first kind we have (in the foregoing note) assigned all those ideas, which are inadequate and confused; therefore this kind of knowledge is the only source of falsity (II. xxxv.). Furthermore, we assigned to the second and third kinds of knowledge those ideas which are adequate; therefore these kinds are necessarily true (II. xxxiv.). *Q.E.D.*

PROP. XLII. *Knowledge of the second and third kinds, not knowledge of the first kind, teaches us to distinguish the true from the false.*

Proof.—This proposition is self-evident. He, who knows how to distinguish between true and false, must have an adequate idea of true and false. That is (II. xl., note ii.), he must know the true and the false by the second or third kind of knowledge.

PROP. XLIII. *He, who has a true idea, simultaneously knows that he has a true idea, and cannot doubt of the truth of the thing perceived.*

Proof.—A true idea in us is an idea which is adequate in God, in so far as he is displayed through the nature of the human mind (II. xi. Coroll.). Let us suppose that there is in God, in so far as he is displayed through the human mind, an adequate idea, A. The idea of this idea must also necessarily be in God, and be referred to him in the same way as the idea A (by II. xx., whereof the proof is of universal application). But the idea A is supposed to be referred to God, in so far as he is displayed through the human mind; therefore, the idea of the idea A must be referred to God in the same manner; that is (by II. xi. Coroll.), the adequate idea of the idea A will be in the mind, which has the adequate idea A; therefore he, who has an adequate idea or knows a thing truly (II. xxxiv.), must at the same time have an adequate idea or true knowledge of his knowledge; that is, obviously, he must be assured. *Q.E.D.*

Note.—I explained in the note to II. xxi. what is meant

by the idea of an idea; but we may remark that the foregoing proposition is in itself sufficiently plain. No one, who has a true idea, is ignorant that a true idea involves the highest certainty. For to have a true idea is only another expression for knowing a thing perfectly, or as well as possible. No one, indeed, can doubt of this, unless he thinks that an idea is something lifeless, like a picture on a panel, and not a mode of thinking—namely, the very act of understanding. And who, I ask, can know that he understands anything, unless he do first understand it? In other words, who can know that he is sure of a thing, unless he be first sure of that thing? Further, what can there be more clear, and more certain, than a true idea as a standard of truth? Even as light displays both itself and darkness, so is truth a standard both of itself and of falsity.

I think I have thus sufficiently answered these questions—namely, if a true idea is distinguished from a false idea, only in so far as it is said to agree with its object, a true idea has no more reality or perfection than a false idea (since the two are only distinguished by an extrinsic mark); consequently, neither will a man who has true ideas have any advantage over him who has only false ideas. Further, how comes it that men have false ideas? Lastly, how can anyone be sure, that he has ideas which agree with their objects? These questions, I repeat, I have, in my opinion, sufficiently answered. The difference between a true idea and a false idea is plain: from what was said in II. xxxv., the former is related to the latter as being is to not-being. The causes of falsity I have set forth very clearly in II. xix. and II. xxxv. with the note. From what is there stated, the difference between a man who has true ideas, and a man who has only false ideas, is made apparent. As for the last question—as to how a man can be sure that he has ideas that agree with their objects, I have just pointed out, with abundant clearness, that his knowledge arises from the simple fact, that he has an idea which corresponds with its object—in other words, that truth is its own standard. We may add that our mind, in so far as it perceives things truly, is part of the infinite intellect of God (II. xi. Coroll.); therefore, the clear and distinct ideas of the mind are as necessarily true as the ideas of God.

PROP. XLIV. *It is not in the nature of reason to regard things as contingent, but as necessary.*

Proof.—It is in the nature of reason to perceive things truly (II. xli.), namely (I. Ax. vi.), as they are in themselves—that is (I. xxix.), not as contingent, but as necessary. *Q.E.D.*

Corollary I.—Hence it follows, that it is only through our imagination that we consider things, whether in respect to the future or the past, as contingent.

Note.—How this way of looking at things arises, I will briefly explain. We have shown above (II. xvii. and Coroll.) that the mind always regards things as present to itself, even though they be not in existence, until some causes arise which exclude their existence and presence. Further (II. xviii.), we showed that, if the human body has once been affected by two external bodies simultaneously, the mind, when it afterwards imagines one of the said external bodies, will straightway remember the other—that is, it will regard both as present to itself, unless there arise causes which exclude their existence and presence. Further, no one doubts that we imagine time, from the fact that we imagine bodies to be moved some more slowly than others, some more quickly, some at equal speed. Thus, let us suppose that a child yesterday saw Peter for the first time in the morning, Paul at noon, and Simon in the evening; then, that to-day he again sees Peter in the morning. It is evident, from II. Prop. xviii., that, as soon as he sees the morning light, he will imagine that the sun will traverse the same parts of the sky, as it did when he saw it on the preceding day; in other words, he will imagine a complete day, and, together with his imagination of the morning, he will imagine Peter; with noon, he will imagine Paul; and with evening, he will imagine Simon—that is, he will imagine the existence of Paul and Simon in relation to a future time; on the other hand, if he sees Simon in the evening, he will refer Peter and Paul to a past time, by imagining them simultaneously with the imagination of a past time. If it should at any time happen, that on some other evening the child should see James instead of Simon, he will, on the following morning, associate with his imagination of evening sometimes Simon, sometimes

James, not both together: for the child is supposed to have seen, at evening, one or other of them, not both together. His imagination will therefore waver; and, with the imagination of future evenings, he will associate first one, then the other—that is, he will imagine them in the future, neither of them as certain, but both as contingent. This wavering of the imagination will be the same, if the imagination be concerned with things which we thus contemplate, standing in relation to time past or time present: consequently, we may imagine things as contingent, whether they be referred to time present, past, or future.

Corollary II.—It is in the nature of reason to perceive things under a certain form of eternity (*sub quâdam æternitatis specie*).

Proof.—It is in the nature of reason to regard things, not as contingent, but as necessary (II. xliv.). Reason perceives this necessity of things (II. xli.) truly—that is (I. Ax. vi.), as it is in itself. But (I. xvi.) this necessity of things is the very necessity of the eternal nature of God; therefore, it is in the nature of reason to regard things under this form of eternity. We may add that the bases of reason are the notions (II. xxxviii.), which answer to things common to all, and which (II. xxxvii.) do not answer to the essence of any particular thing: which must therefore be conceived without any relation to time, under a certain form of eternity.

Prop. XLV. *Every idea of every body, or of every particular thing actually existing, necessarily involves the eternal and infinite essence of God.*

Proof.—The idea of a particular thing actually existing necessarily involves both the existence and the essence of the said thing (II. viii.). Now particular things cannot be conceived without God (I. xv.); but, inasmuch as (II. vi.) they have God for their cause, in so far as he is regarded under the attribute of which the things in question are modes, their ideas must necessarily involve (I. Ax. iv.) the conception of the attribute of those ideas—that is (I. vi.), the eternal and infinite essence of God. *Q.E.D.*

Note.—By existence I do not here mean duration—that is, existence in so far as it is conceived abstractedly, and as a certain form of quantity. I am speaking of the very nature of existence, which is assigned to particular things, because they follow in infinite numbers and in infinite ways from the eternal necessity of God's nature (I. xvi.). I am speaking, I repeat, of the very existence of particular things, in so far as they are in God. For although each particular thing be conditioned by another particular thing to exist in a given way, yet the force whereby each particular thing perseveres in existing follows from the eternal necessity of God's nature (cf. I. xxiv. Coroll.).

PROP. XLVI. *The knowledge of the eternal and infinite essence of God which every idea involves is adequate and perfect.*

Proof.—The proof of the last proposition is universal; and whether a thing be considered as a part or a whole, the idea thereof, whether of the whole or of a part (by the last Prop.), will involve God's eternal and infinite essence. Wherefore, that, which gives knowledge of the eternal and infinite essence of God, is common to all, and is equally in the part and in the whole; therefore (II. xxxviii.) this knowledge will be adequate. *Q.E.D.*

PROP. XLVII. *The human mind has an adequate knowledge of the eternal and infinite essence of God.*

Proof.—The human mind has ideas (II. xxii.), from which (II. xxiii.) it perceives itself and its own body (II. xix.) and external bodies (II. xvi. Coroll. I. and II. xvii.) as actually existing; therefore (II. xlv. xlvi.) it has an adequate knowledge of the eternal and infinite essence of God. *Q.E.D.*

Note.—Hence we see, that the infinite essence and the eternity of God are known to all. Now as all things are in God, and are conceived through God, we can from this knowledge infer many things, which we may adequately know, and we may form that third kind of knowledge of which we spoke in the note to II. xl., and of the excellence and use of which we shall have occasion to speak in Part V. Men have not so clear a knowledge of God as they have of general notions, because they are unable to imagine God as they do bodies, and also because they have associated the name God with images of things that they are in the habit of seeing, as indeed they can hardly avoid doing, being, as they are, men, and continually affected by external bodies. Many errors, in truth, can be traced to this head, namely, that we do not apply names to things rightly. For instance, when a man says that the lines drawn from the centre of a circle to its circumference are not equal, he then, at all events, assuredly attaches a meaning to the word circle different from that assigned by mathematicians. So again, when men make mistakes in calculation, they have one set of figures in their mind, and another on the paper. If we could see into their minds, they do not make a mistake; they seem to do so, because we think, that they have the same numbers in their mind as they have on the paper. If this were not so, we should not believe them to be in error, any more than I thought that a man was in error, whom I lately heard exclaiming that his entrance hall had flown into a neighbour's hen, for his meaning seemed to me sufficiently clear. Very many controversies have arisen from the fact, that men do not rightly explain their meaning, or do not rightly interpret the meaning of others. For, as a matter of fact, as they flatly contradict themselves, they assume now one side, now another, of the argument, so as to oppose the opinions, which they consider mistaken and absurd in their opponents.

PROP. XLVIII. *In the mind there is no absolute or free will; but the mind is determined to wish this or that by a cause, which has also been determined by another cause, and this last by another cause, and so on to infinity.*

Proof.—The mind is a fixed and definite mode of thought (II. xi.), therefore it cannot be the free cause of its actions (I. xvii. Coroll. ii.); in other words, it cannot have an absolute faculty of positive or negative volition; but (by I. xxviii.) it must be determined by a cause, which has also been determined by another cause, and this last by another, &c. *Q.E.D.*

Note.—In the same way it is proved, that there is in the mind no absolute faculty of understanding, desiring, loving, &c. Whence it follows, that these and similar faculties are either entirely fictitious, or are merely abstract or general terms, such as we are accustomed to put together from particular things. Thus the intellect and the will stand in the same relation to this or that idea, or this or that volition, as "lapidity" to this or that stone, or as "man" to Peter and Paul. The cause which leads men to consider themselves free has been set forth in the Appendix to Part I. But, before I proceed further, I would here remark that, by the will to affirm and decide, I mean the faculty, not the desire. I mean, I repeat, the faculty, whereby the mind affirms or denies what is true or false, not the desire, wherewith the mind wishes for or turns away from any given thing. After we have proved, that these faculties of ours are general notions, which cannot be distinguished from the particular instances on which they are based, we must inquire whether volitions themselves are anything besides the ideas of things. We must inquire, I say, whether there is in the mind any affirmation or negation beyond that, which the idea, in so far as it is an idea, involves. On which subject see the following proposition, and II. Def. iii., lest the idea of pictures should suggest itself. For by ideas I do not mean images such as are formed at the back of the eye, or in the midst of the brain, but the conceptions of thought.

PROP. XLIX. *There is in the mind no volition or affirmation and negation, save that which an idea, inasmuch as it is an idea, involves.*

Proof.—There is in the mind no absolute faculty of positive or negative volition, but only particular volitions, namely, this or that affirmation, and this or that negation. Now let us conceive a particular volition, namely, the mode of thinking whereby the mind affirms, that the three interior angles of a triangle are equal to two right angles. This affirmation involves the conception or idea of a triangle, that is, without the idea of a triangle it cannot be conceived. It is the same thing to say, that the concept A must involve the concept B, as it is to say, that A cannot be conceived without B. Further, this affirmation cannot be made (II. Ax. iii.) without the idea of a triangle. Therefore, this affirmation can neither be nor be conceived, without the idea of a triangle. Again, this idea of a triangle must involve this same affirmation, namely, that its three interior angles are equal to two right angles. Wherefore, and *vice versâ*, this idea of a triangle can neither be nor be conceived without this affirmation, therefore, this affirmation belongs to the essence of the idea of a triangle, and is nothing besides. What we have said of this volition (inasmuch as we have selected it at random) may be said of any other volition, namely, that it is nothing but an idea. *Q.E.D.*

Corollary.—Will and understanding are one and the same.

Proof.—Will and understanding are nothing beyond the individual volitions and ideas (II. xlviii. and note). But a particular volition and a particular idea are one and the same (by the foregoing Prop.); therefore, will and understanding are one and the same. *Q.E.D.*

Note.—We have thus removed the cause which is commonly assigned for error. For we have shown above, that falsity consists solely in the privation of knowledge involved in ideas which are fragmentary and confused. Wherefore, a false idea, inasmuch as it is false, does not involve certainty. When we say, then, that a man acquiesces in what is false, and that he has no doubts on the subject, we do not say that he is certain, but only that he does not doubt, or that he acquiesces in what is false, inasmuch as there are no reasons, which should cause his imagination to waver (see II. xliv. note). Thus, although the man be assumed to acquiesce in what is false, we shall never say that he is certain. For by certainty we mean something positive (II. xliii. and note), not merely the absence of doubt.

However, in order that the foregoing proposition may be fully explained, I will draw attention to a few additional points, and I will furthermore answer the objections which may be advanced against our doctrine. Lastly, in order to remove every scruple, I have thought it worth while to point out some of the advantages, which follow therefrom. I say "some," for they will be better appreciated from what we shall set forth in the fifth part.

I begin, then, with the first point, and warn my readers to make an accurate distinction between an idea, or conception of the mind, and the images of things which we imagine. It is further necessary that they should distinguish between idea and words, whereby we signify things. These three—namely, images, words, and ideas—are by many persons either entirely confused together, or not distinguished with sufficient accuracy or care, and hence people are generally in ignorance, how absolutely necessary is a knowledge of this doctrine of the will, both for philosophic purposes and for the wise ordering of life. Those who think that ideas consist in images which are formed in us by contact with external bodies, persuade themselves that the ideas of those things, whereof we can form no mental picture, are not ideas, but only figments, which we invent by the free decree of our will; they thus regard ideas as though they were inanimate pictures on a panel, and, filled with this misconception, do not see that an idea, inasmuch as it is an idea, involves an affirmation or negation. Again, those who confuse words with ideas, or with the affirmation which an idea involves, think that they can wish something contrary to what they feel, affirm, or deny. This misconception will easily be laid aside by one, who reflects on the nature of knowledge, and seeing that it in no wise involves the conception of extension, will therefore clearly understand, that an idea (being a mode of thinking) does not consist in the image of anything, nor in words. The essence of words and images is put together by bodily motions, which in no wise involve the conception of thought.

These few words on this subject will suffice: I will therefore pass on to consider the objections, which may be raised against our doctrine. Of these, the first is advanced by those, who think that the will has a wider scope than the understanding, and that therefore it is different therefrom. The reason for their holding the belief, that the will has wider scope than the understanding, is that they assert, that they have no need of an increase in their faculty of assent, that is of affirmation or negation, in order to assent to an infinity of things which we do not perceive, but that they have need of an increase in their faculty of understanding. The will is thus distinguished from the intellect, the latter being finite and the former infinite. Secondly, it may be objected that experience seems to teach us especially clearly, that we are able to suspend our judgment before assenting to things which we perceive; this is confirmed by the fact that no one is said to be deceived, in so far as he perceives anything, but only in so far as he assents or dissents.

For instance, he who feigns a winged horse, does not therefore admit that a winged horse exists; that is, he is not deceived, unless he admits in addition that a winged horse does exist. Nothing therefore seems to be taught more clearly by experience, than that the will or faculty of assent is free and different from the faculty of understanding. Thirdly, it may be objected that one affirmation does not apparently contain more reality than another; in other words, that we do not seem to need for affirming, that what is true is true, any greater power than for affirming, that what is false is true. We have, however, seen that one idea has more reality or perfectiou than another, for as objects are some more excellent than others, so also are the ideas of them some more excellent than others; this also seems to point to a difference between the understanding and the will. Fourthly, it may be objected, if man does not act from free will, what will happen if the incentives to action are equally balanced, as in the case of Buridan's ass? Will he perish of hunger and thirst? If I say that he would, I shall seem to have in my thoughts an ass or the statue of a man rather than an actual man. If I say that he would not, he would then determine his own action, and would consequently possess the faculty of going and doing whatever he liked. Other objections might also be raised, but, as I am not bound to put in evidence everything that anyone may dream, I will only set myself to the task of refuting those I have mentioned, and that as briefly as possible.

To the *first* objection I answer, that I admit that the will has a wider scope than the understanding, if by the understanding be meant only clear and distinct ideas; but I deny that the will has a wider scope than the perceptions, and the faculty of forming conceptions; nor do I see why the faculty of volition should be called infinite, any more than the faculty of feeling: for, as we are able by the same faculty of volition to affirm an infinite number of things (one after the other, for we cannot affirm an infinite number simultaneously), so also can we, by the same faculty of feeling, feel or perceive (in succession) an infinite number of bodies. If it be said that there is an infinite number of things which we cannot perceive, I answer, that we cannot attain to such things by any thinking, nor, consequently, by any faculty of volition. But, it may still be urged, if God wished to bring it about that we should perceive them, he would be obliged to endow us with a greater faculty of perception, but not a greater faculty of volition than we have already. This is the same as to say that, if God wished to bring it about that we should understand an infinite number of other entities, it would be necessary for him to give us a greater understanding, but not a more universal idea of entity than that which we have already, in order to grasp such infinite entities. We have shown that will is a universal entity or idea, whereby we explain all particular volitions—in other words, that which is common to all such volitions.

As, then, our opponents maintain that this idea, common or universal to all volitions, is a faculty, it is little to be wondered at that they assert, that such a faculty extends itself into the infinite, beyond the limits of the understanding: for what is universal is predicated alike of one, of many, and of an infinite number of individuals.

To the *second* objection I reply by denying, that we have a free power of suspending our judgment: for, when we say that anyone suspends his judgment, we merely mean that he sees, that he does not perceive the matter in question adequately. Suspension of judgment is, therefore, strictly speaking, a perception, and not free will. In order to illustrate the point, let us suppose a boy imagining a horse, and perceiving nothing else. Inasmuch as this imagination involves the existence of the horse (II. xvii. Coroll.), and the boy does not perceive anything which would exclude the existence of the horse, he will necessarily regard the horse as present: he will not be able to doubt of its existence, although he be not certain thereof. We have daily experience of such a state of things in dreams; and I do not suppose that there is anyone, who would maintain that, while he is dreaming, he has the free power of suspending his judgment concerning the things in his dream, and bringing it about that he should not dream those things, which he dreams that he sees; yet it happens, notwithstanding, that even in dreams we suspend our judgment, namely, when we dream that we are dreaming.

Further, I grant that no one can be deceived, so far as actual perception extends—that is, I grant that the mind's imaginations, regarded in themselves, do not involve error (II. xvii., note); but I deny, that a man does not, in the act of perception, make any affirmation. For what is the perception of a winged horse, save affirming that a horse has wings? If the mind could perceive nothing else but the winged horse, it would regard the same as present to itself: it would have no reasons for doubting its existence, nor any faculty of dissent, unless the imagination of a winged horse be joined to an idea which precludes the existence of the said horse, or unless the mind perceives that the idea which it possesses of a winged horse is inadequate, in which case it will either necessarily deny the existence of such a horse, or will necessarily be in doubt on the subject.

I think that I have anticipated my answer to the *third* objection, namely, that the will is something universal which is predicated of all ideas, and that it only signifies that which is common to all ideas, namely, an affirmation, whose adequate essence must, therefore, in so far as it is thus conceived in the abstract, be in every idea, and be, in this respect alone, the same in all, not in so far as it is considered as constituting the idea's essence: for, in this respect, particular affirmations differ one from the other, as much as do ideas. For instance, the affirmation which involves the idea of a circle, differs from that which involves the idea of a triangle, as much as the idea of a circle differs from the idea of a triangle.

Further, I absolutely deny, that we are in need of an equal power of thinking, to affirm that that which is true is true, and to affirm that that which is false is true. These two affirmations, if we regard the mind, are in the same relation to one another as being and not-being; for there is nothing positive in ideas, which constitutes the actual reality of falsehood (II. xxxv. note, and xlvii. note).

We must therefore conclude, that we are easily deceived, when we confuse universals with singulars, and the entities of reason and abstractions with realities. As for the *fourth* objection, I am quite ready to admit, that a man placed in the equilibrium described (namely, as perceiving nothing but hunger and thirst, a certain food and a certain drink, each equally distant from him) would die of hunger and thirst. If I am asked, whether such an one should not rather be considered an ass than a man; I answer, that I do not know, neither do I know how a man should be considered, who hangs himself, or how we should consider children, fools, madmen, &c.

It remains to point out the advantages of a knowledge of this doctrine as bearing on conduct, and this may be easily gathered from what has been said. The doctrine is good,

1. Inasmuch as it teaches us to act solely according to the decree of God, and to be partakers in the Divine nature, and so much the more, as we perform more perfect actions and more and more understand God. Such a doctrine not only completely tranquillizes our spirit, but also shows us where our highest happiness or blessedness is, namely, solely in the knowledge of God, whereby we are led to act only as love and piety shall bid us. We may thus clearly understand, how far astray from a true estimate of virtue are those who expect to be decorated by God with high rewards for their virtue, and their best actions, as for having endured the direst slavery; as if virtue and the service of God were not in itself happiness and perfect freedom.

2. Inasmuch as it teaches us, how we ought to conduct ourselves with respect to the gifts of fortune, or matters which are not in our own power, and do not follow from our nature. For it shows us, that we should await and endure fortune's smiles or frowns with an equal mind, seeing that all things follow from the eternal decree of God by the same necessity, as it follows from the essence of a triangle, that the three angles are equal to two right angles.

3. This doctrine raises social life, inasmuch as it teaches us to hate no man, neither to despise, to deride, to envy, or to be angry with any. Further, as it tells us that each should be content with his own, and helpful to his neighbour, not from any womanish pity, favour, or superstition,

but solely by the guidance of reason, according as the time and occasion demand, as I will show in Part III.

4. Lastly, this doctrine confers no small advantage on the commonwealth; for it teaches how citizens should be governed and led, not so as to become slaves, but so that they may freely do whatsoever things are best.

I have thus fulfilled the promise made at the beginning of this note, and I thus bring the second part of my treatise to a close. I think I have therein explained the nature and properties of the human mind at sufficient length, and, considering the difficulty of the subject, with sufficient clearness. I have laid a foundation, whereon may be raised many excellent conclusions of the highest utility and most necessary to be known, as will, in what follows, be partly made plain.

PART III.

ON THE ORIGIN AND NATURE OF THE EMOTIONS.

MOST writers on the emotions and on human conduct seem to be treating rather of matters outside nature than of natural phenomena following nature's general laws. They appear to conceive man to be situated in nature as a kingdom within a kingdom: for they believe that he disturbs rather than follows nature's order, that he has absolute control over his actions, and that he is determined solely by himself. They attribute human infirmities and fickleness, not to the power of nature in general, but to some mysterious flaw in the nature of man, which accordingly they bemoan, deride, despise, or, as usually happens, abuse: he, who succeeds in hitting off the weakness of the human mind more eloquently or more acutely than his fellows, is looked upon as a seer. Still there has been no lack of very excellent men (to whose toil and industry I confess myself much indebted), who have written many noteworthy things concerning the right way of life, and have given much sage advice to mankind. But no one, so far as I know, has defined the nature and strength of the emotions, and the power of the mind against them for their restraint.

I do not forget, that the illustrious Descartes, though he believed, that the mind has absolute power over its actions, strove to explain human emotions by their primary causes, and, at the same time, to point out a way, by which the mind might attain to absolute dominion over them. However, in my opinion, he accomplishes nothing beyond a display of the acuteness of his own great intellect, as I will show in the proper place. For the present I wish to revert to those, who would rather abuse or deride human emotions than understand them. Such persons will, doubtless think it strange that I should attempt to treat of human vice and folly geometrically, and should wish to set forth with rigid reasoning those matters which they cry out against as repugnant to reason, frivolous, absurd, and dreadful. However, such is my plan. Nothing comes to pass in nature, which can be set down to a flaw therein; for nature is always the same, and everywhere one and the same in her efficacy and power of action; that is, nature's laws and ordinances, whereby all things come to pass and change from one form to another, are everywhere and always the same; so that there should be one and the same method of understanding the nature of all things whatsoever, namely, through nature's universal laws and rules. Thus the passions of hatred, anger, envy, and so on, considered in themselves, follow from this same necessity and efficacy of nature; they answer to certain definite causes, through which they are understood, and possess certain properties as worthy of being known as the properties of anything else, whereof the contemplation in itself affords us delight. I shall, therefore, treat of the nature and strength of the emotions according to the same method, as I employed heretofore in my investigations concerning God and the mind. I shall consider human actions and desires in exactly the same manner, as though I were concerned with lines, planes, and solids.

DEFINITIONS.

I. By an *adequate* cause, I mean a cause through which its effect can be clearly and distinctly perceived. By an *inadequate* or partial cause, I mean a cause through which, by itself, its effect cannot be understood.

II. I say that we *act* when anything takes place, either within us or externally to us, whereof we are the adequate cause; that is (by the foregoing definition) when through our nature something takes place within us or externally to us, which can through our nature alone be clearly and distinctly understood. On the other hand, I say that we are passive as regards something when that something takes place within us, or follows from our nature externally, we being only the partial cause.

III. By *emotion* I mean the modifications of the body, whereby the active power of the said body is increased or diminished, aided or constrained, and also the ideas of such modifications.

N.B. If we can be the adequate cause of any of these modifications, I then call the emotion an activity, otherwise I call it a passion, or state wherein the mind is passive.

Postulates.

I. The human body can be affected in many ways, whereby its power of activity is increased or diminished, and also in other ways which do not render its power of activity either greater or less.

N.B. This postulate or axiom rests on Postulate i. and Lemmas v. and vii., which see after II. xiii.

II. The human body can undergo many changes, and, nevertheless, retain the impressions or traces of objects (cf. II. Post. v.), and, consequently, the same images of things (see note II. xvii.).

Prop. I. *Our mind is in certain cases active, and in certain cases passive. In so far as it has adequate ideas it is necessarily active, and in so far as it has inadequate ideas, it is necessarily passive.*

Proof.—In every human mind there are some adequate ideas, and some ideas that are fragmentary and confused (II. xl. note). Those ideas which are adequate in the mind are adequate also in God, inasmuch as he constitutes the essence of the mind (II. xl. Coroll.), and those which are inadequate in the mind are likewise (by the same Coroll.) adequate in God, not inasmuch as he contains in himself the essence of the given mind alone, but as he, at the same time, contains the minds of other things. Again, from any given idea some effect must necessarily follow (I. 36); of this effect God is the adequate cause (III. Def. i.), not inasmuch as he is infinite, but inasmuch as he is conceived as affected by the given idea (II. ix.). But of that effect whereof God is the cause, inasmuch as he is affected by an idea which is adequate in a given mind, of that effect, I repeat, the mind in question is the adequate cause (II. xi. Coroll.). Therefore our mind, in so far as it has adequate ideas (III. Def. ii.), is in certain cases necessarily active; this was our first point. Again, whatsoever necessarily follows from the idea which is adequate in God, not by virtue of his possessing in himself the mind of one man only, but by virtue of his containing, together with the mind of that one man, the minds of other things also, of such an effect (II. xi. Coroll.) the mind of the given man is not an adequate, but only a partial cause; thus (III. Def. ii.) the mind, inasmuch as it has inadequate ideas, is in certain cases necessarily passive; this was our second point. Therefore our mind, &c. *Q.E.D.*

Corollary.—Hence it follows that the mind is more or less liable to be acted upon, in proportion as it possesses inadequate ideas, and, contrariwise, is more or less active in proportion as it possesses adequate ideas.

PROP. II. *Body cannot determine mind to think, neither can mind determine body to motion or rest or any state different from these, if such there be.*

Proof.—All modes of thinking have for their cause God, by virtue of his being a thinking thing, and not by virtue of his being displayed under any other attribute (II. vi.). That, therefore, which determines the mind to thought is a mode of thought, and not a mode of extension; that is (II. Def. i.), it is not body. This was our first point. Again, the motion and rest of a body must arise from another body, which has also been determined to a state of motion or rest by a third body, and absolutely everything which takes place in a body must spring from God, in so far as he is regarded as affected by some mode of extension, and not by some mode of thought (II. vi.); that is, it cannot spring from the mind, which is a mode of thought. This was our second point. Therefore body cannot determine mind, &c. *Q.E.D.*

Note.—This is made more clear by what was said in the note to II. vii., namely, that mind and body are one and the same thing, conceived first under the attribute of thought, secondly, under the attribute of extension. Thus it follows that the order or concatenation of things is identical, whether nature be conceived under the one attribute or the other; consequently the order of states of activity and passivity in our body is simultaneous in nature with the order of states of activity and passivity in the mind. The same conclusion is evident from the manner in which we proved II. xii.

Nevertheless, though such is the case, and though there be no further room for doubt, I can scarcely believe, until the fact is proved by experience, that men can be induced to consider the question calmly and fairly, so firmly are they convinced that it is merely at the bidding of the mind, that the body is set in motion or at rest, or performs a variety of actions depending solely on the mind's will or the exercise of thought. However, no one has hitherto laid down the limits to the powers of the body, that is, no one has as yet been taught by experience what the body can accomplish solely by the laws of nature, in so far as she is regarded as extension. No one hitherto has gained such an accurate knowledge of the bodily mechanism, that he can explain all its functions; nor need I call attention to the fact that many actions are observed in the lower animals, which far transcend human sagacity, and that somnambulists do many things in their sleep, which they would not venture to do when awake: these instances are enough to show, that the body can by the sole laws of its nature do many things which the mind wonders at.

Again, no one knows how or by what means the mind moves the body, nor how many various degrees of motion it can impart to the body, nor how quickly it can move it. Thus, when men say that this or that physical action has its origin in the mind, which latter has dominion over the body, they are using words without meaning, or are confessing in specious phraseology that they are ignorant of the cause of the said action, and do not wonder at it.

But, they will say, whether we know or do not know the means whereby the mind acts on the body, we have, at any rate, experience of the fact that unless the human mind is in a fit state to think, the body remains inert. Moreover, we have experience, that the mind alone can determine whether we speak or are silent, and a variety of similar states which, accordingly, we say depend on the mind's decree. But, as to the first point, I ask such objectors, whether experience does not also teach, that if the body be inactive the mind is simultaneously unfitted for thinking?

For when the body is at rest in sleep, the mind simultaneously is in a state of torpor also, and has no power of thinking, such as it possesses when the body is awake. Again, I think everyone's experience will confirm the statement, that the mind is not at all times equally fit for thinking on a given subject, but according as the body is more or less fitted for being stimulated by the image of this or that object, so also is the mind more or less fitted for contemplating the said object.

But, it will be urged, it is impossible that solely from the laws of nature considered as extended substance, we should be able to deduce the causes of buildings, pictures, and things of that kind, which are produced only by human art; nor would the human body, unless it were determined and led by the mind, be capable of building a single temple. However, I have just pointed out that the objectors cannot fix the limits of the body's power, or say what can be concluded from a consideration of its sole nature, whereas they have experience of many things being accomplished solely by the laws of nature, which they would never have believed possible except under the direction of mind: such are the actions performed by somnambulists while asleep, and wondered at by their performers when awake. I would further call attention to the mechanism of the human body, which far surpasses in complexity all that has been put together by human art, not to repeat what I have already shown, namely, that from nature, under whatever attribute she be considered, infinite results follow. As for the second objection, I submit that the world would be much happier, if men were as fully able to keep silence as they are to speak. Experience abundantly shows that men can govern anything more easily than their tongues, and restrain anything more easily than their appetites; whence it comes about that many believe, that we are only free in respect to objects which we moderately desire, because our desire for such can easily be controlled by the thought of something else frequently remembered, but that we are by no means free in respect to what we seek with violent emotion, for our desire cannot then be allayed with the remembrance of anything else. However, unless such persons had proved by experience that we do many things which we afterwards repent of, and again that we often, when assailed by contrary emotions, see the better and follow the worse, there would be nothing to prevent their believing that we are free in all things. Thus an infant believes that of its own free will it desires milk, an angry child believes that it freely desires vengeance, a timid child believes that it freely desires to run away; further, a drunken man believes that he utters from the free decision of his mind words which, when he is sober, he would willingly have withheld: thus, too, a delirious man, a garrulous woman, a child, and others of like complexion, believe that they speak from the free decision of their mind, when they are in reality unable to restrain their impulse to talk. Experience teaches us no less clearly than reason, that men believe themselves to be free, simply because they are conscious of their actions, and unconscious of the causes whereby those actions are determined; and, further, it is plain that the dictates of the mind are but another name for the appetites, and therefore vary according to the varying state of the body. Everyone shapes his actions according to his emotion, those who are assailed by conflicting emotions know not what they wish; those who are not attacked by any emotion are readily swayed this way or that. All these considerations clearly show that a mental decision and a bodily appetite, or determined state, are simultaneous, or rather are one and the same thing, which we call decision, when it is regarded under and explained through the attribute of thought, and a conditioned state, when it is regarded under the attribute of extension, and deduced from the laws of motion and rest. This will appear yet more plainly in the sequel. For the present I wish to call attention to another point, namely, that we cannot act by the decision of the mind, unless we have a remembrance of having done so. For instance, we cannot say a word without remembering that we have done so. Again, it is not within the free power of the mind to remember or forget a thing at will. Therefore the freedom of the mind must in any case be limited to the power of uttering or not uttering something which it remembers. But when we dream that we speak, we believe that we speak from a free decision of the mind, yet we do not speak, or. if we do, it is by a spontaneous motion of the body. Again, we dream that we are concealing something, and we seem to act from the same decision of the mind as that, whereby we keep silence when awake concerning something we know. Lastly, we dream that from the free decision of our mind we do something, which we should not dare to do when awake.

Now I should like to know whether there be in the mind two sorts of decisions, one sort illusive, and the other sort free? If our folly does not carry us so far as this, we must necessarily admit, that the decision of the mind, which is believed to be free, is not distinguishable from the imagination or memory, and is nothing more than the affirmation, which an idea, by virtue of being an idea, necessarily involves (II. xlix.). Wherefore these decisions of the mind arise in the mind by the same necessity, as the ideas of things actually existing. Therefore those who believe, that they speak or keep silence or act in any way from the free decision of their mind, do but dream with their eyes open.

PROP. III. *The activities of the mind arise solely from adequate ideas; the passive states of the mind depend solely on inadequate ideas.*

Proof.—The first element, which constitutes the essence of the mind, is nothing else but the idea of the actually existent body (II. xi. and xiii.), which (II. xv.) is compounded of many other ideas, whereof some are adequate and some inadequate (II. xxix. Coroll., II. xxxviii. Coroll.). Whatsoever therefore follows from the nature of mind, and has mind for its proximate cause, through which it must be understood, must necessarily follow either from an adequate or from an inadequate idea. But in so far as the mind (III. i.) has inadequate ideas, it is necessarily passive: wherefore the activities of the mind follow solely from adequate ideas, and accordingly the mind is only passive in so far as it has inadequate ideas. *Q.E.D.*

Note.—Thus we see, that passive states are not attributed to the mind, except in so far as it contains something involving negation, or in so far as it is regarded as a part of nature, which cannot be clearly and distinctly perceived through itself without other parts: I could thus show, that passive states are attributed to individual things in the same way that they are attributed to the mind, and that they cannot otherwise be perceived, but my purpose is solely to treat of the human mind.

PROP. IV. *Nothing can be destroyed, except by a cause external to itself.*

Proof.—This proposition is self-evident, for the definition of anything affirms the essence of that thing, but does not negative it; in other words, it postulates the essence of the thing, but does not take it away. So long therefore as we regard only the thing itself, without taking into account external causes, we shall not be able to find in it anything which could destroy it. *Q.E.D.*

PROP. V. *Things are naturally contrary, that is, cannot exist in the same object, in so far as one is capable of destroying the other.*

Proof.—If they could agree together or co-exist in the same object, there would then be in the said object something which could destroy it; but this, by the foregoing proposition, is absurd, therefore things, &c. *Q.E.D.*

PROP. VI. *Everything, in so far as it is in itself, endeavours to persist in its own being.*

Proof.—Individual things are modes whereby the attributes of God are expressed in a given determinate manner (I. xxv. Coroll.); that is (I. xxxiv.), they are things which express in a given determinate manner the power of God, whereby God is and acts; now no thing contains in itself anything whereby it can be destroyed, or which can take away its existence (III. iv.); but contrariwise it is opposed to all that could take away its existence (III. v.). Therefore, in so far as it can, and in so far as it is in itself, it endeavours to persist in its own being. *Q.E.D.*

PROP. VII. *The endeavour, wherewith everything endeavours to persist in its own being, is nothing else but the actual essence of the thing in question.*

Proof.—From the given essence of any thing certain consequences necessarily follow (I. xxxvi.), nor have things any power save such as necessarily follows from their nature as determined (I. xxix.); wherefore the power of any given thing, or the endeavour whereby, either alone or with other things, it acts, or endeavours to act, that is (III. vi.), the power or endeavour, wherewith it endeavours to persist in its own being, is nothing else but the given or actual essence of the thing in question. *Q.E.D.*

PROP. VIII. *The endeavour, whereby a thing endeavours to persist in its being, involves no finite time, but an indefinite time.*

Proof.—If it involved a limited time, which should determine the duration of the thing, it would then follow solely from that power whereby the thing exists, that the thing could not exist beyond the limits of that time, but that it must be destroyed; but this (III. iv.) is absurd. Wherefore the endeavour wherewith a thing exists involves no definite time; but, contrariwise, since (III. iv.) it will by the same power whereby it already exists always continue to exist, unless it be destroyed by some external cause, this endeavour involves an indefinite time.

PROP. IX. *The mind, both in so far as it has clear and distinct ideas, and also in so far as it has confused ideas, endeavours to persist in its being for an indefinite period, and of this endeavour it is conscious.*

Proof.—The essence of the mind is constituted by adequate and inadequate ideas (III. iii.), therefore (III. vii.), both in so far as it possesses the former, and in so far as it possesses the latter, it endeavours to persist in its own being, and that for an indefinite time (III. viii.). Now as the mind (II. xxiii.) is necessarily conscious of itself through the ideas of the modifications of the body, the mind is therefore (III. vii.) conscious of its own endeavour.

Note.—This endeavour, when referred solely to the mind, is called *will*, when referred to the mind and body in conjunction it is called *appetite;* it is, in fact, nothing else but man's essence, from the nature of which necessarily follow all those results which tend to its preservation; and which man has thus been determined to perform.

Further, between appetite and desire there is no difference, except that the term desire is generally applied to men, in so far as they are conscious of their appetite, and may accordingly be thus defined: *Desire is appetite with consciousness thereof.* It is thus plain from what has been said, that in no case do we strive for, wish for, long for, or desire anything, because we deem it to be good, but on the other hand we deem a thing to be good, because we strive for it, wish for it, long for it, or desire it.

PROP. X. *An idea, which excludes the existence of our body, cannot be postulated in our mind, but is contrary thereto.*

Proof.—Whatsoever can destroy our body, cannot be postulated therein (III. v.). Therefore neither can the idea of such a thing occur in God, in so far as he has the idea of our body (II. ix. Coroll.); that is (II. xi. xiii.), the idea of that thing cannot be postulated as in our mind, but contrariwise, since (II. xi. xiii.) the first element, that constitutes the essence of the mind, is the idea of the human body as actually existing, it follows that the first and chief endeavour of our mind is the endeavour to affirm the existence of our body: thus, an idea, which negatives the existence of our body, is contrary to our mind, &c. *Q.E.D.*

PROP. XI. *Whatsoever increases or diminishes, helps or hinders the power of activity in our body, the idea thereof increases or diminishes, helps or hinders the power of thought in our mind.*

Proof.—This proposition is evident from II. vii. or from II. xiv.

Note.—Thus we see, that the mind can undergo many changes, and can pass sometimes to a state of greater perfection, sometimes to a state of lesser perfection. These passive states of transition explain to us the emotions of pleasure and pain. By *pleasure* therefore in the following propositions I shall signify *a passive state wherein the mind passes to a greater perfection.* By *pain* I shall signify *a passive state wherein the mind passes to a lesser perfection.* Further, the emotion of pleasure in reference to the body and mind together I shall call *stimulation* (*titillatio*) or *merriment* (*hilaritas*), the emotion of pain in the same relation I shall call *suffering* or *melancholy.* But we must bear in mind, that stimulation and suffering are attributed to man, when one part of his nature is more affected than the rest, merriment and melancholy, when all parts are alike affected. What I mean by desire I have explained in the note to Prop. ix. of this part; beyond these three I recognize no other primary emotion; I will show as I proceed, that all other emotions arise from these three. But, before I go further, I should like here to explain at greater length Prop. x. of this part, in order that we may clearly understand how one idea is contrary to another. In the note to II. xvii. we showed that the idea, which constitutes the essence of mind, involves the existence of body, so long as the body itself exists. Again, it follows from what we pointed out in the Coroll. to II. viii., that the present existence of our mind depends solely on the fact, that the mind involves the actual existence of the body. Lastly, we showed (II. xvii. xviii. and note) that the power of the mind, whereby it imagines and remembers things, also depends on the fact, that it involves the actual existence of the body. Whence it follows, that the present existence of the mind and its power of imagining are removed, as soon as the mind ceases to affirm the present existence of the body. Now the cause, why the mind ceases to affirm this existence of the body, cannot be the mind itself (III. iv.), nor again the fact that the body ceases to exist. For (by II. vi.) the cause, why the mind affirms the existence of the body, is not that the body began to exist; therefore, for the same reason, it does not cease to affirm the existence of the body, because the body ceases to exist; but (II. xvii.) this result follows from another idea, which excludes the present existence of our body and, consequently, of our mind, and which is therefore contrary to the idea constituting the essence of our mind.

PROP. XII. *The mind, as far as it can, endeavours to conceive those things, which increase or help the power of activity in the body.*

Proof.—So long as the human body is affected in a mode, which involves the nature of any external body, the human mind will regard that external body as present (II. xvii.), and consequently (II. vii.), so long as the human mind regards an external body as present, that is (II. xvii. note), conceives it, the human body is affected in a mode, which involves the nature of the said external body; thus so long as the mind conceives things, which increase or help the power of activity in our body, the body is affected in modes which increase or help its power of activity (III. Post i.); consequently (III. xi.) the mind's power of thinking is for that period increased or helped. Thus (III. vi. ix.) the mind, as far as it can, endeavours to imagine such things. *Q.E.D.*

PROP. XIII. *When the mind conceives things which di-*

minish or hinder the body's power of activity, it endeavours, as far as possible, to remember things which exclude the existence of the first-named things.

Proof.—So long as the mind conceives anything of the kind alluded to, the power of the mind and body is diminished or constrained (cf. III. xii. Proof); nevertheless it will continue to conceive it, until the mind conceives something else, which excludes the present existence thereof (II. xvii.); that is (as I have just shown), the power of the mind and of the body is diminished, or constrained, until the mind conceives something else, which excludes the existence of the former thing conceived: therefore the mind (III. ix.), as far as it can, will endeavour to conceive or remember the latter. *Q.E.D.*

Corollary.—Hence it follows, that the mind shrinks from conceiving those things, which diminish or constrain the power of itself and of the body.

Note.—From what has been said we may clearly understand the nature of Love and Hate. *Love* is nothing else but *pleasure accompanied by the idea of an external cause: Hate* is nothing else but *pain accompanied by the idea of an external cause.* We further see, that he who loves necessarily endeavours to have, and to keep present to him, the object of his love; while he who hates endeavours to remove and destroy the object of his hatred. But I will treat of these matters at more length hereafter.

PROP. XIV. *If the mind has once been affected by two emotions at the same time, it will, whenever it is afterwards affected by one of the two, be also affected by the other.*

Proof.—If the human body has once been affected by two bodies at once, whenever afterwards the mind conceives one of them, it will straightway remember the other also (II. xviii.). But the mind's conceptions indicate rather the emotions of our body than the nature of external bodies (II. xvi. Coroll. ii.); therefore, if the body, and consequently the mind (III. Def. iii.) has been once affected by two emotions at the same time, it will, whenever it is afterwards affected by one of the two, be also affected by the other.

PROP. XV. *Anything can, accidentally, be the cause of pleasure, pain, or desire.*

Proof.—Let it be granted that the mind is simultaneously

affected by two emotions, of which one neither increases nor diminishes its power of activity, and the other does either increase or diminish the said power (III. Post. i.). From the foregoing proposition it is evident that, whenever the mind is afterwards affected by the former, through its true cause, which (by hypothesis) neither increases nor diminishes its power of action, it will be at the same time affected by the latter, which does increase or diminish its power of activity, that is (III. xi. note) it will be affected with pleasure or pain. Thus the former of the two emotions will, not through itself, but accidentally, be the cause of pleasure or pain. In the same way also it can be easily shown, that a thing may be accidentally the cause of desire. *Q.E.D.*

Corollary.—Simply from the fact that we have regarded a thing with the emotion of pleasure or pain, though that thing be not the efficient cause of the emotion, we can either love or hate it.

Proof.—For from this fact alone it arises (III. xiv.), that the mind afterwards conceiving the said thing is affected with the emotion of pleasure or pain, that is (III. xi. note), according as the power of the mind and body may be increased or diminished, &c.; and consequently (III. xii.), according as the mind may desire or shrink from the conception of it (III. xiii. Coroll.), in other words (III. xiii. note), according as it may love or hate the same. *Q.E.D.*

Note.—Hence we understand how it may happen, that we love or hate a thing without any cause for our emotion being known to us; merely, as the phrase is, from *sympathy* or *antipathy*. We should refer to the same category those objects, which affect us pleasurably or painfully, simply because they resemble other objects which affect us in the same way. This I will show in the next Prop. I am aware that certain authors, who were the first to introduce these terms "sympathy" and "antipathy," wished to signify thereby some occult qualities in things; nevertheless I think we may be permitted to use the same terms to indicate known or manifest qualities.

PROP. XVI. *Simply from the fact that we conceive, that a given object has some point of resemblance with another object which is wont to affect the mind pleasurably or painfully, although the point of resemblance be not the efficient cause of the said emotions, we shall still regard the first-named object with love or hate.*

Proof.—The point of resemblance was in the object (by hypothesis), when we regarded it with pleasure or pain, thus (III. xiv.), when the mind is affected by the image thereof, it will straightway be affected by one or the other emotion, and consequently the thing, which we perceive to have the same point of resemblance, will be accidentally (III. xv.) a cause of pleasure or pain. Thus (by the foregoing Corollary), although the point in which the two objects resemble one another be not the efficient cause of the emotion, we shall still regard the first-named object with love or hate. *Q.E.D.*

PROP. XVII. *If we conceive that a thing, which is wont to affect us painfully, has any point of resemblance with another thing which is wont to affect us with an equally strong emotion of pleasure, we shall hate the first-named thing, and at the same time we shall love it.*

Proof.—The given thing is (by hypothesis) in itself a cause of pain, and (III. xiii. note), in so far as we imagine it with this emotion, we shall hate it: further, inasmuch as we conceive that it has some point of resemblance to something else, which is wont to affect us with an equally strong emotion of pleasure, we shall with an equally strong impulse of pleasure love it (III. xvi.); thus we shall both hate and love the same thing. *Q.E.D.*

Note.—This disposition of the mind, which arises from two contrary emotions, is called *vacillation;* it stands to the emotions in the same relation as doubt does to the imagination (II. xliv. note); vacillation and doubt do not differ one from the other, except as greater differs from less. But we must bear in mind that I have deduced this vacillation from causes, which give rise through themselves to one of the emotions, and to the other accidentally. I have done this, in order that they might be more easily deduced from what went before; but I do not deny that vacillation of the disposition generally arises from an object, which is the efficient cause of both emotions. The human body is composed (II. Post. i.) of a variety of individual parts of different nature, and may therefore (Ax. i. after Lemma iii. after II. xiii.) be affected in a variety of different ways by one and the same body; and contrariwise, as one and the same thing can be affected in many ways, it can also in many different ways affect one and the same part of the body. Hence we can easily conceive, that one and the same object may be the cause of many and conflicting emotions.

PROP. XVIII. *A man is as much affected pleasurably or painfully by the image of a thing past or future as by the image of a thing present.*

Proof.—So long as a man is affected by the image of anything, he will regard that thing as present, even though it be non-existent (II. xvii. and Coroll.), he will not conceive it as past or future, except in so far as its image is joined to the image of time past or future (II. xliv. note). Wherefore the image of a thing, regarded in itself alone, is identical, whether it be referred to time past, time future, or time present; that is (II. xvi. Coroll.), the disposition or emotion of the body is identical, whether the image be of a thing past, future, or present. Thus the emotion of pleasure or pain is the same, whether the image be of a thing past or future. *Q.E.D.*

Note I.—I call a thing past or future, according as we either have been or shall be affected thereby. For instance, according as we have seen it, or are about to see it, according as it has recreated us, or will recreate us, according as it has harmed us, or will harm us. For, as we thus conceive it, we affirm its existence; that is, the body is affected by no emotion which excludes the existence of the thing, and therefore (II. xvii.) the body is affected by the image of the thing, in the same way as if the thing were actually present. However, as it generally happens that those, who have had many experiences, vacillate, so long as they regard a thing as future or past, and are usually in doubt about its issue (II. xliv. note); it follows that the emotions which arise from similar images of things are not so constant, but are generally disturbed by the images of other things, until men become assured of the issue.

Note II.—From what has just been said, we understand what is meant by the terms Hope, Fear, Confidence,

Despair, Joy, and Disappointment.[1] *Hope* is nothing else but *an inconstant pleasure, arising from the image of something future or past, whereof we do not yet know the issue. Fear*, on the other hand, is *an inconstant pain also arising from the image of something concerning which we are in doubt.* If the element of doubt be removed from these emotions, hope becomes *Confidence* and fear becomes *Despair.* In other words, *Pleasure or Pain arising from the image of something concerning which we have hoped or feared.* Again, *Joy* is *Pleasure arising from the image of something past whereof we doubted the issue. Disappointment* is the *Pain opposed to Joy.*

PROP. XIX. *He who conceives that the object of his love is destroyed will feel pain; if he conceives that it is preserved he will feel pleasure.*

Proof.—The mind, as far as possible, endeavours to conceive those things which increase or help the body's power of activity (III. xii.); in other words (III. xii. note), those things which it loves. But conception is helped by those things which postulate the existence of a thing, and contrariwise is hindered by those which exclude the existence of a thing (II. xvii.); therefore the images of things, which postulate the existence of an object of love, help the mind's endeavour to conceive the object of love, in other words (III. xi. note), affect the mind pleasurably; contrariwise those things, which exclude the existence of an object of love, hinder the aforesaid mental endeavour; in other words, affect the mind painfully. He, therefore, who conceives that the object of his love is destroyed will feel pain, &c. *Q.E.D.*

PROP. XX. *He who conceives that the object of his hate is destroyed will feel pleasure.*

Proof.—The mind (III. xiii.) endeavours to conceive those things, which exclude the existence of things whereby the body's power of activity is diminished or constrained; that is (III. xiii. note), it endeavours to conceive such things as exclude the existence of what it hates; therefore the image of a thing, which excludes the existence of what the mind hates, helps the aforesaid mental effort, in

[1] *Conscientiæ morsus*—thus rendered by Mr. Pollock.

other words (III. xi. note), affects the mind pleasurably. Thus he who conceives that the object of his hate is destroyed will feel pleasure. *Q.E.D.*

Prop. XXI. *He who conceives, that the object of his love is affected pleasurably or painfully, will himself be affected pleasurably or painfully; and the one or the other emotion will be greater or less in the lover according as it is greater or less in the thing loved.*

Proof.—The images of things (as we showed in III. xix.) which postulate the existence of the object of love, help the mind's endeavour to conceive the said object. But pleasure postulates the existence of something feeling pleasure, so much the more in proportion as the emotion of pleasure is greater; for it is (III. xi. note) a transition to a greater perfection; therefore the image of pleasure in the object of love helps the mental endeavour of the lover; that is, it affects the lover pleasurably, and so much the more, in proportion as this emotion may have been greater in the object of love. This was our first point. Further, in so far as a thing is affected with pain, it is to that extent destroyed, the extent being in proportion to the amount of pain (III. xi. note); therefore (III. xix.) he who conceives, that the object of his love is affected painfully, will himself be affected painfully, in proportion as the said emotion is greater or less in the object of love. *Q.E.D.*

Prop. XXII. *If we conceive that anything pleasurably affects some object of our love, we shall be affected with love towards that thing. Contrariwise, if we conceive that it affects an object of our love painfully, we shall be affected with hatred towards it.*

Proof.—He, who affects pleasurably or painfully the object of our love, affects us also pleasurably or painfully—that is, if we conceive the loved object as affected with the said pleasure or pain (III. xxi.). But this pleasure or pain is postulated to come to us accompanied by the idea of an external cause; therefore (III. xiii. note), if we conceive that anyone affects an object of our love pleasurably or painfully, we shall be affected with love or hatred towards him. *Q.E.D.*

Note.—Prop. xxi. explains to us the nature of *Pity*, which we may define as *pain arising from another's hurt.* What term we can use for pleasure arising from another's gain, I know not.

We will call the *love towards him who confers a benefit on another, Approval;* and the *hatred towards him who injures another,* we will call *Indignation.* We must further remark, that we not only feel pity for a thing which we have loved (as shown in III. xxi.), but also for a thing which we have hitherto regarded without emotion, provided that we deem that it resembles ourselves (as I will show presently). Thus, we bestow approval on one who has benefited anything resembling ourselves, and, contrariwise, are indignant with him who has done it an injury.

PROP. XXIII. *He who conceives, that an object of his hatred is painfully affected, will feel pleasure. Contrariwise, if he thinks that the said object is pleasurably affected, he will feel pain. Each of these emotions will be greater or less, according as its contrary is greater or less in the object of hatred.*

Proof.—In so far as an object of hatred is painfully affected, it is destroyed, to an extent proportioned to the strength of the pain (III. xi. note). Therefore, he (III. xx.) who conceives, that some object of his hatred is painfully affected, will feel pleasure, to an extent proportioned to the amount of pain he conceives in the object of his hatred. This was our first point. Again, pleasure postulates the existence of the pleasurably affected thing (III. xi. note), in proportion as the pleasure is greater or less. If anyone imagines that an object of his hatred is pleasurably affected, this conception (III. xiii.) will hinder his own endeavour to persist; in other words (III. xi. note), he who hates will be painfully affected. *Q.E.D.*

Note.—This pleasure can scarcely be felt unalloyed, and without any mental conflict. For (as I am about to show in Prop. xxvii.), in so far as a man conceives that something similar to himself is affected by pain, he will himself be affected in like manner; and he will have the contrary emotion in contrary circumstances. But here we are regarding hatred only.

PROP. XXIV. *If we conceive that anyone pleasurably affects an object of our hate, we shall feel hatred towards him also. If we conceive that he painfully affects the said object, we shall feel love towards him.*

Proof.—This proposition is proved in the same way as III. xxii., which see.

Note.—These and similar emotions of hatred are attributable to *envy*, which, accordingly, is nothing else but *hatred, in so far as it is regarded as disposing a man to rejoice in another's hurt, and to grieve at another's advantage.*

PROP. XXV. *We endeavour to affirm, concerning ourselves, and concerning what we love, everything that we conceive to affect pleasurably ourselves, or the loved object. Contrariwise, we endeavour to negative everything, which we conceive to affect painfully ourselves or the loved object.*

Proof.—That, which we conceive to affect an object of our love pleasurably or painfully, affects us also pleasurably or painfully (III. xxi.). But the mind (III. xii.) endeavours, as far as possible, to conceive those things which affect us pleasurably; in other words (II. xvii. and Coroll.), it endeavours to regard them as present. And, contrariwise (III. xiii.), it endeavours to exclude the existence of such things as affect us painfully; therefore, we endeavour to affirm concerning ourselves, and concerning the loved object, whatever we conceive to affect ourselves, or the loved object pleasurably. *Q.E.D.*

PROP. XXVI. *We endeavour to affirm, concerning that which we hate, everything which we conceive to affect it painfully; and, contrariwise, we endeavour to deny, concerning it, everything which we conceive to affect it pleasurably.*

Proof.—This proposition follows from III. xxiii., as the foregoing proposition followed from III. xxi.

Note.—Thus we see that it may readily happen, that a man may easily think too highly of himself, or a loved object, and, contrariwise, too meanly of a hated object. This feeling is called *pride*, in reference to the man who thinks too highly of himself, and is a species of madness, wherein a man dreams with his eyes open, thinking that he can accomplish all things that fall within the scope of his conception, and thereupon accounting them real, and exulting in them, so long as he is unable to conceive anything which excludes their existence, and determines his own power of action. *Pride*, therefore, is *pleasure springing from a man thinking too highly of himself.* Again, the *pleasure which arises from a man thinking too highly of another* is called *over-esteem.* Whereas the *pleasure which arises from thinking too little of a man* is called *disdain.*

PROP. XXVII. *By the very fact that we conceive a thing, which is like ourselves, and which we have not regarded with any emotion, to be affected with any emotion, we are ourselves affected with a like emotion* (*affectus*).

Proof.—The images of things are modifications of the human body, whereof the ideas represent external bodies as present to us (II. xvii.); in other words (II. x.), whereof the ideas involve the nature of our body, and, at the same time, the nature of external bodies as present. If, therefore, the nature of the external body be similar to the nature of our body, then the idea which we form of the external body will involve a modification of our own body similar to the modification of the external body. Consequently, if we conceive anyone similar to ourselves as affected by any emotion, this conception will express a modification of our body similar to that emotion. Thus, from the fact of conceiving a thing like ourselves to be affected with any emotion, we are ourselves affected with a like emotion. If, however, we hate the said thing like ourselves, we shall, to that extent, be affected by a contrary, and not similar, emotion. *Q.E.D.*

Note I.—This imitation of emotions, when it is referred to pain, is called *compassion* (cf. III. xxii. note); when it is referred to desire, it is called *emulation*, which is nothing else but *the desire of anything, engendered in us by the fact that we conceive that others have the like desire.*

Corollary I.—If we conceive that anyone, whom we have hitherto regarded with no emotion, pleasurably affects something similar to ourselves, we shall be affected with love towards him. If, on the other hand, we conceive that he painfully affects the same, we shall be affected with hatred towards him.

Proof.—This is proved from the last proposition in the same manner as III. xxii. is proved from III. xxi.

Corollary II.—We cannot hate a thing which we pity, because its misery affects us painfully.

Proof.—If we could hate it for this reason, we should rejoice in its pain, which is contrary to the hypothesis.

Corollary III.—We seek to free from misery, as far as we can, a thing which we pity.

Proof.—That, which painfully affects the object of our pity, affects us also with similar pain (by the foregoing proposition); therefore, we shall endeavour to recall everything which removes its existence, or which destroys it (cf. III. xiii.); in other words (III. ix. note), we shall desire to destroy it, or we shall be determined for its destruction; thus, we shall endeavour to free from misery a thing which we pity. *Q.E.D.*

Note II.—This will or appetite for doing good, which arises from pity of the thing whereon we would confer a benefit, is called *benevolence*, and is nothing else but *desire arising from compassion.* Concerning love or hate towards him who has done good or harm to something, which we conceive to be like ourselves, see III. xxii. note.

Prop. XXVIII. *We endeavour to bring about whatsoever we conceive to conduce to pleasure; but we endeavour to remove or destroy whatsoever we conceive to be truly repugnant thereto, or to conduce to pain.*

Proof.—We endeavour, as far as possible, to conceive that which we imagine to conduce to pleasure (III. xii.); in other words (II. xvii.) we shall endeavour to conceive it as far as possible as present or actually existing. But the endeavour of the mind, or the mind's power of thought, is equal to, and simultaneous with, the endeavour of the body, or the body's power of action. (This is clear from II. vii. Coroll. and II. xi. Coroll.). Therefore we make an absolute endeavour for its existence, in other words (which by III. ix. note come to the same thing) we desire and strive for it; this was our first point. Again, if we conceive that something, which we believed to be the cause of pain, that is (III. xiii. note), which we hate, is destroyed, we shall rejoice (III. xx.). We shall, therefore (by the first part of this proof), endeavour to destroy the same, or (III. xiii.) to remove it from us, so that we may not regard it as present; this was our second point. Wherefore whatsoever conduces to pleasure, &c. *Q.E.D.*

Prop. XXIX. *We shall also endeavour to do whatsoever*

we conceive men[1] *to regard with pleasure, and contrariwise we shall shrink from doing that which we conceive men to shrink from.*

Proof.—From the fact of imagining, that men love or hate anything, we shall love or hate the same thing (III. xxvii.). That is (III. xiii. note), from this mere fact we shall feel pleasure or pain at the thing's presence. And so we shall endeavour to do whatever we conceive men to love or regard with pleasure, etc. *Q.E.D.*

Note.—This endeavour to do a thing or leave it undone, solely in order to please men, we call *ambition*, especially when we so eagerly endeavour to please the vulgar, that we do or omit certain things to our own or another's hurt: in other cases it is generally called *kindliness*. Furthermore I give the name of *praise* to the *pleasure, with which we conceive the action of another, whereby he has endeavoured to please us;* but of *blame* to the *pain wherewith we feel aversion to his action.*

Prop. XXX. *If anyone has done something which he conceives as affecting other men pleasurably, he will be affected by pleasure, accompanied by the idea of himself as cause; in other words, he will regard himself with pleasure. On the other hand, if he has done anything which he conceives as affecting others painfully, he will regard himself with pain.*

Proof.—He who conceives, that he affects others with pleasure or pain, will, by that very fact, himself be affected with pleasure or pain (III. xxvii.), but, as a man (II. xix. and xxiii.) is conscious of himself through the modifications whereby he is determined to action, it follows that he who conceives, that he affects others pleasurably, will be affected with pleasure accompanied by the idea of himself as cause; in other words, will regard himself with pleasure. And so *mutatis mutandis* in the case of pain. *Q.E.D.*

Note.—As love (III. xiii.) is pleasure accompanied by the idea of an external cause, and hatred is pain accompanied by the idea of an external cause; the pleasure and pain in question will be a species of love and hatred. But, as the terms love and hatred are used in reference to external objects, we will employ other names for the emotions now under discussion: pleasure accompanied by the idea

[1] N.B. By "men" in this and the following propositions, I mean men whom we regard without any particular emotion.

of an external cause[1] we will style *Honour*, and the emotion contrary thereto we will style *Shame:* I mean in such cases as where pleasure or pain arises from a man's belief, that he is being praised or blamed: otherwise pleasure accompanied by the idea of an external cause[1] is called *self-complacency*, and its contrary pain is called *repentance.* Again, as it may happen (II. xvii. Coroll.) that the pleasure, wherewith a man conceives that he affects others, may exist solely in his own imagination, and as (III. xxv.) everyone endeavours to conceive concerning himself that which he conceives will affect him with pleasure, it may easily come to pass that a vain man may be proud and may imagine that he is pleasing to all, when in reality he may be an annoyance to all.

PROP. XXXI. *If we conceive that anyone loves, desires, or hates anything which we ourselves love, desire, or hate, we shall thereupon regard the thing in question with more steadfast love, &c. On the contrary, if we think that anyone shrinks from something that we love, we shall undergo vacillation of soul.*

Proof.—From the mere fact of conceiving that anyone loves anything we shall ourselves love that thing (III. xxvii.): but we are assumed to love it already; there is, therefore, a new cause of love, whereby our former emotion is fostered; hence we shall thereupon love it more steadfastly. Again, from the mere fact of conceiving that anyone shrinks from anything, we shall ourselves shrink from that thing (III. xxvii.). If we assume that we at the same time love it, we shall then simultaneously love it and shrink from it; in other words, we shall be subject to vacillation (III. xvii. note). *Q.E.D.*

Corollary.—From the foregoing, and also from III. xxviii. it follows that everyone endeavours, as far as possible, to cause others to love what he himself loves, and to hate what he himself hates: as the poet says: "As lovers let us share every hope and every fear: ironhearted were he who should love what the other leaves.[2]"

[1] So Van Vloten and Bruder. The Dutch version and Camerer read, "an internal cause." "Honour" = *Gloria.*

[2] Ovid. Amores, II. xix. 4, 5. Spinoza transposes the verses.

"Speremus pariter, pariter metuamus amantes;
Ferreus est, si quis, quod sinit alter, amat."

Note.—This endeavour to bring it about, that our own likes and dislikes should meet with universal approval, is really ambition (see III. xxix. note); wherefore we see that everyone by nature desires (*appetere*), that the rest of mankind should live according to his own individual disposition: when such a desire is equally present in all, everyone stands in everyone else's way, and in wishing to be loved or praised by all, all become mutually hateful.

PROP. XXXII. *If we conceive that anyone takes delight in something, which only one person can possess, we shall endeavour to bring it about that the man in question shall not gain possession thereof.*

Proof.—From the mere fact of our conceiving that another person takes delight in a thing (III. xxvii. and Coroll.) we shall ourselves love that thing and desire to take delight therein. But we assumed that the pleasure in question would be prevented by another's delight in its object; we shall, therefore, endeavour to prevent his possession thereof (III. xxviii.). *Q.E.D.*

Note.—We thus see that man's nature is generally so constituted, that he takes pity on those who fare ill, and envies those who fare well with an amount of hatred proportioned to his own love for the goods in their possession. Further, we see that from the same property of human nature, whence it follows that men are merciful, it follows also that they are envious and ambitious. Lastly, if we make appeal to Experience, we shall find that she entirely confirms what we have said; more especially if we turn our attention to the first years of our life. We find that children, whose body is continually, as it were, in equilibrium, laugh or cry simply because they see others laughing or crying; moreover, they desire forthwith to imitate whatever they see others doing, and to possess themselves whatever they conceive as delighting others: inasmuch as the images of things are, as we have said, modifications of the human body, or modes wherein the human body is affected and disposed by external causes to act in this or that manner.

PROP. XXXIII. *When we love a thing similar to ourselves we endeavour, as far as we can, to bring about that it should love us in return.*

Proof.—That which we love we endeavour, as far as we can, to conceive in preference to anything else (III. xii.). If the thing be similar to ourselves, we shall endeavour to affect it pleasurably in preference to anything else (III. xxix.). In other words, we shall endeavour, as far as we can, to bring it about, that the thing should be affected with pleasure accompanied by the idea of ourselves, that is (III. xiii. note), that it should love us in return. *Q.E.D.*

PROP. XXXIV. *The greater the emotion with which we conceive a loved object to be affected towards us, the greater will be our complacency.*

Proof.—We endeavour (III. xxxiii.), as far as we can, to bring about, that what we love should love us in return: in other words, that what we love should be affected with pleasure accompanied by the idea of ourself as cause. Therefore, in proportion as the loved object is more pleasurably affected because of us, our endeavour will be assisted.—that is (III. xi. and note) the greater will be our pleasure. But when we take pleasure in the fact, that we pleasurably affect something similar to ourselves, we regard ourselves with pleasure (III. 30); therefore the greater the emotion with which we conceive a loved object to be affected, &c. *Q.E.D.*

PROP. XXXV. *If anyone conceives, that an object of his love joins itself to another with closer bonds of friendship than he himself has attained to, he will be affected with hatred towards the loved object and with envy towards his rival.*

Proof.—In proportion as a man thinks, that a loved object is well affected towards him, will be the strength of his self-approval (by the last Prop.), that is (III. xxx. note), of his pleasure; he will, therefore (III. xxviii.), endeavour, as far as he can, to imagine the loved object as most closely bound to him: this endeavour or desire will be increased, if he thinks that someone else has a similar desire (III. xxxi.). But this endeavour or desire is assumed to be checked by the image of the loved object in conjunction with the image of him whom the loved object has joined to itself; therefore (III. xi. note) he will for that reason be affected with pain, accompanied by the idea of the loved object as a cause in conjunction with the image of his rival; that is, he will be (III. xiii.) affected with hatred towards the loved object and also towards his rival (III. xv. Coroll.), which latter he will envy as enjoying the beloved object. *Q.E.D.*

Note.—This hatred towards an object of love joined with envy is called *Jealousy*, which accordingly is nothing else but a wavering of the disposition arising from combined love and hatred, accompanied by the idea of some rival who is envied. Further, this hatred towards the object of love will be greater, in proportion to the pleasure which the jealous man had been wont to derive from the reciprocated love of the said object; and also in proportion to the feelings he had previously entertained towards his rival. If he had hated him, he will forthwith hate the object of his love, because he conceives it is pleasurably affected by one whom he himself hates: and also because he is compelled to associate the image of his loved one with the image of him whom he hates. This condition generally comes into play in the case of love for a woman: for he who thinks, that a woman whom he loves prostitutes herself to another, will feel pain, not only because his own desire is restrained, but also because, being compelled to associate the image of her he loves with the parts of shame and the excreta of another, he therefore shrinks from her.

We must add, that a jealous man is not greeted by his beloved with the same joyful countenance as before, and this also gives him pain as a lover, as I will now show.

PROP. XXXVI. *He who remembers a thing, in which he has once taken delight, desires to possess it under the same circumstances as when he first took delight therein.*

Proof.—Everything, which a man has seen in conjunction with the object of his love, will be to him accidentally a cause of pleasure (III. xv.); he will, therefore, desire to possess it, in conjunction with that wherein he has taken delight; in other words, he will desire to possess the object of his love under the same circumstances as when he first took delight therein. *Q.E.D.*

Corollary.—A lover will, therefore, feel pain if one of the aforesaid attendant circumstances be missing.

Proof.—For, in so far as he finds some circumstance to be missing, he conceives something which excludes its existence. As he is assumed to be desirous for love's sake of that thing or circumstance (by the last Prop.), he will, in so far as he conceives it to be missing, feel pain (III. xix.). *Q.E.D.*

Note.—This pain, in so far as it has reference to the absence of the object of love, is called *Regret.*

Prop. XXXVII. *Desire arising through pain or pleasure, hatred or love, is greater in proportion as the emotion is greater.*

Proof.—Pain diminishes or constrains man's power of activity (III. xi. note), in other words (III. vii.), diminishes or constrains the effort, wherewith he endeavours to persist in his own being; therefore (III. v.) it is contrary to the said endeavour: thus all the endeavours of a man affected by pain are directed to removing that pain. But (by the definition of pain), in proportion as the pain is greater, so also is it necessarily opposed to a greater part of man's power of activity; therefore the greater the pain, the greater the power of activity employed to remove it; that is, the greater will be the desire or appetite in endeavouring to remove it. Again, since pleasure (III. xi. note) increases or aids a man's power of activity, it may easily be shown in like manner, that a man affected by pleasure has no desire further than to preserve it, and his desire will be in proportion to the magnitude of the pleasure.

Lastly, since hatred and love are themselves emotions of pain and pleasure, it follows in like manner that the endeavour, appetite, or desire, which arises through hatred or love, will be greater in proportion to the hatred or love. *Q.E.D.*

Prop. XXXVIII. *If a man has begun to hate an object of his love, so that love is thoroughly destroyed, he will, causes being equal, regard it with more hatred than if he had never loved it, and his hatred will be in proportion to the strength of his former love.*

Proof.—If a man begins to hate that which he had loved, more of his appetites are put under restraint than if he had never loved it. For love is a pleasure (III. xiii. note) which a man endeavours as far as he can to render permanent (III. xxviii.); he does so by regarding the object of his love as present, and by affecting it as far as he can pleasurably; this endeavour is greater in proportion as the love is greater, and so also is the endeavour to bring about that the beloved should return his affection (III. xxxiii.).

Now these endeavours are constrained by hatred towards the object of love (III. xiii. Coroll. and III. xxiii.); wherefore the lover (III. xi. note) will for this cause also be affected with pain, the more so in proportion as his love has been greater; that is, in addition to the pain caused by hatred, there is a pain caused by the fact that he has loved the object; wherefore the lover will regard the beloved with greater pain, or in other words, will hate it more than if he had never loved it, and with the more intensity in proportion as his former love was greater. *Q.E.D.*

PROP. XXXIX. *He who hates anyone will endeavour to do him an injury, unless he fears that a greater injury will thereby accrue to himself; on the other hand, he who loves anyone will, by the same law, seek to benefit him.*

Proof.—To hate a man is (III. xiii. note) to conceive him as a cause of pain; therefore he who hates a man will endeavour to remove or destroy him. But if anything more painful, or, in other words, a greater evil, should accrue to the hater thereby—and if the hater thinks he can avoid such evil by not carrying out the injury, which he planned against the object of his hate—he will desire to abstain from inflicting that injury (III. xxviii.), and the strength of his endeavour (III. xxxvii.) will be greater than his former endeavour to do injury, and will therefore prevail over it, as we asserted. The second part of this proof proceeds in the same manner. Wherefore he who hates another, etc. *Q.E.D.*

Note.—By *good* I here mean every kind of pleasure, and all that conduces thereto, especially that which satisfies our longings, whatsoever they may be. By *evil*, I mean every kind of pain, especially that which frustrates our longings. For I have shown (III. ix. note) that we in no case desire a thing because we deem it good, but, contrariwise, we deem a thing good because we desire it: consequently we deem evil that which we shrink from; everyone, therefore, according to his particular emotions, judges or estimates what is good, what is bad, what is better, what is worse, lastly, what is best, and what is worst. Thus a miser thinks that abundance of money is the best, and want of money the worst; an ambitious man desires nothing so much as glory, and fears nothing so much as shame. To an envious man nothing is more delightful than another's misfortune, and nothing more painful than another's success. So every man, according to his emotions, judges a thing to be good or bad, useful or useless. The emotion, which induces a man to turn from that which he wishes, or to wish for that which he turns from, is called *timidity*, which may accordingly be defined as *the fear whereby a man is induced to avoid an evil which he regards as future by encountering a lesser evil* (III. xxviii.). But if the evil which he fears be shame, timidity becomes *bashfulness*. Lastly, if the desire to avoid a future evil be checked by the fear of another evil, so that the man knows not which to choose, fear becomes *consternation*, especially if both the evils feared be very great.

PROP. XL. *He, who conceives himself to be hated by another, and believes that he has given him no cause for hatred, will hate that other in return.*

Proof.—He who conceives another as affected with hatred, will thereupon be affected himself with hatred (III. xxvii.), that is, with pain, accompanied by the idea of an external cause. But, by the hypothesis, he conceives no cause for this pain except him who is his enemy; therefore, from conceiving that he is hated by some one, he will be affected with pain, accompanied by the idea of his enemy; in other words, he will hate his enemy in return. *Q.E.D.*

Note.—He who thinks that he has given just cause for hatred will (III. xxx. and note) be affected with shame; but this case (III. xxv.) rarely happens. This reciprocation of hatred may also arise from the hatred, which follows an endeavour to injure the object of our hate (III. xxxix.). He therefore who conceives that he is hated by another will conceive his enemy as the cause of some evil or pain; thus he will be affected with pain or fear, accompanied by the idea of his enemy as cause; in other words, he will be affected with hatred towards his enemy, as I said above.

Corollary I.—He who conceives, that one whom he loves hates him, will be a prey to conflicting hatred and love. For, in so far as he conceives that he is an object of hatred, he is determined to hate his enemy in return. But, by the hypothesis, he nevertheless loves him: wherefore he will be a prey to conflicting hatred and love.

Corollary II.—If a man conceives that one, whom he has hitherto regarded without emotion, has done him any injury from motives of hatred, he will forthwith seek to repay the injury in kind.

Proof.—He who conceives, that another hates him, will (by the last proposition) hate his enemy in return, and (III. xxvi.) will endeavour to recall everything which can affect him painfully; he will moreover endeavour to do him an injury (III. xxxix.). Now the first thing of this sort which he conceives is the injury done to himself; he will, therefore, forthwith endeavour to repay it in kind. *Q.E.D.*

Note.—The endeavour to injure one whom we hate is called *Anger;* the endeavour to repay in kind injury done to ourselves is called *Revenge.*

Prop. XLI. *If anyone conceives that he is loved by another, and believes that he has given no cause for such love, he will love that other in return.* (Cf. III. xv. Coroll., and III. xvi.)

Proof.—This proposition is proved in the same way as the preceding one. See also the note appended thereto.

Note.—If he believes that he has given just cause for the love, he will take pride therein (III. xxx. and note); this is what most often happens (III. xxv.), and we said that its contrary took place whenever a man conceives himself to be hated by another. (See note to preceding proposition.) This reciprocal love, and consequently the desire of benefiting him who loves us (III. xxxix.), and who endeavours to benefit us, is called *gratitude* or *thankfulness.* It thus appears that men are much more prone to take vengeance than to return benefits.

Corollary.—He who imagines, that he is loved by one whom he hates, will be a prey to conflicting hatred and love. This is proved in the same way as the first corollary of the preceding proposition.

Note.—If hatred be the prevailing emotion, he will endeavour to injure him who loves him; this emotion is called cruelty, especially if the victim be believed to have given no ordinary cause for hatred.

Prop. XLII. *He who has conferred a benefit on anyone from motives of love or honour will feel pain, if he sees that the benefit is received without gratitude.*

Proof.—When a man loves something similar to himself, he endeavours, as far as he can, to bring it about that he should be loved thereby in return (III. xxxiii.). Therefore he who has conferred a benefit confers it in obedience to the desire, which he feels of being loved in return; that is (III. xxxiv.) from the hope of honour or (III. xxx. note) pleasure; hence he will endeavour, as far as he can, to conceive this cause of honour, or to regard it as actually existing. But, by the hypothesis, he conceives something else, which excludes the existence of the said cause of honour: wherefore he will thereat feel pain (III. xix.). *Q.E.D.*

Prop. XLIII. *Hatred is increased by being reciprocated, and can on the other hand be destroyed by love.*

Proof.—He who conceives, that an object of his hate hates him in return, will thereupon feel a new hatred, while the former hatred (by hypothesis) still remains (III. xl.). But if, on the other hand, he conceives that the object of hate loves him, he will to this extent (III. xxxviii.) regard himself with pleasure, and (III. xxix.) will endeavour to please the cause of his emotion. In other words, he will endeavour not to hate him (III. xli.), and not to affect him painfully; this endeavour (III. xxxvii.) will be greater or less in proportion to the emotion from which it arises. Therefore, if it be greater than that which arises from hatred, and through which the man endeavours to affect painfully the thing which he hates, it will get the better of it and banish the hatred from his mind. *Q.E.D.*

Prop. XLIV. *Hatred which is completely vanquished by love passes into love: and love is thereupon greater than if hatred had not preceded it.*

Proof.—The proof proceeds in the same way as Prop. xxxviii. of this Part: for he who begins to love a thing, which he was wont to hate or regard with pain, from the very fact of loving feels pleasure. To this pleasure involved in love is added the pleasure arising from aid given to the endeavour to remove the pain involved in hatred (III. xxxvii.), accompanied by the idea of the former object of hatred as cause.

Note.—Though this be so, no one will endeavour to hate anything, or to be affected with pain, for the sake of enjoying this greater pleasure; that is, no one will desire that he should be injured, in the hope of recovering from the injury, nor long to be ill for the sake of getting well. For everyone will always endeavour to persist in his being, and to ward off pain as far as he can. If the contrary is conceivable, namely, that a man should desire to hate someone, in order that he might love him the more thereafter, he will always desire to hate him. For the strength of the love is in proportion to the strength of the hatred, wherefore the man would desire, that the hatred be continually increased more and more, and, for a similar reason, he would desire to become more and more ill, in order that he might take a greater pleasure in being restored to health: in such a case he would always endeavour to be ill, which (III. vi.) is absurd.

Prop. XLV. *If a man conceives, that anyone similar to himself hates anything also similar to himself, which he loves, he will hate that person.*

Proof.—The beloved object feels reciprocal hatred towards him who hates it (III. xl.); therefore the lover, in conceiving that anyone hates the beloved object, conceives the beloved thing as affected by hatred, in other words (III. xiii.), by pain; consequently he is himself affected by pain accompanied by the idea of the hater of the beloved thing as cause; that is, he will hate him who hates anything which he himself loves (III. xiii. note). *Q.E.D.*

Prop. XLVI. *If a man has been affected pleasurably or painfully by anyone, of a class or nation different from his own, and if the pleasure or pain has been accompanied by the idea of the said stranger as cause, under the general category of the class or nation: the man will feel love or hatred, not only to the individual stranger, but also to the whole class or nation whereto he belongs.*

Proof.—This is evident from III. xvi.

Prop. XLVII. *Joy arising from the fact, that anything we hate is destroyed, or suffers other injury, is never unaccompanied by a certain pain in us.*

Proof.—This is evident from III. xxvii. For in so far as we conceive a thing similar to ourselves to be affected with pain, we ourselves feel pain.

Note.—This proposition can also be proved from the Corollary to II. xvii. Whenever we remember anything, even if it does not actually exist, we regard it only as present, and the body is affected in the same manner; wherefore, in so far as the remembrance of the thing is strong, a man is determined to regard it with pain; this determination, while the image of the thing in question lasts, is indeed checked by the remembrance of other things excluding the existence of the aforesaid thing, but is not destroyed: hence, a man only feels pleasure in so far as the said determination is checked: for this reason the joy arising from the injury done to what we hate is repeated, every time we remember that object of hatred. For, as we have said, when the image of the thing in question is aroused, inasmuch as it involves the thing's existence, it determines the man to regard the thing with the same pain as he was wont to do, when it actually did exist. However, since he has joined to the image of the thing other images, which exclude its existence, this determination to pain is forthwith checked, and the man rejoices afresh as often as the repetition takes place. This is the cause of men's pleasure in recalling past evils, and delight in narrating dangers from which they have escaped. For when men conceive a danger, they conceive it as still future, and are determined to fear it; this determination is checked afresh by the idea of freedom, which became associated with the idea of the danger when they escaped therefrom: this renders them secure afresh: therefore they rejoice afresh.

Prop. XLVIII. *Love or hatred towards, for instance, Peter is destroyed, if the pleasure involved in the former, or the pain involved in the latter emotion, be associated with the idea of another cause: and will be diminished in proportion as we conceive Peter not to have been the sole cause of either emotion.*

Proof.—This Prop. is evident from the mere definition of love and hatred (III. xiii. note). For pleasure is called love towards Peter, and pain is called hatred towards Peter, simply in so far as Peter is regarded as the cause of one emotion or the other. When this condition of causality is either wholly or partly removed, the emotion towards Peter also wholly or in part vanishes. *Q.E.D.*

Prop. XLIX. *Love or hatred towards a thing, which we conceive to be free, must, other conditions being similar, be greater than if it were felt towards a thing acting by necessity.*

Proof.—A thing which we conceive as free must (I. Def. vii.) be perceived through itself without anything else. If, therefore, we conceive it as the cause of pleasure or pain, we shall therefore (III. xiii. note) love it or hate it, and shall do so with the utmost love or hatred that can arise from the given emotion. But if the thing which causes the emotion be conceived as acting by necessity, we shall then (by the same Def. vii. Part I.) conceive it not as the sole cause, but as one of the causes of the emotion, and therefore our love or hatred towards it will be less. *Q.E.D.*

Note.—Hence it follows, that men, thinking themselves to be free, feel more love or hatred towards one another than towards anything else: to this consideration we must add the imitation of emotions treated of in III. xxvii. xxxiv. xl. and xliii.

PROP. L. *Anything whatever can be, accidentally, a cause of hope or fear.*

Proof.—This proposition is proved in the same way as III. xv., which see, together with the note to III. xviii.

Note.—Things which are accidentally the causes of hope or fear are called good or evil omens. Now, in so far as such omens are the cause of hope or fear, they are (by the definitions of hope and fear given in III. xviii. note) the causes also of pleasure and pain; consequently we, to this extent, regard them with love or hatred, and endeavour either to invoke them as means towards that which we hope for, or to remove them as obstacles, or causes of that which we fear. It follows, further, from III. xxv., that we are naturally so constituted as to believe readily in that which we hope for, and with difficulty in that which we fear; moreover, we are apt to estimate such objects above or below their true value. Hence there have arisen superstitions, whereby men are everywhere assailed. However, I do not think it worth while to point out here the vacillations springing from hope and fear; it follows from the definition of these emotions, that there can be no hope without fear, and no fear without hope, as I will duly explain in the proper place. Further, in so far as we hope for or fear anything, we regard it with love or hatred; thus everyone can apply by himself to hope and fear what we have said concerning love and hatred.

Prop. LI. *Different men may be differently affected by the same object, and the same man may be differently affected at different times by the same object.*

Proof.—The human body is affected by external bodies in a variety of ways (II. Post. iii.). Two men may therefore be differently affected at the same time, and therefore (by Ax. i. after Lemma iii. after II. xiii.) may be differently affected by one and the same object. Further (by the same Post.) the human body can be affected sometimes in one way, sometimes in another; consequently (by the same Axiom) it may be differently affected at different times by one and the same object. *Q.E.D.*

Note.—We thus see that it is possible, that what one man loves another may hate, and that what one man fears another may not fear; or, again, that one and the same man may love what he once hated, or may be bold where he once was timid, and so on. Again, as everyone judges according to his emotions what is good, what bad, what better, and what worse (III. xxxix. note), it follows that men's judgments may vary no less than their emotions,[1] hence when we compare some with others, we distinguish them solely by the diversity of their emotions, and style some intrepid, others timid, others by some other epithet. For instance, I shall call a man *intrepid*, if he despises an evil which I am accustomed to fear; if I further take into consideration, that, in his desire to injure his enemies and to benefit those whom he loves, he is not restrained by the fear of an evil which is sufficient to restrain me, I shall call him *daring*. Again, a man will appear *timid* to me, if he fears an evil which I am accustomed to despise; and if I further take into consideration that his desire is restrained by the fear of an evil, which is not sufficient to restrain me, I shall say that he is *cowardly;* and in like manner will everyone pass judgment.

Lastly, from this inconstancy in the nature of human judgment, inasmuch as a man often judges of things solely by his emotions, and inasmuch as the things which

[1] This is possible, though the human mind is part of the divine intellect, as I have shown in II. xiii. note.

he believes cause pleasure or pain, and therefore endeavours to promote or prevent, are often purely imaginary, not to speak of the uncertainty of things alluded to in III. xxviii.; we may readily conceive that a man may be at one time affected with pleasure, and at another with pain, accompanied by the idea of himself as cause. Thus we can easily understand what are *Repentance* and *Self-complacency. Repentance is pain, accompanied by the idea of one's self as cause; Self-complacency is pleasure accompanied by the idea of one's self as cause,* and these emotions are most intense because men believe themselves to be free (III. xlix.).

PROP. LII. *An object which we have formerly seen in conjunction with others, and which we do not conceive to have any property that is not common to many, will not be regarded by us for so long, as an object which we conceive to have some property peculiar to itself.*

Proof.—As soon as we conceive an object which we have seen in conjunction with others, we at once remember those others (II. xviii. and note), and thus we pass forthwith from the contemplation of one object to the contemplation of another object. And this is the case with the object, which we conceive to have no property that is not common to many. For we thereupon assume that we are regarding therein nothing, which we have not before seen in conjunction with other objects. But when we suppose that we conceive in an object something special, which we have never seen before, we must needs say that the mind, while regarding that object, has in itself nothing which it can fall to regarding instead thereof; therefore it is determined to the contemplation of that object only. Therefore an object, &c. *Q.E.D.*

Note.—This mental modification, or imagination of a particular thing, in so far as it is alone in the mind, is called *Wonder;* but if it be excited by an object of fear, it is called *Consternation,* because wonder at an evil keeps a man so engrossed in the simple contemplation thereof, that he has no power to think of anything else whereby he might avoid the evil. If, however, the object of wonder be a man's prudence, industry, or anything of that sort, inasmuch as the said man is thereby regarded as far surpassing ourselves, wonder is called *Veneration;* otherwise, if a man's anger, envy, &c., be what we wonder at, the emotion is called *Horror*. Again, if it be the prudence, industry, or what not, of a man we love, that we wonder at, our love will on this account be the greater (III. xii.), and when joined to wonder or veneration is called *Devotion*. We may in like manner conceive hatred, hope, confidence, and the other emotions, as associated with wonder; and we should thus be able to deduce more emotions than those which have obtained names in ordinary speech. Whence it is evident, that the names of the emotions have been applied in accordance rather with their ordinary manifestations than with an accurate knowledge of their nature.

To wonder is opposed *Contempt*, which generally arises from the fact that, because we see someone wondering at, loving, or fearing something, or because something, at first sight, appears to be like things, which we ourselves wonder at, love, fear, &c., we are, in consequence (III. xv. Coroll. and iii. xxvii.), determined to wonder at, love, or fear that thing. But if from the presence, or more accurate contemplation of the said thing, we are compelled to deny concerning it all that can be the cause of wonder, love, fear, &c., the mind then, by the presence of the thing, remains determined to think rather of those qualities which are not in it, than of those which are in it; whereas, on the other hand, the presence of the object would cause it more particularly to regard that which is therein. As devotion springs from wonder at a thing which we love, so does *Derision* spring from contempt of a thing which we hate or fear, and *Scorn* from contempt of folly, as veneration from wonder at prudence. Lastly, we can conceive the emotions of love, hope, honour, &c., in association with contempt, and can thence deduce other emotions, which are not distinguished one from another by any recognized name.

PROP. LIII. *When the mind regards itself and its own power of activity, it feels pleasure: and that pleasure is greater in proportion to the distinctness wherewith it conceives itself and its own power of activity.*

Proof.—A man does not know himself except through the modifications of his body, and the ideas thereof (II. xix. and xxiii.). When, therefore, the mind is able to contemplate itself, it is thereby assumed to pass to a greater perfection, or (III. xi. note) to feel pleasure; and the pleasure will be greater in proportion to the distinctness, wherewith it is able to conceive itself and its own power of activity. *Q.E.D.*

Corollary.—This pleasure is fostered more and more, in proportion as a man conceives himself to be praised by others. For the more he conceives himself as praised by others, the more will he imagine them to be affected with pleasure, accompanied by the idea of himself (III. xxix. note); thus he is (III. xxvii.) himself affected with greater pleasure, accompanied by the idea of himself. *Q.E.D.*

PROP. LIV. *The mind endeavours to conceive only such things as assert its power of activity.*

Proof.—The endeavour or power of the mind is the actual essence thereof (III. vii.); but the essence of the mind obviously only affirms that which the mind is and can do; not that which it neither is nor can do; therefore the mind endeavours to conceive only such things as assert or affirm its power of activity. *Q.E.D.*

PROP. LV. *When the mind contemplates its own weakness, it feels pain thereat.*

Proof.—The essence of the mind only affirms that which the mind is, or can do; in other words, it is the mind's nature to conceive only such things as assert its power of activity (last Prop.). Thus, when we say that the mind contemplates its own weakness, we are merely saying that while the mind is attempting to conceive something which asserts its power of activity, it is checked in its endeavour—in other words (III. xi. note), it feels pain. *Q.E.D.*

Corollary.—This pain is more and more fostered, if a man conceives that he is blamed by others; this may be proved in the same way as the corollary to III. liii.

Note.—This pain, accompanied by the idea of our own weakness, is called *humility;* the pleasure, which springs from the contemplation of ourselves, is called *self-love* or *self-complacency.* And inasmuch as this feeling is renewed as often as a man contemplates his own virtues, or his own power of activity, it follows that everyone is fond of narrating his own exploits, and displaying the force both of his body and mind, and also that, for this reason, men are troublesome one to another. Again, it follows that men are naturally envious (III. xxiv. note, and III. xxxii. note), rejoicing in the shortcomings of their equals, and feeling pain at their virtues. For whenever a man conceives his own actions, he is affected with pleasure (III. liii.), in proportion as his actions display more perfection, and he conceives them more distinctly—that is (II. xl. note), in proportion as he can distinguish them from others, and regard them as something special. Therefore, a man will take most pleasure in contemplating himself, when he contemplates some quality which he denies to others. But, if that which he affirms of himself be attributable to the idea of man or animals in general, he will not be so greatly pleased: he will, on the contrary, feel pain, if he conceives that his own actions fall short when compared with those of others. This pain (III. xxviii.) he will endeavour to remove, by putting a wrong construction on the actions of his equals, or by, as far as he can, embellishing his own.

It is thus apparent that men are naturally prone to hatred and envy, which latter is fostered by their education. For parents are accustomed to incite their children to virtue solely by the spur of honour and envy. But, perhaps, some will scruple to assent to what I have said, because we not seldom admire men's virtues, and venerate their possessors. In order to remove such doubts, I append the following corollary.

Corollary.—No one envies the virtue of anyone who is not his equal.

Proof.—Envy is a species of hatred (III. xxiv. note) or (III. xiii. note) pain, that is (III. xi. note), a modification whereby a man's power of activity, or endeavour towards activity, is checked. But a man does not endeavour or desire to do anything, which cannot follow from his nature as it is given; therefore a man will not desire any power of activity or virtue (which is the same thing) to be attributed to him, that is appropriate to another's nature and foreign to his own; hence his desire cannot be checked, nor he himself pained by the contemplation of virtue in some one unlike himself, consequently he cannot envy such an one. But he can envy his equal, who is assumed to have the same nature as himself. *Q.E.D.*

Note.—When, therefore, as we said in the note to III. lii., we venerate a man, through wonder at his prudence, fortitude, &c., we do so, because we conceive those qualities to be peculiar to him, and not as common to our nature; we, therefore, no more envy their possessor, than we envy trees for being tall, or lions for being courageous.

PROP. LVI. *There are as many kinds of pleasure, of pain, of desire, and of every emotion compounded of these, such as vacillations of spirit, or derived from these, such as love, hatred, hope, fear, &c., as there are kinds of objects whereby we are affected.*

Proof.—Pleasure and pain, and consequently the emotions compounded thereof, or derived therefrom, are passions, or passive states (III. xi. note); now we are necessarily passive (III. i.), in so far as we have inadequate ideas; and only in so far as we have such ideas are we passive (III. iii.); that is, we are only necessarily passive (II. xl. note), in so far as we conceive, or (II. xvii. and note) in so far as we are affected by an emotion, which involves the nature of our own body, and the nature of an external body. Wherefore the nature of every passive state must necessarily be so explained, that the nature of the object whereby we are affected be expressed. Namely, the pleasure, which arises from, say, the object A, involves the nature of that object A, and the pleasure, which arises from the object B, involves the nature of the object B; wherefore these two pleasurable emotions are by nature different, inasmuch as the causes whence they arise are by nature different. So again the emotion of pain, which arises from one object, is by nature different from the pain arising from another object, and, similarly, in the case of love, hatred, hope, fear, vacillation, &c.

Thus, there are necessarily as many kinds of pleasure, pain, love, hatred, &c., as there are kinds of objects whereby we are affected. Now desire is each man's essence or nature, in so far as it is conceived as determined to a particular action by any given modification of itself (III. ix. note); therefore, according as a man is affected through external causes by this or that kind of pleasure, pain, love, hatred, &c., in other words, according as his nature is disposed in this or that manner, so will his desire be of one kind or another, and the nature of one desire must necessarily differ from the nature of another desire, as widely as the emotions differ, wherefrom each desire arose. Thus there are as many kinds of desire, as there are kinds of pleasure, pain, love, &c., consequently (by what has been shown) there are as many kinds of desire, as there are kinds of objects whereby we are affected. *Q.E.D.*

Note.—Among the kinds of emotions, which, by the last proposition, must be very numerous, the chief are *luxury, drunkenness, lust, avarice,* and *ambition,* being merely species of love or desire, displaying the nature of those emotions in a manner varying according to the object, with which they are concerned. For by luxury, drunkenness, lust, avarice, ambition, &c., we simply mean the immoderate love of feasting, drinking, venery, riches, and fame. Furthermore, these emotions, in so far as we distinguish them from others merely by the objects wherewith they are concerned, have no contraries. For *temperance, sobriety,* and *chastity,* which we are wont to oppose to luxury, drunkenness, and lust, are not emotions or passive states, but indicate a power of the mind which moderates the last-named emotions. However, I cannot here explain the remaining kinds of emotions (seeing that they are as numerous as the kinds of objects), nor, if I could, would it be necessary. It is sufficient for our purpose, namely, to determine the strength of the emotions, and the mind's power over them, to have a general definition of each emotion. It is sufficient, I repeat, to understand the general properties of the emotions and the mind, to enable us to determine the quality and extent of the mind's power in moderating and checking the emotions. Thus, though there is a great difference between various emotions of love, hatred, or desire, for instance between love felt towards children, and love felt towards a wife, there is no need for us to take cognizance of such differences, or to track out further the nature and origin of the emotions.

PROP. LVII. *Any emotion of a given individual differs from the emotion of another individual, only in so far as the essence of the one individual differs from the essence of the other.*

Proof.—This proposition is evident from Ax. i. (which

see after Lemma iii. Prop. xiii. Part ii.). Nevertheless, we will prove it from the nature of the three primary emotions.

All emotions are attributable to desire, pleasure, or pain, as their definitions above given show. But desire is each man's nature or essence (III. ix. note); therefore desire in one individual differs from desire in another individual, only in so far as the nature or essence of the one differs from the nature or essence of the other. Again, pleasure and pain are passive states or passions, whereby every man's power or endeavour to persist in his being is increased or diminished, helped or hindered (III. xi. and note). But by the endeavour to persist in its being, in so far as it is attributable to mind and body in conjunction, we mean appetite and desire (III. ix. note); therefore pleasure and pain are identical with desire or appetite, in so far as by external causes they are increased or diminished, helped or hindered, in other words, they are every man's nature; wherefore the pleasure and pain felt by one man differ from the pleasure and pain felt by another man, only in so far as the nature or essence of the one man differs from the essence of the other; consequently, any emotion of one individual only differs, &c. *Q.E.D.*

Note.—Hence it follows, that the emotions of the animals which are called irrational (for after learning the origin of mind we cannot doubt that brutes feel) only differ from man's emotions, to the extent that brute nature differs from human nature. Horse and man are alike carried away by the desire of procreation; but the desire of the former is equine, the desire of the latter is human. So also the lusts and appetites of insects, fishes, and birds must needs vary according to the several natures. Thus, although each individual lives content and rejoices in that nature belonging to him wherein he has his being, yet the life, wherein each is content and rejoices, is nothing else but the idea, or soul, of the said individual, and hence the joy of one only differs in nature from the joy of another, to the extent that the essence of one differs from the essence of another. Lastly, it follows from the foregoing proposition, that there is no small difference between the joy which actuates, say, a drunkard, and the joy possessed by a philosopher, as I just mention here by the way. Thus far I have treated of the emotions attributable to man, in so far as he is passive. It remains to add a few words on those attributable to him in so far as he is active.

PROP. LVIII. *Besides pleasure and desire, which are passivities or passions, there are other emotions derived from pleasure and desire, which are attributable to us in so far as we are active.*

Proof.—When the mind conceives itself and its power of activity, it feels pleasure (III. liii.): now the mind necessarily contemplates itself, when it conceives a true or adequate idea (II. xliii). But the mind does conceive certain adequate ideas (II. xl. note 2). Therefore, it feels pleasure in so far as it conceives adequate ideas; that is, in so far as it is active (III. i). Again, the mind, both in so far as it has clear and distinct ideas, and in so far as it has confused ideas, endeavours to persist in its own being (III. ix.); but by such an endeavour we mean desire (by the note to the same Prop.); therefore, desire is also attributable to us, in so far as we understand, or (III. i.) in so far as we are active. *Q.E.D.*

PROP. LIX. *Among all the emotions attributable to the mind as active, there are none which cannot be referred to pleasure or desire.*

Proof.—All emotions can be referred to desire, pleasure, or pain, as their definitions, already given, show. Now by pain we mean that the mind's power of thinking is diminished or checked (III. xi. and note); therefore, in so far as the mind feels pain, its power of understanding, that is, of activity, is diminished or checked (III. i.); therefore, no painful emotions can be attributed to the mind in virtue of its being active, but only emotions of pleasure and desire, which (by the last Prop.) are attributable to the mind in that condition. *Q.E.D.*

Note.—All actions following from emotion, which are attributable to the mind in virtue of its understanding, I set down to *strength of character* (*fortitudo*), which I divide into *courage* (*animositas*) and *highmindedness* (*generositas*). By *courage* I mean *the desire whereby every man strives to preserve his own being in accordance solely with the dictates of reason.* By *highmindedness* I mean *the desire whereby every man endeavours, solely under the dictates of reason, to aid other men and to unite them to himself in friendship.* Those actions, therefore, which have regard solely to the good of the agent I set down to courage, those which aim at the good of others I set down to highmindedness. Thus temperance, sobriety, and presence of mind in danger, &c., are varieties of courage; courtesy, mercy, &c., are varieties of highmindedness.

I think I have thus explained, and displayed through their primary causes the principal emotions and vacillations of spirit, which arise from the combination of the three primary emotions, to wit, desire, pleasure, and pain. It is evident from what I have said, that we are in many ways driven about by external causes, and that like waves of the sea driven by contrary winds we toss to and fro unwitting of the issue and of our fate. But I have said, that I have only set forth the chief conflicting emotions, not all that might be given. For, by proceeding in the same way as above, we can easily show that love is united to repentance, scorn, shame, &c. I think everyone will agree from what has been said, that the emotions may be compounded one with another in so many ways, and so many variations may arise therefrom, as to exceed all possibility of computation. However, for my purpose, it is enough to have enumerated the most important; to reckon up the rest which I have omitted would be more curious than profitable. It remains to remark concerning love, that it very often happens that while we are enjoying a thing which we longed for, the body, from the act of enjoyment, acquires a new disposition, whereby it is determined in another way, other images of things are aroused in it, and the mind begins to conceive and desire something fresh. For example, when we conceive something which generally delights us with its flavour, we desire to enjoy, that is, to eat it. But whilst we are thus enjoying it, the stomach is filled and the body is otherwise disposed. If, therefore, when the body is thus otherwise disposed, the image of the food which is present be stimulated, and consequently the endeavour or desire to eat it be stimulated also, the new disposition of the body will feel repugnance to the desire or attempt, and consequently the presence of the food which we formerly longed for will become odious. This revulsion of feeling is called *satiety* or weariness. For the rest, I have neglected the outward modifications of the body observable in emotions, such, for instance, as trembling, pallor, sobbing, laughter, &c., for these are attributable to the body only, without any reference to the mind. Lastly, the definitions of the emotions require to be supplemented in a few points; I will therefore repeat them, interpolating such observations as I think should here and there be added.

DEFINITIONS OF THE EMOTIONS.

I. *Desire* is the actual essence of man, in so far as it is conceived, as determined to a particular activity by some given modification of itself.

Explanation.—We have said above, in the note to Prop. ix. of this part, that desire is appetite, with consciousness thereof; further, that appetite is the essence of man, in so far as it is determined to act in a way tending to promote its own persistence. But, in the same note, I also remarked that, strictly speaking, I recognize no distinction between appetite and desire. For whether a man be conscious of his appetite or not, it remains one and the same appetite. Thus, in order to avoid the appearance of tautology, I have refrained from explaining desire by appetite; but I have taken care to define it in such a manner, as to comprehend, under one head, all those endeavours of human nature, which we distinguish by the terms appetite, will, desire, or impulse. I might, indeed, have said, that desire is the essence of man, in so far as it is conceived as determined to a particular activity; but from such a definition (cf. II. xxiii.) it would not follow that the mind can be conscious of its desire or appetite. Therefore, in order to imply the cause of such consciousness, it was necessary to add, *in so far as it is determined by some given modification*, &c. For, by a modification of man's essence, we understand every disposition of the said essence, whether such disposition be innate, or whether it be conceived solely under the attribute of thought, or solely under the attribute of extension, or whether, lastly, it be referred simultaneously to both these attributes. By the term desire, then, I here mean all man's endeavours, impulses, appetites, and volitions, which vary according to each man's disposition, and are, therefore, not seldom opposed one to another, according as a man is drawn in different directions, and knows not where to turn.

II. *Pleasure* is the transition of a man from a less to a greater perfection.

III. *Pain* is the transition of a man from a greater to a less perfection.

Explanation.—I say transition: for pleasure is not perfection itself. For, if man were born with the perfection to which he passes, he would possess the same, without the emotion of pleasure. This appears more clearly from the consideration of the contrary emotion, pain. No one can deny, that pain consists in the transition to a less perfection, and not in the less perfection itself: for a man cannot be pained, in so far as he partakes of perfection of any degree. Neither can we say, that pain consists in the absence of a greater perfection. For absence is nothing, whereas the emotion of pain is an activity; wherefore this activity can only be the activity of transition from a greater to a less perfection—in other words, it is an activity whereby a man's power of action is lessened or constrained (cf. III. xi. note). I pass over the definitions of merriment, stimulation, melancholy, and grief, because these terms are generally used in reference to the body, and are merely kinds of pleasure or pain.

IV. *Wonder* is the conception (*imaginatio*) of anything, wherein the mind comes to a stand, because the particular concept in question has no connection with other concepts (cf. III. lii. and note).

Explanation.—In the note to II. xviii. we showed the reason, why the mind, from the contemplation of one thing, straightway falls to the contemplation of another thing, namely, because the images of the two things are so associated and arranged, that one follows the other. This state of association is impossible, if the image of the thing be new; the mind will then be at a stand in the contemplation thereof, until it is determined by other causes to think of something else.

Thus the conception of a new object, considered in itself, is of the same nature as other conceptions; hence, I do not include wonder among the emotions, nor do I see why I should so include it, inasmuch as this distraction of the mind arises from no positive cause drawing away the mind from other objects, but merely from the absence of a cause, which should determine the mind to pass from the contemplation of one object to the contemplation of another.

I, therefore, recognize only three primitive or primary emotions (as I said in the note to III. xi.), namely, pleasure, pain, and desire. I have spoken of wonder, simply because it is customary to speak of certain emotions springing from the three primitive ones by different names, when they are referred to the objects of our wonder. I am led by the same motive to add a definition of contempt.

V. *Contempt* is the conception of anything which touches the mind so little, that its presence leads the mind to imagine those qualities which are not in it rather than such as are in it (cf. III. lii. note).

The definitions of veneration and scorn I here pass over, for I am not aware that any emotions are named after them.

VI. *Love* is pleasure, accompanied by the idea of an external cause.

Explanation.—This definition explains sufficiently clearly the essence of love; the definition given by those authors who say that love is *the lover's wish to unite himself to the loved object* expresses a property, but not the essence of love; and, as such authors have not sufficiently discerned love's essence, they have been unable to acquire a true conception of its properties, accordingly their definition is on all hands admitted to be very obscure. It must, however, be noted, that when I say that it is a property of love, that the lover should wish to unite himself to the beloved object, I do not here mean by *wish* consent, or conclusion, or a free decision of the mind (for I have shown such, in II. xlviii., to be fictitious); neither do I mean a desire of being united to the loved object when it is absent, or of continuing in its presence when it is at hand; for love can be conceived without either of these desires; but by *wish* I mean the contentment, which is in the lover, on account of the presence of the beloved object, whereby the pleasure of the lover is strengthened, or at least maintained.

VII. *Hatred* is pain, accompanied by the idea of an external cause.

Explanation.—These observations are easily grasped after what has been said in the explanation of the preceding definition (cf. also III. xiii. note).

VIII. *Inclination* is pleasure, accompanied by the idea of something which is accidentally a cause of pleasure.

IX. *Aversion* is pain, accompanied by the idea of something which is accidentally the cause of pain (cf. III. xv. note).

X. *Devotion* is love towards one whom we admire.

Explanation.—Wonder (*admiratio*) arises (as we have shown, III. lii.) from the novelty of a thing. If, therefore, it happens that the object of our wonder is often conceived by us, we shall cease to wonder at it; thus we see, that the emotion of devotion readily degenerates into simple love.

XI. *Derision* is pleasure arising from our conceiving the presence of a quality, which we despise, in an object which we hate.

Explanation.—In so far as we despise a thing which we hate, we deny existence thereof (III. lii. note), and to that extent rejoice (III. xx.). But since we assume that man hates that which he derides, it follows that the pleasure in question is not without alloy (cf. III. xlvii. note).

XII. *Hope* is an inconstant pleasure, arising from the idea of something past or future, whereof we to a certain extent doubt the issue.

XIII. *Fear* is an inconstant pain arising from the idea of something past or future, whereof we to a certain extent doubt the issue (cf. III. xviii. note).

Explanation.—From these definitions it follows, that there is no hope unmingled with fear, and no fear unmingled with hope. For he, who depends on hope and doubts concerning the issue of anything, is assumed to conceive something, which excludes the existence of the said thing in the future; therefore he, to this extent, feels pain (cf. III. xix.); consequently, while dependent on hope, he fears for the issue. Contrariwise he, who fears, in other words doubts, concerning the issue of something which he hates, also conceives something which excludes the existence of the thing in question; to this extent he feels pleasure, and consequently to this extent he hopes that it will turn out as he desires (III. xx.).

XIV. *Confidence* is pleasure arising from the idea of something past or future, wherefrom all cause of doubt has been removed.

XV. *Despair* is pain arising from the idea of something past or future, wherefrom all cause of doubt has been removed.

Explanation.—Thus confidence springs from hope, and despair from fear, when all cause for doubt as to the issue of an event has been removed: this comes to pass, because man conceives something past or future as present and regards it as such, or else because he conceives other things, which exclude the existence of the causes of his doubt. For, although we can never be absolutely certain of the issue of any particular event (II. xxxi. Coroll.), it may nevertheless happen that we feel no doubt concerning it. For we have shown, that to feel no doubt concerning a thing is not the same as to be quite certain of it (II. xlix. note). Thus it may happen that we are affected by the same emotion of pleasure or pain concerning a thing past or future, as concerning the conception of a thing present; this I have already shown in III. xviii., to which, with its note, I refer the reader.

XVI. *Joy* is pleasure accompanied by the idea of something past, which has had an issue beyond our hope.

XVII. *Disappointment* is pain accompanied by the idea of something past, which has had an issue contrary to our hope.

XVIII. *Pity* is pain accompanied by the idea of evil, which has befallen someone else whom we conceive to be like ourselves (cf. III. xxii. note, and III. xxvii. note).

Explanation.—Between pity and sympathy (*misericordia*) there seems to be no difference, unless perhaps that the former term is used in reference to a particular action, and the latter in reference to a disposition.

XIX. *Approval* is love towards one who has done good to another.

XX. *Indignation* is hatred towards one who has done evil to another.

Explanation.—I am aware that these terms are employed in senses somewhat different from those usually assigned. But my purpose is to explain, not the meaning of words, but the nature of things. I therefore make use of such terms, as may convey my meaning without any violent departure from their ordinary signification. One statement of my method will suffice. As for the cause of the above-named emotions see III. xxvii. Coroll. i., and III. xxii. note.

XXI. *Partiality* is thinking too highly of anyone because of the love we bear him.

XXII. *Disparagement* is thinking too meanly of anyone, because we hate him.

Explanation.—Thus partiality is an effect of love, and disparagement an effect of hatred: so that *partiality* may also be defined as *love, in so far as it induces a man to think too highly of a beloved object.* Contrariwise, *disparagement* may be defined as *hatred, in so far as it induces a man to think too meanly of a hated object.* Cf. III. xxvi. note.

XXIII. *Envy* is hatred, in so far as it induces a man to be pained by another's good fortune, and to rejoice in another's evil fortune.

Explanation.—Envy is generally opposed to sympathy, which, by doing some violence to the meaning of the word, may therefore be thus defined:

XXIV. *Sympathy* (*misericordia*) is love, in so far as it induces a man to feel pleasure at another's good fortune, and pain at another's evil fortune.

Explanation.—Concerning envy see the notes to III. xxiv. and xxxii. These emotions also arise from pleasure or pain accompanied by the idea of something external, as cause either in itself or accidentally. I now pass on to other emotions, which are accompanied by the idea of something within as a cause.

XXV. *Self-approval* is pleasure arising from a man's contemplation of himself and his own power of action.

XXVI. *Humility* is pain arising from a man's contemplation of his own weakness of body or mind.

Explanation.—Self-complacency is opposed to humility,

in so far as we thereby mean pleasure arising from a contemplation of our own power of action; but, in so far as we mean thereby pleasure accompanied by the idea of any action which we believe we have performed by the free decision of our mind, it is opposed to repentance, which we may thus define:

XXVII. *Repentance* is pain accompanied by the idea of some action, which we believe we have performed by the free decision of our mind.

Explanation.—The causes of these emotions we have set forth in III. li. note, and in III. liii. liv. lv. and note. Concerning the free decision of the mind see II. xxxv. note. This is perhaps the place to call attention to the fact, that it is nothing wonderful that all those actions, which are commonly called *wrong*, are followed by pain, and all those, which are called *right*, are followed by pleasure. We can easily gather from what has been said, that this depends in great measure on education. Parents, by reprobating the former class of actions, and by frequently chiding their children because of them, and also by persuading to and praising the latter class, have brought it about, that the former should be associated with pain and the latter with pleasure. This is confirmed by experience. For custom and religion are not the same among all men, but that which some consider sacred others consider profane, and what some consider honourable others consider disgraceful. According as each man has been educated, he feels repentance for a given action or glories therein.

XXVIII. *Pride* is thinking too highly of one's self from self-love.

Explanation.—Thus pride is different from partiality, for the latter term is used in reference to an external object, but pride is used of a man thinking too highly of himself. However, as partiality is the effect of love, so is pride the effect or property of *self-love*, which may therefore be thus defined, *love of self or self-approval, in so far as it leads a man to think too highly of himself.* To this emotion there is no contrary. For no one thinks too meanly of himself because of self-hatred; I say that no one thinks too meanly of himself, in so far as he conceives that he is incapable of doing this or that. For whatsoever a man imagines that he is incapable of doing, he imagines this of necessity, and by that notion he is so disposed, that he really cannot do that which he conceives that he cannot do. For, so long as he conceives that he cannot do it, so long is he not determined to do it, and consequently so long is it impossible for him to do it. However, if we consider such matters as only depend on opinion, we shall find it conceivable that a man may think too meanly of himself; for it may happen, that a man, sorrowfully regarding his own weakness, should imagine that he is despised by all men, while the rest of the world are thinking of nothing less than of despising him. Again, a man may think too meanly of himself, if he deny of himself in the present something in relation to a future time of which he is uncertain. As, for instance, if he should say that he is unable to form any clear conceptions, or that he can desire and do nothing but what is wicked and base, &c. We may also say, that a man thinks too meanly of himself, when we see him from excessive fear of shame refusing to do things which others, his equals, venture. We can, therefore, set down as a contrary to pride an emotion which I will call self-abasement, for as from self-complacency springs pride, so from humility springs self-abasement, which I will accordingly thus define:

XXIX. *Self-abasement* is thinking too meanly of one's self by reason of pain.

Explanation.—We are nevertheless generally accustomed to oppose pride to humility, but in that case we pay more attention to the effect of either emotion than to its nature. We are wont to call *proud* the man who boasts too much (III. xxx. note), who talks of nothing but his own virtues and other people's faults, who wishes to be first; and lastly who goes through life with a style and pomp suitable to those far above him in station. On the other hand, we call *humble* the man who too often blushes, who confesses his faults, who sets forth other men's virtues, and who, lastly, walks with bent head and is negligent of his attire. However, these emotions, humility and self-abasement, are extremely rare. For human nature, considered in itself, strives against them as much as it can (see III. xiii. liv.);

hence those, who are believed to be most self-abased and humble, are generally in reality the most ambitious and envious.

XXX. *Honour*[1] is pleasure accompanied by the idea of some action of our own, which we believe to be praised by others.

XXXI. *Shame* is pain accompanied by the idea of some action of our own, which we believe to be blamed by others.

Explanation.—On this subject see the note to III. xxx. But we should here remark the difference which exists between shame and modesty. Shame is the pain following the deed whereof we are ashamed. Modesty is the fear or dread of shame, which restrains a man from committing a base action. Modesty is usually opposed to shamelessness, but the latter is not an emotion, as I will duly show; however, the names of the emotions (as I have remarked already) have regard rather to their exercise than to their nature.

I have now fulfilled my task of explaining the emotions arising from pleasure and pain. I therefore proceed to treat of those which I refer to desire.

XXXII. *Regret* is the desire or appetite to possess something, kept alive by the remembrance of the said thing, and at the same time constrained by the remembrance of other things which exclude the existence of it.

Explanation.—When we remember a thing, we are by that very fact, as I have already said more than once, disposed to contemplate it with the same emotion as if it were something present; but this disposition or endeavour, while we are awake, is generally checked by the images of things which exclude the existence of that which we remember. Thus when we remember something which affected us with a certain pleasure, we by that very fact endeavour to regard it with the same emotion of pleasure as though it were present, but this endeavour is at once checked by the remembrance of things which exclude the existence of the thing in question. Wherefore regret is, strictly speaking, a pain opposed to that pleasure, which arises from the absence of something we hate (cf. III. xlvii. note). But, as the name regret seems to refer to desire, I set

[1] *Gloria.*

this emotion down, among the emotions springing from desire.

XXXIII. *Emulation* is the desire of something, engendered in us by our conception that others have the same desire.

Explanation.—He who runs away, because he sees others running away, or he who fears, because he sees others in fear; or again, he who, on seeing that another man has burnt his hand, draws towards him his own hand, and moves his body as though his own hand were burnt; such an one can be said to imitate another's emotion, but not to emulate him; not because the causes of emulation and imitation are different, but because it has become customary to speak of emulation only in him, who imitates that which we deem to be honourable, useful, or pleasant. As to the cause of emulation, cf. III. xxvii. and note. The reason why this emotion is generally coupled with envy may be seen from III. xxxii. and note.

XXXIV. *Thankfulness* or *Gratitude* is the desire or zeal springing from love, whereby we endeavour to benefit him, who with similar feelings of love has conferred a benefit on us. Cf. III. xxxix. note and xl.

XXXV. *Benevolence* is the desire of benefiting one whom we pity. Cf. III. xxvii. note.

XXXVI. *Anger* is the desire, whereby through hatred we are induced to injure one whom we hate, III. xxxix.

XXXVII. *Revenge* is the desire whereby we are induced, through mutual hatred, to injure one who, with similar feelings, has injured us. (See III. xl. Coroll. ii. and note.)

XXXVIII. *Cruelty* or *savageness* is the desire, whereby a man is impelled to injure one whom we love or pity.

Explanation.—To cruelty is opposed clemency, which is not a passive state of the mind, but a power whereby man restrains his anger and revenge.

XXXIX. *Timidity* is the desire to avoid a greater evil, which we dread, by undergoing a lesser evil. Cf. III. xxxix. note.

XL. *Daring* is the desire, whereby a man is set on to do something dangerous which his equals fear to attempt.

XLI. *Cowardice* is attributed to one, whose desire is

checked by the fear of some danger which his equals dare to encounter.

Explanation.—Cowardice is, therefore, nothing else but the fear of some evil, which most men are wont not to fear; hence I do not reckon it among the emotions springing from desire. Nevertheless, I have chosen to explain it here, because, in so far as we look to the desire, it is truly opposed to the emotion of daring.

XLII. *Consternation* is attributed to one, whose desire of avoiding evil is checked by amazement at the evil which he fears.

Explanation.—Consternation is, therefore, a species of cowardice. But, inasmuch as consternation arises from a double fear, it may be more conveniently defined as a fear which keeps a man so bewildered and wavering, that he is not able to remove the evil. I say bewildered, in so far as we understand his desire of removing the evil to be constrained by his amazement. I say wavering, in so far as we understand the said desire to be constrained by the fear of another evil, which equally torments him: whence it comes to pass that he knows not, which he may avert of the two. On this subject, see III. xxxix. note, and III. lii. note. Concerning cowardice and daring, see III. li. note.

XLIII. *Courtesy*, or *deference* (*Humanitas seu modestia*), is the desire of acting in a way that should please men, and refraining from that which should displease them.

XLIV. *Ambition* is the immoderate desire of power.

Explanation.—Ambition is the desire, whereby all the emotions (cf. III. xxvii. and xxxi.) are fostered and strengthened; therefore this emotion can with difficulty be overcome. For, so long as a man is bound by any desire, he is at the same time necessarily bound by this. "The best men," says Cicero, "are especially led by honour. Even philosophers, when they write a book contemning honour, sign their names thereto," and so on.

XLV. *Luxury* is excessive desire, or even love of living sumptuously.

XLVI. *Intemperance* is the excessive desire and love of drinking.

XLVII. *Avarice* is the excessive desire and love of riches.

XLVIII. *Lust* is desire and love in the matter of sexual intercourse.

Explanation.—Whether this desire be excessive or not, it is still called lust. These last five emotions (as I have shown in III. lvi.) have no contraries. For deference is a species of ambition Cf. III. xxix. note.

Again, I have already pointed out, that temperance, sobriety, and chastity indicate rather a power than a passivity of the mind. It may, nevertheless, happen, that an avaricious, an ambitious, or a timid man may abstain from excess in eating, drinking, or sexual indulgence, yet avarice, ambition, and fear are not contraries to luxury, drunkenness, and debauchery. For an avaricious man often is glad to gorge himself with food and drink at another man's expense. An ambitious man will restrain himself in nothing, so long as he thinks his indulgences are secret; and if he lives among drunkards and debauchees, he will, from the mere fact of being ambitious, be more prone to those vices. Lastly, a timid man does that which he would not. For though an avaricious man should, for the sake of avoiding death, cast his riches into the sea, he will none the less remain avaricious; so, also, if a lustful man is downcast, because he cannot follow his bent, he does not, on the ground of abstention, cease to be lustful. In fact, these emotions are not so much concerned with the actual feasting, drinking, &c., as with the appetite and love of such. Nothing, therefore, can be opposed to these emotions, but high-mindedness and valour, whereof I will speak presently.

The definitions of jealousy and other waverings of the mind I pass over in silence, first, because they arise from the compounding of the emotions already described; secondly, because many of them have no distinctive names, which shows that it is sufficient for practical purposes to have merely a general knowledge of them. However, it is established from the definitions of the emotions, which we have set forth, that they all spring from desire, pleasure, or pain, or, rather, that there is nothing besides these three; wherefore each is wont to be called by a variety of names in accordance with its various relations and extrinsic tokens. If we now direct our attention to these primitive emotions, and to what has been said concerning the nature of the mind, we shall be able thus to define the emotions, in so far as they are referred to the mind only.

General Definition of the Emotions.

Emotion, which is called a passivity of the soul, is a confused idea, whereby the mind affirms concerning its body, or any part thereof, a force for existence (*existendi vis*) greater or less than before, and by the presence of which the mind is determined to think of one thing rather than another.

Explanation.—I say, first, that emotion or passion of the soul is *a confused idea.* For we have shown that the mind is only passive, in so far as it has inadequate or confused ideas. (III. iii.) I say, further, *whereby the mind affirms concerning its body or any part thereof a force for existence greater than before.* For all the ideas of bodies, which we possess, denote rather the actual disposition of our own body (II. xvi. Coroll. ii.) than the nature of an external body. But the idea which constitutes the reality of an emotion must denote or express the disposition of the body, or of some part thereof, which is possessed by the body, or some part thereof, because its power of action or force for existence is increased or diminished, helped or hindered. But it must be noted that, when I say *a greater or less force for existence* than before, I do not mean that the mind compares the present with the past disposition of the body, but that the idea which constitutes the reality of an emotion affirms something of the body, which, in fact, involves more or less of reality than before.

And inasmuch as the essence of mind consists in the fact (II. xi. xiii.), that it affirms the actual existence of its own body, and inasmuch as we understand by perfection the very essence of a thing, it follows that the mind passes to greater or less perfection, when it happens to affirm concerning its own body, or any part thereof, something involving more or less reality than before.

When, therefore, I said above that the power of the mind is increased or diminished, I merely meant that the mind had formed of its own body, or of some part thereof, an idea involving more or less of reality, than it had already affirmed concerning its own body. For the excellence of ideas, and the actual power of thinking are measured by the excellence of the object. Lastly, I have added *by the presence of which the mind is determined to think of one thing rather than another*, so that, besides the nature of pleasure and pain, which the first part of the definition explains, I might also express the nature of desire.

PART IV.

OF HUMAN BONDAGE, OR THE STRENGTH OF THE EMOTIONS.

PREFACE.

HUMAN infirmity in moderating and checking the emotions I name bondage: for, when a man is a prey to his emotions, he is not his own master, but lies at the mercy of fortune: so much so, that he is often compelled, while seeing that which is better for him, to follow that which is worse. Why this is so, and what is good or evil in the emotions, I propose to show in this part of my treatise. But, before I begin, it would be well to make a few prefatory observations on perfection and imperfection, good and evil.

When a man has purposed to make a given thing, and has brought it to perfection, his work will be pronounced perfect, not only by himself, but by everyone who rightly knows, or thinks that he knows, the intention and aim of its author. For instance, suppose anyone sees a work (which I assume to be not yet completed), and knows that the aim of the author of that work is to build a house, he will call the work imperfect; he will, on the other hand, call it perfect, as soon as he sees that it is carried through to the end, which its author had purposed for it. But if a man sees a work, the like whereof he has never seen before, and if he knows not the intention of the artificer, he plainly cannot know, whether that work be perfect or imperfect. Such seems to be the primary meaning of these terms.

But, after men began to form general ideas, to think out types of houses, buildings, towers, &c., and to prefer certain types to others, it came about, that each man called perfect that which he saw agree with the general idea he had formed of the thing in question, and called imperfect that which he saw agree less with his own preconceived type, even though it had evidently been completed in accordance with the idea of its artificer. This seems to be the only reason for calling natural phenomena, which, indeed, are not made with human hands, perfect or imperfect: for men are wont to form general ideas of things natural, no less than of things artificial, and such ideas they hold as types, believing that Nature (who they think does nothing without an object) has them in view, and has set them as types before herself. Therefore, when they behold something in Nature, which does not wholly conform to the preconceived type which they have formed of the thing in question, they say that Nature has fallen short or has blundered, and has left her work incomplete. Thus we see that men are wont to style natural phenomena perfect or imperfect rather from their own prejudices, than from true knowledge of what they pronounce upon.

Now we showed in the Appendix to Part I., that Nature does not work with an end in view. For the eternal and infinite Being, which we call God or Nature, acts by the same necessity as that whereby it exists. For we have shown, that by the same necessity of its nature, whereby it exists, it likewise works (I. xvi.). The reason or cause why God or Nature exists, and the reason why he acts, are one and the same. Therefore, as he does not exist for the sake of an end, so neither does he act for the sake of an end; of his existence and of his action there is neither origin nor end. Wherefore, a cause which is called final is nothing else but human desire, in so far as it is considered as the origin or cause of anything. For example, when we say that to be inhabited is the final cause of this or that house, we mean nothing more than that a man, conceiving the conveniences of household life, had a desire to build a house. Wherefore, the being inhabited, in so far as it is regarded as a final cause, is nothing else but this particular desire, which is really the efficient cause; it is regarded as the primary cause, because men are generally ignorant of the causes of their desires They are, as I have often said already, conscious of their own actions and appetites, but ignorant of the causes whereby they are determined to any particular desire. Therefore, the common saying that Nature sometimes falls short, or blunders, and produces things which are imperfect, I set down among the glosses treated of in the Appendix to Part I. Perfection and imperfection, then, are in reality merely modes of thinking, or notions which we form from a comparison among one another of individuals of the same species; hence I said above (II. Def. vi.), that by reality and perfection I mean the same thing. For we are wont to refer all the individual things in nature to one genus, which is called the highest genus, namely, to the category of Being, whereto absolutely all individuals in nature belong. Thus, in so far as we refer the individuals in nature to this category, and comparing them one with another, find that some possess more of being or reality than others, we, to this extent, say that some are more perfect than others. Again, in so far as we attribute to them anything implying negation—as term, end, infirmity, etc.,—we, to this extent, call them imperfect, because they do not affect our mind so much as the things which we call perfect, not because they have any intrinsic deficiency, or because Nature has blundered. For nothing lies within the scope of a thing's nature, save that which follows from the necessity of the nature of its efficient cause, and whatsoever follows from the necessity of the nature of its efficient cause necessarily comes to pass.

As for the terms *good* and *bad*, they indicate no positive quality in things regarded in themselves, but are merely modes of thinking, or notions which we form from the comparison of things one with another. Thus one and the same thing can be at the same time good, bad, and indifferent. For instance, music is good for him that is melancholy, bad for him that mourns; for him that is deaf, it is neither good nor bad.

Nevertheless, though this be so, the terms should still be retained. For, inasmuch as we desire to form an idea of man as a type of human nature which we may hold in view, it will be useful for us to retain the terms in question, in the sense I have indicated.

In what follows, then, I shall mean by "good" that which we certainly know to be a means of approaching more nearly to the type of human nature, which we have set before ourselves; by "bad," that which we certainly know to be a hindrance to us in approaching the said type.

Again, we shall say that men are more perfect, or more imperfect, in proportion as they approach more or less nearly to the said type. For it must be specially remarked that, when I say that a man passes from a lesser to a greater perfection, or *vice versâ*, I do not mean that he is changed from one essence or reality to another; for instance, a horse would be as completely destroyed by being changed into a man, as by being changed into an insect. What I mean is, that we conceive the thing's power of action, in so far as this is understood by its nature, to be increased or diminished. Lastly, by perfection in general I shall, as I have said, mean reality—in other words, each thing's essence, in so far as it exists, and operates in a particular manner, and without paying any regard to its duration. For no given thing can be said to be more perfect, because it has passed a longer time in existence. The duration of things cannot be determined by their essence, for the essence of things involves no fixed and definite period of existence; but everything, whether it be more perfect or less perfect, will always be able to persist in existence with the same force wherewith it began to exist; wherefore, in this respect, all things are equal.

DEFINITIONS.

I. By *good* I mean that which we certainly know to be useful to us.

II. By *evil* I mean that which we certainly know to be a hindrance to us in the attainment of any good.

(Concerning these terms see the foregoing preface towards the end.)

III. Particular things I call *contingent* in so far as, while regarding their essence only, we find nothing therein, which necessarily asserts their existence or excludes it.

IV. Particular things I call *possible* in so far as, while regarding the causes whereby they must be produced, we know not, whether such causes be determined for producing them.

(In I. xxxiii. note i., I drew no distinction between possible and contingent, because there was in that place no need to distinguish them accurately.)

V. By *conflicting emotions* I mean those which draw a man in different directions, though they are of the same kind, such as luxury and avarice, which are both species of love, and are contraries, not by nature, but by accident.

VI. What I mean by emotion felt towards a thing, future, present, and past, I explained in III. xviii., notes i. and ii., which see.

(But I should here also remark, that we can only distinctly conceive distance of space or time up to a certain definite limit; that is, all objects distant from us more than two hundred feet, or whose distance from the place where we are exceeds that which we can distinctly conceive, seem to be an equal distance from us, and all in the same plane; so also objects, whose time of existing is conceived as removed from the present by a longer interval than we can distinctly conceive, seem to be all equally distant from the present, and are set down, as it were, to the same moment of time.)

VII. By an *end*, for the sake of which we do something, I mean a desire.

VIII. By *virtue* (*virtus*) and *power* I mean the same thing; that is (III. vii.), virtue, in so far as it is referred to man, is a man's nature or essence, in so far as it has the power of effecting what can only be understood by the laws of that nature.

AXIOM.

There is no individual thing in nature, than which there is not another more powerful and strong. Whatsoever thing be given, there is something stronger whereby it can be destroyed.

PROP. I. *No positive quality possessed by a false idea is removed by the presence of what is true, in virtue of its being true.*

Proof.—Falsity consists solely in the privation of knowledge which inadequate ideas involve (II. xxxv.), nor have they any positive quality on account of which they are called false (II. xxxiii.); contrariwise, in so far as they are referred to God, they are true (II. xxxii.). Wherefore, if the positive quality possessed by a false idea were removed by the presence of what is true, in virtue of its being true, a true idea would then be removed by itself, which (IV. iii.) is absurd. Therefore, no positive quality possessed by a false idea, &c. *Q.E.D.*

Note.—This proposition is more clearly understood from II. xvi. Coroll. ii. For imagination is an idea, which indicates rather the present disposition of the human body than the nature of the external body; not indeed distinctly, but confusedly; whence it comes to pass, that the mind is said to err. For instance, when we look at the sun, we conceive that it is distant from us about two hundred feet; in this judgment we err, so long as we are in ignorance of its true distance; when its true distance is known, the error is removed, but not the imagination; or, in other words, the idea of the sun, which only explains the nature of that luminary, in so far as the body is affected thereby: wherefore, though we know the real distance, we shall still nevertheless imagine the sun to be near us. For, as we said in II. xxxv. note, we do not imagine the sun to be so near us, because we are ignorant of its true distance, but because the mind conceives the magnitude of the sun to the extent that the body is affected thereby. Thus, when the rays of the sun falling on the surface of water are reflected into our eyes, we imagine the sun as if it were in the water, though we are aware of its real position; and similarly other imaginations, wherein the mind is deceived, whether they indicate the natural disposition of the body, or that its power of activity is increased or diminished, are not contrary to the truth, and do not vanish at its presence. It happens indeed that, when we mistakenly fear an evil, the fear vanishes when we hear the true tidings; but the contrary also happens, namely, that we fear an evil which will certainly come, and our fear vanishes when we hear false tidings; thus imaginations do not vanish at the presence of the truth, in virtue of its being true, but because other imaginations, stronger than the first, supervene and exclude the present existence of that which we imagined, as I have shown in II. xvii.

PROP. II. *We are only passive, in so far as we are a part of Nature, which cannot be conceived by itself without other parts.*

Proof.—We are said to be passive, when something

arises in us, whereof we are only a partial cause (III. Def. ii.), that is (III. Def. i.), something which cannot be deduced solely from the laws of our nature. We are passive therefore, in so far as we are a part of Nature, which cannot be conceived by itself without other parts. *Q.E.D.*

PROP. III. *The force whereby a man persists in existing is limited, and is infinitely surpassed by the power of external causes.*

Proof.—This is evident from the axiom of this part. For, when man is given, there is something else—say A—more powerful; when A is given, there is something else—say B—more powerful than A, and so on to infinity; thus the power of man is limited by the power of some other thing, and is infinitely surpassed by the power of external causes. *Q.E.D.*

PROP. IV. *It is impossible, that man should not be a part of Nature, or that he should be capable of undergoing no changes, save such as can be understood through his nature only as their adequate cause.*

Proof.—The power, whereby each particular thing, and consequently man, preserves his being, is the power of God or of Nature (I. xxiv. Coroll.); not in so far as it is infinite, but in so far as it can be explained by the actual human essence (III. vii.). Thus the power of man, in so far as it is explained through his own actual essence, is a part of the infinite power of God or Nature, in other words, of the essence thereof (I. xxxiv.). This was our first point. Again, if it were possible, that man should undergo no changes save such as can be understood solely through the nature of man, it would follow that he would not be able to die, but would always necessarily exist; this would be the necessary consequence of a cause whose power was either finite or infinite; namely, either of man's power only, inasmuch as he would be capable of removing from himself all changes which could spring from external causes; or of the infinite power of Nature, whereby all individual things would be so ordered, that man should be incapable of undergoing any changes save such as tended towards his own preservation. But the first alternative is absurd (by the last Prop., the proof of which is universal, and can be applied to all individual things). Therefore, if it be possible, that man should not be capable of undergoing any changes, save such as can be explained solely through his own nature, and consequently that he must always (as we have shown) necessarily exist; such a result must follow from the infinite power of God, and consequently (I. xvi.) from the necessity of the divine nature, in so far as it is regarded as affected by the idea of any given man, the whole order of nature as conceived under the attributes of extension and thought must be deducible. It would therefore follow (I. xxi.) that man is infinite, which (by the first part of this proof) is absurd. It is, therefore, impossible, that man should not undergo any changes save those whereof he is the adequate cause. *Q.E.D.*

Corollary.—Hence it follows, that man is necessarily always a prey to his passions, that he follows and obeys the general order of nature, and that he accommodates himself thereto, as much as the nature of things demands.

PROP. V. *The power and increase of every passion, and its persistence in existing are not defined by the power, whereby we ourselves endeavour to persist in existing, but by the power of an external cause compared with our own.*

Proof.—The essence of a passion cannot be explained through our essence alone (III. Deff. i. and ii.), that is (III. vii.), the power of a passion cannot be defined by the power, whereby we ourselves endeavour to persist in existing, but (as is shown in II. xvi.) must necessarily be defined by the power of an external cause compared with our own. *Q.E.D.*

PROP. VI. *The force of any passion or emotion can overcome the rest of a man's activities or power, so that the emotion becomes obstinately fixed to him.*

Proof.—The force and increase of any passion and its persistence in existing are defined by the power of an external cause compared with our own (by the foregoing Prop.); therefore (IV. iii.) it can overcome a man's power, &c. *Q.E.D.*

PROP. VII. *An emotion can only be controlled or destroyed by another emotion contrary thereto, and with more power for controlling emotion.*

Proof.—Emotion, in so far as it is referred to the mind, is an idea, whereby the mind affirms of its body a greater or less force of existence than before (cf. the general Definition of the Emotions at the end of Part III.). When, therefore, the mind is assailed by any emotion, the body is at the same time affected with a modification whereby its power of activity is increased or diminished. Now this modification of the body (IV. v.) receives from its cause the force for persistence in its being; which force can only be checked or destroyed by a bodily cause (II. vi.), in virtue of the body being affected with a modification contrary to (III. v.) and stronger than itself (IV. Ax.); wherefore (II. xii.) the mind is affected by the idea of a modification contrary to, and stronger than the former modification, in other words, (by the general definition of the emotions) the mind will be affected by an emotion contrary to and stronger than the former emotion, which will exclude or destroy the existence of the former emotion; thus an emotion cannot be destroyed nor controlled except by a contrary and stronger emotion. *Q.E.D.*

Corollary.—An emotion, in so far as it is referred to the mind, can only be controlled or destroyed through an idea of a modification of the body contrary to, and stronger than, that which we are undergoing. For the emotion which we undergo can only be checked or destroyed by an emotion contrary to, and stronger than, itself, in other words, (by the general Definition of the Emotions) only by an idea of a modification of the body contrary to, and stronger than, the modification which we undergo.

PROP. VIII. *The knowledge of good and evil is nothing else but the emotions of pleasure or pain, in so far as we are conscious thereof.*

Proof.—We call a thing good or evil, when it is of service or the reverse in preserving our being (IV. Deff. i. and ii.), that is (III. vii.), when it increases or diminishes, helps or hinders, our power of activity. Thus, in so far as we perceive that a thing affects us with pleasure or pain, we call it good or evil; wherefore the knowledge of good and evil is nothing else but the idea of the pleasure or pain, which necessarily follows from that pleasurable or painful emotion (II. xxii.). But this idea is united to the emotion in the same way as mind is united to body (II. xxi.); that is, there is no real distinction between this idea and the emotion or idea of the modification of the body, save in conception only. Therefore the knowledge of good and evil is nothing else but the emotion, in so far as we are conscious thereof. *Q.E.D.*

Prop. IX. *An emotion, whereof we conceive the cause to be with us at the present time, is stronger than if we did not conceive the cause to be with us.*

Proof.—Imagination or conception is the idea, by which the mind regards a thing as present (II. xvii. note), but which indicates the disposition of the mind rather than the nature of the external thing (II. xvi. Coroll. ii). An emotion is therefore a conception, in so far as it indicates the disposition of the body. But a conception (by II. xvii.) is stronger, so long as we conceive nothing which excludes the present existence of the external object; wherefore an emotion is also stronger or more intense, when we conceive the cause to be with us at the present time, than when we do not conceive the cause to be with us. *Q.E.D.*

Note.—When I said above in III. xviii. that we are affected by the image of what is past or future with the same emotion as if the thing conceived were present, I expressly stated, that this is only true in so far as we look solely to the image of the thing in question itself; for the thing's nature is unchanged, whether we have conceived it or not; I did not deny that the image becomes weaker, when we regard as present to us other things which exclude the present existence of the future object: I did not expressly call attention to the fact, because I purposed to treat of the strength of the emotions in this part of my work.

Corollary.—The image of something past or future, that is, of a thing which we regard as in relation to time past or time future, to the exclusion of time present, is, when other conditions are equal, weaker than the image of something present; consequently an emotion felt towards what is past or future is less intense, other conditions being equal, than an emotion felt towards something present.

Prop. X. *Towards something future, which we conceive as close at hand, we are affected more intensely, than if we conceive that its time for existence is separated from the present by a longer interval; so too by the remembrance of what we conceive to have not long passed away we are affected more intensely, than if we conceive that it has long passed away.*

Proof.—In so far as we conceive a thing as close at hand, or not long passed away, we conceive that which excludes the presence of the object less, than if its period of future existence were more distant from the present, or if it had long passed away (this is obvious); therefore (by the foregoing Prop.) we are, so far, more intensely affected towards it. *Q.E.D.*

Corollary.—From the remarks made in Def. vi. of this part it follows that, if objects are separated from the present by a longer period than we can define in conception, though their dates of occurrence be widely separated one from the other, they all affect us equally faintly.

PROP. XI. *An emotion towards that which we conceive as necessary is, when other conditions are equal, more intense than an emotion towards that which is possible, or contingent, or non-necessary.*

Proof.—In so far as we conceive a thing to be necessary, we, to that extent, affirm its existence; on the other hand we deny a thing's existence, in so far as we conceive it not to be necessary (I. xxxiii. note i.); wherefore (IV. ix.) an emotion towards that which is necessary is, other conditions being equal, more intense than an emotion towards that which is non-necessary. *Q.E.D.*

PROP. XII. *An emotion towards a thing, which we know not to exist at the present time, and which we conceive as possible, is more intense, other conditions being equal, than an emotion towards a thing contingent.*

Proof.—In so far as we conceive a thing as contingent, we are affected by the conception of some further thing, which would assert the existence of the former (IV. Def. iii.); but, on the other hand, we (by hypothesis) conceive certain things, which exclude its present existence. But, in so far as we conceive a thing to be possible in the future, we thereby conceive things which assert its existence (IV. iv.), that is (III. xviii.), things which promote hope or fear: wherefore an emotion towards something possible is more vehement. *Q.E.D.*

Corollary.—An emotion towards a thing, which we know not to exist in the present, and which we conceive as contingent, is far fainter, than if we conceive the thing to be present with us.

Proof.—Emotion towards a thing, which we conceive to exist, is more intense than it would be, if we conceived the thing as future (IV. ix. Coroll.), and is much more vehement, than if the future time be conceived as far distant from the present (IV. x.). Therefore an emotion towards a thing, whose period of existence we conceive to be far distant from the present, is far fainter, than if we conceive the thing as present; it is, nevertheless, more intense, than if we conceived the thing as contingent, wherefore an emotion towards a thing, which we regard as contingent, will be far fainter, than if we conceived the thing to be present with us. *Q.E.D.*

PROP. XIII. *Emotion towards a thing contingent, which we know not to exist in the present, is, other conditions being equal, fainter than an emotion towards a thing past.*

Proof.—In so far as we conceive a thing as contingent, we are not affected by the image of any other thing, which asserts the existence of the said thing (IV. Def. iii.), but, on the other hand (by hypothesis), we conceive certain things excluding its present existence. But, in so far as we conceive it in relation to time past, we are assumed to conceive something, which recalls the thing to memory, or excites the image thereof (II. xviii. and note), which is so far the same as regarding it as present (II. xvii. Coroll.). Therefore (IV. ix.) an emotion towards a thing contingent, which we know does not exist in the present, is fainter, other conditions being equal, than an emotion towards a thing past. *Q.E.D.*

PROP. XIV. *A true knowledge of good and evil cannot check any emotion by virtue of being true, but only in so far as it is considered as an emotion.*

Proof.—An emotion is an idea, whereby the mind affirms of its body a greater or less force of existing than before (by the general Definition of the Emotions); therefore it has no positive quality, which can be destroyed by the presence of what is true; consequently the knowledge of good and evil cannot, by virtue of being true, restrain any emotion. But, in so far as such knowledge is an emotion (IV. viii.) if it have more strength for restraining emotion, it will to that extent be able to restrain the given emotion. *Q.E.D.*

PROP. XV. *Desire arising from the knowledge of good and*

bad can be quenched or checked by many of the other desires arising from the emotions whereby we are assailed.

Proof.—From the true knowledge of good and evil, in so far as it is an emotion, necessarily arises desire (Def. of the Emotions, i.), the strength of which is proportioned to the strength of the emotion wherefrom it arises (III. xxxvii.). But, inasmuch as this desire arises (by hypothesis) from the fact of our truly understanding anything, it follows that it is also present with us, in so far as we are active (III. i.), and must therefore be understood through our essence only (III. Def. ii.); consequently (III. vii.) its force and increase can be defined solely by human power. Again, the desires arising from the emotions whereby we are assailed are stronger, in proportion as the said emotions are more vehement; wherefore their force and increase must be defined solely by the power of external causes, which, when compared with our own power, indefinitely surpass it (IV. iii.); hence the desires arising from like emotions may be more vehement, than the desire which arises from a true knowledge of good and evil, and may, consequently, control or quench it. *Q.E.D.*

Prop. XVI. *Desire arising from the knowledge of good and evil, in so far as such knowledge regards what is future, may be more easily controlled or quenched, than the desire for what is agreeable at the present moment.*

Proof.—Emotion towards a thing, which we conceive as future, is fainter than emotion towards a thing that is present (IV. ix. Coroll.). But desire, which arises from the true knowledge of good and evil, though it be concerned with things which are good at the moment, can be quenched or controlled by any headstrong desire (by the last Prop., the proof whereof is of universal application). Wherefore desire arising from such knowledge, when concerned with the future, can be more easily controlled or quenched, &c. *Q.E.D.*

Prop. XVII. *Desire arising from the true knowledge of good and evil, in so far as such knowledge is concerned with what is contingent, can be controlled far more easily still, than desire for things that are present.*

Proof.—This Prop. is proved in the same way as the last Prop. from IV. xii. Coroll.

Note.—I think I have now shown the reason, why men are moved by opinion more readily than by true reason, why it is that the true knowledge of good and evil stirs up conflicts in the soul, and often yields to every kind of passion. This state of things gave rise to the exclamation of the poet:[1]—

"The better path I gaze at and approve,
The worse—I follow."

Ecclesiastes seems to have had the same thought in his mind, when he says, "He who increaseth knowledge increaseth sorrow." I have not written the above with the object of drawing the conclusion, that ignorance is more excellent than knowledge, or that a wise man is on a par with a fool in controlling his emotions, but because it is necessary to know the power and the infirmity of our nature, before we can determine what reason can do in restraining the emotions, and what is beyond her power. I have said, that in the present part I shall merely treat of human infirmity. The power of reason over the emotions I have settled to treat separately.

PROP. XVIII. *Desire arising from pleasure is, other conditions being equal, stronger than desire arising from pain.*

Proof.—Desire is the essence of a man (Def. of the Emotions, i.), that is, the endeavour whereby a man endeavours to persist in his own being. Wherefore desire arising from pleasure is, by the fact of pleasure being felt, increased or helped; on the contrary, desire arising from pain is, by the fact of pain being felt, diminished or hindered; hence the force of desire arising from pleasure must be defined by human power together with the power of an external cause, whereas desire arising from pain must be defined by human power only. Thus the former is the stronger of the two. *Q.E.D.*

Note.—In these few remarks I have explained the causes of human infirmity and inconstancy, and shown why men do not abide by the precepts of reason. It now remains for me to show what course is marked out for us by reason, which of the emotions are in harmony with the rules of human reason, and which of them are contrary thereto.

[1] Ov. Met. vii. 20, "Video meliora proboque, Deteriora sequor."

But, before I begin to prove my propositions in detailed geometrical fashion, it is advisable to sketch them briefly in advance, so that everyone may more readily grasp my meaning.

As reason makes no demands contrary to nature, it demands, that every man should love himself, should seek that which is useful to him—I mean, that which is really useful to him, should desire everything which really brings man to greater perfection, and should, each for himself, endeavour as far as he can to preserve his own being. This is as necessarily true, as that a whole is greater than its part. (Cf. III. iv.)

Again, as virtue is nothing else but action in accordance with the laws of one's own nature (IV. Def. viii.), and as no one endeavours to preserve his own being, except in accordance with the laws of his own nature, it follows, *first*, that the foundation of virtue is the endeavour to preserve one's own being, and that happiness consists in man's power of preserving his own being; *secondly*, that virtue is to be desired for its own sake, and that there is nothing more excellent or more useful to us, for the sake of which we should desire it; *thirdly* and lastly, that suicides are weak-minded, and are overcome by external causes repugnant to their nature. Further, it follows from Postulate iv. Part II., that we can never arrive at doing without all external things for the preservation of our being or living, so as to have no relations with things which are outside ourselves. Again, if we consider our mind, we see that our intellect would be more imperfect, if mind were alone, and could understand nothing besides itself. There are, then, many things outside ourselves, which are useful to us, and are, therefore, to be desired. Of such none can be discerned more excellent, than those which are in entire agreement with our nature. For if, for example, two individuals of entirely the same nature are united, they form a combination twice as powerful as either of them singly.

Therefore, to man there is nothing more useful than man—nothing, I repeat, more excellent for preserving their being can be wished for by men, than that all should so in all points agree, that the minds and bodies of all should form, as it were, one single mind and one single body, and that all should, with one consent, as far as they are able, endeavour to preserve their being, and all with one consent seek what is useful to them all. Hence, men who are governed by reason—that is, who seek what is useful to them in accordance with reason,—desire for themselves nothing, which they do not also desire for the rest of mankind, and, consequently, are just, faithful, and honourable in their conduct.

Such are the dictates of reason, which I purposed thus briefly to indicate, before beginning to prove them in greater detail. I have taken this course, in order, if possible, to gain the attention of those who believe, that the principle that every man is bound to seek what is useful for himself is the foundation of impiety, rather than of piety and virtue.

Therefore, after briefly showing that the contrary is the case, I go on to prove it by the same method, as that whereby I have hitherto proceeded.

PROP. XIX. *Every man, by the laws of his nature, necessarily desires or shrinks from that which he deems to be good or bad.*

Proof.—The knowledge of good and evil is (IV. viii.) the emotion of pleasure or pain, in so far as we are conscious thereof; therefore, every man necessarily desires what he thinks good, and shrinks from what he thinks bad. Now this appetite is nothing else but man's nature or essence (cf. the Definition of Appetite, III. ix. note, and Def. of the Emotions, i.). Therefore, every man, solely by the laws of his nature, desires the one, and shrinks from the other, &c. *Q.E.D.*

PROP. XX. *The more every man endeavours, and is able to seek what is useful to him—in other words, to preserve his own being—the more is he endowed with virtue; on the contrary, in proportion as a man neglects to seek what is useful to him, that is, to preserve his own being, he is wanting in power.*

Proof.—Virtue is human power, which is defined solely by man's essence (IV. Def. viii.), that is, which is defined solely by the endeavour made by man to persist in his own being. Wherefore, the more a man endeavours, and is able to preserve his own being, the more is he endowed with virtue, and, consequently (III. iv. and vi.), in so far as a man neglects to preserve his own being, he is wanting in power. *Q.E.D.*

Note.—No one, therefore, neglects seeking his own good, or preserving his own being, unless he be overcome by causes external and foreign to his nature. No one, I say, from the necessity of his own nature, or otherwise than under compulsion from external causes, shrinks from food, or kills himself: which latter may be done in a variety of ways. A man, for instance, kills himself under the compulsion of another man, who twists round his right hand, wherewith he happened to have taken up a sword, and forces him to turn the blade against his own heart; or, again, he may be compelled, like Seneca, by a tyrant's command, to open his own veins—that is, to escape a greater evil by incurring a lesser; or, lastly, latent external causes may so disorder his imagination, and so affect his body, that it may assume a nature contrary to its former one, and whereof the idea cannot exist in the mind (III. x.) But that a man, from the necessity of his own nature, should endeavour to become non-existent, is as impossible as that something should be made out of nothing, as everyone will see for himself, after a little reflection.

PROP. XXI. *No one can desire to be blessed, to act rightly, and to live rightly, without at the same time wishing to be, to act, and to live—in other words, to actually exist.*

Proof.—The proof of this proposition, or rather the proposition itself, is self-evident, and is also plain from the definition of desire. For the desire of living, acting, &c., blessedly or rightly, is (Def. of the Emotions, i.) the essence of man—that is (III. vii.), the endeavour made by everyone to preserve his own being. Therefore, no one can desire, &c. *Q.E.D.*

PROP. XXII. *No virtue can be conceived as prior to this endeavour to preserve one's own being.*

Proof.—The effort for self-preservation is the essence of a thing (III. vii.); therefore, if any virtue could be conceived as prior thereto, the essence of a thing would have to be conceived as prior to itself, which is obviously absurd. Therefore no virtue, &c. *Q.E.D.*

Corollary.—The effort for self-preservation is the first

and only foundation of virtue. For prior to this principle nothing can be conceived, and without it no virtue can be conceived.

PROP. XXIII. *Man, in so far as he is determined to a particular action because he has inadequate ideas, cannot be absolutely said to act in obedience to virtue; he can only be so described, in so far as he is determined for the action because he understands.*

Proof.—In so far as a man is determined to an action through having inadequate ideas, he is passive (III. i.), that is (III. Deff. i. and iii.), he does something, which cannot be perceived solely through his essence, that is (by IV. Def. viii.), which does not follow from his virtue. But, in so far as he is determined for an action because he understands, he is active; that is, he does something, which is perceived through his essence alone, or which adequately follows from his virtue. *Q.E.D.*

PROP. XXIV. *To act absolutely in obedience to virtue is in us the same thing as to act, to live, or to preserve one's being (these three terms are identical in meaning) in accordance with the dictates of reason on the basis of seeking what is useful to one's self.*

Proof.—To act absolutely in obedience to virtue is nothing else but to act according to the laws of one's own nature. But we only act, in so far as we understand (III. iii.): therefore to act in obedience to virtue is in us nothing else but to act, to live, or to preserve one's being in obedience to reason, and that on the basis of seeking what is useful for us (IV. xxii. Coroll.). *Q.E.D.*

PROP. XXV. *No one wishes to preserve his being for the sake of anything else.*

Proof.—The endeavour, wherewith everything endeavours to persist in its being, is defined solely by the essence of the thing itself (III. vii.); from this alone, and not from the essence of anything else, it necessarily follows (III. vi.) that everyone endeavours to preserve his being. Moreover, this proposition is plain from IV. xxii. Coroll., for if a man should endeavour to preserve his being for the sake of anything else, the last-named thing would obviously be the basis of virtue, which, by the foregoing corollary, is absurd. Therefore no one, &c. *Q.E.D.*

PROP. XXVI. *Whatsoever we endeavour in obedience to reason is nothing further than to understand; neither does the mind, in so far as it makes use of reason, judge anything to be useful to it, save such things as are conducive to understanding.*

Proof.—The effort for self-preservation is nothing else but the essence of the thing in question (III. vii.), which, in so far as it exists such as it is, is conceived to have force for continuing in existence (III. vi.) and doing such things as necessarily follow from its given nature (see the Def. of Appetite, III. ix. note). But the essence of reason is nought else but our mind, in so far as it clearly and distinctly understands (see the definition in II. xl. note ii.); therefore (II. xl.) whatsoever we endeavour in obedience to reason is nothing else but to understand. Again, since this effort of the mind wherewith the mind endeavours, in so far as it reasons, to preserve its own being is nothing else but understanding; this effort at understanding is (IV. xxii. Coroll.) the first and single basis of virtue, nor shall we endeavour to understand things for the sake of any ulterior object (IV. xxv.); on the other hand, the mind, in so far as it reasons, will not be able to conceive any good for itself, save such things as are conducive to understanding.

PROP. XXVII. *We know nothing to be certainly good or evil, save such things as really conduce to understanding, or such as are able to hinder us from understanding.*

Proof.—The mind, in so far as it reasons, desires nothing beyond understanding, and judges nothing to be useful to itself, save such things as conduce to understanding (by the foregoing Prop.). But the mind (II. xli. xliii. and note) cannot possess certainty concerning anything, except in so far as it has adequate ideas, or (what by II. xl. note, is the same thing) in so far as it reasons. Therefore we know nothing to be good or evil save such things as really conduce, &c. *Q.E.D.*

PROP. XXVIII. *The mind's highest good is the knowledge of God, and the mind's highest virtue is to know God.*

Proof.—The mind is not capable of understanding anything higher than God, that is (I. Def. vi.), than a Being absolutely infinite, and without which (I. xv.) nothing can either be or be conceived; therefore (IV. xxvi. and xxvii.), the mind's highest utility or (IV. Def. i.) good is the knowledge of God. Again, the mind is active, only in so far as it understands, and only to the same extent can it be said absolutely to act virtuously. The mind's absolute virtue is therefore to understand. Now, as we have already shown, the highest that the mind can understand is God; therefore the highest virtue of the mind is to understand or to know God. *Q.E.D.*

PROP. XXIX. *No individual thing, which is entirely different from our own nature, can help or check our power of activity, and absolutely nothing can do us good or harm, unless it has something in common with our nature.*

Proof.—The power of every individual thing, and consequently the power of man, whereby he exists and operates, can only be determined by an individual thing (I. xxviii.), whose nature (II. vi.) must be understood through the same nature as that, through which human nature is conceived. Therefore our power of activity, however it be conceived, can be determined and consequently helped or hindered by the power of any other individual thing, which has something in common with us, but not by the power of anything, of which the nature is entirely different from our own; and since we call good or evil that which is the cause of pleasure or pain (IV. viii.), that is (III. xi. note), which increases or diminishes, helps or hinders, our power of activity; therefore, that which is entirely different from our nature can neither be to us good nor bad. *Q.E.D.*

PROP. XXX. *A thing cannot be bad for us through the quality which it has in common with our nature, but it is bad for us in so far as it is contrary to our nature.*

Proof.—We call a thing bad when it is the cause of pain (IV. viii.), that is (by the Def., which see in III. xi. note), when it diminishes or checks our power of action. Therefore, if anything were bad for us through that quality which it has in common with our nature, it would be able itself to diminish or check that which it has in common with our nature, which (III. iv.) is absurd. Wherefore nothing can be bad for us through that quality which it has in common with us, but, on the other hand, in so far as it is bad for us, that is (as we have just shown), in so far as it can diminish or check our power of action, it is contrary to our nature. *Q.E.D.*

PROP. XXXI. *In so far as a thing is in harmony with our nature, it is necessarily good.*

Proof.—In so far as a thing is in harmony with our nature, it cannot be bad for it. It will therefore necessarily be either good or indifferent. If it be assumed that it be neither good nor bad, nothing will follow from its nature (IV. Def. i.), which tends to the preservation of our nature, that is (by the hypothesis), which tends to the preservation of the thing itself; but this (III. vi.) is absurd; therefore, in so far as a thing is in harmony with our nature, it is necessarily good. *Q.E.D.*

Corollary.—Hence it follows, that, in proportion as a thing is in harmony with our nature, so is it more useful or better for us, and *vice versâ*, in proportion as a thing is more useful for us, so is it more in harmony with our nature. For, in so far as it is not in harmony with our nature, it will necessarily be different therefrom or contrary thereto. If different, it can neither be good nor bad (IV. xxix); if contrary, it will be contrary to that which is in harmony with our nature, that is, contrary to what is good—in short, bad. Nothing, therefore, can be good, except in so far as it is in harmony with our nature; and hence a thing is useful, in proportion as it is in harmony with our nature, and *vice versâ*. *Q.E.D.*

PROP. XXXII. *In so far as men are a prey to passion, they cannot, in that respect, be said to be naturally in harmony.*

Proof.—Things, which are said to be in harmony naturally, are understood to agree in power (III. vii.), not in want of power or negation, and consequently not in passion (III. iii. note); wherefore men, in so far as they are a prey to their passions, cannot be said to be naturally in harmony. *Q.E.D.*

Note.—This is also self-evident; for, if we say that white and black only agree in the fact that neither is red, we absolutely affirm that they do not agree in any respect. So, if we say that a man and a stone only agree in the fact that both are finite—wanting in power, not existing by the necessity of their own nature, or, lastly, indefinitely surpassed by the power of external causes—we should certainly affirm that a man and a stone are in no respect alike;

therefore, things which agree only in negation, or in qualities which neither possess, really agree in no respect.

PROP. XXXIII. *Men can differ in nature, in so far as they are assailed by those emotions, which are passions, or passive states; and to this extent one and the same man is variable and inconstant.*

Proof.—The nature or essence of the emotions cannot be explained solely through our essence or nature (III. Deff. i. ii.), but it must be defined by the power, that is (III. vii.), by the nature of external causes in comparison with our own; hence it follows, that there are as many kinds of each emotion as there are external objects whereby we are affected (III. lvi.), and that men may be differently affected by one and the same object (III. li), and to this extent differ in nature; lastly, that one and the same man may be differently affected towards the same object, and may therefore be variable and inconstant. *Q.E.D.*

PROP. XXXIV. *In so far as men are assailed by emotions which are passions, they can be contrary one to another.*

Proof.—A man, for instance Peter, can be the cause of Paul's feeling pain, because he (Peter) possesses something similar to that which Paul hates (III. xvi.), or because Peter has sole possession of a thing which Paul also loves (III. xxxii. and note), or for other causes (of which the chief are enumerated in III. lv. note); it may therefore happen that Paul should hate Peter (Def. of Emotions, vii.), consequently it may easily happen also, that Peter should hate Paul in return, and that each should endeavour to do the other an injury (III. xxxix.), that is (IV. xxx.), that they should be contrary one to another. But the emotion of pain is always a passion or passive state (III. lix.); hence men, in so far as they are assailed by emotions which are passions, can be contrary one to another. *Q.E.D.*

Note.—I said that Paul may hate Peter, because he conceives that Peter possesses something which he (Paul) also loves; from this it seems, at first sight, to follow, that these two men, through both loving the same thing, and, consequently, through agreement of their respective natures, stand in one another's way; if this were so, Props. xxx. and xxxi. of this Part would be untrue. But if we give the matter our unbiassed attention, we shall see that the discrepancy vanishes. For the two men are not in one another's way in virtue of the agreement of their natures, that is, through both loving the same thing, but in virtue of one differing from the other. For, in so far as each loves the same thing, the love of each is fostered thereby (III. xxxi.), that is (Def. of the Emotions, vi.) the pleasure of each is fostered thereby. Wherefore it is far from being the case, that they are at variance through both loving the same thing, and through the agreement in their natures. The cause for their opposition lies, as I have said, solely in the fact that they are assumed to differ. For we assume that Peter has the idea of the loved object as already in his possession, while Paul has the idea of the loved object as lost. Hence the one man will be affected with pleasure, the other will be affected with pain, and thus they will be at variance one with another. We can easily show in like manner, that all other causes of hatred depend solely on differences, and not on the agreement between men's natures.

PROP. XXXV. *In so far only as men live in obedience to reason, do they always necessarily agree in nature.*

Proof.—In so far as men are assailed by emotions that are passions, they can be different in nature (IV. xxxiii.), and at variance one with another. But men are only said to be active, in so far as they act in obedience to reason (III. iii.); therefore, whatsoever follows from human nature in so far as it is defined by reason must (III. Def. ii.) be understood solely through human nature as its proximate cause. But, since every man by the laws of his nature desires that which he deems good, and endeavours to remove that which he deems bad (IV. xix.); and further, since that which we, in accordance with reason, deem good or bad, necessarily is good or bad (II. xli.); it follows that men, in so far as they live in obedience to reason, necessarily do only such things as are necessarily good for human nature, and consequently for each individual man (IV. xxxi. Coroll.); in other words, such things as are in harmony with each man's nature. Therefore, men in so far as they live in obedience to reason, necessarily live always in harmony one with another. *Q.E.D.*

Corollary I.—There is no individual thing in nature, which is more useful to man, than a man who lives in obedience to reason. For that thing is to man most useful, which is most in harmony with his nature (IV. xxxi. Coroll); that is, obviously, man. But man acts absolutely according to the laws of his nature, when he lives in obedience to reason (III. Def. ii.), and to this extent only is always necessarily in harmony with the nature of another man (by the last Prop.); wherefore among individual things nothing is more useful to man, than a man who lives in obedience to reason. *Q.E.D.*

Corollary II.—As every man seeks most that which is useful to him, so are men most useful one to another. For the more a man seeks what is useful to him and endeavours to preserve himself, the more is he endowed with virtue (IV. xx.), or, what is the same thing (IV. Def. viii.), the more is he endowed with power to act according to the laws of his own nature, that is to live in obedience to reason. But men are most in natural harmony, when they live in obedience to reason (by the last Prop.); therefore (by the foregoing Coroll.) men will be most useful one to another, when each seeks most that which is useful to him. *Q.E.D.*

Note.—What we have just shown is attested by experience so conspicuously, that it is in the mouth of nearly everyone: "Man is to man a God." Yet it rarely happens that men live in obedience to reason, for things are so ordered among them, that they are generally envious and troublesome one to another. Nevertheless they are scarcely able to lead a solitary life, so that the definition of man as a social animal has met with general assent; in fact, men do derive from social life much more convenience than injury. Let satirists then laugh their fill at human affairs, let theologians rail, and let misanthropes praise to their utmost the life of untutored rusticity, let them heap contempt on men and praises on beasts; when all is said, they will find that men can provide for their wants much more easily by mutual help, and that only by uniting their forces can they escape from the dangers that on every side beset them: not to say how much more excellent and worthy of our knowledge it is, to study the actions of men than the actions of beasts. But I will treat of this more at length elsewhere.

PROP. XXXVI. *The highest good of those who follow virtue is common to all, and therefore all can equally rejoice therein.*

Proof.—To act virtuously is to act in obedience with reason (IV. xxiv.), and whatsoever we endeavour to do in obedience to reason is to understand (IV. xxvi.); therefore (IV. xxviii.) the highest good for those who follow after virtue is to know God; that is (II. xlvii. and note) a good which is common to all and can be possessed by all men equally, in so far as they are of the same nature. *Q.E.D.*

Note.—Someone may ask how it would be, if the highest good of those who follow after virtue were not common to all? Would it not then follow, as above (IV. xxxiv.), that men living in obedience to reason, that is (IV. xxxv.), men in so far as they agree in nature, would be at variance one with another? To such an inquiry I make answer, that it follows not accidentally but from the very nature of reason, that man's highest good is common to all, inasmuch as it is deduced from the very essence of man, in so far as defined by reason; and that a man could neither be, nor be conceived without the power of taking pleasure in this highest good. For it belongs to the essence of the human mind (II. xlvii.), to have an adequate knowledge of the eternal and infinite essence of God.

PROP. XXXVII. *The good which every man, who follows after virtue, desires for himself he will also desire for other men, and so much the more, in proportion as he has a greater knowledge of God.*

Proof.—Men, in so far as they live in obedience to reason, are most useful to their fellow men (IV. xxxv; Coroll. i.); therefore (IV. xix.), we shall in obedience to reason necessarily endeavour to bring about that men should live in obedience to reason. But the good which every man, in so far as he is guided by reason, or, in other words, follows after virtue, desires for himself, is to understand (IV. xxvi.); wherefore the good, which each follower of virtue seeks for himself, he will desire also for others. Again, desire, in so far as it is referred to the mind, is the very essence of the mind (Def. of the Emotions, i.); now the essence of the mind consists in knowledge (II. xi.), which involves the knowledge of God (II. xlvii.), and without it

(I. xv.), can neither be, nor be conceived; therefore, in proportion as the mind's essence involves a greater knowledge of God, so also will be greater the desire of the follower of virtue, that other men should possess that which he seeks as good for himself.—*Q.E.D.*

Another Proof.—The good, which a man desires for himself and loves, he will love more constantly, if he sees that others love it also (III. xxxi.); he will therefore endeavour that others should love it also; and as the good in question is common to all, and therefore all can rejoice therein, he will endeavour, for the same reason, to bring about that all should rejoice therein, and this he will do the more (III. xxxvii.), in proportion as his own enjoyment of the good is greater.

Note I.—He who, guided by emotion only, endeavours to cause others to love what he loves himself, and to make the rest of the world live according to his own fancy, acts solely by impulse, and is, therefore, hateful, especially to those who take delight in something different, and accordingly study and, by similar impulse, endeavour, to make men live in accordance with what pleases themselves. Again, as the highest good sought by men under the guidance of emotion is often such, that it can only be possessed by a single individual, it follows that those who love it are not consistent in their intentions, but, while they delight to sing its praises, fear to be believed. But he, who endeavours to lead men by reason, does not act by impulse but courteously and kindly, and his intention is always consistent. Again, whatsoever we desire and do, whereof we are the cause in so far as we possess the idea of God, or know God, I set down to *Religion.* The desire of well-doing, which is engendered by a life according to reason, I call *piety.* Further, the desire, whereby a man living according to reason is bound to associate others with himself in friendship, I call *honour;*[1] by *honourable* I mean that which is praised by men living according to reason, and by *base* I mean that which is repugnant to the gaining of friendship. I have also shown in addition what are the foundations of a state; and the difference between true virtue and infirmity may be readily gathered from what I have said; namely, that true virtue is nothing else but

[1] *Honestas.*

living in accordance with reason; while infirmity is nothing else but man's allowing himself to be led by things which are external to himself, and to be by them determined to act in a manner demanded by the general disposition of things rather than by his own nature considered solely in itself.

Such are the matters which I engaged to prove in Prop. xviii. of this Part, whereby it is plain that the law against the slaughtering of animals is founded rather on vain superstition and womanish pity than on sound reason. The rational quest of what is useful to us further teaches us the necessity of associating ourselves with our fellow-men, but not with beasts, or things, whose nature is different from our own; we have the same rights in respect to them as they have in respect to us. Nay, as everyone's right is defined by his virtue, or power, men have far greater rights over beasts than beasts have over men. Still I do not deny that beasts feel: what I deny is, that we may not consult our own advantage and use them as we please, treating them in the way which best suits us; for their nature is not like ours, and their emotions are naturally different from human emotions (III. lvii. note). It remains for me to explain what I mean by just and unjust, sin and merit. On these points see the following note.

Note II.—In the Appendix to Part I. I undertook to explain praise and blame, merit and sin, justice and injustice.

Concerning praise and blame I have spoken in III. xxix. note: the time has now come to treat of the remaining terms. But I must first say a few words concerning man in the state of nature and in society.

Every man exists by sovereign natural right, and, consequently, by sovereign natural right performs those actions which follow from the necessity of his own nature; therefore by sovereign natural right every man judges what is good and what is bad, takes care of his own advantage according to his own disposition (IV. xix. and xx.), avenges the wrongs done to him (III. xl. Coroll. ii.), and endeavours to preserve that which he loves and to destroy that which he hates (III. xxviii.). Now, if men lived under the guidance of reason, everyone would remain in possession of this his right, without any injury being done to his neighbour (IV. xxxv. Coroll. i.). But seeing that they are a prey to their emotions, which far surpass human power or virtue (IV. vi.), they are often drawn in different directions, and being at variance one with another (IV. xxxiii. xxxiv.), stand in need of mutual help (IV. xxxv. note). Wherefore, in order that men may live together in harmony, and may aid one another, it is necessary that they should forego their natural right, and, for the sake of security, refrain from all actions which can injure their fellow-men. The way in which this end can be attained, so that men who are necessarily a prey to their emotions (IV. iv. Coroll.), inconstant, and diverse, should be able to render each other mutually secure, and feel mutual trust, is evident from IV. vii. and III. xxxix. It is there shown, that an emotion can only be restrained by an emotion stronger than, and contrary to itself, and that men avoid inflicting injury through fear of incurring a greater injury themselves.

On this law society can be established, so long as it keeps in its own hand the right, possessed by everyone, of avenging injury, and pronouncing on good and evil; and provided it also possesses the power to lay down a general rule of conduct, and to pass laws sanctioned, not by reason, which is powerless in restraining emotion, but by threats (IV. xvii. note). Such a society established with laws and the power of preserving itself is called a *State*, while those who live under its protection are called *citizens*. We may readily understand that there is in the state of nature nothing, which by universal consent is pronounced good or bad; for in the state of nature everyone thinks solely of his own advantage, and according to his disposition, with reference only to his individual advantage, decides what is good or bad, being bound by no law to anyone besides himself.

In the state of nature, therefore, sin is inconceivable; it can only exist in a state, where good and evil are pronounced on by common consent, and where everyone is bound to obey the State authority. *Sin*, then, is nothing else but disobedience, which is therefore punished by the right of the State only. Obedience, on the other hand, is set down as *merit*, inasmuch as a man is thought worthy of merit, if he takes delight in the advantages which a State provides.

Again, in the state of nature, no one is by common consent master of anything, nor is there anything in nature, which can be said to belong to one man rather than another: all things are common to all. Hence, in the state of nature, we can conceive no wish to render to every man his own, or to deprive a man of that which belongs to him; in other words, there is nothing in the state of nature answering to justice and injustice. Such ideas are only possible in a social state, when it is decreed by common consent what belongs to one man and what to another.

From all these considerations it is evident, that justice and injustice, sin and merit, are extrinsic ideas, and not attributes which display the nature of the mind. But I have said enough.

PROP. XXXVIII. *Whatsoever disposes the human body, so as to render it capable of being affected in an increased number of ways, or of affecting external bodies in an increased number of ways, is useful to man; and is so, in proportion as the body is thereby rendered more capable of being affected or affecting other bodies in an increased number of ways; contrariwise, whatsoever renders the body less capable in this respect is hurtful to man.*

Proof.—Whatsoever thus increases the capabilities of the body increases also the mind's capability of perception (II. xiv.); therefore, whatsoever thus disposes the body and thus renders it capable, is necessarily good or useful (IV. xxvi. xxvii.); and is so in proportion to the extent to which it can render the body capable; contrariwise (II. xiv. IV. xxvi. xxvii.), it is hurtful, if it renders the body in this respect less capable. *Q.E.D.*

PROP. XXXIX. *Whatsoever brings about the preservation of the proportion of motion and rest, which the parts of the human body mutually possess, is good; contrariwise, whatsoever causes a change in such proportion is bad.*

Proof.—The human body needs many other bodies for its preservation (II. Post. iv.). But that which constitutes the specific reality (*forma*) of a human body is, that its parts communicate their several motions one to another in a certain fixed proportion (Def. before Lemma iv. after II. xiii.). Therefore, whatsoever brings about the preservation of the proportion between motion and rest, which the parts of the human body mutually possess, preserves the specific reality of the human body, and consequently renders the human body capable of being affected in many ways and of affecting external bodies in many ways; consequently it is good (by the last Prop.). Again, whatsoever brings about a change in the aforesaid proportion causes the human body to assume another specific character, in other words (see Preface to this Part towards the end, though the point is indeed self-evident), to be destroyed, and consequently totally incapable of being affected in an increased numbers of ways; therefore it is bad. *Q.E.D.*

Note.—The extent to which such causes can injure or be of service to the mind will be explained in the Fifth Part. But I would here remark that I consider that a body undergoes death, when the proportion of motion and rest which obtained mutually among its several parts is changed. For I do not venture to deny that a human body, while keeping the circulation of the blood and other properties, wherein the life of a body is thought to consist, may none the less be changed into another nature totally different from its own. There is no reason, which compels me to maintain that a body does not die, unless it becomes a corpse; nay, experience would seem to point to the opposite conclusion. It sometimes happens, that a man undergoes such changes, that I should hardly call him the same. As I have heard tell of a certain Spanish poet, who had been seized with sickness, and though he recovered therefrom yet remained so oblivious of his past life, that he would not believe the plays and tragedies he had written to be his own: indeed, he might have been taken for a grown-up child, if he had also forgotten his native tongue. If this instance seems incredible, what shall we say of infants? A man of ripe age deems their nature so unlike his own, that he can only be persuaded that he too has been an infant by the analogy of other men. However, I prefer to leave such questions undiscussed, lest I should give ground to the superstitious for raising new issues.

PROP. XL. *Whatsoever conduces to man's social life, or*

causes men to live together in harmony, is useful, whereas whatsoever brings discord into a State is bad.

Proof.—For whatsoever causes men to live together in harmony also causes them to live according to reason (IV. xxxv.), and is therefore (IV. xxvi. and xxvii.) good, and (for the same reason) whatsoever brings about discord is bad. *Q.E.D.*

PROP. XLI. *Pleasure in itself is not bad but good: contrariwise, pain in itself is bad.*

Proof.—Pleasure (III. xi. and note) is emotion, whereby the body's power of activity is increased or helped; pain is emotion, whereby the body's power of activity is diminished or checked; therefore (IV. xxxviii.) pleasure in itself is good, &c. *Q.E.D.*

PROP. XLII. *Mirth cannot be excessive, but is always good; contrariwise, Melancholy is always bad.*

Proof.—Mirth (see its Def. in III. xi. note) is pleasure. which, in so far as it is referred to the body, consists in all parts of the body being affected equally: that is (III. xi.), the body's power of activity is increased or aided in such a manner, that the several parts maintain their former proportion of motion and rest; therefore Mirth is always good (IV. xxxix.), and cannot be excessive. But Melancholy (see its Def. in the same note to III. xi.) is pain, which, in so far as it is referred to the body, consists in the absolute decrease or hindrance of the body's power of activity; therefore (IV. xxxviii.) it is always bad. *Q.E.D.*

PROP. XLIII. *Stimulation may be excessive and bad; on the other hand, grief may be good, in so far as stimulation or pleasure is bad.*

Proof.—Localized pleasure or stimulation (*titillatio*) is pleasure, which, in so far as it is referred to the body, consists in one or some of its parts being affected more than the rest (see its Definition, III. xi. note); the power of this emotion may be sufficient to overcome other actions of the body (IV. vi.), and may remain obstinately fixed therein, thus rendering it incapable of being affected in a variety of other ways: therefore (IV. xxxviii.) it may be bad. Again, grief, which is pain, cannot as such be good (IV. xli.). But, as its force and increase is defined by the power of an external cause compared with our own (IV. v.), we can conceive infinite degrees and modes of strength in this emotion (IV. iii.); we can, therefore, conceive it as capable of restraining stimulation, and preventing its becoming excessive, and hindering the body's capabilities; thus, to this extent, it will be good. *Q.E.D.*

PROP. XLIV. *Love and desire may be excessive.*

Proof.—Love is pleasure, accompanied by the idea of an external cause (Def. of Emotions, vi.); therefore stimulation, accompanied by the idea of an external cause is love (III. xi. note); hence love may be excessive. Again, the strength of desire varies in proportion to the emotion from which it arises (III. xxxvii.). Now emotion may overcome all the rest of men's actions (IV. vi.); so, therefore, can desire, which arises from the same emotion, overcome all other desires, and become excessive, as we showed in the last proposition concerning stimulation.

Note.—Mirth, which I have stated to be good, can be conceived more easily than it can be observed. For the emotions, whereby we are daily assailed, are generally referred to some part of the body which is affected more than the rest; hence the emotions are generally excessive, and so fix the mind in the contemplation of one object, that it is unable to think of others; and although men, as a rule, are a prey to many emotions—and very few are found who are always assailed by one and the same—yet there are cases, where one and the same emotion remains obstinately fixed. We sometimes see men so absorbed in one object, that, although it be not present, they think they have it before them; when this is the case with a man who is not asleep, we say he is delirious or mad; nor are those persons who are inflamed with love, and who dream all night and all day about nothing but their mistress, or some woman, considered as less mad, for they are made objects of ridicule. But when a miser thinks of nothing but gain or money, or when an ambitious man thinks of nothing but glory, they are not reckoned to be mad, because they are generally harmful, and are thought worthy of being hated. But, in reality, Avarice, Ambition, Lust, &c., are species of madness, though they may not be reckoned among diseases.

PROP. XLV. *Hatred can never be good.*

Proof.—When we hate a man, we endeavour to destroy

him (III. xxxix.), that is (IV. xxxvii.), we endeavour to do something that is bad. Therefore, &c. *Q.E.D.*

N.B. Here, and in what follows, I mean by hatred only hatred towards men.

Corollary I.—Envy, derision, contempt, anger, revenge, and other emotions attributable to hatred, or arising therefrom, are bad; this is evident from III. xxxix. and IV. xxxvii.

Corollary II.—Whatsoever we desire from motives of hatred is base, and in a State unjust. This also is evident from III. xxxix., and from the definitions of baseness and injustice in IV. xxxvii. note.

Note.—Between derision (which I have in Coroll. I. stated to be bad) and laughter I recognize a great difference. For laughter, as also jocularity, is merely pleasure; therefore, so long as it be not excessive, it is in itself good (IV. xli.). Assuredly nothing forbids man to enjoy himself, save grim and gloomy superstition. For why is it more lawful to satiate one's hunger and thirst than to drive away one's melancholy? I reason, and have convinced myself as follows: No deity, nor anyone else, save the envious, takes pleasure in my infirmity and discomfort, nor sets down to my virtue the tears, sobs, fear, and the like, which are signs of infirmity of spirit; on the contrary, the greater the pleasure wherewith we are affected, the greater the perfection whereto we pass; in other words, the more must we necessarily partake of the divine nature. Therefore, to make use of what comes in our way, and to enjoy it as much as possible (not to the point of satiety, for that would not be enjoyment) is the part of a wise man. I say it is the part of a wise man to refresh and recreate himself with moderate and pleasant food and drink, and also with perfumes, with the soft beauty of growing plants, with dress, with music, with many sports, with theatres, and the like, such as every man may make use of without injury to his neighbour. For the human body is composed of very numerous parts, of diverse nature, which continually stand in need of fresh and varied nourishment, so that the whole body may be equally capable of performing all the actions, which follow from the necessity of its own nature; and, consequently, so that the mind may also be equally capable of understanding many things simultaneously. This way of life, then, agrees best with our principles, and also with general practice; therefore, if there be any question of another plan, the plan we have mentioned is the best, and in every way to be commended. There is no need for me to set forth the matter more clearly or in more detail.

PROP. XLVI. *He, who lives under the guidance of reason, endeavours, as far as possible, to render back love, or kindness, for other men's hatred, anger, contempt, &c., towards him.*

Proof.—All emotions of hatred are bad (IV. xlv. Coroll. i.); therefore he who lives under the guidance of reason will endeavour, as far as possible, to avoid being assailed by such emotions (IV. xix.); consequently, he will also endeavour to prevent others being so assailed (IV. xxxvii.). But hatred is increased by being reciprocated, and can be quenched by love (III. xliii.), so that hatred may pass into love (III. xliv.); therefore he who lives under the guidance of reason will endeavour to repay hatred with love, that is, with kindness. *Q.E.D.*

Note.—He who chooses to avenge wrongs with hatred is assuredly wretched. But he, who strives to conquer hatred with love, fights his battle in joy and confidence; he withstands many as easily as one, and has very little need of fortune's aid. Those whom he vanquishes yield joyfully, not through failure, but through increase in their powers; all these consequences follow so plainly from the mere definitions of love and understanding, that I have no need to prove them in detail.

PROP. XLVII. *Emotions of hope and fear cannot be in themselves good.*

Proof.—Emotions of hope and fear cannot exist without pain. For fear is pain (Def. of the Emotions, xiii.), and hope (Def. of the Emotions, Explanation xii. and xiii.) cannot exist without fear; therefore (IV. xli.) these emotions cannot be good in themselves, but only in so far as they can restrain excessive pleasure (IV. xliii.). *Q.E.D.*

Note.—We may add, that these emotions show defective knowledge and an absence of power in the mind; for the same reason confidence, despair, joy, and disappointment are signs of a want of mental power. For although confidence and joy are pleasurable emotions, they nevertheless imply a preceding pain, namely, hope and fear.

Wherefore the more we endeavour to be guided by reason, the less do we depend on hope; we endeavour to free ourselves from fear, and, as far as we can, to dominate fortune, directing our actions by the sure counsels of wisdom.

PROP. XLVIII. *The emotions of over-esteem and disparagement are always bad.*

Proof.—These emotions (see Def. of the Emotions, xxi. xxii.) are repugnant to reason; and are therefore (IV. xxvi. xxvii.) bad. *Q.E.D.*

PROP. XLIX. *Over-esteem is apt to render its object proud.*

Proof.—If we see that any one rates us too highly, for love's sake, we are apt to become elated (III. xli.), or to be pleasurably affected (Def. of the Emotions, xxx.); the good which we hear of ourselves we readily believe (III. xxv.); and therefore, for love's sake, rate ourselves too highly; in other words, we are apt to become proud. *Q.E.D.*

PROP. L. *Pity, in a man who lives under the guidance of reason, is in itself bad and useless.*

Proof.—Pity (Def. of the Emotions, xviii.) is a pain, and therefore (IV. xli.) is in itself bad. The good effect which follows, namely, our endeavour to free the object of our pity from misery, is an action which we desire to do solely at the dictation of reason (IV. xxxvii.); only at the dictation of reason are we able to perform any action, which we know for certain to be good (IV. xxvii.); thus, in a man who lives under the guidance of reason, pity in itself is useless and bad. *Q.E.D.*

Note.—He who rightly realizes, that all things follow from the necessity of the divine nature, and come to pass in accordance with the eternal laws and rules of nature, will not find anything worthy of hatred, derision, or contempt, nor will he bestow pity on anything, but to the utmost extent of human virtue he will endeavour to do well, as the saying is, and to rejoice. We may add, that he, who is easily touched with compassion, and is moved by another's sorrow or tears, often does something which he afterwards regrets; partly because we can never be sure that an action caused by emotion is good, partly because we are easily deceived by false tears. I am in this place expressly speaking of a man living under the guidance of reason. He who is moved to help others neither by reason nor by compassion, is rightly styled inhuman, for (III. xxvii.) he seems unlike a man.

PROP. LI. *Approval is not repugnant to reason, but can agree therewith and arise therefrom.*

Proof.—Approval is love towards one who has done good to another (Def. of the Emotions, xix.); therefore it may be referred to the mind, in so far as the latter is active (III. lix.), that is (III. iii.), in so far as it understands; therefore, it is in agreement with reason, &c. *Q.E.D.*

Another Proof.—He, who lives under the guidance of reason, desires for others the good which he seeks for himself (IV. xxxvii.); wherefore from seeing someone doing good to his fellow his own endeavour to do good is aided; in other words, he will feel pleasure (III. xi. note) accompanied by the idea of the benefactor. Therefore he approves of him. *Q.E.D.*

Note.—Indignation as we defined it (Def. of the Emotions, xx.) is necessarily evil (IV. xlv.); we may, however, remark that, when the sovereign power for the sake of preserving peace punishes a citizen who has injured another, it should not be said to be indignant with the criminal, for it is not incited by hatred to ruin him, it is led by a sense of duty to punish him.

PROP. LII. *Self-approval may arise from reason, and that which arises from reason is the highest possible.*

Proof.—Self-approval is pleasure arising from a man's contemplation of himself and his own power of action (Def. of the Emotions, xxv.). But a man's true power of action or virtue is reason herself (III. iii.), as the said man clearly and distinctly contemplates her (II. xl. xliii.); therefore self-approval arises from reason. Again, when a man is contemplating himself, he only perceives clearly and distinctly or adequately, such things as follow from his power of action (III. Def. ii.), that is (III. iii.), from his power of understanding; therefore in such contemplation alone does the highest possible self-approval arise. *Q.E.D.*

Note.—Self-approval is in reality the highest object for which we can hope. For (as we showed in IV. xxv.) no one endeavours to preserve his being for the sake of any ulterior object, and, as this approval is more and more fostered and strengthened by praise (III. liii. Coroll.), and on the contrary (III. lv. Coroll.) is more and more disturbed by blame, fame becomes the most powerful of incitements to action, and life under disgrace is almost unendurable.

PROP. LIII. *Humility is not a virtue, or does not arise from reason.*

Proof.—Humility is pain arising from a man's contemplation of his own infirmities (Def. of the Emotions, xxvi.). But, in so far as a man knows himself by true reason, he is assumed to understand his essence, that is, his power (III. vii.). Wherefore, if a man in self-contemplation perceives any infirmity in himself, it is not by virtue of his understanding himself, but (III. lv.) by virtue of his power of activity being checked. But, if we assume that a man perceives his own infirmity by virtue of understanding something stronger than himself, by the knowledge of which he determines his own power of activity, this is the same as saying that we conceive that a man understands himself distinctly (IV. xxvi.), because[1] his power of activity is aided. Wherefore humility, or the pain which arises from a man's contemplation of his own infirmity, does not arise from the contemplation or reason, and is not a virtue but a passion. *Q.E.D.*

PROP. LIV. *Repentance is not a virtue, or does not arise from reason; but he who repents of an action is doubly wretched or infirm.*

Proof.—The first part of this proposition is proved like the foregoing one. The second part is proved from the mere definition of the emotion in question (Def. of the Emotions, xxvii.). For the man allows himself to be overcome, first, by evil desires; secondly, by pain.

Note.—As men seldom live under the guidance of reason, these two emotions, namely, Humility and Repentance, as also Hope and Fear, bring more good than harm; hence, as we must sin, we had better sin in that direction. For, if all men who are a prey to emotion were all equally proud, they would shrink from nothing, and would fear nothing; how then could they be joined and linked together in bonds of union? The crowd plays the tyrant, when it is not in

[1] Land reads: "Quod ipsius agendi potentia juvatur"—which I have translated above. He suggests as alternative readings to 'quod' 'quo' (= whereby) and 'quodque' (= and that).

fear; hence we need not wonder that the prophets, who consulted the good, not of a few, but of all, so strenuously commended Humility, Repentance, and Reverence. Indeed those who are a prey to these emotions may be led much more easily than others to live under the guidance of reason, that is, to become free and to enjoy the life of the blessed.

PROP. LV. *Extreme pride or dejection indicates extreme ignorance of self.*

Proof.—This is evident from Def. of the Emotions, xxviii. and xxix.

PROP. LVI. *Extreme pride or dejection indicates extreme infirmity of spirit.*

Proof.—The first foundation of virtue is self-preservation (IV. xxii. Coroll.) under the guidance of reason (IV. xxiv.). He, therefore, who is ignorant of himself, is ignorant of the foundation of all virtues, and consequently of all virtues. Again, to act virtuously is merely to act under the guidance of reason (IV. xxiv.): now he, that acts under the guidance of reason, must necessarily know that he so acts (II. xliii.). Therefore he who is in extreme ignorance of himself, and consequently of all virtues, acts least in obedience to virtue; in other words (IV. Def. viii.), is most infirm of spirit. Thus extreme pride or dejection indicates extreme infirmity of spirit. *Q.E.D.*

Corollary.—Hence it most clearly follows, that the proud and the dejected specially fall a prey to the emotions.

Note.—Yet dejection can be more easily corrected than pride; for the latter being a pleasurable emotion, and the former a painful emotion, the pleasurable is stronger than the painful (IV. xviii.).

PROP. LVII. *The proud man delights in the company of flatterers and parasites, but hates the company of the high-minded.*

Proof.—Pride is pleasure arising from a man's over-estimation of himself (Def. of the Emotions, xxviii. and vi.); this estimation the proud man will endeavour to foster by all the means in his power (III. xiii. note); he will therefore delight in the company of flatterers and parasites (whose character is too well known to need definition here), and will avoid the company of high-minded men, who value him according to his deserts. *Q.E.D.*

Note.—It would be too long a task to enumerate here all the evil results of pride, inasmuch as the proud are a prey to all the emotions, though to none of them less than to love and pity. I cannot, however, pass over in silence the fact, that a man may be called proud from his underestimation of other people; and, therefore, pride in this sense may be defined as pleasure arising from the false opinion, whereby a man may consider himself superior to his fellows. The dejection, which is the opposite quality to this sort of pride, may be defined as pain arising from the false opinion, whereby a man may think himself inferior to his fellows. Such being the case, we can easily see that a proud man is necessarily envious (III. xli. note), and only takes pleasure in the company, who fool his weak mind to the top of his bent, and make him insane instead of merely foolish.

Though dejection is the emotion contrary to pride, yet is the dejected man very near akin to the proud man. For, inasmuch as his pain arises from a comparison between his own infirmity and other men's power or virtue, it will be removed, or, in other words, he will feel pleasure, if his imagination be occupied in contemplating other men's faults; whence arises the proverb, "The unhappy are comforted by finding fellow-sufferers." Contrariwise, he will be the more pained in proportion as he thinks himself inferior to others; hence none are so prone to envy as the dejected, they are specially keen in observing men's actions, with a view to fault-finding rather than correction, in order to reserve their praises for dejection, and to glory therein, though all the time with a dejected air. These effects follow as necessarily from the said emotion, as it follows from the nature of a triangle, that the three angles are equal to two right angles. I have already said that I call these and similar emotions bad, solely in respect to what is useful to man. The laws of nature have regard to nature's general order, whereof man is but a part. I mention this, in passing, lest any should think that I have wished to set forth the faults and irrational deeds of men rather than the nature and properties of things. For, as I said in the preface to the third Part, I regard human emotions and their properties as on the same footing with other natural phenomena. Assuredly human emotions indicate the power and ingenuity of nature, if not of human nature, quite as fully as other things which we admire, and which we delight to contemplate. But I pass on to note those qualities in the emotions, which bring advantage to man, or inflict injury upon him.

PROP. LVIII. *Honour (gloria) is not repugnant to reason, but may arise therefrom.*

Proof.—This is evident from Def. of the Emotions, xxx., and also from the definition of an honourable man (IV. xxxvii. note i.).

Note.—Empty honour, as it is styled, is self-approval, fostered only by the good opinion of the populace; when this good opinion ceases there ceases also the self-approval, in other words, the highest object of each man's love (IV. lii. note); consequently, he whose honour is rooted in popular approval must, day by day, anxiously strive, act, and scheme in order to retain his reputation. For the populace is variable and inconstant, so that, if a reputation be not kept up, it quickly withers away. Everyone wishes to catch popular applause for himself, and readily represses the fame of others. The object of the strife being estimated as the greatest of all goods, each combatant is seized with a fierce desire to put down his rivals in every possible way, till he who at last comes out victorious is more proud of having done harm to others than of having done good to himself. This sort of honour, then, is really empty, being nothing.

The points to note concerning shame may easily be inferred from what was said on the subject of mercy and repentance. I will only add that shame, like compassion, though not a virtue, is yet good, in so far as it shows, that the feeler of shame is really imbued with the desire to live honourably; in the same way as suffering is good, as showing that the injured part is not mortified. Therefore, though a man who feels shame is sorrowful, he is yet more perfect than he, who is shameless, and has no desire to live honourably.

Such are the points which I undertook to remark upon concerning the emotions of pleasure and pain; as for the desires, they are good or bad according as they spring from good or evil emotions. But all, in so far as they are engendered in us by emotions wherein the mind is passive, are blind (as is evident from what was said in IV. xliv. note), and would be useless, if men could easily be induced to live by the guidance of reason only, as I will now briefly show.

PROP. LIX. *To all the actions, whereto we are determined by emotion wherein the mind is passive; we can be determined without emotion by reason.*

Proof.—To act rationally is nothing else (III. iii. and Def. ii.) but to perform those actions, which follow from the necessity of our nature considered in itself alone. But pain is bad, in so far as it diminishes or checks the power of action (IV. xli.); wherefore we cannot by pain be determined to any action, which we should be unable to perform under the guidance of reason. Again, pleasure is bad only in so far as it hinders a man's capability for action (IV. xli. xliii.); therefore to this extent we could not be determined by it to any action, which we could not perform under the guidance of reason. Lastly, pleasure, in so far as it is good, is in harmony with reason (for it consists in the fact that a man's capability for action is increased or aided); nor is the mind passive therein, except in so far as a man's power of action is not increased to the extent of affording him an adequate conception of himself and his actions (III. iii. and note).

Wherefore, if a man who is pleasurably affected be brought to such a state of perfection, that he gains an adequate conception of himself and his own actions, he will be equally, nay more, capable of those actions, to which he is determined by emotion wherein the mind is passive. But all emotions are attributable to pleasure, to pain, or to desire (Def. of the Emotions, iv. explanation); and desire (Def. of the Emotions, i.) is nothing else but the attempt to act; therefore, to all actions, &c. *Q.E.D.*

Another Proof.—A given action is called bad, in so far as it arises from one being affected by hatred or any evil emotion. But no action, considered in itself alone, is either good or bad (as we pointed out in the preface to Pt. IV.), one and the same action being sometimes good, sometimes bad; wherefore to the action which is sometimes bad, or arises from some evil emotion, we may be led by reason (IV. xix.). *Q.E.D.*

Note.—An example will put this point in a clearer light. The action of striking, in so far as it is considered physically, and in so far as we merely look to the fact that a man raises his arm, clenches his fist, and moves his whole arm violently downwards, is a virtue or excellence which is conceived as proper to the structure of the human body. If, then, a man, moved by anger or hatred, is led to clench his fist or to move his arm, this result takes place (as we showed in Pt. II.), because one and the same action can be associated with various mental images of things; therefore we may be determined to the performance of one and the same action by confused ideas, or by clear and distinct ideas. Hence it is evident that every desire which springs from emotion, wherein the mind is passive, would become useless, if men could be guided by reason. Let us now see why desire which arises from emotion, wherein the mind is passive, is called by us blind.

PROP. LX. *Desire arising from a pleasure or pain, that is not attributable to the whole body, but only to one or certain parts thereof, is without utility in respect to a man as a whole.*

Proof.—Let it be assumed, for instance, that A, a part of a body, is so strengthened by some external cause, that it prevails over the remaining parts (IV. vi.). This part will not endeavour to do away with its own powers, in order that the other parts of the body may perform its office; for this it would be necessary for it to have a force or power of doing away with its own powers, which (III. vi.) is absurd. The said part, and, consequently, the mind also, will endeavour to preserve its condition. Wherefore desire arising from a pleasure of the kind aforesaid has no utility in reference to a man as a whole. If it be assumed, on the other hand, that the part, A, be checked so that the remaining parts prevail, it may be proved in the same manner that desire arising from pain has no utility in respect to a man as a whole. *Q.E.D.*

Note.—As pleasure is generally (IV. xliv. note) attributed to one part of the body, we generally desire to preserve our being without taking into consideration our health as a whole: to which it may be added, that the desires which have most hold over us (IV. ix.) take account of the present and not of the future.

PROP. LXI. *Desire which springs from reason cannot be excessive.*

Proof.—Desire (Def. of the Emotions, i.) considered absolutely is the actual essence of man, in so far as it is conceived as in any way determined to a particular activity by some given modification of itself. Hence desire, which arises from reason, that is (III. iii.), which is engendered in us in so far as we act, is the actual essence or nature of man, in so far as it is conceived as determined to such activities as are adequately conceived through man's essence only (III. Def. ii.). Now, if such desire could be excessive, human nature considered in itself alone would be able to exceed itself, or would be able to do more than it can, a manifest contradiction. Therefore, such desire cannot be excessive. *Q.E.D.*

PROP. LXII. *In so far as the mind conceives a thing under the dictates of reason, it is affected equally, whether the idea be of a thing future, past, or present.*

Proof.—Whatsoever the mind conceives under the guidance of reason, it conceives under the form of eternity or necessity (II. xliv. Coroll. ii.), and is therefore affected with the same certitude (II. xliii. and note). Wherefore, whether the thing be present, past, or future, the mind conceives it under the same necessity and is affected with the same certitude; and whether the idea be of something present, past, or future, it will in all cases be equally true (II. xli.); that is, it will always possess the same properties of an adequate idea (II. Def. iv.); therefore, in so far as the mind conceives things under the dictates of reason, it is affected in the same manner, whether the idea be of a thing future, past, or present. *Q.E.D.*

Note.—If we could possess an adequate knowledge of the duration of things, and could determine by reason their periods of existence, we should contemplate things future with the same emotion as things present; and the mind would desire as though it were present the good which it conceived as future; consequently it would necessarily neglect a lesser good in the present for the sake of a greater good in the future, and would in no wise desire that which is good in the present but a source of evil in the future, as we shall presently show. However, we can have but a very inadequate knowledge of the duration of things (II. xxxi.); and the periods of their existence (II. xliv. note) we can only determine by imagination, which is not so powerfully affected by the future as by the present. Hence such true knowledge of good and evil as we possess is merely abstract or general, and the judgment which we pass on the order of things and the connection of causes, with a view to determining what is good or bad for us in the present, is rather imaginary than real. Therefore it is nothing wonderful, if the desire arising from such knowledge of good and evil, in so far as it looks on into the future, be more readily checked than the desire of things which are agreeable at the present time. (Cf. IV. xvi.)

PROP. LXIII. *He who is led by fear, and does good in order to escape evil, is not led by reason.*

Proof.—All the emotions which are attributable to the mind as active, or in other words to reason, are emotions of pleasure and desire (III. lix.); therefore, he who is led by fear, and does good in order to escape evil, is not led by reason.

Note.—Superstitious persons, who know better how to rail at vice than how to teach virtue, and who strive not to guide men by reason, but so to restrain them that they would rather escape evil than love virtue, have no other aim but to make others as wretched as themselves; wherefore it is nothing wonderful, if they be generally troublesome and odious to their fellow-men.

Corollary.—Under desire which springs from reason, we seek good directly, and shun evil indirectly.

Proof.—Desire which springs from reason can only spring from a pleasurable emotion, wherein the mind is not passive (III. lix.), in other words, from a pleasure which cannot be excessive (IV. lxi.), and not from pain; wherefore this desire springs from the knowledge of good, not of evil (IV. viii.); hence under the guidance of reason we seek good directly and only by implication shun evil. *Q.E.D.*

Note.—This Corollary may be illustrated by the example of a sick and a healthy man. The sick man through fear of death eats what he naturally shrinks from, but the healthy man takes pleasure in his food, and thus gets a better enjoyment out of life, than if he were in fear of death, and desired directly to avoid it. So a judge, who condemns a criminal to death, not from hatred or anger but from love of the public well-being, is guided solely by reason.

PROP. LXIV. *The knowledge of evil is an inadequate knowledge.*

Proof.—The knowledge of evil (IV. viii.) is pain, in so far as we are conscious thereof. Now pain is the transition to a lesser perfection (Def. of the Emotions, iii.) and therefore cannot be understood through man's nature (III. vi. and vii.); therefore it is a passive state (III. Def. ii.) which (III. iii.) depends on inadequate ideas; consequently the knowledge thereof (II. xxix.), namely, the knowledge of evil, is inadequate. *Q.E.D.*

Corollary.—Hence it follows that, if the human mind possessed only adequate ideas, it would form no conception of evil.

PROP. LXV. *Under the guidance of reason we should pursue the greater of two goods and the lesser of two evils.*

Proof.—A good which prevents our enjoyment of a greater good is in reality an evil; for we apply the terms good and bad to things, in so far as we compare them one with another (see preface to this Part); therefore, evil is in reality a lesser good; hence under the guidance of reason we seek or pursue only the greater good and the lesser evil. *Q.E.D.*

Corollary.—We may, under the guidance of reason, pursue the lesser evil as though it were the greater good, and we may shun the lesser good, which would be the cause of the greater evil. For the evil, which is here called the lesser, is really good, and the lesser good is really evil, wherefore we may seek the former and shun the latter. *Q.E.D.*

PROP. LXVI. *We may, under the guidance of reason, seek a greater good in the future in preference to a lesser good in the present, and we may seek a lesser evil in the present in preference to a greater evil in the future.*[1]

Proof.—If the mind could have an adequate knowledge

[1] "Malum præsens minus præ majori futuro." (Van Vloten). Bruder reads: "Malum præsens minus, quod causa est futuri alicujus mali." The last word of the latter is an obvious misprint, and is corrected by the Dutch translator into "majoris boni." (Pollock, p. 268, note.)

of things future, it would be affected towards what is future in the same way as towards what is present (IV. lxii.); wherefore, looking merely to reason, as in this proposition we are assumed to do, there is no difference, whether the greater good or evil be assumed as present, or assumed as future; hence (IV. lxv.) we may seek a greater good in the future in preference to a lesser good in the present, &c. *Q.E.D.*

Corollary.—We may, under the guidance of reason, seek a lesser evil in the present, because it is the cause of a greater good in the future, and we may shun a lesser good in the present, because it is the cause of a greater evil in the future. This Corollary is related to the foregoing Proposition as the Corollary to IV. lxv. is related to the said IV. lxv.

Note.—If these statements be compared with what we have pointed out concerning the strength of the emotions in this Part up to Prop. xviii., we shall readily see the difference between a man, who is led solely by emotion or opinion, and a man, who is led by reason. The former, whether he will or no, performs actions whereof he is utterly ignorant; the latter is his own master and only performs such actions, as he knows are of primary importance in life, and therefore chiefly desires; wherefore I call the former a slave, and the latter a free man, concerning whose disposition and manner of life it will be well to make a few observations.

PROP. LXVII. *A free man thinks of death least of all things; and his wisdom is a meditation not of death but of life.*

Proof.—A free man is one who lives under the guidance of reason, who is not led by fear (IV. lxiii.), but who directly desires that which is good (IV. lxiii. Coroll.), in other words (IV. xxiv.), who strives to act, to live, and to preserve his being on the basis of seeking his own true advantage; wherefore such an one thinks of nothing less than of death, but his wisdom is a meditation of life. *Q.E.D.*

PROP. LXVIII. *If men were born free, they would, so long as they remained free, form no conception of good and evil.*

Proof.—I call free him who is led solely by reason; he, therefore, who is born free, and who remains free, has only adequate ideas; therefore (IV. lxiv. Coroll.) he has no conception of evil, or consequently (good and evil being correlative) of good. *Q.E.D.*

Note.—It is evident, from IV. iv., that the hypothesis of this Proposition is false and inconceivable, except in so far as we look solely to the nature of man, or rather to God; not in so far as the latter is infinite, but only in so far as he is the cause of man's existence.

This, and other matters which we have already proved, seem to have been signified by Moses in the history of the first man. For in that narrative no other power of God is conceived, save that whereby he created man, that is the power wherewith he provided solely for man's advantage; it is stated that God forbade man, being free, to eat of the tree of the knowledge of good and evil, and that, as soon as man should have eaten of it, he would straightway fear death rather than desire to live. Further, it is written that when man had found a wife, who was in entire harmony with his nature, he knew that there could be nothing in nature which could be more useful to him; but that after he believed the beasts to be like himself, he straightway began to imitate their emotions (III. xxvii.), and to lose his freedom; this freedom was afterwards recovered by the patriarchs, led by the spirit of Christ; that is, by the idea of God, whereon alone it depends, that man may be free, and desire for others the good which he desires for himself, as we have shown above (IV. xxxvii.).

PROP. LXIX. *The virtue of a free man is seen to be as great, when it declines dangers, as when it overcomes them.*

Proof.—Emotion can only be checked or removed by an emotion contrary to itself, and possessing more power in restraining emotion (IV. vii.). But blind daring and fear are emotions, which can be conceived as equally great (IV. v. and iii.): hence, no less virtue or firmness is required in checking daring than in checking fear (III. lix. note); in other words (Def. of the Emotions, xl. and xli.), the free man shows as much virtue, when he declines dangers, as when he strives to overcome them. *Q.E.D.*

Corollary.—The free man is as courageous in timely retreat as in combat; or, a free man shows equal courage or presence of mind, whether he elect to give battle or to retreat.

Note.—What courage (*animositas*) is, and what I mean thereby, I explained in III. lix. note. By danger I mean everything, which can give rise to any evil, such as pain, hatred, discord, &c.

PROP. LXX. *The free man, who lives among the ignorant, strives, as far as he can, to avoid receiving favours from them.*

Proof.—Everyone judges what is good according to his disposition (III. xxxix. note); wherefore an ignorant man, who has conferred a benefit on another, puts his own estimate upon it, and, if it appears to be estimated less highly by the receiver, will feel pain (III. xlii.). But the free man only desires to join other men to him in friendship (IV. xxxvii.), not repaying their benefits with others reckoned as of like value, but guiding himself and others by the free decision of reason, and doing only such things as he knows to be of primary importance. Therefore the free man, lest he should become hateful to the ignorant, or follow their desires rather than reason, will endeavour, as far as he can, to avoid receiving their favours.

Note.—I say, *as far as he can.* For though men be ignorant, yet are they men, and in cases of necessity could afford us human aid, the most excellent of all things: therefore it is often necessary to accept favours from them, and consequently to repay such favours in kind; we must, therefore, exercise caution in declining favours, lest we should have the appearance of despising those who bestow them, or of being, from avaricious motives, unwilling to requite them, and so give ground for offence by the very fact of striving to avoid it. Thus, in declining favours, we must look to the requirements of utility and courtesy.

PROP. LXXI. *Only free men are thoroughly grateful one to another.*

Proof.—Only free men are thoroughly useful one to another, and associated among themselves by the closest necessity of friendship (IV. xxxv. and Coroll. i.), only such men endeavour, with mutual zeal of love, to confer benefits on each other (IV. xxxvii.), and, therefore, only they are thoroughly grateful one to another. *Q.E.D.*

Note.—The goodwill, which men who are led by blind desire have for one another, is generally a bargaining or enticement, rather than pure goodwill. Moreover, ingratitude is not an emotion. Yet it is base, inasmuch as it generally shows, that a man is affected by excessive hatred, anger, pride, avarice, &c. He who, by reason of his folly, knows not how to return benefits, is not ungrateful, much less he who is not gained over by the gifts of a courtesan to serve her lust, or by a thief to conceal his thefts, or by any similar persons. Contrariwise, such an one shows a constant mind, inasmuch as he cannot by any gifts be corrupted, to his own or the general hurt.

PROP. LXXII. *The free man never acts fraudently, but always in good faith.*

Proof.—If it be asked: What should a man's conduct be in a case where he could by breaking faith free himself from the danger of present death? Would not his plan of self-preservation completely persuade him to deceive? this may be answered by pointing out that, if reason persuaded him to act thus, it would persuade all men to act in a similar manner, in which case reason would persuade men not to agree in good faith to unite their forces, or to have laws in common, that is, not to have any general laws, which is absurd.

PROP. LXXIII. *The man, who is guided by reason, is more free in a State, where he lives under a general system of law, than in solitude, where he is independent.*

Proof.—The man, who is guided by reason, does not obey through fear (IV. lxiii.): but, in so far as he endeavours to preserve his being according to the dictates of reason, that is (IV. lxvi. note), in so far as he endeavours to live in freedom, he desires to order his life according to the general good (IV. xxxvii.), and, consequently (as we showed in IV. xxxvii. note ii.), to live according to the laws of his country. Therefore the free man, in order to enjoy greater freedom, desires to possess the general rights of citizenship. *Q.E.D.*

Note.—These and similar observations, which we have made on man's true freedom, may be referred to strength, that is, to courage and nobility of character (III. lix. note). I do not think it worth while to prove separately all the properties of strength; much less need I show, that he that is strong hates no man, is angry with no man, envies no man, is indignant with no man, despises no man, and least of all things is proud. These propositions, and all that relate to the true way of life and religion, are easily proved from IV. xxxvii. and xlvi.; namely, that hatred should be overcome with love, and that every man should desire for others the good which he seeks for himself. We may also repeat what we drew attention to in the note to IV. l., and in other places; namely, that the strong man has ever first in his thoughts, that all things follow from the necessity of the divine nature; so that whatsoever he deems to be hurtful and evil, and whatsoever, accordingly, seems to him impious, horrible, unjust, and base, assumes that appearance owing to his own disordered, fragmentary, and confused view of the universe. Wherefore he strives before all things to conceive things as they really are, and to remove the hindrances to true knowledge, such as are hatred, anger, envy, derision, pride, and similar emotions, which I have mentioned above. Thus he endeavours, as we said before, as far as in him lies, to do good, and to go on his way rejoicing. How far human virtue is capable of attaining to such a condition, and what its powers may be, I will prove in the following Part.

Appendix.

What I have said in this Part concerning the right way of life has not been arranged, so as to admit of being seen at one view, but has been set forth piece-meal, according as I thought each Proposition could most readily be deduced from what preceded it. I propose, therefore, to rearrange my remarks and to bring them under leading heads.

I. All our endeavours or desires so follow from the necessity of our nature, that they can be understood either through it alone, as their proximate cause, or by virtue of our being a part of nature, which cannot be adequately conceived through itself without other individuals.

II. Desires, which follow from our nature in such a

manner, that they can be understood through it alone, are those which are referred to the mind, in so far as the latter is conceived to consist of adequate ideas: the remaining desires are only referred to the mind, in so far as it conceives things inadequately, and their force and increase are generally defined not by the power of man, but by the power of things external to us: wherefore the former are rightly called actions, the latter passions, for the former always indicate our power, the latter, on the other hand, show our infirmity and fragmentary knowledge.

III. Our actions, that is, those desires which are defined by man's power or reason, are always good. The rest may be either good or bad.

IV. Thus in life it is before all things useful to perfect the understanding, or reason, as far as we can, and in this alone man's highest happiness or blessedness consists, indeed blessedness is nothing else but the contentment of spirit, which arises from the intuitive knowledge of God: now, to perfect the understanding is nothing else but to understand God, God's attributes, and the actions which follow from the necessity of his nature. Wherefore of a man, who is led by reason, the ultimate aim or highest desire, whereby he seeks to govern all his fellows, is that whereby he is brought to the adequate conception of himself and of all things within the scope of his intelligence.

V. Therefore, without intelligence there is not rational life: and things are only good, in so far as they aid man in his enjoyment of the intellectual life, which is defined by intelligence. Contrariwise, whatsoever things hinder man's perfecting of his reason, and capability to enjoy the rational life, are alone called evil.

VI. As all things whereof man is the efficient cause are necessarily good, no evil can befall man except through external causes; namely, by virtue of man being a part of universal nature, whose laws human nature is compelled to obey, and to conform to in almost infinite ways.

VII. It is impossible, that man should not be a part of nature, or that he should not follow her general order; but if he be thrown among individuals whose nature is in harmony with his own, his power of action will thereby be aided and fostered, whereas, if he be thrown among such as are but very little in harmony with his nature, he will hardly be able to accommodate himself to them without undergoing a great change himself.

VIII. Whatsoever in nature we deem to be evil, or to be capable of injuring our faculty for existing and enjoying the rational life, we may endeavour to remove in whatever way seems safest to us; on the other hand, whatsoever we deem to be good or useful for preserving our being, and enabling us to enjoy the rational life, we may appropriate to our use and employ as we think best. Everyone without exception may, by sovereign right of nature, do whatsoever he thinks will advance his own interest.

IX. Nothing can be in more harmony with the nature of any given thing than other individuals of the same species; therefore (cf. vii.) for man in the preservation of his being and the enjoyment of the rational life there is nothing more useful than his fellow-man who is led by reason. Further, as we know not anything among individual things which is more excellent than a man led by reason, no man can better display the power of his skill and disposition, than in so training men, that they come at last to live under the dominion of their own reason.

X. In so far as men are influenced by envy or any kind of hatred, one towards another, they are at variance, and are therefore to be feared in proportion, as they are more powerful than their fellows.

XI. Yet minds are not conquered by force, but by love and high-mindedness.

XII. It is before all things useful to men to associate their ways of life, to bind themselves together with such bonds as they think most fitted to gather them all into unity, and generally to do whatsoever serves to strengthen friendship.

XIII. But for this there is need of skill and watchfulness. For men are diverse (seeing that those who live under the guidance of reason are few), yet are they generally envious and more prone to revenge than to sympathy. No small force of character is therefore required to take everyone as he is, and to restrain one's self from imitating the emotions of others. But those who carp at mankind, and are more skilled in railing at vice than in instilling virtue, and who break rather than strengthen men's dispositions, are hurtful both to themselves and others. Thus many from too great impatience of spirit, or from misguided religious zeal, have preferred to live among brutes rather than among men; as boys or youths, who cannot peaceably endure the chidings of their parents, will enlist as soldiers and choose the hardships of war and the despotic discipline in preference to the comforts of home and the admonitions of their father: suffering any burden to be put upon them, so long as they may spite their parents.

XIV. Therefore, although men are generally governed in everything by their own lusts, yet their association in common brings many more advantages than drawbacks. Wherefore it is better to bear patiently the wrongs they may do us, and to strive to promote whatsoever serves to bring about harmony and friendship.

XV. Those things, which beget harmony, are such as are attributable to justice, equity, and honourable living. For men brook ill not only what is unjust or iniquitous, but also what is reckoned disgraceful, or that a man should slight the received customs of their society. For winning love those qualities are especially necessary which have regard to religion and piety (cf. IV. xxxvii. notes, i. ii.; xlvi. note; and lxxiii. note).

XVI. Further, harmony is often the result of fear: but such harmony is insecure. Further, fear arises from infirmity of spirit, and moreover belongs not to the exercise of reason: the same is true of compassion, though this latter seems to bear a certain resemblance to piety.

XVII. Men are also gained over by liberality, especially such as have not the means to buy what is necessary to sustain life. However, to give aid to every poor man is far beyond the power and the advantage of any private person. For the riches of any private person are wholly inadequate to meet such a call. Again, an individual man's resources of character are too limited for him to be able to make all men his friends. Hence providing for the poor is a duty, which falls on the State as a whole, and has regard only to the general advantage.

XVIII. In accepting favours, and in returning gratitude our duty must be wholly different (cf. IV. lxx. note; lxxi. note).

XIX. Again, meretricious love, that is, the lust of generation arising from bodily beauty, and generally every sort of love, which owns anything save freedom of soul as its cause, readily passes into hate; unless indeed, what is worse, it is a species of madness; and then it promotes discord rather than harmony (cf. III. xxxi. Coroll.).

XX. As concerning marriage, it is certain that this is in harmony with reason, if the desire for physical union be not engendered solely by bodily beauty, but also by the desire to beget children and to train them up wisely; and moreover, if the love of both, to wit, of the man and of the woman, is not caused by bodily beauty only, but also by freedom of soul.

XXI. Furthermore, flattery begets harmony; but only by means of the vile offence of slavishness or treachery. None are more readily taken with flattery than the proud, who wish to be first, but are not.

XXII. There is in abasement a spurious appearance of piety and religion. Although abasement is the opposite to pride, yet is he that abases himself most akin to the proud (IV. lvii. note).

XXIII. Shame also brings about harmony, but only in such matters as cannot be hid. Further, as shame is a species of pain, it does not concern the exercise of reason.

XXIV. The remaining emotions of pain towards men are directly opposed to justice, equity, honour, piety, and religion; and, although indignation seems to bear a certain resemblance to equity, yet is life but lawless, where every man may pass judgment on another's deeds, and vindicate his own or other men's rights.

XXV. Correctness of conduct (*modestia*), that is, the desire of pleasing men which is determined by reason, is attributable to piety (as we said in IV. xxxvii. note i.). But, if it spring from emotion, it is ambition, or the desire whereby men, under the false cloak of piety, generally stir up discords and seditions. For he who desires to aid his fellows either in word or in deed, so that they may together enjoy the highest good, he, I say, will before all things strive to win them over with love: not to draw them into admiration, so that a system may be called after his name, nor to give any cause for envy. Further, in his conversation he will shrink from talking of men's faults, and will be careful to speak but sparingly of human infirmity: but he will dwell at length on human virtue or power, and the way whereby it may be perfected. Thus will men be stirred not by fear, nor by aversion, but only by the emotion of joy, to endeavour, so far as in them lies, to live in obedience to reason.

XXVI. Besides men, we know of no particular thing in nature in whose mind we may rejoice, and whom we can associate with ourselves in friendship or any sort of fellowship; therefore, whatsoever there be in nature besides man, a regard for our advantage does not call on us to preserve, but to preserve or destroy according to its various capabilities, and to adapt to our use as best we may.

XXVII. The advantage which we derive from things external to us, besides the experience and knowledge which we acquire from observing them, and from recombining their elements in different forms, is principally the preservation of the body; from this point of view, those things are most useful which can so feed and nourish the body, that all its parts may rightly fulfil their functions. For, in proportion as the body is capable of being affected in a greater variety of ways, and of affecting external bodies in a great number of ways, so much the more is the mind capable of thinking (IV. xxxviii. xxxix.). But there seem to be very few things of this kind in nature; wherefore for the due nourishment of the body we must use many foods of diverse nature. For the human body is composed of very many parts of different nature, which stand in continual need of varied nourishment, so that the whole body may be equally capable of doing everything that can follow from its own nature, and consequently that the mind also may be equally capable of forming many perceptions.

XXVIII. Now for providing these nourishments the strength of each individual would hardly suffice, if men did not lend one another mutual aid. But money has furnished us with a token for everything: hence it is with the notion of money, that the mind of the multitude is chiefly engrossed: nay, it can hardly conceive any kind of pleasure, which is not accompanied with the idea of money as cause.

XXIX. This result is the fault only of those, who seek money, not from poverty or to supply their necessary wants, but because they have learned the arts of gain, wherewith they bring themselves to great splendour. Certainly they nourish their bodies, according to custom, but scantily, believing that they lose as much of their wealth as they spend on the preservation of their body. But they who know the true use of money, and who fix the measure of wealth solely with regard to their actual needs, live content with little.

XXX. As, therefore, those things are good which assist the various parts of the body, and enable them to perform their functions; and as pleasure consists in an increase of, or aid to, man's power, in so far as he is composed of mind and body; it follows that all those things which bring pleasure are good. But seeing that things do not work with the object of giving us pleasure, and that their power of action is not tempered to suit our advantage, and, lastly, that pleasure is generally referred to one part of the body more than to the other parts; therefore most emotions of pleasure (unless reason and watchfulness be at hand), and consequently the desires arising therefrom, may become excessive. Moreover we may add that emotion leads us to pay most regard to what is agreeable in the present, nor can we estimate what is future with emotions equally vivid. (IV. xliv. note, and lx. note.)

XXXI. Superstition, on the other hand, seems to account as good all that brings pain, and as bad all that brings pleasure. However, as we said above (IV. xlv. note), none but the envious take delight in my infirmity and trouble. For the greater the pleasure whereby we are affected, the greater is the perfection whereto we pass, and consequently the more do we partake of the divine nature: no pleasure can ever be evil, which is regulated by a true regard for our advantage. But contrariwise he, who is led by fear and does good only to avoid evil, is not guided by reason.

XXXII. But human power is extremely limited, and is infinitely surpassed by the power of external causes; we have not, therefore, an absolute power of shaping to our use those things which are without us. Nevertheless, we shall bear with an equal mind all that happens to us in contravention to the claims of our own advantage, so long as we are conscious, that we have done our duty, and that the power which we possess is not sufficient to enable us to protect ourselves completely; remembering that we are a part of universal nature, and that we follow her order. If we have a clear and distinct understanding of this, that part of our nature which is defined by intelligence, in other words the better part of ourselves, will assuredly acquiesce in what befalls us, and in such acquiescence will endeavour to persist. For, in so far as we are intelligent beings, we cannot desire anything save that which is necessary, nor yield absolute acquiescence to anything, save to that which is true: wherefore, in so far as we have a right understanding of these things, the endeavour of the better part of ourselves is in harmony with the order of nature as a whole.

PART V.

OF THE POWER OF THE UNDERSTANDING, OR OF HUMAN FREEDOM.

PREFACE.

AT length I pass to the remaining portion of my Ethics, which is concerned with the way leading to freedom. I shall therefore treat therein of the power of the reason, showing how far the reason can control the emotions, and what is the nature of Mental Freedom or Blessedness; we shall then be able to see, how much more powerful the wise man is than the ignorant. It is no part of my design to point out the method and means whereby the understanding may be perfected, nor to show the skill whereby the body may be so tended, as to be capable of the due performance of its functions. The latter question lies in the province of Medicine, the former in the province of Logic. Here, therefore, I repeat, I shall treat only of the power of the mind, or of reason; and I shall mainly show the extent and nature of its dominion over the emotions, for their control and moderation. That we do not possess absolute dominion over them, I have already shown. Yet the Stoics have thought, that the emotions depended absolutely on our will, and that we could absolutely govern them. But these philosophers were compelled, by the protest of experience, not from their own principles, to confess, that no slight practice and zeal is needed to control and moderate them: and this someone endeavoured to illustrate by the example (if I remember rightly) of two dogs, the one a house-dog and the other a hunting-dog. For by long training it could be brought about, that the house-dog should become accustomed to hunt, and the hunting-dog to cease from running after hares. To this opinion Descartes not a little inclines. For he maintained, that the soul or mind is specially united to a particular part of the brain, namely, to that part called the pineal gland, by the aid of which the mind is enabled to feel all the movements which are set going in the body, and also external objects, and which the mind by a simple act of volition can put in motion in various ways. He asserted, that this gland is so suspended in the midst of the brain, that it could be moved by the slightest motion of the animal spirits: further, that this gland is suspended in the midst of the brain in as many different manners, as the animal spirits can impinge thereon ; and, again, that as many different marks are impressed on the said gland, as there are different external objects which impel the animal spirits towards it ; whence it follows, that if the will of the soul suspends the gland in a position, wherein it has already been suspended once before by the animal spirits driven in one way or another, the gland in its turn reacts on the said spirits, driving and determining them to the condition wherein they were, when repulsed before by a similar position of the gland. He further asserted, that every act of mental volition is united in nature to a certain given motion of the gland. For instance, whenever anyone desires to look at a remote object, the act of volition causes the pupil of the eye to dilate, whereas, if the person in question had only thought of the dilatation of the pupil, the mere wish to dilate it would not have brought about the result, inasmuch as the motion of the gland, which serves to impel the animal spirits towards the optic nerve in a way which would dilate or contract the pupil, is not associated in nature with the wish to dilate or contract the pupil, but with the wish to look at remote or very near objects. Lastly, he maintained that, although every motion of the aforesaid gland seems to have been united by nature to one particular thought out of the whole number of our thoughts from the very beginning of our life, yet it can nevertheless become through habituation associated with other thoughts; this he endeavours to prove in the *Passions de l'âme*, I. 50. He thence concludes, that there is no soul so weak, that it cannot, under proper direction, acquire absolute power over its passions. For passions as defined by him are "perceptions, or feelings, or disturbances of the soul, which are referred to the soul as species, and which (mark the expression) are produced, preserved, and strengthened through some movement of the spirits." (*Passions de l'âme*, I. 27.) But, seeing that we can join any motion of the gland, or consequently of the spirits, to any volition, the determination of the will depends entirely on our own powers; if, therefore, we determine our will with sure and firm decisions in the direction to which we wish our actions to tend, and associate the motions of the passions which we wish to acquire with the said decisions, we shall acquire an absolute dominion over our passions. Such is the doctrine of this illustrious philosopher (in so far as I gather it from his own words); it is one which, had it been less ingenious, I could hardly believe to have proceeded from so great a man. Indeed, I am lost in wonder, that a philosopher, who had stoutly asserted, that he would draw no conclusions which do not follow from self-evident premisses, and would affirm nothing which he did not clearly and distinctly perceive, and who had so often taken to task the scholastics for wishing to explain obscurities through occult qualities, could maintain a hypothesis, beside which occult qualities are commonplace. What does he understand, I ask, by the union of the mind and the body? What clear and distinct conception has he got of thought in most intimate union with a certain particle of extended matter? Truly I should like him to explain this union through its proximate cause. But he had so distinct a conception of mind being distinct from body, that he could not assign any particular cause of the union between the two, or of the mind itself, but was obliged to have recourse to the cause of the whole universe, that is to God. Further, I should much like to know, what degree of motion the mind can impart to this pineal gland, and with what force can it hold it suspended? For I am in ignorance, whether this gland can be agitated more slowly or more quickly by the mind than by the animal spirits, and whether the motions of the passions, which we have closely united with firm decisions, cannot be again disjoined therefrom by physical causes; in which case it would follow that, although the mind firmly intended to face a given danger, and had united to this decision the motions of boldness, yet at the sight of the danger the gland might become suspended in a way, which would preclude the mind thinking of anything except running away. In truth, as there is no common standard of volition and motion, so is there no comparison possible between the powers of the mind and the power or strength of the body; consequently the strength of one cannot in any wise be determined by the strength of the other. We may also add, that there is no gland discoverable in the midst of the brain, so placed that it can thus easily be set in motion in so many ways, and also that all the nerves are not prolonged so far as the cavities of the brain. Lastly, I omit all the assertions which he makes concerning the will and its freedom, inasmuch as I have abundantly proved that his premisses are false. Therefore, since the power of the mind, as I have shown above, is defined by the understanding only, we shall determine solely by the knowledge of the mind the remedies against the emotions, which I believe all have had experience of, but do not accurately observe or distinctly see, and from the same basis we shall deduce all those conclusions, which have regard to the mind's blessedness.

Axioms.

I. If two contrary actions be started in the same subject, a change must necessarily take place, either in both, or in one of the two, and continue until they cease to be contrary.

II. The power of an effect is defined by the power of its cause, in so far as its essence is explained or defined by the essence of its cause.

(This axiom is evident from III. vii.)

Prop. I. *Even as thoughts and the ideas of things are arranged and associated in the mind, so are the modifications of body or the images of things precisely in the same way arranged and associated in the body.*

Proof.—The order and connection of ideas is the same (II. vii.) as the order and connection of things, and *vice versâ* the order and connection of things is the same (II. vi. Coroll. and vii.) as the order and connection of ideas. Wherefore, even as the order and connection of ideas in the mind takes place according to the order and association of modifications of the body (II. xviii.), so *vice versâ* (III. ii.)

the order and connection of modifications of the body takes place in accordance with the manner, in which thoughts and the ideas of things are arranged and associated in the mind. *Q.E.D.*

PROP. II. *If we remove a disturbance of the spirit, or emotion, from the thought of an external cause, and unite it to other thoughts, then will the love or hatred towards that external cause, and also the vacillations of spirit which arise from these emotions, be destroyed.*

Proof.—That, which constitutes the reality of love or hatred, is pleasure or pain, accompanied by the idea of an external cause (Def. of the Emotions, vi. vii.); wherefore, when this cause is removed, the reality of love or hatred is removed with it; therefore these emotions and those which arise therefrom are destroyed. *Q.E.D.*

PROP. III. *An emotion, which is a passion, ceases to be a passion, as soon as we form a clear and distinct idea thereof.*

Proof.—An emotion, which is a passion, is a confused idea (by the general Def. of the Emotions). If, therefore, we form a clear and distinct idea of a given emotion, that idea will only be distinguished from the emotion, in so far as it is referred to the mind only, by reason (II. xxi. and note); therefore (III. iii.), the emotion will cease to be a passion. *Q.E.D.*

Corollary.—An emotion therefore becomes more under our control, and the mind is less passive in respect to it, in proportion as it is more known to us.

PROP. IV. *There is no modification of the body, whereof we cannot form some clear and distinct conception.*

Proof.—Properties which are common to all things can only be conceived adequately (II. xxxviii.); therefore (II. xii. and Lemma ii. after II. xiii.) there is no modification of the body, whereof we cannot form some clear and distinct conception. *Q.E.D.*

Corollary.—Hence it follows that there is no emotion, whereof we cannot form some clear and distinct conception. For an emotion is the idea of a modification of the body (by the general Def. of the Emotions), and must therefore (by the preceding Prop.) involve some clear and distinct conception.

Note.—Seeing that there is nothing which is not followed

by an effect (I. xxxvi.), and that we clearly and distinctly understand whatever follows from an idea, which in us is adequate (II. xl.), it follows that everyone has the power of clearly and distinctly understanding himself and his emotions, if not absolutely, at any rate in part, and consequently of bringing it about, that he should become less subject to them. To attain this result, therefore, we must chiefly direct our efforts to acquiring, as far as possible, a clear and distinct knowledge of every emotion, in order that the mind may thus, through emotion, be determined to think of those things which it clearly and distinctly perceives, and wherein it fully acquiesces: and thus that the emotion itself may be separated from the thought of an external cause, and may be associated with true thoughts; whence it will come to pass, not only that love, hatred, &c. will be destroyed (V. ii.), but also that the appetites or desires, which are wont to arise from such emotion, will become incapable of being excessive (IV. lxi.). For it must be especially remarked, that the appetite through which a man is said to be active, and that through which he is said to be passive is one and the same. For instance, we have shown that human nature is so constituted, that everyone desires his fellow-men to live after his own fashion (III. xxxi. note); in a man, who is not guided by reason, this appetite is a passion which is called ambition, and does not greatly differ from pride; whereas in a man, who lives by the dictates of reason, it is an activity or virtue which is called piety (IV. xxxvii. note i. and second proof). In like manner all appetites or desires are only passions, in so far as they spring from inadequate ideas; the same results are accredited to virtue, when they are aroused or generated by adequate ideas. For all desires, whereby we are determined to any given action, may arise as much from adequate as from inadequate ideas (IV. lix.). Than this remedy for the emotions (to return to the point from which I started), which consists in a true knowledge thereof, nothing more excellent, being within our power, can be devised. For the mind has no other power save that of thinking and of forming adequate ideas, as we have shown above (III. iii.).

PROP. V. *An emotion towards a thing, which we conceive*

simply, and not as necessary, or as contingent, or as possible, is, other conditions being equal, greater than any other emotion.

Proof.—An emotion towards a thing, which we conceive to be free, is greater than one towards what we conceive to be necessary (III. xlix.), and, consequently, still greater than one towards what we conceive as possible, or contingent (IV. xi.). But to conceive a thing as free can be nothing else than to conceive it simply, while we are in ignorance of the causes whereby it has been determined to action (II. xxxv. note); therefore, an emotion towards a thing which we conceive simply is, other conditions being equal, greater than one, which we feel towards what is necessary, possible, or contingent, and, consequently, it is the greatest of all. *Q.E.D.*

Prop. VI. *The mind has greater power over the emotions and is less subject thereto, in so far as it understands all things as necessary.*

Proof.—The mind understands all things to be necessary (I. xxix.) and to be determined to existence and operation by an infinite chain of causes; therefore (by the foregoing Proposition), it thus far brings it about, that it is less subject to the emotions arising therefrom, and (III. xlviii.) feels less emotion towards the things themselves. *Q.E.D.*

Note.—The more this knowledge, that things are necessary, is applied to particular things, which we conceive more distinctly and vividly, the greater is the power of the mind over the emotions, as experience also testifies. For we see, that the pain arising from the loss of any good is mitigated, as soon as the man who has lost it perceives, that it could not by any means have been preserved. So also we see that no one pities an infant, because it cannot speak, walk, or reason, or lastly, because it passes so many years, as it were, in unconsciousness. Whereas, if most people were born full-grown and only one here and there as an infant, everyone would pity the infants; because infancy would not then be looked on as a state natural and necessary, but as a fault or delinquency in Nature; and we may note several other instances of the same sort.

Prop. VII. *Emotions which are aroused or spring from reason, if we take account of time, are stronger than those, which are attributable to particular objects that we regard as absent.*

Proof.—We do not regard a thing as absent, by reason of the emotion wherewith we conceive it, but by reason of the body being affected by another emotion excluding the existence of the said thing (II. xvii.). Wherefore, the emotion, which is referred to the thing which we regard as absent, is not of a nature to overcome the rest of a man's activities and power (IV. vi.), but is, on the contrary, of a nature to be in some sort controlled by the emotions, which exclude the existence of its external cause (IV. ix.). But an emotion which springs from reason is necessarily referred to the common properties of things (see the def. of reason in II. xl. note ii.), which we always regard as present (for there can be nothing to exclude their present existence), and which we always conceive in the same manner (II. xxxviii.). Wherefore an emotion of this kind always remains the same; and consequently (V. Ax. i.) emotions, which are contrary thereto and are not kept going by their external causes, will be obliged to adapt themselves to it more and more, until they are no longer contrary to it; to this extent the emotion which springs from reason is more powerful. *Q.E.D.*

PROP. VIII. *An emotion is stronger in proportion to the number of simultaneous concurrent causes whereby it is aroused.*

Proof.—Many simultaneous causes are more powerful than a few (III. vii.): therefore (IV. v.), in proportion to the increased number of simultaneous causes whereby it is aroused, an emotion becomes stronger. *Q.E.D.*

Note.—This proposition is also evident from V. Ax. ii.

PROP. IX. *An emotion, which is attributable to many and diverse causes which the mind regards as simultaneous with the emotion itself, is less hurtful, and we are less subject thereto and less affected towards each of its causes, than if it were a different and equally powerful emotion attributable to fewer causes or to a single cause.*

Proof.—An emotion is only bad or hurtful, in so far as it hinders the mind from being able to think (IV. xxvi. xxvii.); therefore, an emotion, whereby the mind is determined to the contemplation of several things at once, is less hurtful than another equally powerful emotion, which so engrosses the mind in the single contemplation of a few objects or of one, that it is unable to think of anything else; this was our first point. Again, as the mind's essence, in other words, its power (III. vii.), consists solely in thought (II. xi.), the mind is less passive in respect to an emotion, which causes it to think of several things at once, than in regard to an equally strong emotion, which keeps it engrossed in the contemplation of a few or of a single object: this was our second point. Lastly, this emotion (III. xlviii.), in so far as it is attributable to several causes, is less powerful in regard to each of them. *Q.E.D.*

PROP. X. *So long as we are not assailed by emotions contrary to our nature, we have the power of arranging and associating the modifications of our body according to the intellectual order.*

Proof.—The emotions, which are contrary to our nature, that is (IV. xxx.), which are bad, are bad in so far as they impede the mind from understanding (IV. xxvii.). So long, therefore, as we are not assailed by emotions contrary to our nature, the mind's power, whereby it endeavours to understand things (IV. xxvi.), is not impeded, and therefore it is able to form clear and distinct ideas and to deduce them one from another (II. xl. note ii. and xlvii. note); consequently we have in such cases the power of arranging and associating the modifications of the body according to the intellectual order. *Q.E.D.*

Note.—By this power of rightly arranging and associating the bodily modifications we can guard ourselves from being easily affected by evil emotions. For (V. vii.) a greater force is needed for controlling the emotions, when they are arranged and associated according to the intellectual order, than when they are uncertain and unsettled. The best we can do, therefore, so long as we do not possess a perfect knowledge of our emotions, is to frame a system of right conduct, or fixed practical precepts, to commit it to memory, and to apply it forthwith[1] to the particular cir-

[1] *Continuo.* Rendered "constantly" by Mr. Pollock on the ground that the classical meaning of the word does not suit the context. I venture to think, however, that a tolerable sense may be obtained without doing violence to Spinoza's scholarship.

cumstances which now and again meet us in life, so that our imagination may become fully imbued therewith, and that it may be always ready to our hand. For instance, we have laid down among the rules of life (IV. xlvi. and note), that hatred should be overcome with love or high-mindedness, and not requited with hatred in return. Now, that this precept of reason may be always ready to our hand in time of need, we should often think over and reflect upon the wrongs generally committed by men, and in what manner and way they may be best warded off by high-mindedness: we shall thus associate the idea of wrong with the idea of this precept, which accordingly will always be ready for use when a wrong is done to us (II. xviii.) If we keep also in readiness the notion of our true advantage, and of the good which follows from mutual friendships, and common fellowships; further, if we remember that complete acquiescence is the result of the right way of life (IV. lii.), and that men, no less than everything else, act by the necessity of their nature: in such case I say the wrong, or the hatred, which commonly arises therefrom, will engross a very small part of our imagination and will be easily overcome; or, if the anger which springs from a grievous wrong be not overcome easily, it will nevertheless be overcome, though not without a spiritual conflict, far sooner than if we had not thus reflected on the subject beforehand. As is indeed evident from V. vi. vii. viii. We should, in the same way, reflect on courage as a means of overcoming fear; the ordinary dangers of life should frequently be brought to mind and imagined, together with the means whereby through readiness of resource and strength of mind we can avoid and overcome them. But we must note, that in arranging our thoughts and conceptions we should always bear in mind that which is good in every individual thing (IV. lxiii. Coroll. and III. lix.), in order that we may always be determined to action by an emotion of pleasure. For instance, if a man sees that he is too keen in the pursuit of honour, let him think over its right use, the end for which it should be pursued, and the means whereby he may attain it. Let him not think of its misuse, and its emptiness, and the fickleness of mankind, and the like, whereof no man thinks except through a morbidness of disposition; with thoughts like these do the most ambitious most torment themselves, when they despair of gaining the distinctions they hanker after, and in thus giving vent to their anger would fain appear wise. Wherefore it is certain that those, who cry out the loudest against the misuse of honour and the vanity of the world, are those who most greedily covet it. This is not peculiar to the ambitious, but is common to all who are ill-used by fortune, and who are infirm in spirit. For a poor man also, who is miserly, will talk incessantly of the misuse of wealth and of the vices of the rich; whereby he merely torments himself, and shows the world that he is intolerant, not only of his own poverty, but also of other people's riches. So, again, those who have been ill received by a woman they love think of nothing but the inconstancy, treachery, and other stock faults of the fair sex; all of which they consign to oblivion, directly they are again taken into favour by their sweetheart. Thus he who would govern his emotions and appetite solely by the love of freedom strives, as far as he can, to gain a knowledge of the virtues and their causes, and to fill his spirit with the joy which arises from the true knowledge of them: he will in no wise desire to dwell on men's faults, or to carp at his fellows, or to revel in a false show of freedom. Whosoever will diligently observe and practise these precepts (which indeed are not difficult) will verily, in a short space of time, be able, for the most part, to direct his actions according to the commandments of reason.

PROP. XI. *In proportion as a mental image is referred to more objects, so is it more frequent, or more often vivid, and occupies the mind more.*

Proof.—In proportion as a mental image or an emotion is referred to more objects, so are there more causes whereby it can be aroused and fostered, all of which (by hypothesis) the mind contemplates simultaneously in association with the given emotion; therefore the emotion is more frequent, or is more often in full vigour, and (V. viii.) occupies the mind more. *Q.E.D.*

PROP. XII. *The mental images of things are more easily associated with the images referred to things which we clearly and distinctly understand, than with others.*

Proof.—Things, which we clearly and distinctly understand, are either the common properties of things or deductions therefrom (see definition of Reason, II. xl. note ii.), and are consequently (by the last Prop.) more often aroused in us. Wherefore it may more readily happen, that we should contemplate other things in conjunction with these than in conjunction with something else, and consequently (II. xviii.) that the images of the said things should be more often associated with the images of these than with the images of something else. *Q.E.D.*

PROP. XIII. *A mental image is more often vivid, in proportion as it is associated with a greater number of other images.*

Proof.—In proportion as an image is associated with a greater number of other images, so (II. xviii.) are there more causes whereby it can be aroused. *Q.E.D.*

PROP. XIV. *The mind can bring it about, that all bodily modifications or images of things may be referred to the idea of God.*

Proof.—There is no modification of the body, whereof the mind may not form some clear and distinct conception (V. iv.); wherefore it can bring it about, that they should all be referred to the idea of God (I. xv.). *Q.E.D.*

PROP. XV. *He who clearly and distinctly understands himself and his emotions loves God, and so much the more in proportion as he more understands himself and his emotions.*

Proof.—He who clearly and distinctly understands himself and his emotions feels pleasure (III. liii.), and this pleasure is (by the last Prop.) accompanied by the idea of God; therefore (Def. of the Emotions, vi.) such an one loves God, and (for the same reason) so much the more in proportion as he more understands himself and his emotions. *Q.E.D.*

PROP. XVI. *This love towards God must hold the chief place in the mind.*

Proof.—For this love is associated with all the modifications of the body (V. xiv.) and is fostered by them all (V. xv.); therefore (V. xi.), it must hold the chief place in the mind. *Q.E.D.*

PROP. XVII. *God is without passions, neither is he affected by any emotion of pleasure or pain.*

Proof.—All ideas, in so far as they are referred to God, are true (II. xxxii.), that is (II. Def. iv.) adequate; and therefore (by the general Def. of the Emotions) God is without passions. Again, God cannot pass either to a greater or to a lesser perfection (I. xx. Coroll. ii.); therefore (by Def. of the Emotions, ii. iii.) he is not affected by any emotion of pleasure or pain.

Corollary.—Strictly speaking, God does not love or hate anyone. For God (by the foregoing Prop.) is not affected by any emotion of pleasure or pain, consequently (Def. of the Emotions, vi. vii.) he does not love or hate anyone.

PROP. XVIII. *No one can hate God.*

Proof.—The idea of God which is in us is adequate and perfect (II. xlvi. xlvii.); wherefore, in so far as we contemplate God, we are active (III. iii.); consequently (III. lix.) there can be no pain accompanied by the idea of God, in other words (Def. of the Emotions, vii.), no one can hate God. *Q.E.D.*

Corollary.—Love towards God cannot be turned into hate.

Note.—It may be objected that, as we understand God as the cause of all things, we by that very fact regard God as the cause of pain. But I make answer, that, in so far as we understand the causes of pain, it to that extent (V. iii.) ceases to be a passion, that is, it ceases to be pain (III. lix.); therefore, in so far as we understand God to be the cause of pain, we to that extent feel pleasure.

PROP. XIX. *He, who loves God, cannot endeavour that God should love him in return.*

Proof.—For, if a man should so endeavour, he would desire (V. xvii. Coroll.) that God, whom he loves, should not be God, and consequently he would desire to feel pain (III. xix.); which is absurd (III. xxviii.). Therefore, he who loves God, &c. *Q.E.D.*

PROP. XX. *This love towards God cannot be stained by the emotion of envy or jealousy: contrariwise, it is the more fostered, in proportion as we conceive a greater number of men to be joined to God by the same bond of love.*

Proof.—This love towards God is the highest good which we can seek for under the guidance of reason (IV. xxviii.), it is common to all men (IV. xxxvi.), and we desire that all should rejoice therein (IV. xxxvii.); therefore (Def. of the Emotions, xxiii.), it cannot be stained by the emotion of envy, nor by the emotion of jealousy (V. xviii. see definition of Jealousy, III. xxxv. note); but, contrariwise, it must needs be the more fostered, in proportion as we conceive a greater number of men to rejoice therein. *Q.E.D.*

Note.—We can in the same way show, that there is no emotion directly contrary to this love, whereby this love can be destroyed; therefore we may conclude, that this love towards God is the most constant of all the emotions, and that, in so far as it is referred to the body, it cannot be destroyed, unless the body be destroyed also. As to its nature, in so far as it is referred to the mind only, we shall presently inquire.

I have now gone through all the remedies against the emotions, or all that the mind, considered in itself alone, can do against them. Whence it appears that the mind's power over the emotions consists :—

I. In the actual knowledge of the emotions (V. iv. note).

II. In the fact that it separates the emotions from the thought of an external cause, which we conceive confusedly (V. ii. and iv. note).

III. In the fact, that, in respect to time, the emotions referred to things, which we distinctly understand, surpass those referred to what we conceive in a confused and fragmentary manner (V. vii.).

IV. In the number of causes whereby those modifications[1] are fostered, which have regard to the common properties of things or to God (V. ix. xi.).

V. Lastly, in the order wherein the mind can arrange and associate, one with another, its own emotions (V. x. note and xii. xiii. xiv.).

But, in order that this power of the mind over the emotions may be better understood, it should be specially observed that the emotions are called by us strong, when we compare the emotion of one man with the emotion of another, and see that one man is more troubled than another by the same emotion; or when we are comparing the various emotions of the same man one with another, and

[1] *Affectiones.* Camerer reads *affectus*—emotions.

find that he is more affected or stirred by one emotion than by another. For the strength of every emotion is defined by a comparison of our own power with the power of an external cause. Now the power of the mind is defined by knowledge only, and its infirmity or passion is defined by the privation of knowledge only: it therefore follows, that that mind is most passive, whose greatest part is made up of inadequate ideas, so that it may be characterized more readily by its passive states than by its activities: on the other hand, that mind is most active, whose greatest part is made up of adequate ideas, so that, although it may contain as many inadequate ideas as the former mind, it may yet be more easily characterized by ideas attributable to human virtue, than by ideas which tell of human infirmity. Again, it must be observed, that spiritual unhealthiness and misfortunes can generally be traced to excessive love for something which is subject to many variations, and which we can never become masters of. For no one is solicitous or anxious about anything, unless he loves it; neither do wrongs, suspicions, enmities, &c. arise, except in regard to things whereof no one can be really master.

We may thus readily conceive the power which clear and distinct knowledge, and especially that third kind of knowledge (II. xlvii. note), founded on the actual knowledge of God, possesses over the emotions: if it does not absolutely destroy them, in so far as they are passions (V. iii. and iv. note); at any rate, it causes them to occupy a very small part of the mind (V. xiv.). Further, it begets a love towards a thing immutable and eternal (V. xv.), whereof we may really enter into possession (II. xlv.); neither can it be defiled with those faults which are inherent in ordinary love; but it may grow from strength to strength, and may engross the greater part of the mind, and deeply penetrate it.

And now I have finished with all that concerns this present life: for, as I said in the beginning of this note, I have briefly described all the remedies against the emotions. And this everyone may readily have seen for himself, if he has attended to what is advanced in the present note, and also to the definitions of the mind and its emotions, and, lastly, to Propositions i. and iii. of Part III. It is now, therefore, time to pass on to those matters, which appertain to the duration of the mind, without relation to the body.

PROP. XXI. *The mind can only imagine anything, or remember what is past, while the body endures.*

Proof.—The mind does not express the actual existence of its body, nor does it imagine the modifications of the body as actual, except while the body endures (II. viii. Coroll.); and, consequently (II. xxvi.), it does not imagine any body as actually existing, except while its own body endures. Thus it cannot imagine anything (for definition of Imagination, see II. xvii. note), or remember things past, except while the body endures (see definition of Memory, II. xviii. note). *Q.E.D.*

PROP. XXII. *Nevertheless in God there is necessarily an idea, which expresses the essence of this or that human body under the form of eternity.*

Proof.—God is the cause, not only of the existence of this or that human body, but also of its essence (I. xxv.). This essence, therefore, must necessarily be conceived through the very essence of God (I. Ax. iv.), and be thus conceived by a certain eternal necessity (I. xvi.); and this conception must necessarily exist in God (II. iii.). *Q.E.D.*

PROP. XXIII. *The human mind cannot be absolutely destroyed with the body, but there remains of it something which is eternal.*

Proof.—There is necessarily in God a concept or idea, which expresses the essence of the human body (last Prop.), which, therefore, is necessarily something appertaining to the essence of the human mind (II. xiii.). But we have not assigned to the human mind any duration, definable by time, except in so far as it expresses the actual existence of the body, which is explained through duration, and may be defined by time—that is (II. viii. Coroll.), we do not assign to it duration, except while the body endures. Yet, as there is something, notwithstanding, which is conceived by a certain eternal necessity through the very essence of God (last Prop.); this something, which appertains to the essence of the mind, will necessarily be eternal. *Q.E.D.*

Note.—This idea, which expresses the essence of the body under the form of eternity, is, as we have said, a certain mode of thinking, which belongs to the essence of the mind, and is necessarily eternal. Yet it is not possible that we should remember that we existed before our body, for our body can bear no trace of such existence, neither can eternity be defined in terms of time, or have any relation to time. But, notwithstanding, we feel and know that we are eternal. For the mind feels those things that it conceives by understanding, no less than those things that it remembers. For the eyes of the mind, whereby it sees and observes things, are none other than proofs. Thus, although we do not remember that we existed before the body, yet we feel that our mind, in so far as it involves the essence of the body, under the form of eternity, is eternal, and that thus its existence cannot be defined in terms of time, or explained through duration. Thus our mind can only be said to endure, and its existence can only be defined by a fixed time, in so far as it involves the actual existence of the body. Thus far only has it the power of determining the existence of things by time, and conceiving them under the category of duration.

PROP. XXIV. *The more we understand particular things, the more do we understand God.*

Proof.—This is evident from I. xxv. Coroll.

PROP. XXV. *The highest endeavour of the mind, and the highest virtue is to understand things by the third kind of knowledge.*

Proof.—The third kind of knowledge proceeds from an adequate idea of certain attributes of God to an adequate knowledge of the essence of things (see its definition II. xl. note ii.); and, in proportion as we understand things more in this way, we better understand God (by the last Prop.); therefore (IV. xxviii.) the highest virtue of the mind, that is (IV. Def. viii.) the power, or nature, or (III. vii.) highest endeavour of the mind, is to understand things by the third kind of knowledge. *Q.E.D.*

PROP. XXVI. *In proportion as the mind is more capable of understanding things by the third kind of knowledge, it desires more to understand things by that kind.*

Proof.—This is evident. For, in so far as we conceive the mind to be capable of conceiving things by this kind of knowledge, we, to that extent, conceive it as determined thus to conceive things; and consequently (Def. of the Emotions, i.), the mind desires so to do, in proportion as it is more capable thereof. *Q.E.D.*

PROP. XXVII. *From this third kind of knowledge arises the highest possible mental acquiescence.*

Proof.—The highest virtue of the mind is to know God (IV. xxviii.), or to understand things by the third kind of knowledge (V. xxv.), and this virtue is greater in proportion as the mind knows things more by the said kind of knowledge (V. xxiv.): consequently, he who knows things by this kind of knowledge passes to the summit of human perfection, and is therefore (Def. of the Emotions, ii.) affected by the highest pleasure, such pleasure being accompanied by the idea of himself and his own virtue; thus (Def. of the Emotions, xxv.), from this kind of knowledge arises the highest possible acquiescence. *Q.E.D.*

PROP. XXVIII. *The endeavour or desire to know things by the third kind of knowledge cannot arise from the first, but from the second kind of knowledge.*

Proof.—This proposition is self-evident. For whatsoever we understand clearly and distinctly, we understand either through itself, or through that which is conceived through itself; that is, ideas which are clear and distinct in us, or which are referred to the third kind of knowledge (II. xl. note ii.) cannot follow from ideas that are fragmentary and confused, and are referred to knowledge of the first kind, but must follow from adequate ideas, or ideas of the second and third kind of knowledge; therefore (Def. of the Emotions, i.), the desire of knowing things by the third kind of knowledge cannot arise from the first, but from the second kind. *Q.E.D.*

PROP. XXIX. *Whatsoever the mind understands under the form of eternity, it does not understand by virtue of conceiving the present actual existence of the body, but by virtue of conceiving the essence of the body under the form of eternity.*

Proof.—In so far as the mind conceives the present existence of its body, it to that extent conceives duration which can be determined by time, and to that extent only has it the power of conceiving things in relation to time (V. xxi. II. xxvi.). But eternity cannot be explained in terms of duration (I. Def. viii. and explanation). Therefore to this extent the mind has not the power of conceiving things under the form of eternity, but it possesses such power, because it is of the nature of reason to conceive things under the form of eternity (II. xliv. Coroll. ii.), and also because it is of the nature of the mind to conceive the essence of the body under the form of eternity (V. xxiii.), for besides these two there is nothing which belongs to the essence of mind (II. xiii.). Therefore this power of conceiving things under the form of eternity only belongs to the mind in virtue of the mind's conceiving the essence of the body under the form of eternity. *Q.E.D.*

Note.—Things are conceived by us as actual in two ways; either as existing in relation to a given time and place, or as contained in God and following from the necessity of the divine nature. Whatsoever we conceive in this second way as true or real, we conceive under the form of eternity, and their ideas involve the eternal and infinite essence of God, as we showed in II. xlv. and note, which see.

PROP. XXX. *Our mind, in so far as it knows itself and the body under the form of eternity, has to that extent necessarily a knowledge of God, and knows that it is in God, and is conceived through God.*

Proof.—Eternity is the very essence of God, in so far as this involves necessary existence (I. Def. viii.). Therefore to conceive things under the form of eternity, is to conceive things in so far as they are conceived through the essence of God as real entities, or in so far as they involve existence through the essence of God; wherefore our mind, in so far as it conceives itself and the body under the form of eternity, has to that extent necessarily a knowledge of God, and knows, &c. *Q.E.D.*

PROP. XXXI. *The third kind of knowledge depends on the mind, as its formal cause, in so far as the mind itself is eternal.*

Proof.—The mind does not conceive anything under the form of eternity, except in so far as it conceives its own body under the form of eternity (V. xxix.); that is, except in so far as it is eternal (V. xxi. xxiii.); therefore (by the last Prop.), in so far as it is eternal, it possesses the knowledge of God, which knowledge is necessarily adequate (II. xlvi.); hence the mind, in so far as it is eternal, is capable of knowing everything which can follow from this given knowledge of God (II. xl.), in other words, of knowing things by the third kind of knowledge (see Def. in II. xl. note ii.), whereof accordingly the mind (III. Def. i.), in so far as it is eternal, is the adequate or formal cause of such knowledge. *Q.E.D.*

Note.—In proportion, therefore, as a man is more potent in this kind of knowledge, he will be more completely conscious of himself and of God; in other words, he will be more perfect and blessed, as will appear more clearly in the sequel. But we must here observe that, although we are already certain that the mind is eternal, in so far as it conceives things under the form of eternity, yet, in order that what we wish to show may be more readily explained and better understood, we will consider the mind itself, as though it had just begun to exist and to understand things under the form of eternity, as indeed we have done hitherto; this we may do without any danger of error, so long as we are careful not to draw any conclusion, unless our premisses are plain.

PROP. XXXII. *Whatsoever we understand by the third kind of knowledge, we take delight in, and our delight is accompanied by the idea of God as cause.*

Proof.—From this kind of knowledge arises the highest possible mental acquiescence, that is (Def. of the Emotions, xxv.), pleasure, and this acquiescence is accompanied by the idea of the mind itself (V. xxvii.), and consequently (V. xxx.) the idea also of God as cause. *Q.E.D.*

Corollary.—From the third kind of knowledge necessarily arises the intellectual love of God. From this kind of knowledge arises pleasure accompanied by the idea of God as cause, that is (Def. of the Emotions, vi.), the love of God; not in so far as we imagine him as present (V. xxix.), but in so far as we understand him to be eternal; this is what I call the intellectual love of God.

PROP. XXXIII. *The intellectual love of God, which arises from the third kind of knowledge, is eternal.*

Proof.—The third kind of knowledge is eternal (V. xxxi. I. Ax. iii.); therefore (by the same Axiom) the love which arises therefrom is also necessarily eternal. *Q.E.D.*

Note.—Although this love towards God has (by the foregoing Prop.) no beginning, it yet possesses all the perfections of love, just as though it had arisen as we feigned in the Coroll. of the last Prop. Nor is there here any difference, except that the mind possesses as eternal those same perfections which we feigned to accrue to it, and they are accompanied by the idea of God as eternal cause. If pleasure consists in the transition to a greater perfection, assuredly blessedness must consist in the mind being endowed with perfection itself.

PROP. XXXIV. *The mind is, only while the body endures, subject to those emotions which are attributable to passions.*

Proof.—Imagination is the idea wherewith the mind contemplates a thing as present (II. xvii. note); yet this idea indicates rather the present disposition of the human body than the nature of the external thing (II. xvi. Coroll. ii.). Therefore emotion (see general Def. of Emotions) is imagination, in so far as it indicates the present disposition of the body; therefore (V. xxi.) the mind is, only while the body endures, subject to emotions which are attributable to passions. *Q.E.D.*

Corollary.—Hence it follows that no love save intellectual love is eternal.

Note.—If we look to men's general opinion, we shall see that they are indeed conscious of the eternity of their mind, but that they confuse eternity with duration, and ascribe it to the imagination or the memory which they believe to remain after death.

PROP. XXXV. *God loves himself with an infinite intellectual love.*

Proof.—God is absolutely infinite (I. Def. vi.), that is (II. Def. vi.), the nature of God rejoices in infinite perfection; and such rejoicing is (II. iii.) accompanied by the idea of himself, that is (I. xi. and Def. i.), the idea of his own cause: now this is what we have (in V. xxxii. Coroll.) described as intellectual love.

PROP. XXXVI. *The intellectual love of the mind towards God is that very love of God whereby God loves himself, not in so far as he is infinite, but in so far as he can be explained through the essence of the human mind regarded under the form of eternity; in other words, the intellectual love of the mind towards God is part of the infinite love wherewith God loves himself.*

Proof.—This love of the mind must be referred to the activities of the mind (V. xxxii. Coroll. and III. iii.); it is itself, indeed, an activity whereby the mind regards itself accompanied by the idea of God as cause (V. xxxii. and Coroll.); that is (I. xxv. Coroll. and II. xi. Coroll.), an activity whereby God, in so far as he can be explained through the human mind, regards himself accompanied by the idea of himself; therefore (by the last Prop.), this love of the mind is part of the infinite love wherewith God loves himself. *Q.E.D.*

Corollary.—Hence it follows that God, in so far as he loves himself, loves man, and, consequently, that the love of God towards men, and the intellectual love of the mind towards God are identical.

Note.—From what has been said we clearly understand, wherein our salvation, or blessedness, or freedom, consists: namely, in the constant and eternal love towards God, or in God's love towards men. This love or blessedness is, in the Bible, called Glory, and not undeservedly. For whether this love be referred to God or to the mind, it may rightly be called acquiescence of spirit, which (Def. of the Emotions, xxv. xxx.) is not really distinguished from glory. In so far as it is referred to God, it is (V. xxxv.) pleasure, if we may still use that term, accompanied by the idea of itself, and, in so far as it is referred to the mind, it is the same (V. xxvii.).

Again, since the essence of our mind consists solely in knowledge, whereof the beginning and the foundation is God (I. xv. and II. xlvii. note), it becomes clear to us, in what manner and way our mind, as to its essence and existence, follows from the divine nature and constantly depends on God. I have thought it worth while here to call attention to this, in order to show by this example how the knowledge of particular things, which I have called intuitive or of the third kind (II. xl. note ii.), is potent, and more powerful than the universal knowledge, which I have styled knowledge of the second kind. For, although in Part I. I showed in general terms, that all things (and consequently, also, the human mind) depend as to their essence and existence on God, yet that demonstration, though legitimate and placed beyond the chances of doubt, does not affect our mind so much, as when the same conclusion is derived from the actual essence of some particular thing, which we say depends on God.

PROP. XXXVII. *There is nothing in nature, which is contrary to this intellectual love, or which can take it away,*

Proof.—This intellectual love follows necessarily from the nature of the mind, in so far as the latter is regarded through the nature of God as an eternal truth (V. xxxiii. and xxix.). If, therefore, there should be anything which would be contrary to this love, that thing would be contrary to that which is true; consequently, that, which should be able to take away this love, would cause that which is true to be false; an obvious absurdity. Therefore there is nothing in nature which, &c. *Q.E.D.*

Note.—The Axiom of Part IV. has reference to particular things, in so far as they are regarded in relation to a given time and place: of this, I think, no one can doubt.

PROP. XXXVIII. *In proportion as the mind understands more things by the second and third kind of knowledge, it is less subject to those emotions which are evil, and stands in less fear of death.*

Proof.—The mind's essence consists in knowledge (II. xi.); therefore, in proportion as the mind understands more things by the second and third kinds of knowledge, the greater will be the part of it that endures (V. xxix. and xxiii.), and, consequently (by the last Prop.), the greater will be the part that is not touched by the emotions, which are contrary to our nature, or in other words, evil (IV. xxx.). Thus, in proportion as the mind understands more things by the second and third kinds of knowledge, the greater will be the part of it, that remains unimpaired, and, consequently, less subject to emotions, &c. *Q.E.D.*

Note.—Hence we understand that point which I touched on in IV. xxxix. note, and which I promised to explain in this Part; namely, that death becomes less hurtful, in proportion as the mind's clear and distinct knowledge is greater, and, consequently, in proportion as the mind loves God more. Again, since from the third kind of knowledge arises the highest possible acquiescence (V. xxvii.), it follows that the human mind can attain to being of such a nature, that the part thereof which we have shown to perish with the body (V. xxi.) should be of little importance when compared with the part which endures. But I will soon treat of the subject at greater length.

PROP. XXXIX. *He, who possesses a body capable of the greatest number of activities, possesses a mind whereof the greatest part is eternal.*

Proof.—He, who possesses a body capable of the greatest number of activities, is least agitated by those emotions which are evil (IV. xxxviii.)—that is (IV. xxx.), by those emotions which are contrary to our nature; therefore (V. x.), he possesses the power of arranging and associating the modifications of the body according to the intellectual order, and, consequently, of bringing it about, that all the modifications of the body should be referred to the idea of God; whence it will come to pass that (V. xv.) he will be affected with love towards God, which (V. xvi.) must occupy or constitute the chief part of the mind; therefore (V. xxxiii.), such a man will possess a mind whereof the chief part is eternal. *Q.E.D.*

Note.—Since human bodies are capable of the greatest number of activities, there is no doubt but that they may be of such a nature, that they may be referred to minds possessing a great knowledge of themselves and of God, and whereof the greatest or chief part is eternal, and, therefore, that they should scarcely fear death. But, in order that this may be understood more clearly, we must here call to mind, that we live in a state of perpetual variation, and, according as we are changed for the better or the worse, we are called happy or unhappy.

For he, who, from being an infant or a child, becomes a corpse, is called unhappy; whereas it is set down to happiness, if we have been able to live through the whole period of life with a sound mind in a sound body. And, in reality, he, who, as in the case of an infant or a child, has a body capable of very few activities, and depending, for the most part, on external causes, has a mind which, considered in itself alone, is scarcely conscious of itself, or of

God, or of things; whereas, he, who has a body capable of very many activities, has a mind which, considered in itself alone, is highly conscious of itself, of God, and of things. In this life, therefore, we primarily endeavour to bring it about, that the body of a child, in so far as its nature allows and conduces thereto, may be changed into something else capable of very many activities, and referable to a mind which is highly conscious of itself, of God, and of things; and we desire so to change it, that what is referred to its imagination and memory may become insignificant, in comparison with its intellect, as I have already said in the note to the last Proposition.

PROP. XL. *In proportion as each thing possesses more of perfection, so is it more active, and less passive; and, vice versâ, in proportion as it is more active, so is it more perfect.*

Proof.—In proportion as each thing is more perfect, it possesses more of reality (II. Def. vi.), and, consequently (III. iii. and note), it is to that extent more active and less passive. This demonstration may be reversed, and thus prove that, in proportion as a thing is more active, so is it more perfect. *Q.E.D.*

Corollary.—Hence it follows that the part of the mind which endures, be it great or small, is more perfect than the rest. For the eternal part of the mind (V. xxiii. xxix.) is the understanding, through which alone we are said to act (III. iii.); the part which we have shown to perish is the imagination (V. xxi.), through which only we are said to be passive (III. iii. and general Def. of the Emotions); therefore, the former, be it great or small, is more perfect than the latter. *Q.E.D.*

Note.—Such are the doctrines which I had purposed to set forth concerning the mind, in so far as it is regarded without relation to the body; whence, as also from I. xxi. and other places, it is plain that our mind, in so far as it understands, is an eternal mode of thinking, which is determined by another eternal mode of thinking, and this other by a third, and so on to infinity; so that all taken together at once constitute the eternal and infinite intellect of God.

PROP. XLI. *Even if we did not know that our mind is*

eternal, we should still consider as of primary importance piety and religion, and generally all things which, in Part IV., we showed to be attributable to courage and high-mindedness.

Proof.—The first and only foundation of virtue, or the rule of right living is (IV. xxii. Coroll. and xxiv.) seeking one's own true interest. Now, while we determined what reason prescribes as useful, we took no account of the mind's eternity, which has only become known to us in this Fifth Part. Although we were ignorant at that time that the mind is eternal, we nevertheless stated that the qualities attributable to courage and high-mindedness are of primary importance. Therefore, even if we were still ignorant of this doctrine, we should yet put the aforesaid precepts of reason in the first place. *Q.E.D.*

Note.—The general belief of the multitude seems to be different. Most people seem to believe that they are free, in so far as they may obey their lusts, and that they cede their rights, in so far as they are bound to live according to the commandments of the divine law. They therefore believe that piety, religion, and, generally, all things attributable to firmness of mind, are burdens, which, after death, they hope to lay aside, and to receive the reward for their bondage, that is, for their piety and religion; it is not only by this hope, but also, and chiefly, by the fear of being horribly punished after death, that they are induced to live according to the divine commandments, so far as their feeble and infirm spirit will carry them.

If men had not this hope and this fear, but believed that the mind perishes with the body, and that no hope of prolonged life remains for the wretches who are broken down with the burden of piety, they would return to their own inclinations, controlling everything in accordance with their lusts, and desiring to obey fortune rather than themselves. Such a course appears to me not less absurd than if a man, because he does not believe that he can by wholesome food sustain his body for ever, should wish to cram himself with poisons and deadly fare; or if, because he sees that the mind is not eternal or immortal, he should prefer to be out of his mind altogether, and to live without the use of reason; these ideas are so absurd as to be scarcely worth refuting.

PROP. XLII. *Blessedness is not the reward of virtue, but virtue itself; neither do we rejoice therein, because we control our lusts, but, contrariwise, because we rejoice therein, we are able to control our lusts.*

Proof.—Blessedness consists in love towards God (V. xxxvi. and note), which love springs from the third kind of knowledge (V. xxxii. Coroll.); therefore this love (III. iii. lix.) must be referred to the mind, in so far as the latter is active; therefore (IV. Def. viii.) it is virtue itself. This was our first point. Again, in proportion as the mind rejoices more in this divine love or blessedness, so does it the more understand (V. xxxii.); that is (V. iii. Coroll.), so much the more power has it over the emotions, and (V. xxxviii.) so much the less is it subject to those emotions which are evil; therefore, in proportion as the mind rejoices in this divine love or blessedness, so has it the power of controlling lusts. And, since human power in controlling the emotions consists solely in the understanding, it follows that no one rejoices in blessedness, because he has controlled his lusts, but, contrariwise, his power of controlling his lusts arises from this blessedness itself. *Q.E.D.*

Note.—I have thus completed all I wished to set forth touching the mind's power over the emotions and the mind's freedom. Whence it appears, how potent is the wise man, and how much he surpasses the ignorant man, who is driven only by his lusts. For the ignorant man is not only distracted in various ways by external causes without ever gaining the true acquiescence of his spirit, but moreover lives, as it were unwitting of himself, and of God, and of things, and as soon as he ceases to suffer, ceases also to be.

Whereas the wise man, in so far as he is regarded as such, is scarcely at all disturbed in spirit, but, being conscious of himself, and of God, and of things, by a certain eternal necessity, never ceases to be, but always possesses true acquiescence of his spirit.

If the way which I have pointed out as leading to this result seems exceedingly hard, it may nevertheless be discovered. Needs must it be hard, since it is so seldom found. How would it be possible, if salvation were ready to our hand, and could without great labour be found, that it should be by almost all men neglected? But all things excellent are as difficult as they are rare.

CORRESPONDENCE.

CORRESPONDENCE.

LETTER I. (I.[1])

HENRY OLDENBURG[2] TO B. DE SPINOZA.

[*Oldenburg, after complimenting Spinoza, asks him to enter into a philosophical correspondence.*]

ILLUSTRIOUS SIR, AND MOST WORTHY FRIEND,—So painful to me was the separation from you the other day after our meeting in your retreat at Rhijnsburg, that it is my first endeavour, now that I am returned to England, to renew, as far as is possible by correspondence, my intercourse with you. Solid learning, conjoined with courtesy and refinement of manners (wherewith both nature and art have most amply endowed you), carries with it such charms as to command the love of every honourable and liberally-educated man. Let us then, most excellent sir, join hands in sincere friendship, and let us foster the feeling with every zealous endeavour and kind office in our power. Whatever my poor means can furnish I beg you to look on as your own. Allow me in return to claim a share in the riches of your talents, as I may do without inflicting any loss on yourself.

We conversed at Rhijnsburg of God, of extension, of infinite thought, of the differences and agreements between these, of the nature of the connection between the human soul and body, and further, of the principles of the Cartesian and Baconian philosophies.

But, as we then spoke of these great questions merely cursorily and by the way, and as my mind has been not a

[1] The number of each letter as arranged in Van Vloten's edition is given in brackets.

[2] See Introduction, p. xvi.

little tormented with them since, I will appeal to the rights of our newly cemented friendship, and most affectionately beg you to give me at somewhat greater length your opinion on the subjects I have mentioned. On two points especially I ask for enlightenment, if I may presume so far; *first:* In what do you place the true distinction between thought and matter? *secondly:* What do you consider to be the chief defects in the Cartesian and Baconian philosophies, and how do you think they might best be removed, and something more sound substituted? The more freely you write to me on these and similar subjects, the more closely will you tie the bonds of our friendship, and the stricter will be the obligation laid on me to repay you, as far as possible, with similar services.

There is at present in the press a collection of physiological discourses written by an Englishman of noble family and distinguished learning.[1] They treat of the nature and elasticity of the air, as proved by forty-three experiments; also of its fluidity, solidity, and other analogous matters. As soon as the work is published, I shall make a point of sending it to you by any friend who may be crossing the sea. Meanwhile, farewell, and remember your friend, who is

Yours, in all affection and zeal,

HENRY OLDENBURG.

London, $\frac{16}{26}$ Aug., 1661.

LETTER II. (II.)

SPINOZA TO OLDENBURG.

[*Answer to Letter I. Spinoza defines "God," and "attribute," and sends definitions, axioms, and first four propositions of Book I. of Ethics. Some errors of Bacon and Descartes discussed.*]

ILLUSTRIOUS SIR,—How pleasant your friendship is to me, you may yourself judge, if your modesty will allow you to reflect on the abundance of your own excellences. In-

[1] Robert Boyle.

deed the thought of these makes me seem not a little bold in entering into such a compact, the more so when I consider that between friends all things, and especially things spiritual, ought to be in common. However, this must lie at the charge of your modesty and kindness rather than of myself. You have been willing to lower yourself through the former and to fill me with the abundance of the latter, till I am no longer afraid to accept the close friendship, which you hold out to me, and which you deign to ask of me in return; no effort on my part shall be spared to render it lasting.

As for my mental endowments, such as they are, I would willingly allow you to share them, even though I knew it would be to my own great hindrance. But this is not meant as an excuse for denying to you what you ask by the rights of friendship. I will therefore endeavour to explain my opinions on the topics you touched on; though I scarcely hope, unless your kindness intervene, that I shall thus draw the bonds of our friendship closer.

I will then begin by speaking briefly of God, Whom I define as a Being consisting in infinite attributes, whereof each is infinite or supremely perfect after its kind. You must observe that by attribute I mean everything, which is conceived through itself and in itself, so that the conception of it does not involve the conception of anything else. For instance, extension is conceived through itself and in itself, but motion is not. The latter is conceived through something else, for the conception of it implies extension.

That the definition above given of God is true appears from the fact, that by God we mean a Being supremely perfect and absolutely infinite. That such a Being exists may easily be proved from the definition; but as this is not the place for such proof, I will pass it over. What I am bound here to prove, in order to satisfy the first inquiry of my distinguished questioner, are the following consequences; *first*, that in the universe there cannot exist two substances without their differing utterly in essence; *secondly*, that substance cannot be produced or created—existence pertains to its actual essence; *thirdly*, that all substance must be infinite or supremely perfect after its kind.

When these points have been demonstrated, my distinguished questioner will readily perceive my drift, if he reflects at the same time on the definition of God. In order to prove them clearly and briefly, I can think of nothing better than to submit them to the bar of your judgment proved in the geometrical method.[1] I therefore enclose them separately and await your verdict upon them.

Again, you ask me what errors I detect in the Cartesian and Baconian philosophies. It is not my custom to expose the errors of others, nevertheless I will yield to your request. The first and the greatest error is, that these philosophers have strayed so far from the knowledge of the first cause and origin of all things; the second is, that they did not know the true nature of the human mind; the third, that they never grasped the true cause of error. The necessity for correct knowledge on these three points can only be ignored by persons completely devoid of learning and training.

That they have wandered astray from the knowledge of the first cause, and of the human mind, may easily be gathered from the truth of the three propositions given above; I therefore devote myself entirely to the demonstration of the third error. Of Bacon I shall say very little, for he speaks very confusedly on the point, and works out scarcely any proofs: he simply narrates. In the first place he assumes, that the human intellect is liable to err, not only through the fallibility of the senses, but also solely through its own nature, and that it frames its conceptions in accordance with the analogy of its own nature, not with the analogy of the universe, so that it is like a mirror receiving rays from external objects unequally, and mingling its own nature with the nature of things, &c.

Secondly, that the human intellect is, by reason of its own nature, prone to abstractions; such things as are in flux it feigns to be constant, &c.

Thirdly, that the human intellect continually augments, and is unable to come to a stand or to rest content. The other causes which he assigns may all be reduced to the

[1] The allusion is to Eth. I., Beginning—Prop. iv.

one Cartesian principle, that the human will is free and more extensive than the intellect, or, as Verulam himself more confusedly puts it, that "the understanding is not a dry light, but receives infusion from the will."[1] (We may here observe that Verulam often employs "intellect" as synonymous with mind, differing in this respect from Descartes). This cause, then, leaving aside the others as unimportant, I shall show to be false; indeed its falsity would be evident to its supporters, if they would consider, that will in general differs from this or that particular volition in the same way as whiteness differs from this or that white object, or humanity from this or that man. It is, therefore, as impossible to conceive, that will is the cause of a given volition, as to conceive that humanity is the cause of Peter and Paul.

Hence, as will is merely an entity of the reason, and cannot be called the cause of particular volitions, and as some cause is needed for the existence of such volitions, these latter cannot be called free, but are necessarily such as they are determined by their causes; lastly, according to Descartes, errors are themselves particular volitions; hence it necessarily follows that errors, or, in other words, particular volitions, are not free, but are determined by external causes, and in nowise by the will. This is what I undertook to prove.

LETTER III. (III.)

Oldenburg to Spinoza.

[*Oldenburg propounds several questions concerning God and His existence, thought, and the axioms of Eth. I. He also informs Spinoza of a philosophical society, and promises to send Boyle's book.*]

Most excellent Friend,—Your learned letter has been delivered to me, and read with great pleasure.

I highly approve of your geometrical method of proof,

[1] Bacon, Nov. Org. I. Aph. 49.

but I must set it down to my dulness, that I cannot follow with readiness what you set forth with such accuracy. Suffer me, then, I beg, to expose the slowness of my understanding, while I put the following questions, and beg of you to answer them.

First. Do you clearly and indisputably understand solely from the definition you have given of God, that such a Being exists? For my part, when I reflect that definitions contain only the conceptions formed by our minds, and that our mind forms many conceptions of things which do not exist, and is very fertile in multiplying and amplifying what it has conceived, I do not yet see, that from the conception I have of God I can infer God's existence. I am able by a mental combination of all the perfections I perceive in men, in animals, in vegetables, in minerals, &c., to conceive and to form an idea of some single substance uniting in itself all such excellences; indeed my mind is able to multiply and augment such excellences indefinitely; it may thus figure forth for itself a most perfect and excellent Being, but there would be no reason thence to conclude that such a Being actually exists.

Secondly. I wish to ask, whether you think it unquestionable, that body cannot be limited by thought, or thought by body; seeing that it still remains undecided, what thought is, whether it be a physical motion or a spiritual act quite distinct from body?

Thirdly. Do you reckon the axioms, which you have sent to me, as indemonstrable principles known by the light of nature and needing no proof? Perhaps the first is of this nature, but I do not see how the other three can be placed in a like category. The second assumes that nothing exists in the universe save substances and accidents, but many persons would say that time and place cannot be classed either as one or the other. Your third axiom, that *things having different attributes have no quality in common,* is so far from being clear to me, that its contrary seems to be shown in the whole universe. All things known to us agree in certain respects and differ in others. Lastly, your fourth axiom, that *when things have no quality in common, one cannot be produced by another,* is not so plain to my groping intelligence as to stand in need of no further illumination.

God has nothing actually in common with created things, yet nearly all of us believe Him to be their cause.

As you see that in my opinion your axioms are not established beyond all the assaults of doubt, you will readily gather that the propositions you have based upon them do not appear to me absolutely firm. The more I reflect upon them, the more are doubts suggested to my mind concerning them.

As to the first, I submit that two men are two substances with the same attribute, inasmuch as both are rational; whence I infer that there can be two substances with the same attribute.

As to the second, I opine that, as nothing can be its own cause, it is hardly within the scope of our intellect to pronounce on the truth of the proposition, that *substance cannot be produced even by any other substance.* Such a proposition asserts all substances to be self-caused, and all and each to be independent of one another, thus making so many gods, and therefore denying the first cause of all things. This, I willingly confess, I cannot understand, unless you will be kind enough to explain your theory on this sublime subject somewhat more fully and simply, informing me what may be the origin and mode of production of substances, and the mutual interdependence and subordination of things. I most strenuously beg and conjure you by that friendship which we have entered into, to answer me freely and faithfully on these points; you may rest assured, that everything which you think fit to communicate to me will remain untampered with and safe, for I will never allow anything to become public through me to your hurt or disadvantage. In our philosophical society we proceed diligently as far as opportunity offers with our experiments and observations, lingering over the compilation of the history of mechanic arts, with the idea that the forms and qualities of things can best be explained from mechanical principles, and that all natural effects can be produced through motion, shape, and consistency, without reference to inexplicable forms or occult qualities, which are but the refuge of ignorance.

I will send the book I promised, whenever the Dutch Ambassadors send (as they frequently do) a messenger to the Hague, or whenever some other friend whom I can trust goes your way. I beg you to excuse my prolixity and freedom, and simply ask you to take in good part, as one friend from another, the straightforward and unpolished reply I have sent to your letter, believing me to be without deceit or affectation,

Yours most faithfully,

HENRY OLDENBURG.

London, 27 Sept., 1661.

LETTER IV. (IV.)

SPINOZA TO OLDENBURG.

[*Spinoza answers some of Oldenburg's questions and doubts, but has not time to reply to all, as he is just setting out for Amsterdam.*]

ILLUSTRIOUS SIR,—As I was starting for Amsterdam, where I intend staying for a week or two, I received your most welcome letter, and noted the objections you raise to the three propositions I sent you. Not having time to reply fully, I will confine myself to these three.

To the *first* I answer, that not from every definition does the existence of the thing defined follow, but only (as I showed in a note appended to the three propositions) from the definition or idea of an attribute, that is (as I explained fully in the definition given of God) of a thing conceived through and in itself. The reason for this distinction was pointed out, if I mistake not, in the above-mentioned note sufficiently clearly at any rate for a philosopher, who is assumed to be aware of the difference between a fiction and a clear and distinct idea, and also of the truth of the axiom that every definition or clear and distinct idea is true. When this has been duly noted, I do not see what more is required for the solution of your first question.

I therefore proceed to the solution of the *second*, wherein you seem to admit that, if thought does not belong to the nature of extension, then extension will not be limited by thought; your doubt only involves the example given. But observe, I beg, if we say that extension is not limited by extension but by thought, is not this the same as saying that extension is not infinite absolutely, but only as far as extension is concerned, in other words, infinite after its kind? But you say: perhaps thought is a corporeal action: be it so, though I by no means grant it: you, at any rate, will not deny that extension, in so far as it is extension, is not thought, and this is all that is required for explaining my definition and proving the third proposition.

Thirdly. You proceed to object, that my axioms ought not to be ranked as universal notions. I will not dispute this point with you; but you further hesitate as to their truth, seeming to desire to show that their contrary is more probable. Consider, I beg, the definition which I gave of substance and attribute, for on that they all depend. When I say that I mean by substance that which is conceived through and in itself; and that I mean by modification or accident that, which is in something else, and is conceived through that wherein it is, evidently it follows that substance is by nature prior to its accidents. For without the former the latter can neither be nor be conceived. Secondly, it follows that, besides substances and accidents, nothing exists really or externally to the intellect. For everything is conceived either through itself or through something else, and the conception of it either involves or does not involve the conception of something else. Thirdly, it follows that things which possess different attributes have nothing in common. For by attribute I have explained that I mean something, of which the conception does not involve the conception of anything else. Fourthly and lastly, it follows that, if two things have nothing in common, one cannot be the cause of the other. For, as there would be nothing in common between the effect and the cause, the whole effect would spring from nothing. As for your contention that God has nothing actually in common with created things, I have maintained the exact opposite in my definition. I said that God is a Being consisting of infinite attributes, whereof each one is infinite or supremely perfect after its kind. With regard to what you say concerning my first proposition, I beg you, my friend, to bear in mind, that men are not created but born, and that their bodies already exist before birth, though under different forms. You draw the conclusion, wherein I fully concur, that, if one particle of matter be annihilated, the whole of extension would forthwith vanish. My second proposition does not make many gods but only one, to wit, a Being consisting of infinite attributes, &c.

LETTER V. (V.)

OLDENBURG TO SPINOZA.

[*Oldenburg sends Boyle's book, and laments that Spinoza has not been able to answer all his doubts.*]

MOST RESPECTED FRIEND —Please accept herewith the book I promised you, and write me in answer your opinion on it, especially on the remarks about nitre, and about fluidity, and solidity. I owe you the warmest thanks for your learned second letter, which I received to-day, but I greatly grieve that your journey to Amsterdam prevented you from answering all my doubts. I beg you will supply the omission, as soon as you have leisure. You have much enlightened me in your last letter, but have not yet dispelled all my darkness; this result will, I believe, be happily accomplished, when you send me clear and distinct information concerning the first origin of things. Hitherto I have been somewhat in doubt as to the cause from which, and the manner in which things took their origin; also, as to what is the nature of their connection with the first cause, if such there be. All that I hear or read on the subject seems inconclusive. Do you then, my very learned master, act, as it were, as my torch-bearer in the matter. You will have no reason to doubt my confidence and gratitude. Such is the earnest petition of

Yours most faithfully,
HENRY OLDENBURG.

LETTER VI. (VI.)

SPINOZA TO OLDENBURG.

[*Containing detailed criticisms by Spinoza of Robert Boyle's book.*]

Omitted.

LETTER VII. (VII.)

OLDENBURG TO SPINOZA.

[*After thanking Spinoza, in the name of himself and Boyle, Oldenburg mentions the foundation of the Royal Society, and begs his correspondent to publish his theological and philosophical works.*]

* * * * * *

The body of philosophers which I formerly mentioned to you has now, by the king's grace, been constituted as a Royal Society, and furnished with a public charter, whereby distinguished privileges are conferred upon it, and an excellent prospect afforded of endowing it with the necessary revenues.

I would by all means advise you not to begrudge to the learned those works in philosophy and theology, which you have composed with the talent that distinguishes you. Publish them, I beg, whatever be the verdict of petty theologians. Your country is free; the course of philosophy should there be free also. Your own prudence will, doubtless, suggest to you, that your ideas and opinions should be put forth as quietly as possible. For the rest, commit the issue to fortune. Come, then, good sir, cast away all fear of exciting against you the pigmies of our time. Long enough have we sacrificed to ignorance and pedantry. Let us spread the sails of true knowledge, and explore the recesses of nature more thoroughly than heretofore. Your meditations can, I take it, be printed in your country with impunity; nor need any scandal among the learned be dreaded because of them. If these be your patrons and supporters (and I warrant me you will find them so), why should you dread the carpings of ignorance? I will not let you go, my honoured friend, till I have gained my request; nor will I ever, so far as in me lies, allow thoughts of such importance as yours to rest in eternal silence. I earnestly beg you to communicate to me, as soon as you conveniently can, your decision in the matter. Perhaps events will occur here not unworthy of your knowledge. The Society I have mentioned will now proceed more strenuously on its course, and, if peace continues on our shores, will possibly illustrate the republic of letters with some extraordinary achievement. Farewell, excellent sir, and believe me,

Your most zealous and friendly,

HENRY OLDENBURG.

LETTER VIII. (XI.)

OLDENBURG TO SPINOZA.

[*After further replying to Spinoza's criticisms on Boyle's book, Oldenburg again exhorts his correspondent to publish.*]

* * * * * *

I now proceed to the question which has arisen between us. First, permit me to ask you whether you have finished the important little work, in which you treat "of the origin of things and their dependence on the first cause, and of the improvement of our understanding." Truly, my dear sir, I believe nothing more pleasing or acceptable to men of true learning and discrimination could possibly be published than such a treatise. This is what a man of your talent and disposition should look to, far more than the gratification of theologians of our time and fashion. The latter have less regard for truth than for their own convenience. I, therefore, conjure you, by the bond of our friendship, by every duty of increasing and proclaiming the truth, not to begrudge us, or withhold from us your writings on these subjects. If anything of greater importance than I can foresee prevents you from publishing the work, I earnestly charge you to give me a summary of it by letter.

Another book is soon to be published by the learned Boyle, which I will send you as an exchange. I will add papers, which will acquaint you with the whole constitution of our Royal Society, whereof I, with twenty others, am on the Council, and, with one other, am Secretary. I have no time to discourse of any further subjects. All the confidence which honest intentions can inspire, all the readiness to serve, which the smallness of my powers will permit, I pledge to you, and am heartily,

Dear sir, yours wholly,

H. Oldenburg.

London, 3 April, 1663.

LETTER IX. (XIII.)

Spinoza to Oldenburg.

[*Spinoza informs Oldenburg that he has removed to Rhijnsburg, and has spent some time at Amsterdam for the purpose of publishing the " Principles of Cartesian Philosophy." He then replies to Boyle's objections.*]

Distinguished Sir,—I have at length received your long wished for letter, and am at liberty to answer it. But, before I do so, I will briefly tell you, what has prevented my replying before. When I removed my household goods here in April, I set out for Amsterdam. While there certain friends asked me to impart to them a treatise containing, in brief, the second part of the principles of Descartes treated geometrically, together with some of the chief points treated of in metaphysics, which I had formerly dictated to a youth, to whom I did not wish to teach my own opinions openly. They further requested me, at the first opportunity, to compose a similar treatise on the first part. Wishing to oblige my friends, I at once set myself to the task, which I finished in a fortnight, and handed over to them. They then asked for leave to print it, which I readily granted on the condition that one of them should, under my supervision, clothe it in more elegant phraseology, and add a little preface warning readers that I do not acknowledge all the opinions there set forth as my own, inasmuch as I hold the exact contrary to much that is there written, illustrating the fact by one or two examples. All this the friend who took charge of the treatise promised to do, and this is the cause for my prolonged stay in Amsterdam. Since I returned to this village, I have hardly been able to call my time my own, because of the friends who have been kind enough to visit me. At last, my dear friend, a moment has come, when I can relate these occurrences to you, and inform you why I allow this treatise to see the light. It may be that on this occasion some of those, who hold the foremost positions in my country, will be found desirous of seeing the rest of my writings, which I acknowledge as my own; they will thus take care that I am enabled to publish them without any danger of infringing the laws of the land. If this be as I think, I shall doubtless publish at once; if things fall out otherwise, I would rather be silent than obtrude my opinions on men, in defiance of my country, and thus render them hostile to me. I therefore hope, my friend, that you will not chafe at having to wait a short time longer; you shall then receive from me either the treatise printed, or the summary of it which you ask for. If meanwhile you would like to have one or two copies of the work now in the press, I will satisfy your wish, as soon as I know of it and of means to send the book conveniently.

[*The rest of the letter is taken up with criticisms on Boyle's book.*]

LETTERS X.—XIV.[1]

[*Contain further correspondence concerning Boyle's book, and kindred subjects.*]

[1] These letters are numbered by Van Vloten, XIV., XVI., XXV., XXVI., XXXI.

LETTER XIII.A.

OLDENBURG TO SPINOZA.

[*The place of this letter is between Letters XIII. and XIV. It was written apparently in September,* 1665. *It mentions the plague, which was then at its height, the war, and the labours of the Royal Society, and especially of Boyle. Then comes the passage here given. The letter terminates with references to the comets, and to Huyghens.*]

* * * * * *

I see that you are engaged not so much in philosophy as in theology, if I may say so. That is, you are recording your thoughts about angels, prophecy, and miracles, but you are doing this, perhaps, in a philosophical manner; however that may be, I am certain that the work [1] is worthy of you, and that I am most anxious to have it. Since these most difficult times prevent free intercourse, I beg at least that you will not disdain to signify to me in your next letter [2] your design and aim in this writing of yours.

Here we are daily expecting news of a second [3] naval battle, unless indeed your fleet has retired into port. Virtue,[4] the nature of which you hint is being discussed among your friends, belongs to wild beasts not to men. For if men acted according to the guidance of reason, they would not so tear one another in pieces, as they evidently do. But what is the good of my complaining? Vices will exist while men do; [5] but yet they are not continuous, but compensated by the interposition of better things.

* * * * * *

[1] The Tractatus Theologico-Politicus.

[2] Spinoza's answer to this letter is not extant.

[3] The English fleet twice defeated the Dutch in 1665, on June 3rd and Sept. 4th. *Secundo* perhaps means "successful," but this hardly agrees with Oldenburg's politeness.—[TR.]

[4] "Virtus, de quâ disceptare inter vos innuis, ferina est, non humana." I do not think that, in the absence of the previous letter from Spinoza here referred to, the precise meaning of this sentence can be ascertained.—[TR.]

[5] The same phrase occurs in Tract. Pol. I. ii.

LETTER XV. (XXXII.)

SPINOZA TO OLDENBURG.

[*Spinoza writes to his friend concerning the reasons which lead us to believe, that "every part of nature agrees with the whole, and is associated with all other parts." He also makes a few remarks about Huyghens.*]

DISTINGUISHED SIR,—For the encouragement to pursue my speculations given me by yourself and the distinguished R. Boyle, I return you my best thanks. I proceed as far as my slender abilities will allow me, with full confidence in your aid and kindness. When you ask me my opinion on the question raised concerning our knowledge of the means, whereby each part of nature agrees with its whole, and the manner in which it is associated with the remaining parts, I presume you are asking for the reasons which induce us to believe, that each part of nature agrees with its whole, and is associated with the remaining parts. For as to the means whereby the parts are really associated, and each part agrees with its whole, I told you in my former letter that I am in ignorance. To answer such a question, we should have to know the whole of nature and its several parts. I will therefore endeavour to show the reason, which led me to make the statement; but I will premise that I do not attribute to nature either beauty or deformity, order or confusion. Only in relation to our imagination can things be called beautiful or deformed, ordered or confused.

By the association of parts, then, I merely mean that the laws or nature of one part adapt themselves to the laws or nature of another part, so as to cause the least possible inconsistency. As to the whole and the parts, I mean that a given number of things are parts of a whole, in so far as the nature of each of them is adapted to the nature of the rest, so that they all, as far as possible, agree together. On the other hand, in so far as they do not agree, each of them forms, in our mind, a separate idea, and is to that extent considered as a whole, not as a part. For instance, when the parts of lymph, chyle, &c., combine, according to the proportion of the figure and size of each, so as to evidently unite, and form one fluid, the chyle, lymph, &c., considered under this aspect, are part of the blood; but, in so far as we consider the particles of lymph as differing in figure and size from the particles of chyle, we shall consider each of the two as a whole, not as a part.

Let us imagine, with your permission, a little worm, living in the blood, able to distinguish by sight the particles of blood, lymph, &c., and to reflect on the manner in which each particle, on meeting with another particle, either is repulsed, or communicates a portion of its own motion. This little worm would live in the blood, in the same way as we live in a part of the universe, and would consider each particle of blood, not as a part, but as a whole. He would be unable to determine, how all the parts are modified by the general nature of blood, and are compelled by it to adapt themselves, so as to stand in a fixed relation to one another. For, if we imagine that there are no causes external to the blood, which could communicate fresh movements to it, nor any space beyond the blood, nor any bodies whereto the particles of blood could communicate their motion, it is certain that the blood would always remain in the same state, and its particles would undergo no modifications, save those which may be conceived as arising from the relations of motion existing between the lymph, the chyle, &c. The blood would then always have to be considered as a whole, not as a part. But, as there exist, as a matter of fact, very many causes which modify, in a given manner, the nature of the blood, and are, in turn, modified thereby, it follows that other motions and other relations arise in the blood, springing not from the mutual relations of its parts only, but from the mutual relations between the blood as a whole and external causes. Thus the blood comes to be regarded as a part, not as a whole. So much for the whole and the part.

All natural bodies can and ought to be considered in the same way as we have here considered the blood, for all bodies are surrounded by others, and are mutually determined to exist and operate in a fixed and definite proportion, while the relations between motion and rest in the sum total of them, that is, in the whole universe, remain unchanged. Hence it follows that each body, in so far as it exists as modified in a particular manner, must be considered as a part of the whole universe, as agreeing with the whole, and associated with the remaining parts. As the nature of the universe is not limited, like the nature of blood, but is absolutely infinite, its parts are by this nature of infinite power infinitely modified, and compelled to undergo infinite variations. But, in respect to substance, I conceive that each part has a more close union with its whole. For, as I said in my first letter[1] (addressed to you while I was still at Rhijnsburg), substance being infinite in its nature,[2] it follows, as I endeavoured to show, that each part belongs to the nature of substance, and, without it, can neither be nor be conceived.

You see, therefore, how and why I think that the human body is a part of nature. As regards the human mind, I believe that it also is a part of nature; for I maintain that there exists in nature an infinite power of thinking, which, in so far as it is infinite, contains subjectively the whole of nature, and its thoughts proceed in the same manner as nature—that is, in the sphere of ideas.[3] Further, I take the human mind to be identical with this said power, not in so far as it is infinite, and perceives the whole of nature, but in so far as it is finite, and perceives only the human body; in this manner, I maintain that the human mind is a part of an infinite understanding.

But to explain, and accurately prove, all these and kindred questions, would take too long; and I do not think you expect as much of me at present. I am afraid that I may have mistaken your meaning, and given an answer to a different question from that which you asked. Please inform me on this point.

[1] Letter II. [2] Ethics, I. viii.

[3] I have given what seems to be the meaning of this passage. The text is very obscure: "Nempe quia statuo dare etiam in natura potentiam infinitam cogitandi, quæ, quatenus infinita, in se continet totam naturam objective et cujus cogitationes procedunt ac natura ejus, nimirum idearum." M. Saisset in his French translation says here, "In this place I rather interpret than translate Spinoza, as his thought does not seem to me completely expressed."—[TR.]

You write in your last letter, that I hinted that nearly all the Cartesian laws of motion are false. What I said was, if I remember rightly, that Huyghens thinks so; I myself do not impeach any of the laws except the sixth, concerning which I think Huyghens is also in error. I asked you at the same time to communicate to me the experiment made according to that hypothesis in your Royal Society; as you have not replied, I infer that you are not at liberty to do so. The above-mentioned Huyghens is entirely occupied in polishing lenses. He has fitted up for the purpose a handsome workshop, in which he can also construct moulds. What will be the result I know not, nor, to speak the truth, do I greatly care. Experience has sufficiently taught me, that the free hand is better and more sure than any machine for polishing spherical moulds. I can tell you nothing certain as yet about the success of the clocks or the date of Huyghens' journey to France.

LETTER XVI. (XXXIII.)

Oldenburg to Spinoza.

[*After some remarks on Spinoza's last letter, and an account of experiments at the Royal Society and at Oxford, Oldenburg mentions a report about the return of the Jews to Palestine*].

* * * * * *

But I pass on to politics. Everyone here is talking of a report that the Jews, after remaining scattered for more than two thousand years, are about to return to their country. Few here believe in it, but many desire it. Please tell your friend what you hear and think on the matter. For my part, unless the news is confirmed from trustworthy sources at Constantinople, which is the place chiefly concerned, I shall not believe it. I should like to know, what the Jews of Amsterdam have heard about the matter, and how they are affected by such important tidings which, if true, would assuredly seem to harbinger the end of the world. * * * Believe me to be

Yours most zealously,

HENRY OLDENBURG

London, 8 Dec., 1665.

P.S. I will shortly (D.V.) tell you the opinion of our philosophers on the recent comets.

LETTER XVII. (LXI.)

OLDENBURG TO SPINOZA.

[*Oldenburg thanks Spinoza for the Tractatus Theoligico-Politicus despatched but not received, and modifies an adverse verdict expressed in a former letter* (*now lost*).]

I was unwilling to let pass the convenient opportunity offered me by the journey to Holland of the learned Dr. Bourgeois, an adherent of the Reformed religion, for expressing my thanks a few weeks ago for your treatise forwarded to me, but not yet arrived. But I am doubtful whether my letter was duly delivered. I indicated in them my opinion on the treatise; but on deeper and more careful inspection I now think that my verdict was hasty. Certain arguments seemed to me to be urged at the expense of religion, as measured by the standard supplied by the common run of theologians and the received formulas of creeds which are evidently biassed. But a closer consideration of the whole subject convinced me, that you are far from attempting any injury to true religion and sound philosophy, but, on the contrary, strive to exalt and establish the true object of the Christian religion and the divine loftiness of fruitful philosophy.

Now that I believe that this is your fixed purpose, I would most earnestly beg you to have the kindness to write frequently and explain the nature of what you are now preparing and considering with this object to your old and sincere friend, who is all eager for the happy issue of so lofty a design. I sacredly promise you, that I will not divulge a syllable to anyone, if you enjoin silence; I will only endeavour gently to prepare the minds of good and wise men for the reception of those truths, which you will some day bring before a wider public, and I will try to dispel the prejudices, which have been conceived against your doctrines. Unless I am quite mistaken, you have an insight deeper than common into the nature and powers of the human mind, and its union with the human body. I earnestly beg you to favour me with your reflections on this subject. Farewell, most excellent Sir, and favour the devoted admirer of your teaching and virtue,

HENRY OLDENBURG.

London, 8 June, 1675.[1]

LETTER XVIII. (LXII.)

OLDENBURG TO SPINOZA.

[*Oldenburg rejoices at the renewal of correspondence, and alludes to the five books of the Ethics which Spinoza (in a letter now lost) had announced his intention of publishing.*]

Our correspondence being thus happily renewed, I should be unwilling to fall short of a friend's duty in the exchange of letters. I understand from your answer delivered to me on July 5, that you intend to publish your treatise in five parts. Allow me, I beg, to warn you by the sincerity of your affection for me, not to insert any passages which may seem to discourage the practice of religion and virtue; especially as nothing is more sought after in this degenerate and evil age than doctrines of the kind, which seem to give countenance to rampant vice.

However, I will not object to receiving a few copies of the said treatise. I will only ask you that, when the time arrives, they may be entrusted to a Dutch merchant living in London, who will see that they are forwarded to

[1] The old edition gives the date 8 Oct., 1665. but this is obviously incorrect, as the Tractatus Theologico-Politicus was not published till 1670.

me. There is no need to mention, that books of the kind in question have been sent to me: if they arrive safely to my keeping, I do not doubt that I can conveniently dispose of some copies to my friends here and there, and can obtain a just price for them. Farewell, and when you have leisure write to

Yours most zealously,
HENRY OLDENBURG.

London, 22 July, 1675.

LETTER XIX. (LXVIII.)

SPINOZA TO OLDENBURG.

[*Spinoza relates his journey to Amsterdam for the purpose of publishing his Ethics; he was deterred by the dissuasions of theologians and Cartesians. He hopes that Oldenburg will inform him of some of the objections to the Tractatus Theologico-Politicus, made by learned men, so that they may be answered in notes.*]

DISTINGUISHED AND ILLUSTRIOUS SIR,—When I received your letter of the 22nd July, I had set out to Amsterdam for the purpose of publishing the book I had mentioned to you. While I was negotiating, a rumour gained currency that I had in the press a book concerning God, wherein I endeavoured to show that there is no God. This report was believed by many. Hence certain theologians, perhaps the authors of the rumour, took occasion to complain of me before the prince and the magistrates; moreover, the stupid Cartesians, being suspected of favouring me, endeavoured to remove the aspersion by abusing everywhere my opinions and writings, a course which they still pursue. When I became aware of this through trustworthy men, who also assured me that the theologians were everywhere lying in wait for me, I determined to put off publishing till I saw how things were going, and I proposed to inform you of my intentions. But matters seem to get worse and worse, and I am still uncertain what to do.

Meanwhile I do not like to delay any longer answering your letter. I will first thank you heartily for your friendly warning, which I should be glad to have further explained, so that I may know, which are the doctrines which seem to you to be aimed against the practice of religion and virtue. If principles agree with reason, they are, I take it, also most serviceable to virtue. Further, if it be not troubling you too much I beg you to point out the passages in the Tractatus Theologico-Politicus which are objected to by the learned, for I want to illustrate that treatise with notes, and to remove if possible the prejudices conceived against it. Farewell.

LETTER XX. (LXXI.)

Oldenburg to Spinoza.

As I see from your last letter, the book you propose to publish is in peril. It is impossible not to approve your purpose of illustrating and softening down those passages in the Tractatus Theologico-Politicus, which have given pain to its readers. First I would call attention to the ambiguities in your treatment of God and Nature: a great many people think you have confused the one with the other. Again, you seem to many to take away the authority and value of miracles, whereby alone, as nearly all Christians believe, the certainty of the divine revelation can be established.

Again, people say that you conceal your opinion concerning Jesus Christ, the Redeemer of the world, the only Mediator for mankind, and concerning His incarnation and redemption: they would like you to give a clear explanation of what you think on these three subjects. If you do this and thus give satisfaction to prudent and rational Christians, I think your affairs are safe. Farewell.

London, 15 Nov., 1675.

P.S.—Send me a line, I beg, to inform me whether this note has reached you safely.

LETTER XXI. (LXXIII.)

Spinoza to Oldenburg.

Distinguished Sir,—I received on Saturday last your very short letter dated 15th Nov. In it you merely indicate the points in the theological treatise, which have given pain to readers, whereas I had hoped to learn from it, what were the opinions which militated against the practice of religious virtue, and which you formerly mentioned. However, I will speak on the three subjects on which you desire me to disclose my sentiments, and tell you, first, that my opinion concerning God differs widely from that which is ordinarily defended by modern Christians. For I hold that God is of all things the cause immanent, as the phrase is, not transient. I say that all things are in God and move in God, thus agreeing with Paul,[1] and, perhaps, with all the ancient philosophers, though the phraseology may be different; I will even venture to affirm that I agree with all the ancient Hebrews, in so far as one may judge from their traditions, though these are in many ways corrupted. The supposition of some, that I endeavour to prove in the Tractatus Theologico-Politicus the unity of God and Nature (meaning by the latter a certain mass or corporeal matter), is wholly erroneous.

As regards miracles, I am of opinion that the revelation of God can only be established by the wisdom of the doctrine, not by miracles, or in other words by ignorance. This I have shown at sufficient length in Chapter VI. concerning miracles. I will here only add, that I make this chief distinction between religion and superstition, that the latter is founded on ignorance, the former on knowledge; this, I take it, is the reason why Christians are distinguished from the rest of the world, not by faith, nor by charity, nor by the other fruits of the Holy Spirit, but solely by their opinions, inasmuch as they defend their cause, like everyone else, by miracles, that is by ignorance, which is the source of all malice; thus they turn a faith,

[1] See Acts xvii. 28. Cf. 1 Cor. iii. 16, xii. 6; Eph. i. 23.

which may be true, into superstition. Lastly, in order to disclose my opinions on the third point, I will tell you that I do not think it necessary for salvation to know Christ according to the flesh: but with regard to the Eternal Son of God, that is the Eternal Wisdom of God, which has manifested itself in all things and especially in the human mind, and above all in Christ Jesus, the case is far otherwise. For without this no one can come to a state of blessedness, inasmuch as it alone teaches, what is true or false, good or evil. And, inasmuch as this wisdom was made especially manifest through Jesus Christ, as I have said, His disciples preached it, in so far as it was revealed to them through Him, and thus showed that they could rejoice in that spirit of Christ more than the rest of mankind. The doctrines added by certain churches, such as that God took upon Himself human nature, I have expressly said that I do not understand; in fact, to speak the truth, they seem to me no less absurd than would a statement, that a circle had taken upon itself the nature of a square. This I think will be sufficient explanation of my opinions concerning the three points mentioned. Whether it will be satisfactory to Christians you will know better than I. Farewell.

LETTER XXII. (LXXIV.)

OLDENBURG TO SPINOZA.

[*Oldenburg wishes to be enlightened concerning the doctrine of fatalism, of which Spinoza has been accused. He discourses on man's limited intelligence and on the incarnation of the Son of God.*]

As you seem to accuse me of excessive brevity, I will this time avoid the charge by excessive prolixity. You expected, I see, that I should set forth those opinions in your writings, which seem to discourage the practice of religious virtue in your readers. I will indicate the matter which especially pains them. You appear to set up a fatalistic necessity for all things and actions; if such is conceded and asserted, people aver, that the sinews of all laws, of virtue, and of religion, are severed, and that all rewards and punishment are vain. Whatsoever can compel, or involves necessity, is held also to excuse; therefore no one, they think, can be without excuse in the sight of God. If we are driven by fate, and all things follow a fixed and inevitable path laid down by the hard hand of necessity, they do not see where punishment can come in. What wedge can be brought for the untying of this knot, it is very difficult to say. I should much like to know and learn what help you can supply in the matter.

As to the opinions which you have kindly disclosed to me on the three points I mentioned, the following inquiries suggest themselves. First, In what sense do you take *miracles* and *ignorance* to be synonymous and equivalent terms, as you appear to think in your last letter?

The bringing back of Lazarus from the dead, and the resurrection from death of Jesus Christ seem to surpass all the power of created nature, and to fall within the scope of divine power only; it would not be a sign of culpable ignorance, that it was necessary to exceed the limits of finite intelligence confined within certain bounds. But perhaps you do not think it in harmony with the created mind and science, to acknowledge in the uncreated mind and supreme Deity a science and power capable of fathoming, and bringing to pass events, whose reason and manner can neither be brought home nor explained to us poor human pigmies? "We are men;" it appears, that we must "think everything human akin to ourselves." [1]

Again, when you say that you cannot understand that God really took upon Himself human nature, it becomes allowable to ask you, how you understand the texts in the Gospel and the Epistle to the Hebrews, whereof the first says, "The Word was made flesh," [2] and the other, "For verily he took not on him the nature of angels; but he took on him the seed of Abraham." [3] Moreover, the whole tenor of the Gospel infers, as I think, that the only begotten Son of God, the Word (who both was God and was with God), showed Himself in human nature, and by His passion and

[1] Terence, Heaut. I. i. 25. [2] John i. 14. [3] Heb. ii. 16.

death offered up the sacrifice for our sins, the price of the atonement. What you have to say concerning this without impugning the truth of the Gospel and the Christian religion, which I think you approve of, I would gladly learn.

I had meant to write more, but am interrupted by friends on a visit, to whom I cannot refuse the duties of courtesy. But what I have already put on paper is enough, and will perhaps weary you in your philosophizing. Farewell, therefore, and believe me to be ever an admirer of your learning and knowledge.

London, 16 Dec., 1675.

LETTER XXIII. (LXXV.)

Spinoza to Oldenburg.

[*Spinoza expounds to Oldenburg his views on fate and necessity, discriminates between miracles and ignorance, takes the resurrection of Christ as spiritual, and deprecates attributing to the sacred writers Western modes of speech.*]

Distinguished Sir,—At last I see, what it was that you begged me not to publish. However, as it forms the chief foundation of everything in the treatise which I intended to bring out, I should like briefly to explain here, in what sense I assert that a fatal necessity presides over all things and actions. God I in no wise subject to fate: I conceive that all things follow with inevitable necessity from the nature of God, in the same way as everyone conceives that it follows from God's nature that God understands Himself. This latter consequence all admit to follow necessarily from the divine nature, yet no one conceives that God is under the compulsion of any fate, but that He understands Himself quite freely, though necessarily.

Further, this inevitable necessity in things does away neither with divine nor human laws. The principles of morality, whether they receive from God Himself the form of laws or institutions, or whether they do not, are still divine and salutary; whether we receive the good, which flows from virtue and the divine love, as from God in the capacity of a judge, or as from the necessity of the divine nature, it will in either case be equally desirable; on the other hand, the evils following from wicked actions and passions are not less to be feared because they are necessary consequences. Lastly, in our actions, whether they be necessary or contingent, we are led by hope and fear.

Men are only without excuse before God, because they are in God's power, as clay is in the hands of the potter, who from the same lump makes vessels, some to honour, some to dishonour.[1] If you will reflect a little on this, you will, I doubt not, easily be able to reply to any objections which may be urged against my opinion, as many of my friends have already done.

I have taken miracles and ignorance as equivalent terms, because those, who endeavour to establish God's existence and the truth of religion by means of miracles, seek to prove the obscure by what is more obscure and completely unknown, thus introducing a new sort of argument, the reduction, not to the impossible, as the phrase is, but to ignorance. But, if I mistake not, I have sufficiently explained my opinion on miracles in the Theologico-Political treatise. I will only add here, that if you will reflect on the facts; that Christ did not appear to the council, nor to Pilate, nor to any unbeliever, but only to the faithful,; also that God has neither right hand nor left, but is by His essence not in a particular spot, but everywhere; that matter is everywhere the same; that God does not manifest himself in the imaginary space supposed to be outside the world; and lastly, that the frame of the human body is kept within due limits solely by the weight of the air; you will readily see that this apparition of Christ is not unlike that wherewith God appeared to Abraham, when the latter saw men whom he invited to dine with him. But, you will say, all the Apostles thoroughly believed, that Christ rose from the dead and really ascended to heaven: I do not deny it. Abraham, too, believed that God had dined with him, and all the Israelites believed that God descended, surrounded

[1] Romans ix. 21.

with fire, from heaven to Mount Sinai, and there spoke directly with them; whereas, these apparitions or revelations, and many others like them, were adapted to the understanding and opinions of those men, to whom God wished thereby to reveal His will. I therefore conclude, that the resurrection of Christ from the dead was in reality spiritual, and that to the faithful alone, according to their understanding, it was revealed that Christ was endowed with eternity, and had risen from the dead (using *dead* in the sense in which Christ said, "let the dead bury their dead" [1]), giving by His life and death a matchless example of holiness. Moreover, He to this extent raises his disciples from the dead, in so far as they follow the example of His own life and death. It would not be difficult to explain the whole Gospel doctrine on this hypothesis. Nay, 1 Cor. ch. xv. cannot be explained on any other, nor can Paul's arguments be understood: if we follow the common interpretation, they appear weak and can easily be refuted: not to mention the fact, that Christians interpret spiritually all those doctrines which the Jews accepted literally. I join with you in acknowledging human weakness. But on the other hand, I venture to ask you whether we "human pigmies" possess sufficient knowledge of nature to be able to lay down the limits of its force and power, or to say that a given thing surpasses that power? No one could go so far without arrogance. We may, therefore, without presumption explain miracles as far as possible by natural causes. When we cannot explain them, nor even prove their impossibility, we may well suspend our judgment about them, and establish religion, as I have said, solely by the wisdom of its doctrines. You think that the texts in John's Gospel and in Hebrews are inconsistent with what I advance, because you measure oriental phrases by the standards of European speech; though John wrote his gospel in Greek, he wrote it as a Hebrew. However this may be, do you believe, when Scripture says that God manifested Himself in a cloud, or that He dwelt in the tabernacle or the temple, that God actually assumed the nature of a cloud, a tabernacle, or a temple? Yet the utmost that Christ says of Himself is, that He is the Temple

[1] Matt. viii. 22; Luke ix. 60.

of God,[1] because, as I said before, God had specially manifested Himself in Christ. John, wishing to express the same truth more forcibly, said that "the Word was made flesh." But I have said enough on the subject.

LETTER XXIV. (LXXVII.)

Oldenburg to Spinoza.

[*Oldenburg returns to the questions of universal necessity, of miracles, and of the literal and allegorical interpretation of Scripture.*]

εὖ πράττειν.

You hit the point exactly, in perceiving the cause why I did not wish the doctrine of the fatalistic necessity of all things to be promulgated, lest the practice of virtue should thereby be aspersed, and rewards and punishments become ineffectual. The suggestions in your last letter hardly seem sufficient to settle the matter, or to quiet the human mind. For if we men are, in all our actions, moral as well as natural, under the power of God, like clay in the hands of the potter, with what face can any of us be accused of doing this or that, seing that it was impossible for him to do otherwise? Should we not be able to cast all responsibility on God? Your inflexible fate, and your irresistible power, compel us to act in a given manner, nor can we possibly act otherwise. Why, then, and by what right do you deliver us up to terrible punishments, which we can in no way avoid, since you direct and carry on all things through supreme necessity, according to your good will and pleasure? When you say that men are only inexcusable before God, because they are in the power of God, I should reverse the argument, and say, with more show of reason, that men are evidently excusable, since they are in the power of God. Everyone may plead, "Thy power cannot be escaped from, O God; therefore, since I could not act otherwise, I may justly be excused."

[1] John ii. 19. Cf. Matt. xxvi. 60; Mark xiv. 58.

Again, in taking miracles and ignorance as equivalent terms, you seem to bring within the same limits the power of God and the knowledge of the ablest men; for God is, according to you, unable to do or produce anything, for which men cannot assign a reason, if they employ all the strength of their faculties.

Again, the history of Christ's passion, death, burial, and resurrection seems to be depicted in such lively and genuine colours, that I venture to appeal to your conscience, whether you can believe them to be allegorical, rather than literal, while preserving your faith in the narrative? The circumstances so clearly stated by the Evangelists seem to urge strongly on our minds, that the history should be understood literally. I have ventured to touch briefly on these points, and I earnestly beg you to pardon me, and answer me as a friend with your usual candour. Mr. Boyle sends you his kind regards. I will, another time, tell you what the Royal Society is doing. Farewell, and preserve me in your affection.

London, 14 Jan., 1676.

LETTER XXV. (LXXVIII.)

Written 7 Feb., 1676.

SPINOZA TO OLDENBURG.

[*Spinoza again treats of fatalism. He repeats that he accepts Christ's passion, death, and burial literally, but His resurrection spiritually.*]

DISTINGUISHED SIR,—When I said in my former letter that we are inexcusable, because we are in the power of God, like clay in the hands of the potter, I meant to be understood in the sense, that no one can bring a complaint against God for having given him a weak nature, or infirm spirit. A circle might as well complain to God of not being endowed with the properties of a sphere, or a child who is tortured, say, with stone, for not being given a healthy body, as a man of feeble spirit, because God has denied to him fortitude, and the true knowledge and love of the Deity, or because he is endowed with so weak a nature, that he cannot check or moderate his desires. For the nature of each thing is only competent to do that which follows necessarily from its given cause. That every man cannot be brave, and that we can no more command for ourselves a healthy body than a healthy mind, nobody can deny, without giving the lie to experience, as well as to reason. "But," you urge, "if men sin by nature, they are excusable;" but you do not state the conclusion you draw, whether that God cannot be angry with them, or that they are worthy of blessedness—that is, of the knowledge and love of God. If you say the former, I fully admit that God cannot be angry, and that all things are done in accordance with His will; but I deny that all men ought, therefore, to be blessed—men may be excusable, and, nevertheless, be without blessedness and afflicted in many ways. A horse is excusable, for being a horse and not a man; but, nevertheless, he must needs be a horse and not a man. He who goes mad from the bite of a dog is excusable, yet he is rightly suffocated. Lastly, he who cannot govern his desires, and keep them in check with the fear of the laws, though his weakness may be excusable, yet he cannot enjoy with contentment the knowledge and love of God, but necessarily perishes. I do not think it necessary here to remind you, that Scripture, when it says that God is angry with sinners, and that He is a Judge who takes cognizance of human actions, passes sentence on them, and judges them, is speaking humanly, and in a way adapted to the received opinion of the masses, inasmuch as its purpose is not to teach philosophy, nor to render men wise, but to make them obedient.

How, by taking miracles and ignorance as equivalent terms, I reduce God's power and man's knowledge within the same limits, I am unable to discern.

For the rest, I accept Christ's passion, death, and burial literally, as you do, but His resurrection I understand allegorically. I admit, that it is related by the Evangelists in such detail, that we cannot deny that they themselves believed Christ's body to have risen from the dead and ascended to heaven, in order to sit at the right hand of

God, or that they believed that Christ might have been seen by unbelievers, if they had happened to be at hand, in the places where He appeared to His disciples; but in these matters they might, without injury to Gospel teaching, have been deceived, as was the case with other prophets mentioned in my last letter. But Paul, to whom Christ afterwards appeared, rejoices, that he knew Christ not after the flesh, but after the spirit.[1] Farewell, honourable Sir, and believe me yours in all affection and zeal.

LETTER XXV.A.

OLDENBURG TO SPINOZA.

[*Oldenburg adduces certain further objections against Spinoza's doctrine of necessity and miracles, and exposes the inconsistency of a partial allegorization of Scripture.*]

To the most illustrious Master Benedict de Spinoza Henry Oldenburg sends greetings.

In your last letter,[2] written to me on the 7th of February, there are some points which seem to deserve criticism. You say that a man cannot complain, because God has denied him the true knowledge of Himself, and strength sufficient to avoid sins; forasmuch as to the nature of everything nothing is competent, except that which follows necessarily from its cause. But I say, that inasmuch as God, the Creator of men, formed them after His own image, which seems to imply in its concept wisdom, goodness, and power, it appears quite to follow, that it is more within the sphere of man's power[3] to have a sound mind than to have a sound body. For physical soundness of body follows from mechanical causes, but soundness of mind depends on purpose

[1] 2 Cor. v. 16.

[2] Letter XXV.

[3] *Potestas*, as distinguished from *potentia*—the word just above translated power—means power delegated by a rightful superior, as here by God. So it is rendered here "sphere of power," and in Tract. Pol. generally "authority." It would not be proper to say that the "image of God" implied *potestas*.

and design. You add, that men may be inexcusable,[1] and yet suffer pain in many ways. This seems hard at first sight, and what you add by way of proof, namely, that a dog[2] mad from having been bitten is indeed to be excused, but yet is rightly killed, does not seem to settle the question. For the killing of such a dog would argue cruelty, were it not necessary in order to preserve other dogs and animals, and indeed men, from a maddening bite of the same kind.

But if God implanted in man a sound mind, as He is able to do, there would be no contagion of vices to be feared. And, surely, it seems very cruel, that God should devote men to eternal, or at least terrible temporary, torments, for sins which by them could be no wise avoided. Moreover, the tenour of all Holy Scripture seems to suppose and imply, that men can abstain from sins. For it abounds in denunciations and promises, in declarations of rewards and punishments, all of which seem to militate against the necessity of sinning, and infer the possibility of avoiding punishment. And if this were denied, it would have to be said, that the human mind acts no less mechanically than the human body.

Next, when you proceed to take miracles and ignorance to be equivalent, you seem to rely on this foundation, that the creature can and should have perfect insight into the power and wisdom of the Creator: and that the fact is quite otherwise, I have hitherto been firmly persuaded.

Lastly, where you affirm that Christ's passion, death, and burial are to be taken literally, but His resurrection allegorically, you rely, as far as I can see, on no proof at all. Christ's resurrection seems to be delivered in the Gospel as literally as the rest. And on this article of the resurrection the whole Christian religion and its truth rest, and with its removal Christ's mission and heavenly doctrine collapse. It cannot escape you, how Christ, after He was raised from the dead, laboured to convince His disciples

[1] Surely this is a mistake for "excusable."—[TR.]

[2] See Letter XXV. Oldenburg misunderstands Spinoza's illustration, because he takes "canis" in the phrase, "qui ex morsu canis furit," to be nominative instead of genitive; "a dog which goes mad from a bite," instead of "he who goes mad from the bite of a dog."

of the truth of the Resurrection properly so called. To want to turn all these things into allegories is the same thing, as if one were to busy one's self in plucking up the whole truth of the Gospel history.

These few points I wished again to submit in the interest of my liberty of philosophizing, which I earnestly beg you not to take amiss.

Written in London, 11 Feb., 1676.

I will communicate with you shortly on the present studies and experiments of the Royal Society, if God grant me life and health.

LETTER XXVI. (VIII.)

SIMON DE VRIES[1] TO SPINOZA.

[*Simon de Vries, a diligent student of Spinoza's writings and philosophy, describes a club formed for the study of Spinoza's MS. containing some of the matter afterwards worked into the Ethics, and asks questions about the difficulties felt by members of the club.*[2]]

MOST HONOURABLE FRIEND,—I have for a long time wished to be present with you; but the weather and the hard winter have not been propitious to me. I sometimes complain of my lot, in that we are separated from each other by so long a distance. Happy, yes most happy is the fellow-lodger, abiding under the same roof with you, who can talk with you on the best of subjects, at dinner,

[1] For an account of Simon de Vries see Introduction, p. xiv. His letters are written in very indifferent Latin, which is, perhaps, one reason, why the present letter at least has been altered freely by the first editors.

[2] The version of this letter in Bruder's and former editions is much altered by the omission of all mention of the club, and of the reference to Albert Burgh, and by the change throughout of the plural referring to the members of the club into the singular referring to the writer only. The genuine form here followed is to be found in Van Vloten's Supplementum.

at supper, and during your walks.[1] However, though I am far apart from you in body, you have been very frequently present to my mind, especially in your writings, while I read and turn them over. But as they are not all clear to the members of our club, for which reason we have begun a fresh series of meetings, and as I would not have you think me unmindful of you, I have applied my mind to writing this letter.

As regards our club, the following is its order. One of us (that is everyone by turn) reads through and, as far as he understands it, expounds and also demonstrates the whole of your work, according to the sequence and order of your propositions. Then, if it happens that on any point we cannot satisfy one another, we have resolved to make a note of it and write to you, so that, if possible, it may be made clearer to us, and that we may be able under your guidance to defend the truth against those who are superstitiously religious, and against the Christians,[2] and to withstand the attack of the whole world. Well then, since, when we first read through and expounded them, the definitions did not all seem clear to us, we differed about the nature of definition. Next in your absence we consulted as our authority a celebrated mathematician, named Borel:[3] for he makes mention of the nature of definition, axiom, and postulate, and adduces the opinions of others on the subject. But his opinion is as follows: "Definitions are cited in a demonstration as premisses. Wherefore it is necessary, that they should be accurately known; otherwise scientific or accurate knowledge cannot be attained by their means." And elsewhere he says: "The primary and most known construction or passive quality of a given subject should not be chosen rashly, but with the greatest care; if the construction or passive quality be an impossibility, no scientific definition can be obtained. For instance,

[1] This "fellow-lodger," again mentioned in the next letter, is pretty certainly Albert Burgh, concerning whom see Introduction, p. xv, and Letters LXXIII. and LXXIV

[2] Van Vloten infers that the members of the club were chiefly Jews.

[3] Peter Borel, born 1620, physician to the king of France, died 1689. He wrote several medical and philosophical works, and became in 1674 a member of the French Academy of Sciences.

if anyone were to say, let two two straight lines enclosing a space be called figurals, the definition would be of non-existences and impossible: hence ignorance rather than knowledge would be deduced therefrom. Again, if the construction or passive quality be possible and true, but unknown or doubtful to us, the definition will not be good. For conclusions arising from what is unknown or doubtful are themselves uncertain or doubtful; they therefore bring about conjecture or opinion, but not certain knowledge.

Jacquet[1] seems to dissent from this opinion, for he thinks that one may proceed from a false premiss directly to a true conclusion, as you are aware. Clavius,[2] however, whose opinion he quotes, thinks as follows: "Definitions," he says, "are artificial phrases, nor is there any need in reasoning that a thing should be defined in a particular way; but it is sufficient that a thing defined should never be said to agree with another thing, until it has been shown that its definition also agrees therewith."

Thus, according to Borel, the definition of a given thing should consist as regards its construction or passive quality in something thoroughly known to us and true. Clavius, on the other hand, holds that it is a matter of indifference, whether the construction or passive quality be well known and true, or the reverse; so long as we do not assert, that our definition agrees with anything, before it has been proved.

I should prefer Borel's opinion to that of Clavius. I know not which you would assent to, if to either. As these difficulties have occurred to me with regard to the nature of definition, which is reckoned among the cardinal points of demonstration, and as I cannot free my mind from them, I greatly desire, and earnestly beg you, when you have leisure and opportunity, to be kind enough to send me your opinion on the matter, and at the same time to tell me the distinction between axioms and definitions. Borel says that the difference is merely nominal, but I believe you decide otherwise.

[1] Andrew Jacquet, born at Antwerp 1611, was mathematical professor in that town, died 1660.

[2] Christopher Clavius, born at Bamberg 1537, was mathematical professor at Rome, died 1612.

Further, we cannot make up our minds about the third definition.[1] I adduced to illustrate it, what my master said to me at the Hague,[2] to wit, that a thing may be regarded in two ways, either as it is in itself, or as it is in relation to something else; as in the case of the intellect, for that can be regarded either under the head of thought, or as consisting in ideas. But we do not see the point of the distinction thus drawn. For it seems to us, that, if we rightly conceive thought, we must range it under the head of ideas; as, if all ideas were removed from it, we should destroy thought. As we find the illustration of the matter not sufficiently clear, the matter itself remains somewhat obscure, and we need further explanation.

Lastly, in the third note to the eighth proposition,[3] the beginning runs thus:—"Hence it is plain that, although two attributes really distinct be conceived, that is, one without the aid of the other, we cannot therefore infer, that they constitute two entities or two different substances. For it belongs to the nature of substance, that each of its attributes should be conceived through itself, though all the attributes it possesses exist simultaneously in it." Here our master seems to assume, that the nature of substance is so constituted, that it may have several attributes. But this doctrine has not yet been proved, unless you refer to the sixth definition, of absolutely infinite substance or God. Otherwise, if it be asserted that each substance has only one attribute, and I have two ideas of two attributes, I may rightly infer that, where there are two different attributes, there are also different substances. On this point also we beg you to give a further explanation. Besides I thank you very much for your writings communicated to me by P. Balling,[4] which have greatly delighted me, especially

[1] The third definition of the Ethics, as they now exist. See p. 45.

[2] Spinoza must, therefore, have visited the Hague before he lived there.

[3] In the Ethics as they now exist, "in I. x. note, towards the beginning," to which reading the editors consequently altered the text, till the true reading was restored by Van Vloten.

[4] Peter Balling is the correspondent, to whom Spinoza wrote Letter XXX., which see. He translated into Dutch Spinoza's Principia, as to which see Introduction, p. xv.

your note on Proposition XIX.[1] If I can do *you* any service here in anything that is within my power, I am at your dispesal. You have but to let me know. I have begun a course of anatomy, and am nearly half through with it; when it is finished, I shall begin a course of chemistry, and thus under your guidance I shall go through the whole of medicine. I leave off, and await your answer. Accept the greeting of

Your most devoted
S. J. DE VRIES.

Amsterdam, 24 Feb., 1663.

LETTER XXVII. (IX.)

SPINOZA TO SIMON DE VRIES.

[*Spinoza deprecates his correspondent's jealousy of Albert Burgh; and answers that distinction must be made between different kinds of definitions. He explains his opinions more precisely.*]

RESPECTED FRIEND,—I have received[2] your long wished-for letter, for which, and for your affection towards me, I heartily thank you. Your long absence has been no less grievous to me than to you; yet in the meantime I rejoice that my trifling studies are of profit to you and our friends. For thus while you[3] are away, I in my absence speak to you.[3] You need not envy my fellow-lodger. There is no one who is more displeasing to me, nor against whom I have been more anxiously on my guard; and therefore I would have you and all my acquaintance warned not to

[1] There is no note to Ethics, I. xix. As there is nothing to show what proposition is intended, the old version suppressed the whole passage from "Besides I thank you" to "medicine."

[2] The whole beginning of this letter, till after the mention of the club, is omitted in the editions before Van Vloten's Supplementum, to make the letter agree with the altered version of Letter XXVI., to which it is an answer.

[3] "You" in these two places is plural, and refers to the club; so also the second "your" on the next page; elsewhere "you" and "your" refer to De Vries only.

communicate my opinions to him, except when he has come to maturer years. So far he is too childish and inconstant, and is fonder of novelty than of truth. But I hope, that in a few years he will amend these childish faults. Indeed I am almost sure of it, as far as I can judge from his nature. And so his temperament bids me like him.

As for the questions propounded in your club, which is wisely enough ordered, I see that your[1] difficulties arise from not distinguishing between kinds of definition: that is, between a definition serving to explain a thing, of which the essence only is sought and in question, and a definition which is put forward only for purposes of inquiry. The former having a definite object ought to be true, the latter need not. For instance, if someone asks me for a description of Solomon's temple, I am bound to give him a true description, unless I want to talk nonsense with him. But if I have constructed, in my mind, a temple which I desire to build, and infer from the description of it that I must buy such and such a site and so many thousand stones and other materials, will any sane person tell me that I have drawn a wrong conclusion because my definition is possibly untrue? or will anyone ask me to prove my definition? Such a person would simply be telling me, that I had not conceived that which I had conceived, or be requiring me to prove, that I had conceived that which I had conceived; in fact, evidently trifling. Hence a definition either explains a thing, in so far as it is external to the intellect, in which case it ought to be true and only to differ from a proposition or an axiom in being concerned merely with the essences of things, or the modifications of things, whereas the latter has a wider scope and extends also to eternal truths. Or else it explains a thing, as it is conceived or can be conceived by us; and then it differs from an axiom or proposition, inasmuch as it only requires to be conceived absolutely, and not like an axiom as true. Hence a bad definition is one which is not conceived. To explain my meaning, I will take Borel's example—a man saying that two straight lines enclosing a space shall be called "figurals." If the man means by a straight line the same as the rest of the world means by

[1] See Note 3 on previous page.

a curved line, his definition is good (for by the definition would be meant some such figure as (), or the like); so long as he does not afterwards mean a square or other kind of figure. But, if he attaches the ordinary meaning to the words straight line, the thing is evidently inconceivable, and therefore there is no definition. These considerations are plainly confused by Borel, to whose opinion you incline. I give another example, the one you cite at the end of your letter. If I say that each substance has only one attribute, this is an unsupported statement and needs proof. But, if I say that I mean by substance that which consists in only one attribute, the definition will be good, so long as entities consisting of several attributes are afterwards styled by some name other than substance. When you say that I do not prove, that substance (or being) may have several attributes, you do not perhaps pay attention to the proofs given. I adduced two:—First, "that nothing is plainer to us, than that every being may be conceived by us under some attribute, and that the more reality or essence a given being has, the more attributes may be attributed to it. Hence a being absolutely infinite must be defined, &c." Secondly, and I think this is the stronger proof of the two, "the more attributes I assign to any being, the more am I compelled to assign to it existence;" in other words, the more I conceive it as true. The contrary would evidently result, if I were feigning a chimera or some such being.

Your remark, that you cannot conceive thought except as consisting in ideas, because, when ideas are removed, thought is annihilated, springs, I think, from the fact that while you, a thinking thing, do as you say, you abstract all your thoughts and conceptions. It is no marvel that, when you have abstracted all your thoughts and conceptions, you have nothing left for thinking with. On the general subject I think I have shown sufficiently clearly and plainly, that the intellect, although infinite, belongs to nature regarded as passive rather than nature regarded as active (ad naturam naturatam, non vero ad naturam naturantem).

However, I do not see how this helps towards understanding the third definition, nor what difficulty the latter presents. It runs, if I mistake not, as follows: "By substance I mean that, which is in itself and is conceived through itself; that is, of which the conception does not involve the conception of anything else. By attribute I mean the same thing, except that it is called attribute with respect to the understanding, which attributes to substance the particular nature aforesaid." This definition, I repeat, explains with sufficient clearness what I wish to signify by substance or attribute. You desire, though there is no need, that I should illustrate by an example, how one and the same thing can be stamped with two names. In order not to seem miserly, I will give you two. First, I say that by Israel is meant the third patriarch; I mean the same by Jacob, the name Jacob being given, because the patriarch in question had caught hold of the heel of his brother. Secondly, by a colourless surface I mean a surface, which reflects all rays of light without altering them. I mean the same by a white surface, with this difference, that a surface is called white in reference to a man looking at it, &c.

LETTER XXVIII. (X.)

Spinoza to Simon de Vries.

[*Spinoza, in answer to a letter from De Vries now lost, speaks of the experience necessary for proving a definition, and also of eternal truths.*]

Respected Friend,—You ask me if we have need of experience, in order to know whether the definition of a given attribute is true. To this I answer, that we never need experience, except in cases when the existence of the thing cannot be inferred from its definition, as, for instance, the existence of modes (which cannot be inferred from their definition); experience is not needed, when the existence of the things in question is not distinguished from their essence, and is therefore inferred from their definition. This can never be taught us by any experience, for experience does not teach us any essences of things; the utmost it can do is to set our mind thinking about definite essences only. Wherefore, when the existence of attributes does not differ from their essence, no experience is capable of attaining it for us.

To your further question, whether things and their modifications are eternal truths, I answer: Certainly. If you ask me, why I do not call them eternal truths, I answer, in order to distinguish them, in accordance with general usage, from those propositions, which do not make manifest any particular thing or modification of a thing; for example, *nothing comes from nothing*. These and such like propositions are, I repeat, called eternal truths simply, the meaning merely being, that they have no standpoint external to the mind, &c.

LETTER XXIX. (XII.)

Spinoza to L. M.[1] (Lewis Meyer).

Dearest Friend,—I have received two letters from you, one dated Jan. 11, delivered to me by our friend, N. N., the other dated March 26, sent by some unknown friend to Leyden. They were both most welcome to me, especially as I gathered from them, that all goes well with you, and that you are often mindful of me. I also owe and repay you the warmest thanks for the courtesy and consideration, with which you have always been kind enough to treat me: I hope you will believe, that I am in no less degree devoted to you, as, when occasion offers, I will always endeavour to prove, as far as my poor powers will admit. As a first proof, I will do my best to answer the questions you ask in your letters. You request me to tell you, what I think about the infinite; I will most readily do so.

Everyone regards the question of the infinite as most difficult, if not insoluble, through not making a distinction between that which must be infinite from its very nature, or in virtue of its definition, and that which has no limits, not in virtue of its essence, but in virtue of its cause; and also through not distinguishing between that which is called

[1] See Introduction, pp. xv, xx.

infinite, because it has no limits, and that, of which the parts cannot be equalled or expressed by any number, though the greatest and least magnitude of the whole may be known; and, lastly, through not distinguishing between that, which can be understood but not imagined, and that which can also be imagined. If these distinctions, I repeat, had been attended to, inquirers would not have been overwhelmed with such a vast crowd of difficulties. They would then clearly have understood, what kind of infinite is indivisible and possesses no parts; and what kind, on the other hand, may be divided without involving a contradiction in terms. They would further have understood, what kind of infinite may, without solecism, be conceived greater than another infinite, and what kind cannot be so conceived. All this will plainly appear from what I am about to say.

However, I will first briefly explain the terms *substance, mode, eternity*, and *duration.*

The points to be noted concerning substance are these: First, that existence appertains to its essence; in other words, that solely from its essence and definition its existence follows. This, if I remember rightly, I have already proved to you by word of mouth, without the aid of any other propositions. Secondly, as a consequence of the above, that substance is not manifold, but single: there cannot be two of the same nature. Thirdly, every substance must be conceived as infinite.

The modifications of substance I call *modes.* Their definition, in so far as it is not identical with that of substance, cannot involve any existence. Hence, though they exist, we can conceive them as non-existent. From this it follows, that, when we are regarding only the essence of modes, and not the order of the whole of nature, we cannot conclude from their present existence, that they will exist or not exist in the future, or that they have existed or not existed in the past; whence it is abundantly clear, that we conceive the existence of substance as entirely different from the existence of modes. From this difference arises the distinction between *eternity* and *duration. Duration* is only applicable to the existence of modes; *eternity* is applicable to the existence of substance, that is, the infinite faculty of existence or being (*infinitum existendi sive* (*invitâ Latinitate*[1]) *essendi fruitionem*).

From what has been said it is quite clear that, when, as is most often the case, we are regarding only the essence of modes and not the order of nature, we may freely limit the existence and duration of modes without destroying the conception we have formed of them; we may conceive them as greater or less, or may divide them into parts. Eternity and substance, being only conceivable as infinite, cannot be thus treated without our conception of them being destroyed. Wherefore it is mere foolishness, or even insanity, to say that extended substance is made up of parts or bodies really distinct from one another. It is as though one should attempt by the aggregation and addition of many circles to make up a square, or a triangle, or something of totally different essence. Wherefore the whole heap of arguments, by which philosophers commonly endeavour to show that extended substance is finite, falls to the ground by its own weight. For all such persons suppose, that corporeal substance is made up of parts. In the same way, others, who have persuaded themselves that a line is made up of points, have been able to discover many arguments to show that a line is not infinitely divisible. If you ask, why we are by nature so prone to attempt to divide extended substance, I answer, that quantity is conceived by us in two ways, namely, by abstraction or superficially, as we imagine it by the aid of the senses, or as substance, which can only be accomplished through the understanding. So that, if we regard quantity as it exists in the imagination (and this is the more frequent and easy method), it will be found to be divisible, finite, composed of parts, and manifold. But, if we regard it as it is in the understanding, and the thing be conceived as it is in itself (which is very difficult), it will then, as I have sufficiently shown you before, be found to be infinite, indivisible, and single.

Again, from the fact that we can limit duration and quantity at our pleasure, when we conceive the latter ab-

[1] Spinoza apologizes here in the original for the use of the unclassical form "essendi," being. The classical Latin verb of being is, as the ancients themselves admitted, defective in a most inconvenient degree.

stractedly as apart from substance, and separate the former from the manner whereby it flows from things eternal, there arise *time* and *measure ; time* for the purpose of limiting duration, *measure* for the purpose of limiting quantity, so that we may, as far as is possible, the more readily imagine them. Further, inasmuch as we separate the modifications of substance from substance itself, and reduce them to classes, so that we may, as far as is possible, the more readily imagine them, there arises *number*, whereby we limit them. Whence it is clearly to be seen, that measure, time, and number, are merely modes of thinking, or, rather, of imagining. It is not to be wondered at, therefore, that all, who have endeavoured to understand the course of nature by means of such notions, and without fully understanding even them, have entangled themselves so wondrously, that they have at last only been able to extricate themselves by breaking through every rule and admitting absurdities even of the grossest kind. For there are many things which cannot be conceived through the imagination but only through the understanding, for instance, substance, eternity, and the like; thus, if anyone tries to explain such things by means of conceptions which are mere aids to the imagination, he is simply assisting his imagination to run away with him.[1] Nor can even the modes of substance ever be rightly understood, if we confuse them with entities of the kind mentioned, mere aids of the reason or imagination. In so doing we separate them from substance, and the mode of their derivation from eternity, without which they can never be rightly understood. To make the matter yet more clear, take the following example: when a man conceives of duration abstractedly, and, confusing it with time, begins to divide it into parts, he will never be able to understand how an hour, for instance, can elapse. For in order that an hour should elapse, it is necessary that its half should elapse first, and afterwards half of the remainder, and again half of the half of the remainder, and if you go on thus to infinity, subtracting the half of the residue, you will never be able

[1] "Nihilo plus agit, quam si det operam ut sua imaginatione insaniat." Mr. Pollock paraphrases, "It is like applying the intellectual tests of sanity and insanity to acts of pure imagination."

to arrive at the end of the hour. Wherefore many, who are not accustomed to distinguish abstractions from realities, have ventured to assert that duration is made up of instants, and so in wishing to avoid Charybdis have fallen into Scylla. It is the same thing to make up duration out of instants, as it is to make number simply by adding up noughts.

Further, as it is evident from what has been said, that neither number, nor measure, nor time, being mere aids to the imagination, can be infinite (for, otherwise, number would not be number, nor measure measure, nor time time); it is hence abundantly evident, why many who confuse these three abstractions with realities, through being ignorant of the true nature of things, have actually denied the infinite.

The wretchedness of their reasoning may be jndged by mathematicians, who have never allowed themselves to be delayed a moment by arguments of this sort, in the case of things which they clearly and distinctly perceive. For not only have they come across many things, which cannot be expressed by number (thus showing the inadequacy of number for determining all things); but also they have found many things, which cannot be equalled by any number, but surpass every possible number. But they infer hence, that such things surpass enumeration, not because of the multitude of their component parts, but because their nature cannot, without manifest contradiction, be expressed in terms of number. As, for instance, in the case of two circles, non-concentric, whereof one encloses the other, no number can express the inequalities of distance which exist between the two circles, nor all the variations which matter in motion in the intervening space may undergo. This conclusion is not based on the excessive size of the intervening space. However small a portion of it we take, the inequalities of this small portion will surpass all numerical expression. Nor, again, is the conclusion based on the fact, as in other cases, that we do not know the maximum and the minimum of the said space. It springs simply from the fact, that the nature of the space between two non-concentric circles cannot be expressed in number. Therefore, he who would assign a numerical equivalent for the inequalities in question, would be bound, at the same time, to bring about that a circle should not be a circle.

The same result would take place—to return to my subject—if one were to wish to determine all the motions undergone by matter up to the present, by reducing them and their duration to a certain number and time. This would be the same as an attempt to deprive corporeal substance, which we cannot conceive except as existent, of its modifications, and to bring about that it should not possess the nature which it does possess. All this I could clearly demonstrate here, together with many other points touched on in this letter, but I deem it superfluous.

From all that has been said, it is abundantly evident that certain things are in their nature infinite, and can by no means be conceived as finite; whereas there are other things, infinite in virtue of the cause from which they are derived, which can, when conceived abstractedly, be divided into parts, and regarded as finite. Lastly, there are some which are called infinite or, if you prefer, indefinite, because they cannot be expressed in number, which may yet be conceived as greater or less. It does not follow that such are equal, because they are alike incapable of numerical expression. This is plain enough, from the example given, and many others.

Lastly, I have put briefly before you the causes of error and confusion, which have arisen concerning the question of the infinite. I have, if I mistake not, so explained them that no question concerning the infinite remains untreated, or cannot readily be solved from what I have said; wherefore, I do not think it worth while to detain you longer on the matter.

But I should like it first to be observed here, that the later Peripatetics have, I think, misunderstood the proof given by the ancients who sought to demonstrate the existence of God. This, as I find it in a certain Jew named Rabbi Ghasdai, runs as follows:—"If there be an infinite series of causes, all things which are, are caused. But nothing which is caused can exist necessarily in virtue of its own nature. Therefore there is nothing in nature, to whose essence existence necessarily belongs. But this is absurd. Therefore the premise is absurd also." Hence the force of the argument lies not in the impossibility of an actual infinite or an infinite series of causes; but only in the absurdity of the assumption that things, which do not necessarily exist by nature, are not conditioned for existence by a thing, which does by its own nature necessarily exist.

I would now pass on, for time presses, to your second letter: but I shall be able more conveniently to reply to its contents, when you are kind enough to pay me a visit. I therefore beg that you will come as soon as possible; the time for travelling is at hand. Enough. Farewell, and keep in remembrance Yours, &c.

Rhijnsburg, 20 April, 1663.

LETTER XXIX.A.[1]

Spinoza to Lewis Meyer.

Dear Friend,—The preface you sent me by our friend De Vries, I now send back to you by the same hand. Some few things, as you will see, I have marked in the margin; but yet a few remain, which I have judged it better to mention to you by letter. First, where on page 4 you give the reader to know on what occasion I composed the first part; I would have you likewise explain there, or where you please, that I composed it within a fortnight. For when this is explained none will suppose the exposition to be so clear as that it cannot be bettered, and so they will not stick at obscurities in this and that phrase on which they may chance to stumble. Secondly, I would have you explain, that when I prove many points otherwise than they be proved by Descartes, 'tis not to amend Descartes, but the better to preserve my order, and not to multiply

[1] This letter is not given in the *Opera Posthuma*, but was preserved in M. Cousin's library at the Sorbonne. This version is reprinted, by kind permission, from Mr. Pollock's "Spinoza, his Life and Philosophy," Appendix C.

axioms overmuch: and that for this same reason I prove many things which by Descartes are barely alleged without any proof, and must needs add other matters which Descartes let alone. Lastly, I will earnestly beseech you, as my especial friend, to let be everything you have written towards the end against that creature, and wholly strike it out. And though many reasons determine me to this request, I will give but one. I would fain have all men readily believe that these matters are published for the common profit of the world, and that your sole motive in bringing out the book is the love of spreading the truth; and that it is accordingly all your study to make the work acceptable to all, to bid men, with all courtesy to the pursuit of genuine philosophy, and to consult their common advantage. Which every man will be ready to think when he sees that no one is attacked, nor anything advanced where any man can find the least offence. Notwithstanding, if afterwards the person you know of, or any other, be minded to display his ill will, then you may portray his life and character, and gain applause by it. So I ask that you will not refuse to be patient thus far, and suffer yourself to be entreated, and believe me wholly bounden to you, and

Yours with all affection,

B. DE SPINOZA.

Voorburg, Aug. 3, 1663.

Our friend De Vries had promised to take this with him; but seeing he knows not when he will return to you, I send it by another hand.

Along with this I send you part of the scholium to Prop. xxvii. Part II. where page 75 begins, that you may hand it to the printer to be reprinted. The matter I send you must of necessity be reprinted, and fourteen or fifteen lines added, which may easily be inserted.

LETTER XXX. (XVII.)

SPINOZA TO PETER BALLING.[1]

[*Concerning omens and phantoms. The mind may have a confused presentiment of the future.*]

BELOVED FRIEND,—Your last letter, written, if I mistake not, on the 26th of last month, has duly reached me. It caused me no small sorrow and solicitude, though the feeling sensibly diminished when I reflected on the good sense and fortitude, with which you have known how to despise the evils of fortune, or rather of opinion, at a time when they most bitterly assailed you. Yet my anxiety increases daily; I therefore beg and implore you by the claims of our friendship, that you will rouse yourself to write me a long letter. With regard to *Omens*, of which you make mention in telling me that, while your child was still healthy and strong, you heard groans like those he uttered when he was ill and shortly afterwards died, I should judge that these were not real groans, but only the effect of your imagination; for you say that, when you got up and composed yourself to listen, you did not hear them so clearly either as before or as afterwards, when you had fallen asleep again. This, I think, shows that the groans were purely due to the imagination, which, when it was unfettered and free, could imagine groans more forcibly and vividly than when you sat up in order to listen in a particular direction. I think I can both illustrate and confirm what I say by another occurrence, which befell me at Rhijnsburg last winter. When one morning, after the day had dawned, I woke up from a very unpleasant dream, the images, which had presented themselves to me in sleep, remained before my eyes just as vividly as though the things had been real, especially the image of a certain black and leprous Brazilian whom I had never seen before. This image disappeared for the most part when, in order to divert my thoughts, I

[1] This letter is from a Latin version of a Dutch original. For Balling, see Letter XXVI., p. 312, and note there.

cast my eyes on a book, or something else. But, as soon as I lifted my eyes again without fixing my attention on any particular object, the same image of this same negro appeared with the same vividness again and again, until the head of it gradually vanished. I say that the same thing, which occurred with regard to my inward sense of sight, occurred with your hearing; but as the causes were very different, your case was an omen and mine was not. The matter may be clearly grasped by means of what I am about to say. The effects of the imagination arise either from bodily or mental causes. I will proceed to prove this, in order not to be too long, solely from experience. We know that fevers and other bodily ailments are the causes of delirium, and that persons of stubborn disposition imagine nothing but quarrels, brawls, slaughterings, and the like. We also see that the imagination is to a certain extent determined by the character of the disposition, for, as we know by experience, it follows in the tracks of the understanding in every respect, and arranges its images and words, just as the understanding arranges its demonstrations and connects one with another; so that we are hardly at all able to say, what will not serve the imagination as a basis for some image or other. This being so, I say that no effects of imagination springing from physical causes can ever be omens of future events; inasmuch as their causes do not involve any future events. But the effects of imagination, or images originating in the mental disposition, may be omens of some future event; inasmuch as the mind may have a confused presentiment of the future. It may, therefore, imagine a future event as forcibly and vividly, as though it were present; for instance a father (to take an example resembling your own) loves his child so much, that he and the beloved child are, as it were, one and the same. And since (like that which I demonstrated on another occasion) there must necessarily exist in thought the idea of the essence of the child's states and their results, and since the father, through his union with his child, is a part of the said child, the soul of the father must necessarily participate in the ideal essence of the child and his states, and in their results, as I have shown at greater length elsewhere.

Again, as the soul of the father participates ideally in the consequences of his child's essence, he may (as I have said) sometimes imagine some of the said consequences as vividly as if they were present with him, provided that the following conditions are fulfilled:—I. If the occurrence in his son's career be remarkable. II. If it be capable of being readily imagined. III. If the time of its happening be not too remote. IV. If his body be sound, in respect not only of health but of freedom from every care or business which could outwardly trouble the senses. It may also assist the result, if we think of something which generally stimulates similar ideas. For instance, if while we are talking with this or that man we hear groans, it will generally happen that, when we think of the man again, the groans heard when we spoke with him will recur to our mind. This, dear friend, is my opinion on the question you ask me. I have, I confess, been very brief, but I have furnished you with material for writing to me on the first opportunity, &c.

Voorburg, 20 July, 1664.

LETTER XXXI. (XVIII.)

William de Blyenbergh[1] to Spinoza.

Unknown Friend and Sir,—I have already read several times with attention your treatise and its appendix recently published. I should narrate to others more becomingly than to yourself the extreme solidity I found in it, and the pleasure with which I perused it. But I am unable to conceal my feeelings from you, because the more frequently I study the work with attention, the more it pleases me, and I am constantly observing something which I had not before remarked. However, I will not too loudly extol its author, lest I should seem in this letter to be a flatterer. I am aware that the gods grant all things to labour. Not to detain you too long with wondering who I may be, and how it comes to pass that one unknown to you

[1] See Introduction, p. xvi. The correspondence with Blyenbergh was originally conducted in Dutch.

takes the great liberty of writing to you, I will tell you that he is a man who is impelled by his longing for pure and unadulterated truth, and desires during this brief and frail life to fix his feet in the ways of science, so far as our human faculties will allow; one who in the pursuit of truth has no goal before his eyes save truth herself; one who by his science seeks to obtain as the result of truth neither honour nor riches, but simple truth and tranquillity; one who, out of the whole circle of truths and sciences, takes delight in none more than in metaphysics, if not in all branches at any rate in some; one who places the whole delight of his life in the fact, that he can pass in the study of them his hours of ease and leisure. But no one, I rest assured, is so blessed as yourself, no one has carried his studies so far, and therefore no one has arrived at the pitch of perfection which, as I see from your work, you have attained. To add a last word, the present writer is one with whom you may gain a closer acquaintance, if you choose to attach him to you by enlightening and interpenetrating, as it were, his halting meditations.

But I return to your treatise. While I found in it many things which tickled my palate vastly, some of them proved difficult to digest. Perhaps a stranger ought not to report to you his objections, the more so as I know not whether they will meet with your approval. This is the reason for my making these prefatory remarks, and asking you, if you can find leisure in the winter evenings, and, at the same time, will be willing to answer the difficulties which I still find in your book, and to forward me the result, always under the condition that it does not interrupt any occupation of greater importance or pleasure; for I desire nothing more earnestly than to see the promise made in your book fulfilled by a more detailed exposition of your opinions. I should have communicated to you by word of mouth what I now commit to paper; but my ignorance of your address, the infectious disease,[1] and my duties here, prevented me. I must defer the pleasure for the present.

However, in order that this letter may not be quite

[1] The plague, which had prevailed on the Continent during 1664, was introduced into London in the very month in which this letter was written, perhaps from Holland.

empty, and in the hope that it will not be displeasing to you, I will ask you one question. You say in various passages in the "Principia," and in the "Metaphysical Reflections," either as your own opinion, or as explaining the philosophy of Descartes, that creation and preservation are identical (which is, indeed, so evident to those who have considered the question as to be a primary notion); secondly, that God has not only created substances, but also motions in substances—in other words, that God, by a continuous act of creation preserves, not only substances in their normal state, but also the motion and the endeavours of substances. God, for instance, not only brings about by His immediate will and working (whatever be the term employed), that the soul should last and continue in its normal state; but He is also the cause of His will determining, in some way, the movement of the soul—in other words, as God, by a continuous act of creation, brings about that things should remain in existence, so is He also the cause of the movements and endeavours existing in things. In fact, save God, there is no cause of motion. It therefore follows that God is not only the cause of the substance of mind, but also of every endeavour or motion of mind, which we call volition, as you frequently say. From this statement it seems to follow necessarily, either that there is no evil in the motion or volition of the mind, or else that God directly brings about that evil. For that which we call evil comes to pass through the soul, and, consequently, through the immediate influence and concurrence of God. For instance, the soul of Adam wishes to eat of the forbidden fruit. It follows from what has been said above, not only that Adam forms his wish through the influence of God, but also, as will presently be shown, that through that influence he forms it in that particular manner. Hence, either the act forbidden to Adam is not evil, inasmuch as God Himself not only caused the wish, but also the manner of it, or else God directly brought about that which we call evil. Neither you nor Descartes seem to have solved this difficulty by saying that evil is a negative conception, and that, as such, God cannot bring it about. Whence, we may ask, came the wish to eat the forbidden fruit, or the wish of devils to be equal with God?

For since (as you justly observe) the will is not something different from the mind, but is only an endeavour or movement of the mind, the concurrence of God is as necessary to it as to the mind itself. Now the concurrence of God, as I gather from your writings, is merely the determining of a thing in a particular manner through the will of God. It follows that God concurs no less in an evil wish, in so far as it is evil, than in a good wish in so far as it is good, in other words, He determines it. For the will of God being the absolute cause of all that exists, either in substance or in effort, seems to be also the primary cause of an evil wish, in so far as it is evil. Again, no exercise of volition takes place in us, that God has not known from all eternity. If we say that God does not know of a particular exercise of volition, we attribute to Him imperfection. But how could God gain knowledge of it except from His decrees? Therefore His decrees are the cause of our volitions, and hence it seems also to follow that either an evil wish is not evil, or else that God is the direct cause of the evil, and brings it about. There is no room here for the theological distinction between an act and the evil inherent in that act. For God decrees the mode of the act, no less than the act, that is, God not only decreed that Adam should eat, but also that he should necessarily eat contrary to the command given. Thus it seems on all sides to follow, either that Adam's eating contrary to the command was not an evil, or else that God Himself brought it to pass.

These, illustrious Sir, are the questions in your treatise, which I am unable, at present, to elucidate. Either alternative seems to me difficult of acceptance. However, I await a satisfactory answer from your keen judgment and learning, hoping to show you hereafter how deeply indebted I shall be to you. Be assured, illustrious Sir, that I put these questions from no other motive than the desire for truth. I am a man of leisure, not tied to any profession, gaining my living by honest trade, and devoting my spare time to questions of this sort. I humbly hope that my difficulties will not be displeasing to you. If you are minded to send an answer, as I most ardently hope, write to, &c.

WILLIAM DE BLYENBERGH.

Dordrecht, 12 Dec., 1664.

LETTER XXXII. (XIX.)

SPINOZA TO BLYENBERGH.

(Spinoza answers with his usual courtesy the question propounded by Blyenbergh.)

UNKNOWN FRIEND,—I received, at Schiedam, on the 26th of December, your letter dated the 12th of December, enclosed in another written on the 24th of the same month. I gather from it your fervent love of truth, and your making it the aim of all your studies. This compelled me, though by no means otherwise unwilling, not only to grant your petition by answering all the questions you have sent, or may in future send, to the best of my ability, but also to impart to you everything in my power, which can conduce to further knowledge and sincere friendship. So far as in me lies, I value, above all other things out of my own control, the joining hands of friendship with men who are sincere lovers of truth. I believe that nothing in the world, of things outside our own control, brings more peace than the possibility of affectionate intercourse with such men; it is just as impossible that the love we bear them can be disturbed (inasmuch as it is founded on the desire each feels for the knowledge of truth), as that truth once perceived should not be assented to. It is, moreover, the highest and most pleasing source of happiness derivable from things not under our own control. Nothing save truth has power closely to unite different feelings and dispositions. I say nothing of the very great advantages which it brings, lest I should detain you too long on a subject which, doubtless, you know already. I have said thus much, in order to show you better how gladly I shall embrace this and any future opportunity of serving you.

In order to make the best of the present opportunity, I will at once proceed to answer your question. This seems to turn on the point "that it seems to be clear, not only from God's providence, which is identical with His will, but also from God's co-operation and continuous creation of things, either that there are no such things as sin or evil, or that God directly brings sin and evil to pass." You do not, however, explain what you mean by evil. As far as one may judge from the example you give in the predetermined act of volition of Adam, you seem to mean by evil the actual exercise of volition, in so far as it is conceived as predetermined in a particular way, or in so far as it is repugnant to the command of God. Hence you conclude (and I agree with you if this be what you mean) that it is absurd to adopt either alternative, either that God brings to pass anything contrary to His own will, or that what is contrary to God's will can be good.

For my own part, I cannot admit that sin and evil have any positive existence, far less that anything can exist, or come to pass, contrary to the will of God. On the contrary, not only do I assert that sin has no positive existence, I also maintain that only in speaking improperly, or humanly, can we say that we sin against God, as in the expression that men offend God.

As to the first point, we know that whatsoever is, when considered in itself without regard to anything else, possesses perfection, extending in each thing as far as the limits of that thing's essence: for essence is nothing else. I take for an illustration the design or determined will of Adam to eat the forbidden fruit. This design or determined will, considered in itself alone, includes perfection in so far as it expresses reality; hence it may be inferred that we can only conceive imperfection in things, when they are viewed in relation to other things possessing more reality: thus in Adam's decision, so long as we view it by itself and do not compare it with other things more perfect or exhibiting a more perfect state, we can find no imperfection: nay it may be compared with an infinity of other things far less perfect in this respect than itself, such as stones, stocks, &c. This, as a matter of fact, everyone grants. For we all admire in animals qualities which we regard with dislike and aversion in men, such as the pugnacity of bees, the jealousy of doves, &c.; these in human beings are despised, but are nevertheless considered to enhance the value of animals. This being so, it follows that sin, which indicates nothing save imperfection, cannot consist in anything that expresses reality, as we see in the case of Adam's decision and its execution.

Again, we cannot say that Adam's will is at variance with the law of God, and that it is evil because it is displeasing to God; for besides the fact that grave imperfection would be imputed to God, if we say that anything happens contrary to His will, or that He desires anything which He does not obtain, or that His nature resembled that of His creatures in having sympathy with some things more than others; such an occurrence would be at complete variance with the nature of the divine will.

The will of God is identical with His intellect, hence the former can no more be contravened than the latter; in other words, anything which should come to pass against His will must be of a nature to be contrary to His intellect, such, for instance, as a round square. Hence the will or decision of Adam regarded in itself was neither evil nor, properly speaking, against the will of God: it follows that God may—or rather, for the reason you call attention to, must—be its cause; not in so far as it was evil, for the evil in it consisted in the loss of the previous state of being which it entailed on Adam, and it is certain that loss has no positive existence, and is only so spoken of in respect to our and not God's understanding. The difficulty arises from the fact, that we give one and the same definition to all the individuals of a genus, as for instance all who have the outward appearance of men: we accordingly assume all things which are expressed by the same definition to be equally capable of attaining the highest perfection possible for the genus; when we find an individual whose actions are at variance with such perfection, we suppose him to be deprived of it, and to fall short of his nature. We should hardly act in this way, if we did not hark back to the definition and ascribe to the individual a nature in accordance with it. But as God does not know things through abstraction, or form general definitions of the kind above mentioned, and as things have no more reality than the divine understanding and power have put into them and actually endowed them with, it clearly follows that a state of privation can only be spoken of in relation to our intellect, not in relation to God.

Thus, as it seems to me, the difficulty is completely solved. However, in order to make the way still plainer, and remove every doubt, I deem it necessary to answer the two following difficulties:—First, why Holy Scripture says that God wishes for the conversion of the wicked, and also why God forbade Adam to eat of the fruit when He had ordained the contrary? Secondly, that it seems to follow from what I have said, that the wicked by their pride, avarice, and deeds of desperation, worship God in no less degree than the good do by their nobleness, patience, love, &c., inasmuch as both execute God's will.

In answer to the first question, I observe that Scripture, being chiefly fitted for and beneficial to the multitude, speaks popularly after the fashion of men. For the multitude are incapable of grasping sublime conceptions. Hence I am persuaded that all matters, which God revealed to the prophets as necessary to salvation, are set down in the form of laws. With this understanding, the prophets invented whole parables, and represented God as a king and a law-giver, because He had revealed the means of salvation and perdition, and was their cause; the means which were simply causes they styled laws and wrote them down as such; salvation and perdition, which are simply effects necessarily resulting from the aforesaid means, they described as reward and punishment; framing their doctrines more in accordance with such parables than with actual truth. They constantly speak of God as resembling a man, as sometimes angry, sometimes merciful, now desiring what is future, now jealous and suspicious, even as deceived by the devil; so that philosophers and all who are above the law, that is, who follow after virtue, not in obedience to law, but through love, because it is the most excellent of all things, must not be hindered by such expressions.

Thus the command given to Adam consisted solely in this, that God revealed to Adam, that eating of the fruit brought about death; as He reveals to us, through our natural faculties, that poison is deadly. If you ask, for what object did He make this revelation, I answer, in order to render Adam to that extent more perfect in knowledge. Hence, to ask God why He had not bestowed on Adam a more perfect will, is just as absurd as to ask, why the circle has not been endowed with all the properties of a sphere. This follows clearly from what has been said, and I have also proved it in my Principles of Cartesian Philosophy, I. 15.

As to the second difficulty, it is true that the wicked execute after their manner the will of God: but they cannot, therefore, be in any respect compared with the good. The more perfection a thing has, the more does it partici pate in the deity, and the more does it express perfection. Thus, as the good have incomparably more perfection than the bad, their virtue cannot be likened to the virtue of the wicked, inasmuch as the wicked lack the love of God, which proceeds from the knowledge of God, and by which alone we are, according to our human understanding, called the servants of God. The wicked, knowing not God, are but as instruments in the hand of the workman, serving unconsciously, and perishing in the using; the good, on the other hand, serve consciously, and in serving become more perfect.

[1] This, Sir, is all I can now contribute to answering your question, and I have no higher wish than that it may satisfy you. But in case you still find any difficulty, I beg you to let me know of that also, to see if I may be able to remove it. You have nothing to fear on your side, but so long as you are not satisfied, I like nothing better than to be informed of your reasons, so that finally the truth may appear. I could have wished to write in the tongue in which I have been brought up. I should, perhaps, have been able to express my thoughts better. But be pleased to take it as it is, amend the mistakes yourself, and believe me,

Your sincere friend and servant.

Long Orchard, near Amsterdam,
Jan. 5, 1665.

[1] The last paragraph (not found in the Latin version) is reprinted by kind permission from Mr. Pollock's translation from the Dutch original, Pollock's "Spinoza," Appendix C. On page 332 a misprint of "perfectioribus" for "imperfectioribus" is corrected from the original.

LETTER XXXIII. (XX.)

Blyenbergh to Spinoza.

(*A summary only of this letter is here given.*—Tr.)

I have two rules in my philosophic inquiries: i. Conformity to reason; ii. Conformity to scripture. I consider the second the most important. Examining your letter by the first, I observe that your identification of God's creative power with His preservative power seems to involve, either that evil does not exist, or else that God brings about evil. If evil be only a term relative to our imperfect knowledge, how do you explain the state of a man who falls from a state of grace into sin? If evil be a negation, how can we have the power to sin? If God causes an evil act, he must cause the evil as well as the act. You say that every man can only act, as he, in fact, does act. This removes all distinction between the good and the wicked. Both, according to you, are perfect. You remove all the sanctions of virtue and reduce us to automata. Your doctrine, that strictly speaking we cannot sin against God, is a hard saying.

[The rest of the letter is taken up with an examination of Spinoza's arguments in respect to their conformity to Scripture.]

Dordrecht, 16 Jan., 1665.

LETTER XXXIV. (XXI.)

Spinoza to Blyenbergh.

[*Spinoza complains that Blyenbergh has misunderstood him: he sets forth his true meaning.*]

Voorburg, 28 Jan., 1665.

Friend and Sir,—When I read your first letter, I thought that our opinions almost coincided. But from the second, which was delivered to me on the 21st of this month, I see that the matter stands far otherwise, for I perceive that we disagree, not only in remote inferences from first principles, but also in first principles themselves; so that I can hardly think that we can derive any mutual instruction from further correspondence. I see that no proof, though it be by the laws of proof most sound, has any weight with you, unless it agrees with the explanation, which either you yourself, or other theologians known to you, attribute to Holy Scripture. However, if you are convinced that God speaks more clearly and effectually through Holy Scripture than through the natural understanding, which He also has bestowed upon us, and with His divine wisdom keeps continually stable and uncorrupted, you have valid reasons for making your understanding bow before the opinions which you attribute to Holy Scripture; I myself could adopt no different course. For my own part, as I confess plainly, and without circumlocution, that I do not understand the Scriptures, though I have spent some years upon them, and also as I feel that when I have obtained a firm proof, I cannot fall into a state of doubt concerning it, I acquiesce entirely in what is commended to me by my understanding, without any suspicion that I am being deceived in the matter, or that Holy Scripture, though I do not search, could gainsay it: for "truth is not at variance with truth," as I have already clearly shown in my appendix to The Principles of Cartesian Philosophy (I cannot give the precise reference, for I have not the book with me here in the country). But if in any instance I found that a result obtained through my natural understanding was false, I should reckon myself fortunate, for I enjoy life, and try to spend it not in sorrow and sighing, but in peace, joy, and cheerfulness, ascending from time to time a step higher. Meanwhile I know (and this knowledge gives me the highest contentment and peace of mind), that all things come to pass by the power and unchangeable decree of a Being supremely perfect.

To return to your letter, I owe you many and sincere thanks for having confided to me your philosophical opinions; but for the doctrines, which you attribute to me, and seek to infer from my letter, I return you no thanks at at all. What ground, I should like to know, has my letter afforded you for ascribing to me the opinions; that men are like beasts, that they die and perish after the manner of beasts, that our actions are displeasing to God, &c.? Perhaps we are most of all at variance on this third point. You think, as far as I can judge, that God takes pleasure in our actions, as though He were a man, who has attained his object, when things fall out as he desired. For my part, have I not said plainly enough, that the good worship God, that in continually serving Him they become more perfect, and that they love God? Is this, I ask, likening them to beasts, or saying that they perish like beasts, or that their actions are displeasing to God? If you had read my letter with more attention, you would have clearly perceived, that our whole dissension lies in the following alternative:—Either the perfections which the good receive are imparted to them by God in His capacity of God, that is absolutely without any human qualities being ascribed to Him—this is what I believe; or else such perfections are imparted by God as a judge, which is what you maintain. For this reason you defend the wicked, saying that they carry out God's decrees as far as in them lies, and therefore serve God no less than the good. But if my doctrine be accepted, this consequence by no means follows; I do not bring in the idea of God as a judge, and, therefore, I estimate an action by its intrinsic merits, not by the powers of its performer; the recompense which follows the action follows from it as necessarily as from the nature of a triangle it follows, that the three angles are equal to two right angles. This may be understood by everyone, who reflects on the fact, that our highest blessedness consists in love towards God, and that such love flows naturally from the knowledge of God, which is so strenuously enjoined on us. The question may very easily be proved in general terms, if we take notice of the nature of God's decrees, as explained in my appendix. However, I confess that all those, who confuse the divine nature with human nature, are gravely hindered from understanding it.

I had intended to end my letter at this point, lest I should prove troublesome to you in these questions, the discussion of which (as I discover from the extremely pious postscript added to your letter) serves you as a pastime and a jest, but for no serious use. However, that I may not summarily deny your request, I will proceed to explain further the words privation and negation, and briefly point out what is necessary for the elucidation of my former letter.

I say then, first, that *privation* is not the act of depriving, but simply and merely a state of want, which is in itself nothing: it is a mere entity of the reason, a mode of thought framed in comparing one thing with another. We say, for example, that a blind man is deprived of sight, because we readily imagine him as seeing, or else because we compare him with others who can see, or compare his present condition with his past condition when he could see; when we regard the man in this way, comparing his nature either with the nature of others or with his own past nature, we affirm that sight belongs to his nature, and therefore assert that he has been deprived of it. But when we are considering the nature and decree of God, we cannot affirm privation of sight in the case of the aforesaid man any more than in the case of a stone; for at the actual time sight lies no more within the scope of the man than of the stone; *since there belongs to man and forms part of his nature only that which is granted to him by the understanding and will of God.* Hence it follows that God is no more the cause of a blind man not seeing, than he is of a stone not seeing. Not seeing is a pure negation. *So also, when we consider the case of a man who is led by lustful desires, we compare his present desires with those which exist in the good, or which existed in himself at some other time; we then assert that he is deprived of the better desires, because we conceive that virtuous desires lie within the scope of his nature. This we cannot do, if we consider the nature and decree of God. For, from this point of view, virtuous desires lie at that time no more within the scope of the nature of the lustful man, than within the scope of the nature of the devil or a stone.* Hence, from the latter standpoint the virtuous desire is not a privation but a negation.

Thus *privation* is nothing else than denying of a thing something, which we think belongs to its nature; *negation* is denying of a thing something, which we do not think belongs to its nature.

We may now see, how Adam's desire for earthly things

was evil from our standpoint, but not from God's. Although God knew both the present and the past state *of Adam, He did not, therefore, regard Adam as deprived of his past state, that is, He did not regard Adam's past state as within the scope of Adam's present nature.* Otherwise God would have apprehended something contrary to His own will, that is, contrary to His own understanding. If you quite grasp my meaning here and at the same time remember, that I do not grant to the mind the same freedom as Descartes does —L[ewis] M[eyer] bears witness to this in his preface to my book—you will perceive, that there is not the smallest contradiction in what I have said. But I see that I should have done far better to have answered you in my first letter with the words of Descartes, to the effect that we cannot know how our freedom and its consequences agree with the foreknowledge and freedom of God (see several passages in my appendix), that, therefore, we can discover no contradiction between creation by God and our freedom, because we cannot understand how God created the universe, nor (what is the same thing) how He preserves it. I thought that you had read the preface, and that by not giving you my real opinions in reply, I should sin against those duties of friendship which I cordially offered you. But this is of no consequence.

Still, as I see that you have not hitherto thoroughly grasped Descartes' meaning, I will call your attention to the two following points. First, that neither Descartes nor I have ever said, that it appertains to our nature to confine the will within the limits of the understanding; we have only said, that God has endowed us with a determined understanding and an undetermined will, so that we know not the object for which He has created us. Further, that an undetermined or perfect will of this kind not only makes us more perfect, but also, as I will presently show you, is extremely necessary for us.

Secondly: that our freedom is not placed in a certain contingency nor in a certain indifference, but in the method of affirmation or denial; so that, in proportion as we are less indifferent in affirmation or denial, so are we more free. For instance, if the nature of God be known to us, it follows as necessarily from our nature to affirm that God exists, as from the nature of a triangle it follows, that the three angles are equal to two right angles; we are never more free, than when we affirm a thing in this way. As this necessity is nothing else but the decree of God (as I have clearly shown in my appendix), we may hence, after a fashion, understand how we act freely and are the cause of our action, though all the time we are acting necessarily and according to the decree of God. This, I repeat, we may, after a fashion, understand, whenever we affirm something, which we clearly and distinctly perceive, but when we assert something which we do not clearly and distinctly understand, in other words, when we allow our will to pass beyond the limits of our understanding, we no longer perceive the necessity nor the decree of God, we can only see our freedom, which is always involved in our will; in which respect only our actions are called good or evil. If we then try to reconcile our freedom with God's decree and continuous creation, we confuse that which we clearly and distinctly understand with that which we do not perceive, and, therefore, our attempt is vain. It is, therefore, sufficient for us to know that we are free, and that we can be so notwithstanding God's decree, and further that we are the cause of evil, because an act can only be called evil in relation to our freedom. I have said thus much for Descartes in order to show that, in the question we are considering, his words exhibit no contradiction.

I will now turn to what concerns myself, and will first briefly call attention to the advantage arising from my opinion, inasmuch as, according to it, our understanding offers our mind and body to God freed from all superstition. Nor do I deny that prayer is extremely useful to us. For my understanding is too small to determine all the means, whereby God leads men to the love of Himself, that is, to salvation. So far is my opinion from being hurtful, that it offers to those, who are not taken up with prejudices and childish superstitions, the only means for arriving at the highest stage of blessedness.

When you say that, by making men so dependent on God, I reduce them to the likeness of the elements, plants or stones, you sufficiently show that you have thoroughly misunderstood my meaning, and have confused things which regard the understanding with things which regard the imagination. If by your intellect only you had perceived what dependence on God means, you certainly would not think that things, in so far as they depend on God, are dead, corporeal, and imperfect (who ever dared to speak so meanly of the Supremely Perfect Being?); on the contrary, you would understand that for the very reason that they depend on God they are perfect; so that this dependence and necessary operation may best be understood as God's decree, by considering, not stocks and plants, but the most reasonable and perfect creatures. This sufficiently appears from my second observation on the meaning of Descartes, which you ought to have looked to.

I cannot refrain from expressing my extreme astonishment at your remarking, that if God does not punish wrong-doing (that is, as a judge does, with a punishment not intrinsically connected with the offence, for our whole difference lies in this), what reason prevents me from rushing headlong into every kind of wickedness? Assuredly he, who is only kept from vice by the fear of punishment (which I do not think of you), is in no wise acted on by love, and by no means embraces virtue. For my own part, I avoid or endeavour to avoid vice, because it is at direct variance with my proper nature and would lead me astray from the knowledge and love of God.

Again, if you had reflected a little on human nature and the nature of God's decree (as explained in my appendix), and perceived, and known by this time, how a consequence should be deduced from its premises, before a conclusion is arrived at; you would not so rashly have stated that my opinion makes us like stocks, &c.: nor would you have ascribed to me the many absurdities you conjure up.

As to the two points which you say, before passing on to your second rule, that you cannot understand; I answer, that the first may be solved through Descartes, who says that in observing your own nature you feel that you can suspend your judgment. If you say that you do not feel, that you have at present sufficient force to keep your judgment suspended, this would appear to Descartes to be the same as saying that we cannot at present see, that so long as we exist we shall always be thinking things, or retain the nature of thinking things; in fact it would imply a contradiction.

As to your second difficulty, I say with Descartes, that if we cannot extend our will beyond the bounds of our extremely limited understanding, we shall be most wretched —it will not be in our power to eat even a crust of bread, or to walk a step, or to go on living, for all things are uncertain and full of peril.

I now pass on to your second rule, and assert that I believe, though I do not ascribe to Scripture that sort of truth which you think you find in it, I nevertheless assign to it as great if not greater authority than you do. I am far more careful than others not to ascribe to Scripture any childish and absurd doctrines, a precaution which demands either a thorough acquaintance with philosophy or the possession of divine revelations. Hence I pay very little attention to the glosses put upon Scripture by ordinary theologians, especially those of the kind who always interpret Scripture according to the literal and outward meaning: I have never, except among the Socinians, found any theologian stupid enough to ignore that Holy Scripture very often speaks in human fashion of God and expresses its meaning in parables; as for the contradiction which you vainly (in my opinion) endeavour to show, I think you attach to the word parable a meaning different from that usually given. For who ever heard, that a man, who expressed his opinions in parables, had therefore taken leave of his senses? When Micaiah said to King Ahab, that he had seen God sitting on a throne, with the armies of heaven standing on the right hand and the left, and that God asked His angels which of them would deceive Ahab, this was assuredly a parable employed by the prophet on that occasion (which was not fitted for the inculcation of sublime theological doctrines), as sufficiently setting forth the message he had to deliver in the name of God. We cannot say that he had in anywise taken leave of his senses. So also the other prophets of God made manifest God's commands to the people in this fashion as being the best adapted, though not expressly enjoined by

God, for leading the people to the primary object of Scripture, which, as Christ Himself says, is to bid men love God above all things, and their neighbour as themselves. Sublime speculations have, in my opinion, no bearing on Scripture. As far as I am concerned I have never learnt or been able to learn any of God's eternal attributes from Holy Scripture.

As to your fifth argument (that the prophets thus made manifest the word of God, since truth is not at variance with truth), it merely amounts, for those who understand the method of proof, to asking me to prove, that Scripture, as it is, is the true revealed word of God. The mathematical proof of this proposition could only be attained by divine revelation. I, therefore, expressed myself as follows: "*I believe, but I do not mathematically know, that all things revealed by God to the prophets,*" &c. Inasmuch as I firmly believe but do not mathematically know, that the prophets were the most trusted counsellors and faithful ambassadors of God. So that in all I have written there is no contradiction, though several such may be found among holders of the opposite opinion.

The rest of your letter (to wit the passage where you say, "Lastly, the supremely perfect Being knew beforehand," &c; and again, your objections to the illustration from poison, and lastly, the whole of what you say of the appendix and what follows) seems to me beside the question.

As regards Lewis Meyer's preface, the points which were still left to be proved by Descartes before establishing his demonstration of free will, are certainly there set forth; it is added that I hold a contrary opinion, my reasons for doing so being given. I shall, perhaps, in due time give further explanations. For the present I have no such intention.

I have never thought about the work on Descartes, nor given any further heed to it, since it has been translated into Dutch. I have my reasons, though it would be tedious to enumerate them here. So nothing remains for me but to subscribe myself, &c.

LETTER XXXV. (XXII.)

BLYENBERGH TO SPINOZA.

[*This letter (extending over five pages) is only given here in brief summary.*]

The tone of your last letter is very different from that of your first. If our essence is equivalent to our state at a given time, we are as perfect when sinning as when virtuous: God would wish for vice as much as virtue. Both the virtuous and the vicious execute God's will—What is the difference between them? You say some actions are more perfect than others; wherein does this perfection consist? If a mind existed so framed, that vice was in agreement with its proper nature, why should such a mind prefer good to evil? If God makes us all that we are, how can we "go astray"? Can rational substances depend on God in any way except lifelessly? What is the difference between a rational being's dependence on God, and an irrational being's? If we have no free will, are not our actions God's actions, and our will God's will? I could ask several more questions, but do not venture.

P.S. In my hurry I forgot to insert this question: Whether we cannot by foresight avert what would otherwise happen to us?

Dordrecht, 19 Feb., 1665.

LETTER XXXVI. (XXIII.)

SPINOZA TO BLYENBERGH.

[*Spinoza replies, that there is a difference between the theological and the philosophical way of speaking of God and things divine. He proceeds to discuss Blyenbergh's questions.* (Voorburg, 13th March, 1665.)]

FRIEND AND SIR,—I have received two letters from you this week; the second, dated 9th March, only served to inform me of the first written on February 19th, and sent to me at Schiedam. In the former I see that you complain of my saying, that "demonstration carried no weight with you," as though I had spoken of my own arguments, which had failed to convince you. Such was far from my intention. I was referring to your own words, which ran as follows:—"And if after long investigation it comes to pass, that my natural knowledge appears either to be at variance with the word (of Scripture), or not sufficiently well, &c.; the word has so great authority with me, that I would rather doubt of the conceptions, which I think I clearly perceive," &c. You see I merely repeat in brief your own phrase, so that I cannot think you have any cause for anger against me, especially as I merely quoted in order to show the great difference between our standpoints.

Again, as you wrote at the end of your letter that your only hope and wish is to continue in faith and hope, and that all else, which we may become convinced of through our natural faculties, is indifferent to you; I reflected, as I still continue to do, that my letters could be of no use to you, and that I should best consult my own interests by ceasing to neglect my pursuits (which I am compelled while writing to you to interrupt) for the sake of things which could bring no possible benefit. Nor is this contrary to the spirit of my former letter, for in that I looked upon you as simply a philosopher, who (like not a few who call themselves Christians) possesses no touchstone of truth save his natural understanding, and not as a theologian. However, you have taught me to know better, and have also shown me that the foundation, on which I was minded to build up our friendship, has not, as I imagined, been laid.

As for the rest, such are the general accompaniments of controversy, so that I would not on that account transgress the limits of courtesy: I will, therefore, pass over in your second letter, and in this, these and similar expressions, as though they had never been observed. So much for your taking offence; to show you that I have given you no just cause, and, also, that I am quite willing to brook contradiction. I now turn a second time to answering your objections.

I maintain, in the first place, that God is absolutely and really the cause of all things which have essence, whatsoever they may be. If you can demonstrate that evil, error, crime, &c., have any positive existence, which expresses essence, I will fully grant you that God is the cause of crime, evil, error, &c. I believe myself to have sufficiently shown, that that which constitutes the reality of evil, error, crime, &c., does not consist in anything, which expresses essence, and therefore we cannot say that God is its cause. For instance, Nero's matricide, in so far as it comprehended anything positive, was not a crime; the same outward act was perpetrated, and the same matricidal intention was entertained by Orestes; who, nevertheless, is not blamed—at any rate, not so much as Nero. Wherein, then, did Nero's crime consist? In nothing else, but that by his deed he showed himself to be ungrateful, unmerciful, and disobedient. Certainly none of these qualities express aught of essence, therefore God was not the cause of them, though He was the cause of Nero's act and intention.

Further, I would have you observe, that, while we speak philosophically, we ought not to employ theological phrases. For, since theology frequently, and not unwisely, represents God as a perfect man, it is often expedient in theology to say, that God desires a given thing, that He is angry at the actions of the wicked, and delights in those of the good. But in philosophy, when we clearly perceive that the attributes which make men perfect can as ill be ascribed and assigned to God, as the attributes which go to make perfect the elephant and the ass can be ascribed to man; here I say these and similar phrases have no place, nor can we employ them without causing extreme confusion in our conceptions. Hence, in the language of philosophy, it cannot be said that God desires anything of any man, or that anything is displeasing or pleasing to Him: all these are human qualities and have no place in God.

I would have it observed, that although the actions of the good (that is of those who have a clear idea of God, whereby all their actions and their thoughts are determined) and of the wicked (that is of those who do not possess the idea of God, but only the ideas of earthly things, whereby their actions and thoughts are determined), and, in fact, of all things that are, necessarily flow from God's eternal laws and decrees; yet they do not differ from one another in degree only, but also in essence. A mouse no less than an angel, and sorrow no less than joy depend on God; yet a mouse is not a kind of angel, neither is sorrow a kind of joy. I think I have thus answered your objections, if I rightly understand them, for I sometimes doubt, whether the conclusions which you deduce are not foreign to the proposition you are undertaking to prove.

However, this will appear more clearly, if I answer the questions you proposed on these principles. First, Whether murder is as acceptable to God as alms-giving? Secondly, Whether stealing is as good in relation to God as honesty? Thirdly and lastly, Whether if there be a mind so framed, that it would agree with, rather than be repugnant to its proper nature, to give way to lust, and to commit crimes, whether, I repeat, there can be any reason given, why such a mind should do good and eschew evil?

To your first question, I answer, that I do not know, speaking as a philosopher, what you mean by the words "acceptable to God." If you ask, whether God does not hate the wicked, and love the good? whether God does not regard the former with dislike, and the latter with favour? I answer, No. If the meaning of your question is: Are murderers and almsgivers equally good and perfect? my answer is again in the negative. To your second question, I reply: If, by "good in relation to God," you mean that the honest man confers a favour on God, and the thief does Him an injury, I answer that neither the honest man nor the thief can cause God any pleasure or displeasure. If you mean to ask, whether the actions of each, in so far as they posssess reality, and are caused by God, are equally perfect? I reply that, if we merely regard the actions and the manner of their execution, both may be equally perfect. If you, therefore, inquire whether the thief and the honest man are equally perfect and blessed? I answer, No. For, by an honest man, I mean one who always desires, that everyone should possess that which is his. This desire, as I prove in my Ethics (as yet unpublished), necessarily derives its origin in the pious from the clear knowledge which they possess, of God and of themselves. As a thief has no desire of the kind, he is necessarily without the knowledge of God and of himself—in other words, without the chief element of our blessedness. If you further ask, What causes you to perform a given action, which I call virtuous, rather than another? I reply, that I cannot know which method, out of the infinite methods at His disposal, God employs to determine you to the said action. It may be, that God has impressed you with a clear idea of Himself, so that you forget the world for love of Him, and love your fellow-men as yourself; it is plain that such a disposition is at variance with those dispositions which are called bad, and, therefore, could not co-exist with them in the same man.

However, this is not the place to expound all the foundations of my Ethics, or to prove all that I have advanced; I am now only concerned in answering your questions, and defending myself against them.

Lastly, as to your third question, it assumes a contradiction, and seems to me to be, as though one asked: If it agreed better with a man's nature that he should hang himself, could any reasons be given for his not hanging himself? Can such a nature possibly exist? If so, I maintain (whether I do or do not grant free will), that such an one, if he sees that he can live more conveniently on the gallows than sitting at his own table, would act most foolishly, if he did not hang himself. So anyone who clearly saw that, by committing crimes, he would enjoy a really more perfect and better life and existence, than he could attain by the practice of virtue, would be foolish if he did not act on his convictions. For, with such a perverse human nature as his, crime would become virtue.

As to the other question, which you add in your postscript, seeing that one might ask a hundred such in an hour, without arriving at a conclusion about any, and seeing that you yourself do not press for an answer, I will send none.

I will now only subscribe myself, &c.

LETTER XXXVII. (XXIV.)

Blyenbergh to Spinoza.

[*Blyenbergh, who had been to see Spinoza, asks the latter to send him a report of their conversation, and to answer five fresh questions.* (*Dordrecht, 27th March,* 1665.)]

Omitted.

LETTER XXXVIII. (XXVII.)

Spinoza to Blyenbergh.

[*Spinoza declines further correspondence with Blyenbergh, but says he will give explanations of certain points by word of mouth.* (*Voorburg, 3rd June,* 1665.)] [1]

Friend and Sir,—When your letter, dated 27th March, was delivered to me, I was just starting for Amsterdam. I, therefore, after reading half of it, left it at home, to be answered on my return: for I thought it dealt only with questions raised in our first controversy. However, a second perusal showed me, that it embraced a far wider subject, and not only asked me for a proof of what, in my preface to "Principles of Cartesian Philosophy," I wrote (with the object of merely stating, without proving or urging my opinion), but also requested me to impart a great portion of my Ethics, which, as everyone knows, ought to be based on physics and metaphysics. For this reason, I have been unable to allow myself to satisfy your demands. I wished to await an opportunity for begging you, in a most friendly way, by word of mouth, to withdraw your request, for giving you my reasons for refusal, and for showing that your inquiries do not promote the

[1] The true date of this letter is June 3rd, as appears from the Dutch original printed in Van Vloten's Supplementum. The former editors gave April.

solution of our first controversy, but, on the contrary, are for the most part entirely dependent on its previous settlement. So far are they not essential to the understanding of my doctrine concerning necessity, that they cannot be apprehended, unless the latter question is understood first. However, before such an opportunity offered, a second letter reached me this week, appearing to convey a certain sense of displeasure at my delay. Necessity, therefore, has compelled me to write you these few words, to acquaint you more fully with my proposal and decision. I hope that, when the facts of the case are before you, you will, of your own accord, desist from your request, and will still remain kindly disposed towards me. I, for my part, will, in all things, according to my power, prove myself your, &c.

LETTER XXXIX.

Spinoza to Christian Huyghens.

(*Treating of the Unity of God.*)

Distinguished Sir,—The demonstration of the unity of God, on the ground that His nature involves necessary existence, which you asked for, and I took note of, I have been prevented by various business from sending to you before. In order to accomplish my purpose, I will premise—

I. That the true definition of anything includes nothing except the simple nature of the thing defined. From this it follows—

II. That no definition can involve or express a multitude or a given number of individuals, inasmuch as it involves and expresses nothing except the nature of the thing as it is in itself. For instance, the definition of a triangle includes nothing beyond the simple nature of a triangle; it does not include any given number of triangles. In like manner, the definition of the mind as a thinking thing, or the definition of God as a perfect Being, includes nothing beyond the natures of the mind and of God, not a given number of minds or gods.

III. That for everything that exists there must necessarily be a positive cause, through which it exists.

IV. This cause may be situate either in the nature and definition of the thing itself (to wit, because existence belongs to its nature or necessarily includes it), or externally to the thing.

From these premisses it follows, that if any given number of individuals exists in nature, there must be one or more causes, which have been able to produce exactly that number of individuals, neither more nor less. If, for instance, there existed in nature twenty men (in order to avoid all confusion, I will assume that these all exist together as primary entities), it is not enough to investigate the cause of human nature in general, in order to account for the existence of these twenty; we must also inquire into the reason, why there exist exactly twenty men, neither more nor less. For (by our third hypothesis) for each man a reason and a cause must be forthcoming, why he should exist. But this cause (by our second and third hypotheses) cannot be contained in the nature of man himself; for the true definition of man does not involve the number of twenty men. Hence (by our fourth hypothesis) the cause for the existence of these twenty men, and consequently for the existence of each of them, must exist externally to them. We may thus absolutely conclude, that all things, which are conceived to exist in the plural number, must necessarily be produced by external causes and not by the force of their own nature. But since (by our second hypothesis) necessary existence appertains to the nature of God, His true definition must necessarily include necessary existence: therefore from His true definition His necessary existence must be inferred. But from His true definition (as I have already demonstrated from our second and third hypotheses) the necessary existence of many gods cannot be inferred. Therefore there only follows the existence of a single God. Which was to be proved.

This, distinguished Sir, has now seemed to me the best

method for demonstrating the proposition. I have also proved it differently by means of the distinction between essence and existence; but bearing in mind the object you mentioned to me, I have preferred to send you the demonstration given above. I hope it will satisfy you, and I will await your reply, meanwhile remaining, &c.

Voorburg, 7 Jan., 1666.

LETTER XL. (XXXV.)

Spinoza to Christian Huyghens.

Further arguments for the unity of God.

Distinguished Sir,—In your last letter, written on March 30th, you have excellently elucidated the point, which was somewhat obscure to me in your letter of February 10th. As I now know your opinion, I will set forth the state of the question as you conceive it; whether there be only a single Being who subsists by his own sufficiency or force? I not only affirm this to be so, but also undertake to prove it from the fact, that the nature of such a Being necessarily involves existence; perhaps it may also be readily proved from the understanding of God (as I set forth, "Principles of Cartesian Philosophy," I. Prop. i.), or from others of His attributes. Before treating of the subject I will briefly show, as preliminaries, what properties must be possessed by a Being including necessary existence. To wit:—

I. It must be eternal. For if a definite duration be assigned to it, it would beyond that definite duration be conceived as non-existent, or as not involving necessary existence, which would be contrary to its definition.

II. It must be simple, not made up of parts. For parts must in nature and knowledge be prior to the whole they compose: this could not be the case with regard to that which is eternal.

III. It cannot be conceived as determinate, but only as infinite. For, if the nature of the said Being were determinate, and conceived as determinate, that nature would beyond the said limits be conceived as non-existent, which again is contrary to its definition.

IV. It is indivisible. For if it were divisible, it could be divided into parts, either of the same or of different nature. If the latter, it could be destroyed and so not exist, which is contrary to its definition; if the former, each part would in itself include necessary existence, and thus one part could exist without others, and consequently be conceived as so existing. Hence the nature of the Being would be comprehended as finite, which, by what has been said, is contrary to its definition. Thus we see that, in attempting to ascribe to such a Being any imperfection, we straightway fall into contradictions. For, whether the imperfection which we wish to assign to the said Being be situate in any defect, or in limitations possessed by its nature, or in any change which it might, through deficiency of power, undergo from external causes, we are always brought back to the contradiction, that a nature which involves necessary existence, does not exist, or does not necessarily exist. I conclude, therefore—

V. That everything, which includes necessary existence, cannot have in itself any imperfection, but must express pure perfection.

VI. Further, since only from perfection can it come about, that any Being should exist by its own sufficiency and force, it follows that, if we assume a Being to exist by its own nature, but not to express all perfections, we must further suppose that another Being exists, which does comprehend in itself all perfections. For, if the less powerful Being exists by its own sufficiency, how much more must the more powerful so exist?

Lastly, to deal with the question, I affirm that there can only be a single Being, of which the existence belongs to its nature; such a Being which possesses in itself all perfections I will call God. If there be any Being to whose nature existence belongs, such a Being can contain in itself no imperfection, but must (by my fifth premiss) express every perfection; therefore, the nature of such a Being seems to belong to God (whose existence we are bound to affirm by Premiss VI.), inasmuch as He has in Himself all perfections and no imperfections. Nor can it exist externally to God. For if, externally to God, there existed one and the same nature involving necessary existence, such nature would be twofold; but this, by what we have just shown, is absurd. Therefore there is nothing save God, but there is a single God, that involves necessary existence, which was to be proved.

Such, distinguished Sir, are the arguments I can now produce for demonstrating this question. I hope I may also demonstrate to you, that I am, &c.

Voorburg, 10 April, 1666.

LETTER XLI. (XXXVI.)

SPINOZA TO CHRISTIAN HUYGHENS.

[*Further discussion concerning the unity of God. Spinoza asks for advice about polishing lenses.* (*Voorburg, May,* 1666.)]

DISTINGUISHED SIR,—I have been by one means or another prevented from answering sooner your letter, dated 19th May. As I gather that you suspend your judgment with regard to most of the demonstration I sent you (owing, I believe, to the obscurity you find in it), I will here endeavour to explain its meaning more clearly.

First I enumerated four properties, which a Being existing by its own sufficiency or force must possess. These four, and others like them, I reduced in my fifth observation to one. Further, in order to deduce all things necessary for the demonstration from a single premiss, I endeavoured in my sixth observation to demonstrate the existence of God from the given hypothesis; whence, lastly, taking (as you know) nothing beyond the ordinary meaning of the terms, I drew the desired conclusion.

Such, in brief, was my purpose and such my aim. I will now explain the meaning of each step singly, and will first start with the aforesaid four properties.

In the first you find no difficulty, nor is it anything but, as in the case of the second, an axiom. By simple I merely mean not compound, or not made up of parts differing in nature or other parts agreeing in nature. This demonstration is assuredly universal.

The sense of my third observation (that if the Being be thought, it cannot be conceived as limited by thought, but only as infinite, and similarly, if it be extension, it cannot be conceived as limited by extension) you have excellently perceived, though you say you do not perceive the conclusion; this last is based on the fact, that a contradiction is involved in conceiving under the category of non-existence anything, whose definition includes or (what is the same thing) affirms existence. And since determination implies nothing positive, but only a limitation of the existence of the nature conceived as determinate, it follows that that, of which the definition affirms existence, cannot be conceived as determinate. For instance, if the term extension included necessary existence, it would be alike impossible to conceive extension without existence and existence without extension. If this were established, it would be impossible to conceive determinate extension. For, if it be conceived as determinate, it must be determined by its own nature, that is by extension, and this extension, whereby it is determined, must be conceived under the category of non-existence, which by the hypothesis is obviously a contradiction. In my fourth observation, I merely wished to show, that such a Being could neither be divided into parts of the same nature or parts of a different nature, whether those of a different nature involved necessary existence or not. If, I said, we adopt the second view, the Being would be destroyed; for destruction is merely the resolution of a thing into parts so that none of them expresses the nature of the whole; if we adopt the first view, we should be in contradiction with the first three properties.

In my fifth observation, I merely asserted, that perfection consists in being, and imperfection in the privation of being. I say the privation; for although extension denies of itself thought, this argues no imperfection in it. It would be an imperfection in it, if it were in any degree deprived of extension, as it would be, if it were determinate; or again, if it lacked duration, position, &c.

My sixth observation you accept absolutely, and yet you say, that your whole difficulty remains (inasmuch as there may be, you think, several self-existent entities of different nature; as for instance thought and extension are different and perhaps subsist by their own sufficiency). I am, therefore, forced to believe, that you attribute to my observation a meaning quite different from the one intended by me. I think I can discern your interpretation of it; however, in order to save time, I will merely set forth my own meaning. I say then, as regards my sixth observation, that if we assert that anything, which is indeterminate and perfect only after its kind, exists by its own sufficiency, we must also grant the existence of a Being indeterminate and perfect absolutely; such a Being I will call God. If, for example, we wish to assert that extension or thought (which are each perfect after their kind, that is, in a given sphere of being) exists by its own sufficiency, we must grant also the existence of God, who is absolutely perfect, that is of a Being absolutely indeterminate. I would here direct attention to what I have just said with regard to the term *imperfection;* namely, that it signifies that a thing is deficient in some quality, which, nevertheless, belongs to its nature. For instance, extension can only be called imperfect in respect of duration, position, or quantity: that is, as not enduring longer, as not retaining its position, or as not being greater. It can never be called imperfect, because it does not think, inasmuch as its nature requires nothing of the kind, but consists solely in extension, that is in a certain sphere of being. Only in respect to its own sphere can it be called determinate or indeterminate, perfect or imperfect. Now, since the nature of God is not confined to a certain sphere of being, but exists in being, which is absolutely indeterminate, so His nature also demands everything which perfectly expresses being; otherwise His nature would be determinate and deficient.

This being so, it follows that there can be only one Being, namely God, who exists by His own force. If, for the sake of an illustration, we assert, that extension involves existence; it is, therefore, necessary that it should be eternal and indeterminate, and express absolutely no imperfection, but perfection. Hence extension will appertain to God, or will be something which in some fashion expresses the nature of God, since God is a Being, who not only in a certain respect but absolutely is in essence indeterminate and omnipotent. What we have here said by way of illustration regarding extension must be asserted of all that we ascribe a similar existence to. I, therefore, conclude as in my former letter, that there is nothing external to God, but that God alone exists by His own sufficiency. I think I have said enough to show the meaning of my former letter; however, of this you will be the best judge. * * * * *

(*The rest of the letter is occupied with details about the polishing of lenses.*)

LETTER XLI.A.

SPINOZA TO * * * * *[1] (May or June, 1665).

[*Spinoza urges his correspondent to be diligent in studying philosophy, promises to send part of the Ethics, and adds some personal details.*]

DEAR FRIEND,—I do not know whether you have quite forgotten me; but there are many circumstances which lead me to suspect it. First, when I was setting out on my journey,[2] I wished to bid you good-bye; and, after your own invitation, thinking I should certainly find you at home, heard that you had gone to the Hague. I return to Voorburg, nothing doubting but that you would at least have visited me in passing; but you, forsooth, without greeting your friend, went back home. Three weeks have I waited, without getting sight of a letter from you. If you wish this opinion of mine to be changed, you may easily change it by writing; and you can, at the same

[1] Probably J. Bresser, a member of the Spinozistic Society formed at Amsterdam. See note to Letter XLII.

[2] See Letter XXXVIII., which fixes approximately the date of this.

time, point out a means of entering into a correspondence, as we once talked of doing at your house.

Meanwhile, I should like to ask you, nay I do beg and entreat you, by our friendship, to apply yourself to some serious work with real study, and to devote the chief part of your life to the cultivation of your understanding and your soul. Now, while there is time, and before you complain of having let time and, indeed, your own self slip by. Further, in order to set our correspondence on foot, and to give you courage to write to me more freely, I would have you know that I have long thought, and, indeed, been almost certain, that you are somewhat too diffident of your own abilities, and that you are afraid of advancing some question or proposal unworthy of a man of learning. It does not become me to praise you, and expatiate on your talents to your face; but, if you are afraid that I shall show your letters to others, who will laugh at you, I give you my word of honour, that I will religiously keep them, and will show them to no mortal without your leave. On these conditions, you may enter on a correspondence, unless you doubt of my good faith, which I do not in the least believe. I want to hear your opinion on this in your first letter; and you may, at the same time, send me the conserve of red roses, though I am now much better.

After my journey, I was once bled; but the fever did not cease, though I was somewhat more active than before the bleeding, owing, I think, to the change of air; but I was two or three times laid up with a tertian. This, however, by good diet, I have at length driven away, and sent about its business. Where it has gone, I know not; but I am taking care it does not return here.

As regards the third part of my philosophy, I will shortly send it you, if you wish to be its transmitter, or to our friend De Vries; and, although I had settled not to send any of it, till it was finished, yet, as it takes longer than I thought, I am unwilling to keep you waiting. I will send up to the eightieth proposition, or thereabouts.[1]

Of English affairs I hear a good deal, but nothing for certain. The people continue to be apprehensive, and can

[1] The third and fourth part of the Ethics were probably originally united

see no reason, why the fleet should not be despatched; but the matter does not yet seem to be set on foot. I am afraid our rulers want to be overwise and prudent; but the event will show what they intend, and what they will attempt. May the gods turn it all to good. I want to know, what our people think, where you are, and what they know for certain; but, above all things, I want you to believe me, &c.

LETTER XLII. (XXXVII.)

Spinoza to I. B.[1]

[*Concerning the best method, by which we may safely arrive at the knowledge of things.*]

Most learned Sir and dearest Friend,—I have not been able hitherto to answer your last letter, received some time back. I have been so hindered by various occupations and calls on my time, that I am hardly yet free from them. However, as I have a few spare moments, I do not want to fall short of my duty, but take this first opportunity of heartily thanking you for your affection and kindness towards me, which you have often displayed in your actions, and now also abundantly prove by your letter.

I pass on to your question, which runs as follows: "Is there, or can there be, any method by which we may, without hindrance, arrive at the knowledge of the most excellent things? or are our minds, like our bodies, subject to the vicissitudes of circumstance, so that our thoughts are governed rather by fortune than by skill?" I think I shall satisfy you, if I show that there must necessarily be a method, whereby we are able to direct our clear and distinct perceptions, and that our mind is not, like our body, subject to the vicissitudes of circumstance.

[1] I. B. has been identified by some with John Bredenburg, a citizen of Rotterdam, who translated into Latin (1675) a Dutch attack on the Tractatus Theologico-Politicus, but the tone of the letter renders this improbable. Murr and Van Vloten think that I. B. may be the physician, John Bresser, who prefixed some verses to the "Principles of Cartesian Philosophy."

This conclusion may be based simply on the consideration that one clear and distinct perception, or several such together, can be absolutely the cause of another clear and distinct perception. Now, all the clear and distinct perceptions, which we form, can only arise from other clear and distinct perceptions, which are in us; nor do they acknowledge any cause external to us. Hence it follows that the clear and distinct perceptions, which we form, depend solely on our nature, and on its certain and fixed laws; in other words, on our absolute power, not on fortune—that is, not on causes which, although also acting by certain and fixed laws, are yet unknown to us, and alien to our nature and power. As regards other perceptions, I confess that they depend chiefly on fortune. Hence clearly appears, what the true method ought to be like, and what it ought chiefly to consist in—namely, solely in the knowledge of the pure understanding, and its nature and laws. In order that such knowledge may be acquired, it is before all things necessary to distinguish between the understanding and the imagination, or between ideas which are true and the rest, such as the fictitious, the false, the doubtful, and absolutely all which depend solely on the memory. For the understanding of these matters, as far as the method requires, there is no need to know the nature of the mind through its first cause; it is sufficient to put together a short history of the mind, or of perceptions, in the manner taught by Verulam.

I think that in these few words I have explained and demonstrated the true method, and have, at the same time, pointed out the way of acquiring it. It only remains to remind you, that all these questions demand assiduous study, and great firmness of disposition and purpose. In order to fulfil these conditions, it is of prime necessity to follow a fixed mode and plan of living, and to set before one some definite aim. But enough of this for the present, &c.

Voorburg, 10 June, 1666.

LETTER XLIII. (XXXVIII.)

SPINOZA TO I. v. M.[1]

[*Spinoza solves for his friend an arithmetical problem connected with games of chance.* (Voorburg, Oct. 1, 1666.)]

Omitted.

LETTERS XLIV., XLV., XLVI. (XXXIX., XL., XLI.)

SPINOZA TO I. I.[2]

XLIV. [*Remarks on Descartes' treatise on Optics.*]

XLV. [*Remarks on some alchemistic experiments, on the third and fourth meditations of Descartes, and on Optics.*]

XLVI. [*Remarks on Hydrostatics.*]

LETTER XLVII. (XLIV.)

SPINOZA TO I. I.

[*Spinoza begs his friend to stop the printing of the Dutch version of the Tractatus Theologico-Politicus. Some remarks on a pernicious pamphlet, "Homo Politicus," and on Thales of Miletus.*]

MOST COURTEOUS SIR,—When Professor N. N. visited me the other day, he told me that my Theologico-Political Treatise has been translated into Dutch, and that someone, whose name he did not know, was about printing it. With regard to this, I earnestly beg you to inquire carefully into the business, and, if possible, stop the printing. This is the

[1] It is not known who I. v. M. was. Letters XLIII.-XLVII. were written in Dutch.

[2] I. I. Probably Jarig Jellis, a merchant of Amsterdam and a Mennonite. He translated the Opera Posthuma into Dutch, 1677.

request not only of myself, but of many of my friends and acquaintances, who would be sorry to see the book placed under an interdict, as it undoubtedly would be, if published in Dutch. I do not doubt, but that you will do this service to me and the cause.

One of my friends sent me a short time since a pamphlet called "Homo Politicus," of which I had heard much. I have read it, and find it to be the most pernicious work which men could devise or invent. Rank and riches are the author's highest good; he adapts his doctrine accordingly, and shows the means to acquire them; to wit, by inwardly rejecting all religion, and outwardly professing whatever best serves his own advancement, also by keeping faith with no one, except in so far as he himself is profited thereby. For the rest, to feign, to make promises and break them, to lie, to swear falsely, and many such like practices call forth his highest praises. When I had finished reading the book, I debated whether I should write a pamphlet indirectly aimed against its author, wherein I should treat of the highest good and show the troubled and wretched condition of those who are covetous of rank and riches; finally proving by very plain reasoning and many examples, that the insatiable desire for rank and riches must bring and has brought ruin to states.

How much better and more excellent than the doctrines of the aforesaid writer are the reflections of Thales of Miletus, appears from the following. All the goods of friends, he says, are in common; wise men are the friends of the gods, and all things belong to the gods; therefore all things belong to the wise. Thus in a single sentence, this wisest of men accounts himself most rich, rather by nobly despising riches than by sordidly seeking them. In other passages he shows that the wise lack riches, not from necessity, but from choice. For when his friends reproached him with his poverty he answered, "Do you wish me to show you, that I could acquire what I deem unworthy of my labour, but you so diligently seek?" On their answering in the affirmative, he hired every oil-press in the whole of Greece (for being a distinguished astrologer he knew that the olive harvest would be as abundant as in previous years it had been scanty), and sub-let at his own price what he had hired for a very small sum, thus acquiring in a single year a large fortune, which he bestowed liberally as he had gained it industriously, &c.

The Hague, 17 Feb., 1671.

LETTER XLVIII.

Written by a physician, Lambert de Velthuysen, to Isaac Orobio, and forwarded by the latter to Spinoza. It contains a detailed attack on the Tractatus Theologico-Politicus. Its tenor may be sufficiently seen from Spinoza's reply. (Written at Utrecht, January 24th, 1671.) Velthuysen afterwards became more friendly to Spinoza, as appears from Letter LXXV.

LETTER XLIX.

Spinoza to Isaac Orobio.[1]

[*A defence of the Tractatus Theologico-Politicus.* (*The Hague*, 1671.)]

Most learned Sir,—You doubtless wonder why I have kept you so long waiting. I could hardly bring myself to reply to the pamphlet of that person, which you thought fit to send me; indeed I only do so now because of my promise. However, in order as far as possible to humour my feelings, I will fulfil my engagement in as few words as I can, and will briefly show how perversely he has interpreted my meaning; whether through malice or through ignorance I cannot readily say. But to the matter in hand.

First he says, "*that it is of little moment to know what nation I belong to, or what sort of life I lead.*" Truly, if he

[1] The rough copy of this letter is still preserved, and contains many strong expressions of Spinoza's indignation against Velthuysen, which he afterwards suppressed or mitigated.

had known, he would not so easily have persuaded himself that I teach Atheism. For Atheists are wont greedily to covet rank and riches, which I have always despised, as all who know me are aware. Again, in order to smooth his path to the object he has in view, he says that, "*I am possessed of no mean talents,*" so that he may, forsooth, more easily convince his readers, that I have knowingly and cunningly with evil intent argued for the cause of the deists, in order to discredit it. This contention sufficiently shows that he has not understood my reasons. For who could be so cunning and clever, as to be able to advance under false pretences so many and such good reasons for a doctrine which he did not believe in? Who will pass for an honest writer in the eyes of a man, that thinks one may argue as soundly for fiction as for truth? But after all I am not astonished. Descartes was formerly served in the same way by Voët, and the most honourable writers are constantly thus treated.

He goes on to say, "*In order to shun the reproach of superstition, he seems to me to have thrown off all religion.*" What this writer means by religion and what by superstition, I know not. But I would ask, whether a man throws off all religion, who maintains that God must be acknowledged as the highest good, and must, as such, be loved with a free mind? or, again, that the reward of virtue is virtue itself, while the punishment of folly and weakness is folly itself? or, lastly, that every man ought to love his neighbour, and to obey the commands of the supreme power? Such doctrines I have not only expressly stated, but have also demonstrated them by very solid reasoning. However, I think I see the mud wherein this person sticks. He finds nothing in virtue and the understanding in themselves to please him, but would prefer to live in accordance with his passions, if it were not for the single obstacle that he fears punishment. He abstains from evil actions, and obeys the divine commands like a slave, with unwillingness and hesitation, expecting as the reward of his bondage to be recompensed by God with gifts far more pleasing than divine love, and greater in proportion to his dislike to goodness and consequent unwillingness to practise it. Hence it comes to pass, that he believes that all, who are not restrained by this fear, lead a life of licence and throw off all religion. But this I pass over, and proceed to the deduction, whereby he wishes to show, that "*with covert and disguised arguments I teach atheism.*" The foundation of his reasoning is, that he thinks I take away freedom from God, and subject Him to fate. This is flatly false. For I have maintained, that all things follow by inevitable necessity from the nature of God, in the same way as all maintain that it follows from the nature of God, that He understands Himself: no one denies that this latter consequence follows necessarily from the divine nature, yet no one conceives that God is constrained by any fate; they believe that He understands Himself with entire freedom, though necessarily. I find nothing here, that cannot be perceived by everyone; if, nevertheless, my adversary thinks that these arguments are advanced with evil intent, what does he think of his own Descartes, who asserted that nothing is done by us, which has not been pre-ordained by God, nay, that we are newly created as it were by God every moment, though none the less we act according to our own free will? This, as Descartes himself confesses, no one can understand.

Further, this inevitable necessity in things destroys neither divine laws nor human. For moral principles, whether they have received from God the form of laws or not, are nevertheless divine and salutary. Whether we accept the good, which follows from virtue and the divine love, as given us by God as a judge, or as emanating from the necessity of the divine nature, it is not in either case more or less to be desired; nor are the evils which follow from evil actions less to be feared, because they follow necessarily: finally, whether we act under necessity or freedom, we are in either case led by hope and fear. Wherefore the assertion is false, "*that I maintain that there is no room left for precepts and commands.*" Or as he goes on to say, "*that there is no expectation of reward or punishment, since all things are ascribed to fate, and are said to flow with inevitable necessity from God.*"

I do not here inquire, why it is the same, or almost the same to say that all things necessarily flow from God, as to say that God is universal; but I would have you observe the insinuation which he not less maliciously subjoins, "*that I wish that men should practise virtue, not because of the precepts and law of God, or through hope of reward and fear of punishment, but,*" &c. Such a sentiment you will assuredly not find anywhere in my treatise: on the contrary, I have expressly stated in Chap. IV., that the sum of the divine law (which, as I have said in Chap. II., has been divinely inscribed on our hearts), and its chief precept is, to love God as the highest good: not, indeed, from the fear of any punishment, for love cannot spring from fear; nor for the love of anything which we desire for our own delight, for then we should love not God, but the object of our desire.

I have shown in the same chapter, that God revealed this law to the prophets, so that, whether it received from God the form of a command, or whether we conceive it to be like God's other decrees, which involve eternal necessity and truth, it will in either case remain God's decree and a salutary principle. Whether I love God in freedom, or whether I love Him from the necessity of the divine decree, I shall nevertheless love God, and shall be in a state of salvation. Wherefore, I can now declare here, that this person is one of that sort, of whom I have said at the end of my preface, that I would rather that they utterly neglected my book, than that by misinterpreting it after their wont, they should become hostile, and hinder others without benefiting themselves.

Though I think I have said enough to prove what I intended, I have yet thought it worth while to add a few observations—namely, that this person falsely thinks, that I have in view the axiom of theologians, which draws a distinction between the words of a prophet when propounding doctrine, and the same prophet when narrating an event. If by such an axiom he means that which in Chap. XV. I attributed to a certain R. Jehuda Alpakhar, how could he think that I agree with it, when in that very chapter I reject it as false? If he does not mean this, I confess I am as yet in ignorance as to what he does mean, and, therefore, could not have had it in view.

Again, I cannot see why he says, that all will adopt my

opinions, who deny that reason and philosophy should be the interpreters of Scripture; I have refuted the doctrine of such persons, together with that of Maimonides.

It would take too long to review all the indications he gives of not having judged me altogether calmly. I therefore pass on to his conclusion, where he says, "*that I have no arguments left to prove, that Mahomet was not a true prophet.*" This he endeavours to show from my opinions, whereas from them it clearly follows, that Mahomet was an impostor, inasmuch as he utterly forbids that freedom, which the Catholic religion revealed by our natural faculties and by the prophets grants, and which I have shown should be granted in its completeness. Even if this were not so, am I, I should like to know, bound to show that any prophet is false? Surely the burden lies with the prophets, to prove that they are true. But if he retorts, that Mahomet also taught the divine law, and gave certain signs of his mission, as the rest of the prophets did, there is surely no reason why he should deny, that Mahomet also was a true prophet.

As regards the Turks and other non-Christian nations; if they worship God by the practice of justice and charity towards their neighbour, I believe that they have the spirit of Christ, and are in a state of salvation, whatever they may ignorantly hold with regard to Mahomet and oracles.

Thus you see, my friend, how far this man has strayed from the truth; nevertheless, I grant that he has inflicted the greatest injury, not on me but on himself, inasmuch as he has not been ashamed to declare, that "*under disguised and covert arguments I teach atheism.*"

I do not think, that you will find any expressions I have used against this man too severe. However, if there be any of the kind which offend you, I beg you to correct them, as you shall think fit. I have no disposition to irritate him, whoever he may be, and to raise up by my labours enemies against myself; as this is often the result of disputes like the present, I could scarcely prevail on myself to reply—nor should I have prevailed, if I had not promised. Farewell. I commit to your prudence this letter, and myself, who am, &c.

LETTER L. (L.)

SPINOZA TO JARIG JELLIS.

[*Of the difference between the political theories of Hobbes and Spinoza, of the Unity of God, of the notion of figure, of the book of a Utrecht professor against the Tractatus Theologico-Politicus.*]

MOST COURTEOUS SIR,—As regards political theories, the difference which you inquire about between Hobbes and myself, consists in this, that I always preserve natural right intact, and only allot to the chief magistrates in every state a right over their subjects commensurate with the excess of their power over the power of the subjects. This is what always takes place in the state of nature.

Again, with regard to the demonstration which I establish in the appendix to my geometric exposition of Cartesian principles, namely, that God can only with great impropriety be called one or single, I answer that a thing can only be called one or single in respect of existence, not in respect of essence. For we do not conceive things under the category of numbers, unless they have first been reduced to a common genus. For example, he who holds in his hand a penny and a crown piece will not think of the twofold number, unless he can call both the penny and the crown piece by one and the same name, to wit, coins or pieces of money. In the latter case he can say that he holds two coins or pieces of money, inasmuch as he calls the crown as well as the penny, a coin, or piece of money. Hence, it is evident that a thing cannot be called one or single, unless there be afterwards another thing conceived, which (as has been said) agrees with it. Now, since the existence of God is His essence, and of His essence we can form no general idea, it is certain, that he who calls God one or single has no true idea of God, and speaks of Him very improperly.

As to the doctrine that figure is negation and not anything positive, it is plain that the whole of matter considered indefinitely can have no figure, and that figure can only exist in finite and determinate bodies. For he who says, that he perceives a figure, merely indicates thereby, that he conceives a determinate thing, and how it is determinate. This determination, therefore, does not appertain to the thing according to its being, but, on the contrary, is its non-being. As then figure is nothing else than determination, and determination is negation, figure, as has been said, can be nothing but negation.

The book, which a Utrecht professor wrote against mine, and which was published after his death, I saw lying in a bookseller's window. From the little I then read of it, I judged it unworthy of perusal, still less of reply. I, therefore, left the book, and its author. With an inward smile I reflected, that the most ignorant are ever the most audacious and the most ready to rush into print. The Christians seem to me to expose their wares for sale like hucksters, who always show first that which is worst. The devil is said to be very cunning, but to my thinking the tricks of these people are in cunning far beyond his. Farewell.

The Hague, 2 June, 1674.

LETTER LI. (XLV.)

Godfrey Leibnitz to Spinoza.

Distinguished Sir,—Among your other merits spread abroad by fame, I understand that you have remarkable skill in optics. I have, therefore, wished to forward my essay, such as it is, to you, as I am not likely to find a better critic in this branch of learning. The paper, which I send you, and which I have styled "a note on advanced optics," has been published with the view of more conveniently making known my ideas to my friends and the curious in such matters. I hear that * * * * * is very clever in the same subject, doubtless he is well known to you.[1] If you could obtain for me his opinion and kind

[1] Probably the name omitted is Diemerbroech, a learned physician and Cartesian at Utrecht.

attention, you would greatly increase my obligation to you. The paper explains itself.

I believe you have already received the "Prodromo" of Francis Lana[1] the Jesuit, written in Italian. Some remarkable observations on optics are contained in it. John Oltius too, a young Swiss very learned in these matters, has published "Physico-Mechanical Reflections concerning Vision;" in which he announces a machine for the polishing all kinds of glasses, very simple and of universal applicability, and also declares that he has discovered a means of collecting all the rays coming from different points of an object, so as to obtain an equal number of corresponding points, but only under conditions of a given distance and form of object.

My proposal is, not that the rays from all points should be collected and re-arranged (this is with any object or distance impossible at the present stage of our knowledge); the result I aim at is the equal collection of rays from points outside the optic axis and in the optic axis, so that the apertures of glasses could be made of any size desired without impairing the distinctness of vision. But this must stand according to your skilled verdict. Farewell, and believe me, distinguished Sir, your obedient servant,

GODFREY LEIBNITZ,
J. U. D., Councillor of the Elector of Mainz.

Frankfort, 5 Oct., 1671 (new style).

LETTER LII. (XLVI.)

SPINOZA TO LEIBNITZ.

[*Answer to the foregoing letter*].

MOST LEARNED AND DISTINGUISHED SIR,—I have read the paper you were kind enough to send me, and return you many thanks for the communication. I regret that I

[1] Francis Lana, of Brescia, 1631-1687. The title of his book is, "Prodromo premesso all' Arte maestra." He also wrote "Magistræ naturæ et artis."

have not been able quite to follow your meaning, though you explain it sufficiently clearly, whether you think that there is any cause for making the apertures of the glasses small, except that the rays coming from a single point are not collected accurately at another single point, but in a small area which we generally call the mechanical point, and that this small area is greater or less in proportion to the size of the aperture. Further, I ask whether the lenses which you call "pandochæ" correct this fault, so that the mechanical point or small area, on which the rays coming from a single point are after refraction collected, always preserves the same proportional size, whether the aperture be small or large. If so, one may enlarge the aperture as much as one likes, and consequently these lenses will be far superior to those of any other shape known to me; if not, I hardly see why you praise them so greatly beyond common lenses. For circular lenses have everywhere the same axis; therefore, when we employ them, we must regard all the points of an object as placed in the optic axis; although all the points of the object be not at the same distance, the difference arising thence will not be perceptible, when the objects are very remote; because then the rays coming from a single point would, as they enter the glass, be regarded as parallel. I think your lenses might be of service in obtaining a more distinct representation of all the objects, when we wish to include several objects in one view, as we do, when we employ very large convex circular lenses. However, I would rather suspend my judgment about all these details, till you have more clearly explained your meaning, as I heartily beg you to do. I have, as you requested, sent the other copy of your paper to Mr. * * * *. He answers, that he has at present no time to study it, but he hopes to have leisure in a week or two.

I have not yet seen the "Prodromo" of Francis Lana, nor the "Physico-Mechanical Reflections" of John Oltius. What I more regret is, that your "Physical Hypothesis" has not yet come to my hands, nor is there a copy for sale here at the Hague. The gift, therefore, which you so liberally promise me will be most acceptable to me; if I can be of use to you in any other matter, you will always find me most ready. I hope you will not think it too irksome to reply to this short note.

Distinguished Sir,
Yours sincerely,
B. DE SPINOZA.

The Hague, 9 Nov., 1671.

P.S. Mr. Diemerbroech does not live here. I am, therefore, forced to entrust this to an ordinary letter-carrier. I doubt not that you know someone at the Hague, who would take charge of our letters; I should like to hear of such a person, that our correspondence might be more conveniently and securely taken care of. If the "Tractatus Theologico-Politicus" has not yet come to your hands, I will, unless you have any objection, send you a copy. Farewell.

LETTER LIII. (XLVII.)

FABRITIUS TO SPINOZA.

[*Fabritius, under the order and in the name of the Elector Palatine, offers Spinoza the post of Professor of Philosophy at Heidelberg, under very liberal conditions.*]

MOST RENOWNED SIR,—His Most Serene Highness the Elector Palatine,[1] my most gracious master, commands me to write to you, who are, as yet, unknown to me, but most favourably regarded by his Most Serene Highness, and to inquire of you, whether you are willing to accept an ordinary professorship of Philosophy in his illustrious university. An annual salary would be paid to you, equal to that enjoyed at present by the ordinary professors. You will hardly find elsewhere a prince more favourable to distinguished talents, among which he reckons yourself. You will have the most ample freedom in philosophical teaching, which the prince is confident you will not misuse, to disturb the religion publicly established. I cannot refrain from seconding the prince's injunction. I therefore most

[1] Charles Lewis, Elector, 1632-1680.

earnestly beg you to reply as soon as possible, and to address your answer either under cover to the Most Serene Elector's resident at the Hague, Mr. Grotius, or to Mr. Gilles Van der Hele, so that it may come in the packet of letters usually sent to the court, or else to avail yourself of some other convenient opportunity for transmitting it. I will only add, that if you come here, you will live pleasantly a life worthy of a philosopher, unless events turn out quite contrary to our expectation and hope. So farewell.

I remain, illustrious Sir,
Your devoted admirer,
I. LEWIS FABRITIUS.
Professor of the Academy of Heidelberg, and
Councillor of the Elector Palatine.

Heidelberg, 16 Feb., 1673.

LETTER LIV. (XLVIII.)

SPINOZA TO FABRITIUS.

[*Spinoza thanks the Elector for his kind offer, but, owing to his unwillingness to teach in public, and other causes, humbly begs to be allowed time to consider it.*]

DISTINGUISHED SIR,—If I had ever desired to take a professorship in any faculty, I could not have wished for any other than that which is offered to me, through you, by His Most Serene Highness the Elector Palatine, especially because of that freedom in philosophical teaching, which the most gracious prince is kind enough to grant, not to speak of the desire which I have long entertained, to live under the rule of a prince, whom all men admire for his wisdom.

But since it has never been my wish to teach in public, I have been unable to induce myself to accept this splendid opportunity, though I have long deliberated about it. I think, in the first place, that I should abandon philosophical research if I consented to find time for teaching young students. I think, in the second place, that I do not know the limits, within which the freedom of my philosophical teaching would be confined, if I am to avoid all appearance of disturbing the publicly established religion. Religious quarrels do not arise so much from ardent zeal for religion, as from men's various dispositions and love of contradiction, which causes them to habitually distort and condemn everything, however rightly it may have been said. I have experienced these results in my private and secluded station, how much more should I have to fear them after my elevation to this post of honour.

Thus you see, distinguished Sir, that I am not holding back in the hope of getting something better, but through my love of quietness, which I think I can in some measure secure, if I keep away from lecturing in public. I therefore most earnestly entreat you to beg of the Most Serene Elector, that I may be allowed to consider further about this matter, and I also ask you to conciliate the favour of the most gracious prince to his most devoted admirer, thus increasing the obligations of your sincere friend,

B. DE. S.

The Hague, 30 March, 1673.

LETTER LV. (LI.)

HUGO BOXEL TO SPINOZA.

[*A friend asks Spinoza's opinion about Ghosts.*]

DISTINGUISHED SIR,—My reason for writing to you is, that I want to know your opinion about apparitions and ghosts or spectres; if you admit their existence, what do you think about them, and how long does their life last? For some hold them to be mortal, others immortal. As I am doubtful whether you admit their existence, I will proceed no further.

Meanwhile, it is certain, that the ancients believed in

them. The theologians and philosophers of to-day are hitherto agreed as to the existence of some creatures of the kind, though they may not agree as to the nature of their essence. Some assert that they are composed of very thin and subtle matter, others that they are spiritual. But, as I was saying before, we are quite at cross purposes, inasmuch as I am doubtful whether you would grant their existence; though, as you must be aware, so many instances and stories of them are found throughout antiquity, that it would really be difficult either to deny or to doubt them. It is clear that, even if you confess that they exist, you do not believe that some of them are the souls of the dead, as the defenders of the Romish faith would have it. I will here end, and will say nothing about war and rumours, inasmuch as our lot is cast in an age, &c. Farewell.

14 Sept., 1674.

LETTER LVI. (LII.)

Spinoza to Hugo Boxel.

[*Spinoza answers that he does not know what ghosts are, and can gain no information from antiquity.* (*The Hague, Sept.*, 1674.)]

Dear Sir,—Your letter, which I received yesterday, was most welcome to me, both because I wanted to hear news of you, and also because it shows that you have not utterly forgotten me. Although some might think it a bad omen, that ghosts are the cause of your writing to me, I, on the contrary, can discern a deeper meaning in the circumstance; I see that not only truths, but also things trifling and imaginary may be of use to me.

However, let us defer the question, whether ghosts are delusions and imaginary, for I see that not only denial of them, but even doubt about them seems very singular to you, as to one who has been convinced by the numerous histories related by men of to-day and the ancients. The great esteem and honour, in which I have always held and still hold you, does not suffer me to contradict you, still less to humour you. The middle course, which I shall adopt, is to beg you to be kind enough to select from the numerous stories which you have read, one or two of those least open to doubt, and most clearly demonstrating the existence of ghosts. For, to confess the truth, I have never read a trustworthy author, who clearly showed that there are such things. Up to the present time I do not know what they are, and no one has ever been able to tell me. Yet it is evident, that in the case of a thing so clearly shown by experience we ought to know what it is; otherwise we shall have great difficulty in gathering from histories that ghosts exist. We only gather that something exists of nature unknown. If philosophers choose to call things which we do not know "ghosts," I shall not deny the existence of such, for there are an infinity of things, which I cannot make out.

Pray tell me, my dear Sir, before I explain myself further in the matter, What are these ghosts or spectres? Are they children, or fools, or madmen? For all that I have heard of them seems more adapted to the silly than the wise, or, to say the best we can of it, resembles the pastimes of children or of fools. Before I end, I would submit to you one consideration, namely, that the desire which most men have to narrate things, not as they really happened, but as they wished them to happen, can be illustrated from the stories of ghosts and spectres more easily than from any others. The principal reason for this is, I believe, that such stories are only attested by the narrators, and thus a fabricator can add or suppress circumstances, as seems most convenient to him, without fear of anyone being able to contradict him. He composes them to suit special circumstances, in order to justify the fear he feels of dreams and phantoms, or else to confirm his courage, his credit, or his opinion. There are other reasons, which lead me to doubt, if not the actual stories, at least some of the narrated circumstances; and which have a close bearing on the conclusion we are endeavouring to derive from the aforesaid stories. I will here stop, until I have learnt from you what those stories are, which have so completely convinced you, that you regard all doubt about them as absurd, &c.

LETTER LVII. (LIII.)

Hugo Boxel to Spinoza.

Most sagacious Sir,—You have sent me just the answer I expected to receive, from a friend holding an opinion adverse to my own. But no matter. Friends may always disagree on indifferent subjects without injury to their friendship.

You ask me, before you gave an opinion as to what these spectres or spirits are, to tell you whether they are children, fools, or madmen, and you add that everything you have heard of them seems to have proceeded rather from the insane than the sane. It is a true proverb, which says that a preconceived opinion hinders the pursuit of truth.

I, then, believe that ghosts exist for the following reasons: first, because it appertains to the beauty and perfection of the universe, that they should; secondly, because it is probable that the Creator created them, as being more like Himself than are embodied creatures; thirdly, because as body exists without soul, soul exists without body; fourthly and lastly, because in the upper air, region, or space, I believe there is no obscure body without inhabitants of its own; consequently, that the measureless space between us and the stars is not empty, but thronged with spiritual inhabitants. Perhaps the highest and most remote are true spirits, whereas the lowest in the lowest region of the air are creatures of very thin and subtle substance, and also invisible. Thus I think there are spirits of all sorts, but, perhaps, none of the female sex.

This reasoning will in no wise convince those, who rashly believe that the world has been created by chance. Daily experience, if these reasons be dismissed, shows that there are spectres, and many stories, both new and old, are current about them. Such may be found in Plutarch's book "De viris illustribus," and in his other works; in Suetonius's "Lives of the Cæsars," also in Wierus's and Lavater's books about ghosts, where the subject is fully treated and illustrated from writers of all kinds. Cardano, celebrated for his learning, also speaks of them in his books "De

Subtilitate," "De Varietate," and in his "Life;" showing, by experience, that they have appeared to himself, his relations and friends. Melancthon, a wise man and a lover of truth, testifies to his experience of them, as also do many others. A certain burgomaster, learned and wise, who is still living, once told me that he heard by night the noise of working in his mother's brew-house, going on just as it does while beer is being brewed in the day; this he attested as having occurred frequently. The same sort of thing has happened to me, and will never fade from my memory; hence I am convinced by the above-mentioned experiences and reasons, that there are ghosts.

As for evil spirits, who torture wretched men in this life and the next, and who work spells, I believe the stories of them to be fables. In treatises about spirits you will find a host of details. Besides those I have cited, you may refer to Pliny the younger, bk. vii., the letter to Sura; Suetonius, "Life of Julius Cæsar," ch. xxxii.; Valerius Maximus, I. viii. § § 7, 8; and Alexander ab Alexandro, "Dies Geniales." I am sure these books are accessible to you. I say nothing of monks and priests, for they relate so many tales of souls and evil spirits, or as I should rather say of spectres, that the reader becomes wearied with their abundance. Thyræus, a Jesuit, in the book about the apparition of spirits, also treats of the question. But these last-named discourse on such subjects merely for the sake of gain, and to prove that purgatory is not so bad as is supposed, thus treating the question as a mine, from which they dig up plenteous store of gold and silver. But the same cannot be said of the writers mentioned previously, and other moderns, who merit greater credit from their absence of bias.

As an answer to the passage in your letter, where you speak of fools and madmen, I subjoin this sentence from the learned Lavater, who ends with it his first book on ghosts or spectres. "He who is bold enough to gainsay so many witnesses, both ancient and modern, seems to me unworthy of credit. For as it is a mark of frivolity to lend incontinent credence to everyone who says he has seen a ghost; so, on the other hand, rashly and flatly to contradict so many trustworthy historians, Fathers, and other persons placed in authority would argue a remarkable shamelessness."

21 Sept., 1674

LETTER LVIII. (LIV.)

Spinoza to Hugo Boxel.

[*Spinoza treats of the necessary creation of the world—he refutes his friend's arguments and quotations.*]

Dear Sir,—I will rely on what you said in your letter of the 21st of last month, that friends may disagree on indifferent questions, without injury to their friendship, and will frankly tell you my opinion on the reasons and stories, whereon you base your conclusion, that *there are ghosts of every kind, but perhaps none of the female sex.* The reason for my not replying sooner is that the books you quoted are not at hand, in fact I have not found any except Pliny and Suetonius. However, these two have saved me the trouble of consulting any other, for I am persuaded that they all talk in the same strain and hanker after extraordinary tales, which rouse men's astonishment and compel their wonder. I confess that I am not a little amazed, not at the stories, but at those who narrate them. I wonder, that men of talent and judgment should so employ their readiness of speech, and abuse it in endeavouring to convince us of such trifles.

However, let us dismiss the writers, and turn to the question itself. In the first place, we will reason a little about your conclusion. Let us see whether I, who deny that there are spectres or spirits, am on that account less able to understand the authors, who have written on the subject; or whether you, who assert that such beings exist, do not give to the aforesaid writers more credit than they deserve. The distinction you drew, in admitting without hesitation spirits of the male sex, but doubting whether any female spirits exist, seems to me more like a fancy than a genuine doubt. If it were really your opinion, it would resemble the common imagination, that God is masculine, not feminine. I wonder that those, who have seen naked ghosts, have not cast their eyes on those parts of the person, which would remove all doubt; perhaps they were timid, or did not know of this distinction. You would say that this is ridicule, not reasoning: and hence I see, that your reasons appear to you so strong and well founded, that no one can (at least in your judgment) contradict them, unless he be some perverse fellow, who thinks the world has been made by chance. This impels me, before going into your reasons, to set forth briefly my opinion on the question, *whether the world was made by chance.* But I answer, that as it is clear that chance and necessity are two contraries, so is it also clear, that he, who asserts the world to be a necessary effect of the divine nature, must utterly deny that the world has been made by chance; whereas, he who affirms, that God need not have made the world, confirms, though in different language, the doctrine that it has been made by chance; inasmuch as he maintains that it proceeds from a wish, which might never have been formed. However, as this opinion and theory is on the face of it absurd, it is commonly very unanimously admitted, that God's will is eternal, and has never been indifferent; hence it must necessarily be also admitted, you will observe, that the world is a necessary effect of the divine nature. Let them call it will, understanding, or any name they like, they come at last to the same conclusion, that under different names they are expressing one and the same thing. If you ask them, whether the divine will does not differ from the human, they answer, that the former has nothing in common with the latter except its name; especially as they generally admit that God's will, understanding, intellect, essence, and nature are all identical; so I, myself, lest I should confound the divine nature with the human, do not assign to God human attributes, such as will, understanding, attention, hearing, &c. I therefore say, as I have said already, that *the world is a necessary effect of the divine nature, and that it has not been made by chance.* I think this is enough to persuade you, that the opinion of those (if such there be), who say that the world has been made by chance, is entirely contrary to mine; and, relying on this hypothesis, I proceed to examine those reasons which lead you to infer the existence of all kinds of ghosts. I should like to say of these reasons generally, that they seem rather conjectures than reasons, and I can with difficulty believe, that you take them for guiding reasons. However, be they conjectures or be they reasons, let us see whether we can take them for foundations.

Your first reason is, that the existence of ghosts is needful for the beauty and perfection of the universe. Beauty, my dear Sir, is not so much a quality of the object beheld, as an effect in him who beholds it. If our sight were longer or shorter, or if our constitution were different, what now appears beautiful to us would seem misshapen, and what we now think misshapen we should regard as beautiful. The most beautiful hand seen through the microscope will appear horrible. Some things are beautiful at a distance, but ugly near; thus things regarded in themselves, and in relation to God, are neither ugly nor beautiful. Therefore, he who says that God has created the world, so that it might be beautiful, is bound to adopt one of the two alternatives, either that God created the world for the sake of men's pleasure and eyesight, or else that He created men's pleasure and eyesight for the sake of the world. Now, whether we adopt the former or the latter of these views, how God could have furthered His object by the creation of ghosts, I cannot see. Perfection and imperfection are names, which do not differ much from the names beauty and ugliness. I only ask, therefore (not to be tedious), which would contribute most to the perfect adornment of the world, ghosts, or a quantity of monsters, such as centaurs, hydras, harpies, satyrs, gryphons, arguses, and other similar inventions? Truly the world would be handsomely bedecked, if God had adorned and embellished it, in obedience to our fancy, with beings, which anyone may readily imagine and dream of, but no one can understand.

Your second reason is, that because spirits express God's image more than embodied creatures, it is probable that He has created them. I frankly confess, that I am as yet in ignorance, how spirits more than other creatures express God. This I know, that between finite and infinite there is no comparison; so that the difference between God and the greatest and most excellent created thing is no less than the difference between God and the least created thing. This argument, therefore, is beside the mark. If I had as clear an idea of ghosts, as I have of a triangle or a circle, I should not in the least hesitate to affirm that they had been created by God; but as the idea I possess of them is just like the ideas, which my imagination forms of harpies, gryphons, hydras, &c., I cannot consider them as anything but dreams, which differ from God as totally, as that which is not differs from that which is.

Your third reason (that as body exists without soul, so soul should exist without body) seems to me equally absurd. Pray tell me, if it is not also likely, that memory, hearing, sight, &c., exist without bodies, because bodies exist without memory, hearing, sight, &c., or that a sphere exists without a circle, because a circle exists without a sphere?

Your fourth, and last reason, is the same as your first, and I refer you to my answer given above. I will only observe here, that I do not know which are the highest or which the lowest places, which you conceive as existing in infinite matter, unless you take the earth as the centre of the universe. For if the sun or Saturn be the centre of the universe, the sun, or Saturn, not the earth, will be the lowest.

Thus, passing by this argument and what remains, I conclude, that these and similar reasons will convince no one of the existence of all kinds of ghosts and spectres, unless it be those persons, who shut their ears to the understanding, and allow themselves to be led away by superstition. This last is so hostile to right reason, that she lends willing credence to old wives' tales for the sake of discrediting philosophers.

As regards the stories, I have already said in my first letter, that I do not deny them altogether, but only the conclusion drawn from them. To this I may add, that I do not believe them so thoroughly, as not to doubt many of the details, which are generally added rather for ornament than for bringing out the truth of the story or the conclusion drawn from it. I had hoped, that out of so many stories you would at least have produced one or two, which could hardly be questioned, and which would clearly show that ghosts or spectres exist. The case you relate of the burgomaster, who wanted to infer their existence, because he heard spectral brewers working in his mother's brewhouse by night, and making the same noises as he was accustomed to hear by day, seems to me laughable. In like manner it would be tedious here to examine all the stories of people, who have written on these trifles. To be brief, I cite the instance of Julius Cæsar, who, as Suetonius testifies, laughed at such things and yet was happy, if we may trust what Suetonius says in the 59th chapter of his life of that leader. And so should all, who reflect on the human imagination, and the effects of the emotions, laugh at such notions; whatever Lavater and others, who have gone dreaming with him in the matter, may produce to the contrary.

LETTER LIX. (LV.)

Hugo Boxel to Spinoza.

[*A continuation of the arguments in favour of ghosts, which may be summarized as follows:—I say a thing is done by chance, when it has not been the subject of will on the part of the doer; not when it might never have happened.—Necessity and freedom, not necessity and chance, are contraries.—If we do not in some sense attribute human qualities to God, what meaning can we attach to the term?—You ask for absolute proof of the existence of spirits; such proof is not obtainable for many things, which are yet firmly believed.—Some thinys are more beautiful intrinsically than others.—As God is a spirit, spirits resemble Him more than embodied creatures do.—A ghost cannot be conceived as clearly as a triangle: can you say that your own idea of God is as clear as your idea of a triangle?—As a circle exists without a sphere, so a sphere exists without a circle.—We call things higher or lower in proportion to their distance from the earth.—All the Stoics, Pythagoreans, and Platonists, Empedocles, Maximus Tyrius, Apuleius, and others, bear witness to ghosts; and no modern denies them.*

It is presumption to sneer at such a body of testimony. Cæsar did not ridicule ghosts, but omens, and if he had listened to Spurina he would not have been murdered.]

LETTER LX. (LVI.)

Spinoza to Hugo Boxel.

[*Spinoza again answers the argument in favour of ghosts.* (*The Hague*, 1674).]

Dear Sir,—I hasten to answer your letter, received yesterday, for if I delay my reply, I may have to put it off longer than I should like. The state of your health would have made me anxious, if I did not understand that you are better. I hope you are by this time quite well again.

The difficulties experienced by two people following different principles, and trying to agree on a matter, which depends on many other questions, might be shown from this discussion alone, if there were no reason to prove it by. Pray tell me, whether you have seen or read any philosophers, who hold that the world has been made by chance, taking chance in your sense, namely, that God had some design in making the world, and yet has not kept to the plan he had formed. I do not know, that such an idea has ever entered anyone's mind. I am likewise at a loss for the reasons, with which you want to make me believe, that chance and necessity are not contraries. As soon as I affirm that the three angles of a triangle are equal to two right angles necessarily, I deny that they are thus equal by chance. As soon as I affirm that heat is a necessary effect of fire, I deny that it is a chance effect. To say, that necessary and free are two contrary terms, seems to me no less absurd and repugnant to reason. For no one can deny, that God freely knows Himself and all else, yet all with one voice grant that God knows Himself necessarily. Hence, as it seems to me, you draw no distinction between constraint or force and necessity. Man's wishes to live, to love, &c., are not under constraint, but nevertheless are necessary; much more is it necessary, that God wishes to be, to know, and to act. If you will also reflect, that indifference is only another name for ignorance or doubt, and that a will always constant and determined in all things is a necessary property of the understanding, you will see that my words are in complete harmony with truth. If we affirm, that God might have been able not to wish a given event, or not to understand it, we attribute to God two different freedoms, one necessary, the other indifferent; consequently we shall conceive God's will as different from His essence and understanding, and shall thus fall from one absurdity into another.

The attention, which I asked for in my former letter, has not seemed to you necessary. This has been the reason why you have not directed your thoughts to the main issue, and have neglected a point which is very important.

Further, when you say that if I deny, that the operations of seeing, hearing, attending, wishing, &c., can be ascribed to God, or that they exist in Him in any eminent fashion, you do not know what sort of God mine is; I suspect that you believe there is no greater perfection than such as can be explained by the aforesaid attributes. I am not astonished; for I believe that, if a triangle could speak, it would say, in like manner, that God is eminently triangular, while a circle would say that the divine nature is eminently circular. Thus each would ascribe to God its own attributes, would assume itself to be like God, and look on everything else as ill-shaped.

The briefness of a letter and want of time do not allow me to enter into my opinion on the divine nature, or the questions you have propounded. Besides, suggesting difficulties is not the same as producing reasons. That we do many things in the world from conjecture is true, but that our reflections are based on conjecture is false. In practical life we are compelled to follow what is most probable; in speculative thought we are compelled to follow truth. A man would perish of hunger and thirst, if he refused to eat or drink, till he had obtained positive proof that food and drink would be good for him. But in philosophic reflection this is not so. On the contrary, we must take care not to admit as true anything, which is only probable. For when one falsity has been let in, infinite others follow.

Again, we cannot infer that because sciences of things divine and human are full of controversies and quarrels, therefore their whole subject-matter is uncertain; for there have been many persons so enamoured of contradiction, as to turn into ridicule geometrical axioms. Sextus Empiricus and other sceptics, whom you quote, declare, that it is false to say that a whole is greater than its part, and pass similar judgments on other axioms.

However, as I pass over and grant that in default of proof we must be content with probabilities, I say that a probable proof ought to be such that, though we may doubt about it, we cannot maintain its contrary; for that which can be contradicted resembles not truth but falsehood. For instance, if I say that Peter is alive, because I saw him yesterday in good health, this is a probability, in so far as no one can maintain the contrary; but if anyone says that he saw Peter yesterday in a swoon, and that he believed Peter to have departed this life to-day, he will make my statement seem false. That your conjecture about ghosts and spectres seems false, and not even probable, I have shown so clearly, that I can find nothing worthy of answer in your reply.

To your question, whether I have of God as clear an idea as I have of a triangle, I reply in the affirmative. But if you ask me, whether I have as clear a mental image of God as I have of a triangle, I reply in the negative. For we are not able to imagine God, though we can understand Him. You must also here observe, that I do not assert that I thoroughly know God, but that I understand some of His attributes, not all nor the greater part, and it is evident that my ignorance of very many does not hinder the knowledge I have of some. When I learned Euclid's Elements, I understood that the three angles of a triangle are equal to two right angles, and this property of a triangle I perceived clearly, though I might be ignorant of many others.

As regards spectres or ghosts, I have hitherto heard attributed to them no intelligible property: they seem like phantoms, which no one can understand. When you say that spectres, or ghosts, in these lower regions (I adopt your phraseology, though I know not why matter below should be inferior to matter above) consist in a very thin rarefied and subtle substance, you seem to me to be speaking of spiders' webs, air, or vapours. To say, that they are invisible, seems to me to be equivalent to saying that they do not exist, not to stating their nature; unless, perhaps, you wish to indicate, that they render themselves visible or invisible at will, and that the imagination, in these as in other impossibilities, will find a difficulty.

The authority of Plato, Aristotle, and Socrates, does not carry much weight with me. I should have been astonished, if you had brought forward Epicurus, Democritus, Lucretius, or any of the atomists, or upholders of the atomic theory. It is no wonder that persons, who have invented occult qualities, intentional species, substantial forms, and a thousand other trifles, should have also devised spectres and ghosts, and given credence to old wives' tales, in order to take away the reputation of Democritus, whom they were so jealous of, that they burnt all the books which he had published amid so much eulogy. If you are inclined to believe such witnesses, what reason have you for denying the miracles of the Blessed Virgin, and all the Saints? These have been described by so many famous philosophers, theologians, and historians, that I could produce at least a hundred such authorities for every one of the former. But I have gone further, my dear Sir, than I intended: I do not desire to cause any further annoyance by doctrines which I know you will not grant. For the principles which you follow are far different from my own.

LETTER LXI. (LVII.)

* * * * * TO SPINOZA.[1]

[*Philosophers often differ through using words in different senses. Thus in the question of free will Descartes means by free, constrained by no cause. You mean by the same, undetermined in a particular way by a cause. The question of free will is threefold :—I. Have we any power whatever over things external to us? II. Have we absolute power over the intentional movements of our own body? III. Have we free use of our reason? Both Descartes and yourself are right according to the terms employed by each* (8th October, 1674).]

LETTER LXII. (LVIII.)

SPINOZA TO * * * * *[2] (The Hague, October, 1674).

[*Spinoza gives his opinions on liberty and necessity.*]

SIR,—Our friend, J. R.[3] has sent me the letter which you have been kind enough to write to me, and also the judgment of your friend[4] as to the opinions of Descartes and myself regarding free will. Both enclosures were very welcome to me. Though I am, at present, much occupied with other matters, not to mention my delicate health, your singular courtesy, or, to name the chief motive, your love of truth, impels me to satisfy your inquiries, as far as my poor abilities will permit. What your friend wishes to imply by his remark before he appeals to experience, I

[1] This letter is by Van Vloten, followed by Mr. Pollock, assigned to Ehrenfried Walter von Tschirnhausen, a Bohemian nobleman. See Introduction, p. xvi. The correspondence with Tschirnhausen was formerly supposed to be with Lewis Meyer. The letters of Tschirnhausen contain by far the most acute contemporary criticism of Spinoza.

[2] This letter is addressed to G. H. Schaller, who had sent on Letter LXI. to Spinoza.

[3] John Rieuwerts, a bookseller of Amsterdam.

[4] Tschirnhausen; the "judgment" is Letter LXI.

know not. What he adds, that *when one of two disputants affirms something which the other denies, both may be right,* is true, if he means that the two, though using the same terms, are thinking of different things. I once sent several examples of this to our friend J. R.,[1] and am now writing to tell him to communicate them to you.

I, therefore, pass on to that definition of liberty, which he says is my own; but I know not whence he has taken it. I say that a thing is free, which exists and acts solely by the necessity of its own nature. Thus also God understands Himself and all things freely, because it follows solely from the necessity of His nature, that He should understand all things. You see I do not place freedom in free decision, but in free necessity. However, let us descend to created things, which are all determined by external causes to exist and operate in a given determinate manner. In order that this may be clearly understood, let us conceive a very simple thing. For instance, a stone receives from the impulsion of an external cause, a certain quantity of motion, by virtue of which it continues to move after the impulsion given by the external cause has ceased. The permanence of the stone's motion is constrained, not necessary, because it must be defined by the impulsion of an external cause. What is true of the stone is true of any individual, however complicated its nature, or varied its functions, inasmuch as every individual thing is necessarily determined by some external cause to exist and operate in a fixed and determinate manner.

Further conceive, I beg, that a stone, while continuing in motion, should be capable of thinking and knowing, that it is endeavouring, as far as it can, to continue to move. Such a stone, being conscious merely of its own endeavour and not at all indifferent, would believe itself to be completely free, and would think that it continued in motion solely because of its own wish. This is that human freedom, which all boast that they possess, and which consists solely in the fact, that men are conscious of their own desire, but are ignorant of the causes whereby that desire has been determined. Thus an infant believes that it desires milk freely;

[1] John Rieuwerts.

an angry child thinks he wishes freely for vengeance, a timid child thinks he wishes freely to run away. Again, a drunken man thinks, that from the free decision of his mind he speaks words, which afterwards, when sober, he would like to have left unsaid. So the delirious, the garrulous, and others of the same sort think that they act from the free decision of their mind, not that they are carried away by impulse. As this misconception is innate in all men, it is not easily conquered. For, although experience abundantly shows, that men can do anything rather than check their desires, and that very often, when a prey to conflicting emotions, they see the better course and follow the worse, they yet believe themselves to be free; because in some cases their desire for a thing is slight, and can easily be overruled by the recollection of something else, which is frequently present in the mind.

I have thus, if I mistake not, sufficiently explained my opinion regarding free and constrained necessity, and also regarding so-called human freedom: from what I have said you will easily be able to reply to your friend's objections. For when he says, with Descartes, that he who is constrained by no external cause is free, if by being constrained he means acting against one's will, I grant that we are in some cases quite unrestrained, and in this respect possess free will. But if by constrained he means acting necessarily, although not against one's will (as I have explained above), I deny that we are in any instance free.

But your friend, on the contrary, asserts that *we may employ our reason absolutely, that is, in complete freedom;* and is, I think, a little too confident on the point. *For who,* he says, *could deny, without contradicting his own consciousness, that I can think with my thoughts, that I wish or do not wish to write?* I should like to know what consciousness he is talking of, over and above that which I have illustrated by the example of the stone.

As a matter of fact I, without, I hope, contradicting my consciousness, that is my reason and experience, and without cherishing ignorance and misconception, deny that I can by any absolute power of thought think, that I wish or do not wish to write. I appeal to the consciousness, which he has doubtless experienced, that in dreams he has not the power of thinking that he wishes, or does not wish to write; and that, when he dreams that he wishes to write, he has not the power not to dream that he wishes to write. I think he must also have experienced, that the mind is not always equally capable of thinking of the same object, but according as the body is more capable for the image of this or that object being excited in it, so is the mind more capable of thinking of the same object.

When he further adds, that the causes for his applying his mind to writing have led him, but not constrained him to write, he merely means (if he will look at the question impartially), that his disposition was then in a state, in which it could be easily acted on by causes, which would have been powerless under other circumstances, as for instance when he was under a violent emotion. That is, causes, which at other times would not have constrained him, have constrained him in this case, not to write against his will but necessarily to wish to write.

As for his statement, that *if we were constrained by external causes, no one could acquire the habit of virtue,* I know not what is his authority for saying, that firmness and constancy of disposition cannot arise from predestined necessity, but only from free will.

What he finally adds, that *if this were granted, all wickedness would be excusable,* I meet with the question, What then? Wicked men are not less to be feared, and are not less harmful, when they are wicked from necessity. However, on this point I would ask you to refer to my Principles of Cartesian Philosophy, Part II., chap. viii.

In a word, I should like your friend, who makes these objections, to tell me, how he reconciles the human virtue, which he says arises from the free decision of the mind, with God's pre-ordainment of the universe. If, with Descartes, he confesses his inability to do so, he is endeavouring to direct against me the weapon which has already pierced himself. But in vain. For if you examine my opinion attentively, you will see that it is quite consistent, &c.

LETTER LXIII. (LIX.)

* * * * * TO SPINOZA.[1]

[*The writer exhorts Spinoza to publish the treatises on Ethics and on the Improvement of the Understanding.—Remarks on the definition of motion. On the difference between a true and an adequate idea.*]

MOST EXCELLENT SIR,—When shall we have your method of rightly directing the reason in the acquisition of unknown truths, and your general treatise on physics? I know you have already proceeded far with them. The first has already come to my knowledge, and the second I have become aware of from the Lemmas added to the second part of the Ethics; whereby many difficulties in physics are readily solved. If time and opportunity permit, I humbly beg from you a true *definition of motion* and its explanation; also to know how, seeing that extension in so far as it is conceived in itself is indivisible, immutable, &c., we can infer *à priori*, that there can arise so many varieties of it, and consequently the existence of figure in the particles of any given body, which are, nevertheless, in every body various, and distinct from the figures of the parts, which compose the reality of any other body. You have already, by word of mouth, pointed out to me a method, which you employ in the search for truths as yet unknown. I find this method to be very excellent, and at the same time very easy, in so far as I have formed an opinion on it, and I can assert that from this single discovery I have made great progress in mathematics. I wish therefore, that you would give me a true definition of an adequate, a true, a false, a fictitious, and a doubtful idea. I have been in search of the difference between a true and an adequate idea. Hitherto, however, I can ascertain nothing except after inquiring into a thing, and forming a certain concept or idea of it. I then (in order to elicit whether this true idea is also an adequate idea of its object) inquire,

[1] This letter is from Tschirnhausen, who had in the meantime, as appears from its contents, had an interview with Spinoza.

what is the cause of this idea or concept; when this is ascertained, I again ask, What is the cause of this prior concept? and so I go on always inquiring for the causes of the causes of ideas, until I find a cause of such a kind, that I can not find any cause for it, except that among all the ideas which I can command this alone exists. If, for instance, we inquire the true origin of our errors, Descartes will answer, that it consists in our giving assent to things not yet clearly perceived. But supposing this to be the true idea of the thing, I nevertheless shall not yet be able to determine all things necessary to be known concerning it, unless I have also an adequate idea of the thing in question; in order to obtain such, therefore, I inquire into the cause of this concept, how it happens that we give assent to things not clearly understood—and I answer, that it arises from defective knowledge. But here I cannot inquire further, and ask what is the cause, that we are ignorant of certain things; hence I see that I have detected an adequate idea of the origin of our errors. Here meanwhile I ask you, whether, seeing that many things expressed in infinite modes have an adequate idea of themselves, and that from every adequate idea all that can be known of its object can be inferred, though more readily from some ideas than others, whether, I say, this may be the means of knowing which idea is to be preferred? For instance, one adequate idea of a circle consists in the equality of its radii; another adequate idea consists in the infinite right angles equal to one another, made by the intersection of two lines, &c., and thus we have infinite expressions, each giving the adequate nature of a circle, Now, though all the properties of a circle may be inferred from every one of them, they may be deduced much more easily from some than from others. So also he, who considers lines applied to curves, will be able to draw many conclusions as to the measurement of curves, but will do so more readily from the consideration of tangents, &c. Thus I have wished to indicate how far I have progressed in this study; I await perfection in it, or, if I am wrong on any point, correction; also the definition I asked for. Farewell.

5 Jan., 1675.

LETTER LXIV. (LX.)

SPINOZA TO * * * * *.[1]

[*The difference between a true and an adequate idea is merely extrinsic, &c. The Hague, Jan.*, 1675.]

HONOURED SIR.—Between a true and an adequate idea, I recognize no difference, except that the epithet true only has regard to the agreement between the idea and its object, whereas the epithet adequate has regard to the nature of the idea in itself; so that in reality there is no difference between a true and an adequate idea beyond this extrinsic relation. However, in order that I may know, from which idea out of many all the properties of its object may be deduced, I pay attention to one point only, namely, that the idea or definition should express the efficient cause of its object. For instance, in inquiring into the properties of a circle, I ask, whether from the idea of a circle, that it consists of infinite right angles, I can deduce all its properties. I ask, I repeat, whether this idea involves the efficient cause of a circle. If it does not, I look for another, namely, that a circle is the space described by a line, of which one point is fixed, and the other movable. As this definition explains the efficient cause, I know that I can deduce from it all the properties of a circle. So, also, when I define God as a supremely perfect Being, then, since that definition does not express the efficient cause (I mean the efficient cause internal as well as external) I shall not be able to infer therefrom all the properties of God; as I can, when I define God as a Being, &c. (see Ethics, I. Def. vi.). As for your other inquiries, namely, that concerning motion, and those pertaining to method, my observations on them are not yet written out in due order, so I will reserve them for another occasion.

As regards your remark, that he "who considers lines applied to curves makes many deductions with regard to the measurement of curves, but does so with greater

[1] Tschirnhausen.

facility from the consideration of tangents," &c., I think that from the consideration of tangents many deductions will be made with more difficulty, than from the consideration of lines applied in succession; and I assert absolutely, that from certain properties of any particular thing (whatever idea be given) some things may be discovered more readily, others with more difficulty, though all are concerned with the nature of the thing. I think it need only be observed, that an idea should be sought for of such a kind, that all properties may be inferred, as has been said above. He, who is about to deduce all the properties of a particular thing, knows that the ultimate properties will necessarily be the most difficult to discover, &c.

LETTER LXV. (LXIII.)

G. H. SCHALLER TO SPINOZA.[1]

[*Schaller asks for answers to four questions of his friend Tschirnhausen on the attributes of God, and mentions that Tschirnhausen has removed the unfavourable opinion of Spinoza lately conceived by Boyle and Oldenburg.*]

MOST DISTINGUISHED AND EXCELLENT SIR,—I should blush for my silence, which has lasted so long, and has laid me open to the charge of ingratitude for your kindness extended to me beyond my merits, if I did not reflect that your generous courtesy inclines rather to excuse than to accuse, and also know that you devote your leisure, for the common good of your friends, to serious studies, which it would be harmful and injurious to disturb without due cause. For this reason I have been silent, and have meanwhile been content to hear from friends of your good health: I send you this letter to inform you, that our noble friend von Tschirnhausen is enjoying the same in England, and has three times in the letters he has sent me bidden

[1] In the Opera Posthuma this letter is arranged, so as to seem to be from the person who puts the questions himself, and the names of Schaller and Tschirnhausen are suppressed.

me convey his kindest regards to the master, again bidding me request from you the solution of the following questions, and forward to him your hoped-for answer: would the master be pleased to convince him by positive proof, not by a reduction to the impossible, that we cannot know any attributes of God, save thought and extension? Further, whether it follows that creatures constituted under other attributes can form no idea of extension? If so, it would follow that there must be as many worlds as there are attributes of God. For instance, there would be as much room for extension in worlds affected by other attributes, as there actually exists of extension in our world. But as we perceive nothing save thought besides extension, so creatures in the other world would perceive nothing besides the attributes of that world and thought.

Secondly, as the understanding of God differs from our understanding as much in essence as in existence, it has, therefore, nothing in common with it; therefore (by Ethics, I. iii.) God's understanding cannot be the cause of our own.

Thirdly (in Ethics, I. x. note) you say, that *nothing in nature is clearer than that every entity must be conceived under some attribute* (this I thoroughly understand), *and that the more it has of reality or being, the more attributes appertain to it.* It seems to follow from this, that there are entities possessing three, four, or more attributes (though we gather from what has been demonstrated that every being consists only of two attributes, namely, a certain attribute of God and the idea of that attribute).

Fourthly, I should like to have examples of those things which are immediately produced by God, and those which are produced through the means of some infinite modification. Thought and extension seem to be of the former kind; understanding in thought and motion in extension seem to be of the latter.

And these are the points which our said friend von Tschirnhausen joins with me in wishing to have explained by your excellence, if perchance your spare time allows it. He further relates, that Mr. Boyle and Oldenburg had formed a strange idea of your personal character, but that he has not only removed it, but also given reasons, which have not only led them back to a most worthy and favourable opinion thereof, but also made them value most highly the Theologico-Political Treatise. Of this I have not ventured to inform you, because of your health. Be assured that I am, and live,

Most noble sir,
for every good office your most devoted servant,
G. H. SCHALLER.

Amsterdam, 25 July, 1675.

Mr. à Gent and J. Rieuwerts dutifully greet you.

LETTER LXVI. (LXIV.)

SPINOZA TO * * * * *[1]

[*Spinoza answers by references to the first three books of the Ethics.*]

DEAR SIR,—I am glad that you have at last had occasion to refresh me with one of your letters, always most welcome to me. I heartily beg that you will frequently repeat the favour, &c.

I proceed to consider your doubts: to the first I answer, that the human mind can only acquire knowledge of those things which the idea of a body actually existing involves, or of what can be inferred from such an idea. For the power of anything is defined solely by its essence (Ethics, III. vii.); the essence of the mind (Ethics, II. xiii.) consists solely in this, that it is the idea of body actually existing; therefore the mind's power of understanding only extends to things, which this idea of body contains in itself, or which follow therefrom. Now this idea of body does not involve or express any of God's attributes, save extension and thought. For its object (*ideatum*), namely, body (by Ethics, II. vi), has God for its cause, in so far as He is regarded under the attribute of extension, and not in so far as He is regarded under any other; therefore (Ethics, I. ax. vi.) this idea of the body involves the knowledge of God, only

[1] Tschirnhausen.

in so far as He is regarded under the attribute of extension. Further, this idea, in so far as it is a mode of thinking, has also (by the same proposition) God for its cause, in so far as He is regarded as a thinking thing, and not in so far as He is regarded under any other attribute. Hence (by the same axiom) the idea of this idea involves the knowledge of God, in so far as He is regarded under the attribute of thought, and not in so far as He is regarded under any attribute. It is therefore plain, that the human mind, or the idea of the human body neither involves nor expresses any attributes of God save these two. Now from these two attributes, or their modifications, no other attribute of God can (Ethics, I. x.) be inferred or conceived. I therefore conclude, that the human mind cannot attain knowledge of any attribute of God besides these, which is the proposition you inquire about. With regard to your question, whether there must be as many worlds as there are attributes, I refer you to Ethics II. vii. note.

Moreover this proposition might be proved more readily by a reduction to the absurd; I am accustomed, when the proposition is negative, to employ this mode of demonstration as more in character. However, as the question you ask is positive, I make use of the positive method, and ask, whether one thing can be produced from another, from which it differs both in essence and existence; for things which differ to this extent seem to have nothing in common. But since all particular things, except those which are produced from things similar to themselves, differ from their causes both in essence and existence, I see here no reason for doubt.

The sense in which I mean that God is the efficient cause of things, no less of their essence than of their existence, I think has been sufficiently explained in Ethics I. xxv. note and corollary. The axiom in the note to Ethics I. x., as I hinted at the end of the said note, is based on the idea which we have of a Being absolutely infinite, not on the fact, that there are or may be beings possessing three, four, or more attributes.

Lastly, the examples you ask for of the first kind are, in thought, absolutely infinite understanding; in extension, motion and rest; an example of the second kind is the sum of the whole extended universe (*facies totius universi*), which, though it varies in infinite modes, yet remains always the same. Cf. Ethics II. note to Lemma vii. before Prop. xiv.

Thus, most excellent Sir, I have answered, as I think, the objections of yourself and your friend. If you think any uncertainty remains, I hope you will not neglect to tell me, so that I may, if possible, remove it.

The Hague, 29 July, 1675.

LETTER LXVII. (LXV.)

* * * * *[1] TO SPINOZA.

[*A fresh inquiry as to whether there are two or more attributes of God.*]

DISTINGUISHED SIR,—I should like a demonstration of what you say: namely, that the soul cannot perceive any attributes of God, except extension and thought. Though this might appear evident to me, it seems possible that the contrary might be deduced from Ethics II. vii. note; perhaps because I do not rightly grasp the meaning of that passage. I have therefore resolved, distinguished Sir, to show you how I make the deduction, earnestly begging you to aid me with your usual courtesy, wherever I do not rightly represent your meaning. I reason as follows:—Though I gather that the universe is one, it is not less clear from the passage referred to, that it is expressed in infinite modes, and therefore that every individual thing is expressed in infinite modes. Hence it seems to follow, that the modification constituting my mind, and the modification constituting my body, though one and the same modification, is yet expressed in infinite ways—first, through thought; secondly, through extension; thirdly, through some attribute of God unknown to me, and so on to infinity, seeing that there are in God infinite attributes, and the order and connection of the modifications seem to

[1] Tschirnhausen.

be the same in all. Hence arises the question: Why the mind, which represents a certain modification, the same modification being expressed not only in extension, but in infinite other ways,—why, I repeat, does the mind perceive that modification only as expressed through extension, to wit, the human body, and not as expressed through any other attributes? Time does not allow me to pursue the subject further; perhaps my difficulties will be removed by further reflection.

London, 12 Aug., 1675.

LETTER LXVIII. (LXVI.)

SPINOZA TO * * * * *.[1]

[*In this fragment of a letter Spinoza refers his friend to Ethics,* I. x. *and* II. vii. *note.*]

DISTINGUISHED SIR,— . . . But in answer to your objection I say, that although each particular thing be expressed in infinite ways in the infinite understanding of God, yet those infinite ideas, whereby it is expressed, cannot constitute one and the same mind of a particular thing, but infinite minds; seeing that each of these infinite ideas has no connection with the rest, as I have explained in the same note to Ethics, II. vii., and as is also evident from I. x. If you will reflect on these passages a little, you will see that all difficulty vanishes, &c.

The Hague, 18 August, 1675.

[1] Tschirnhausen.

LETTER LXVIII.A.

G. H. Schaller to Spinoza.

[*Schaller relates to Spinoza Tschirnhausen's doings in France, and letter to him, and makes known to Spinoza the answers contained in that letter to Spinoza's objections in Letter LXVIII. and the request of Leibnitz to see Spinoza's unpublished writings.*]

Amsterdam, 14 Nov., 1675.

Most learned and excellent Master, my most venerable Patron,—I hope that you duly received my letter with ——'s method,[1] and likewise, that you are up to the present time in good health, as I am.

But for three months I had no letter from our friend von Tschirnhausen, whence I formed sad conjectures that he had made a fatal journey, when he left England for France. Now that I have received a letter, in my fulness of joy I felt bound, according to his request, to communicate it to the Master, and to let you know, with his most dutiful greeting, that he has arrived safely in Paris, and found there Mr. Huygens, as we had told him, and consequently has in every way sought to please him, and is thus highly esteemed by him. He mentioned, that the Master had recommended to him Huygens's conversation, and made very much of him personally. This greatly pleased Huygens; so he answered that he likewise greatly esteemed you personally, and he has now received from you a copy of the Theologico-Political Treatise, which is esteemed by many there, and it is eagerly inquired, whether there are extant any more of the same writer's works. To this Mr. von Tschirnhausen replied that he knew of none but the Demonstrations in the first and second parts of the Cartesian Principles. But he mentioned nothing about the Master, but what I have said, and so he hopes that he has not displeased you herein.

* * * * * *

To the objection that you last made he replies, that those few words which I wrote at the Master's dicta-

[1] See the next Letter.

tion,[1] explained to him your meaning more thoroughly, and that he has favourably entertained the said reasonings (for by these two methods[2] they best admit of explanation). But two reasons have obliged him to continue in the opinion implied in his recent objection. Of these the first is, that otherwise there appears to be a contradiction between the fifth and seventh propositions of the second book. For in the former of these it is laid down, that the objects of ideas are the efficient causes of the ideas, which yet seems to be refuted by the quotation, in the proof of the latter, of the fourth axiom of Part I. "Or, as I rather think, I do not make the right application of this axiom according to the author's intention, which I would most willingly be told by him, if his leisure permits it. The second cause which prevented me from following the explanation he gives was, that thereby the attribute of thought is pronounced to extend much more widely than other attributes. But since every one of the attributes contributes to make up the essence of God, I do not quite see how this fact does not contradict the opinion just stated. I will say just this more, that if I may judge the minds of others by my own, there will be great difficulty in understanding the seventh and eighth propositions of Book II., and this for no other reason than that the author has been pleased (doubtless because they seemed so plain to him) to accompany the demonstrations annexed to them with such short and laconic explanations."

He further mentions, that he has found at Paris a man called Leibnitz, remarkably learned, and most skilled in various sciences, as also free from the vulgar prejudices of theology. With him he has formed an intimate acquaintance, founded on the fact that Leibnitz labours with him to pursue the perfection of the intellect, and, in fact, reckons nothing better or more useful. Von Tschirnhausen says, that he is most practised in ethics, and speaks without any stimulus of the passions by the sole dictate of reason. He adds, that he is most skilled in physics, and also in meta-

[1] Letter LXVIII.

[2] That is, I think, hearing from the author criticized what his precise meaning is, and attending carefully to his arguments in favour of the opinion thus precisely ascertained.—[Tr.]

physical studies concerning God and the soul. Finally, he concludes that he is most worthy of having communicated to him the Master's writings, if you will first give your permission, for he believes that the author will thence gain a great advantage, as he promises to show at length, if the Master be so pleased. But if not, do not doubt, in the least, that he will honourably keep them concealed as he has promised, as in fact he has not made the slightest mention of them. Leibnitz also highly values the Theologico-Political Treatise, on the subject of which he once wrote the Master a letter, if he is not mistaken. And therefore I would beg my Master, that, unless there is some reason against him, you will not refuse your permission in accordance with your gracious kindness, but will, if possible, open your mind to me, as soon as may be, for after receiving your answers I shall be able to reply to our friend von Tschirnhausen, which I would gladly do on Tuesday evening, unless important hindrances cause my Master to delay.

Mr. Bresser,[1] on his return from Cleves, has sent here a large quantity of the beer of that country; I suggested to him that he should make a present to the Master of half a tun, which he promised to do, and added a most friendly greeting.

Finally, excuse my unpractised style and hurried writing, and give me your orders, that I may have a real occasion of proving myself, most excellent Sir,

Your most ready servant,

G. H. SCHALLER.

LETTER LXVIII.B.

SPINOZA TO SCHALLER.

[*Spinoza answers all the points in Schaller's letter, and hesitates to entrust his writings to Leibnitz.*]

MOST EXPERIENCED SIR, AND VALUED FRIEND,—I was much pleased to learn from your letter, received to-day, that you are well, and that our friend von Tschirnhausen

[1] See Letters XLI.A, XLII.

has happily accomplished his journey to France. In the conversation which he had about me with Mr. Huygens, he behaved, at least in my opinion, very judiciously; and besides, I am very glad that he has found so convenient an opportunity for the purpose which he intended. But what it is he has found in the fourth axiom of Part I. that seems to contradict Proposition v. of Part II. I do not see. For in that proposition it is affirmed, that the essence of every idea has for its cause God, in so far as He is considered as a thinking thing; but in that axiom, that the knowledge or idea of a cause depends on the knowledge or idea of an effect. But, to tell the truth, I do not quite follow, in this matter, the meaning of your letter, and suspect that either in it, or in his copy of the book, there is a slip of the pen. For you write, that it is affirmed in Proposition v. that the objects of ideas are the efficient causes of the ideas, whereas this is exactly what is expressly denied in that proposition, and I now think that this is the cause of the whole confusion.[1] Accordingly it would be useless for me at present to try to write at greater length on this subject, but I must wait, till you explain to me his mind more clearly, and till I know whether he has a correct copy. I believe that I have an epistolary acquaintance with the Leibnitz he mentions. But why he, who was a counsellor at Frankfort, has gone to France, I do not know. As far as I could conjecture from his letters, he seemed to me a man of liberal mind, and versed in every science. But yet I think it imprudent so soon to entrust my writings to him. I should like first to know what is his business in France, and the judgment of our friend von Tschirnhausen, when he has been longer in his company, and knows his character more intimately. However, greet that friend of ours in my name, and let him command me what he pleases, if in anything I can be of service to him, and he will find me most ready to obey him in everything.

I congratulate my most worthy friend Mr. Bresser on his arrival or return, and also thank him heartily for the

[1] It appears to me, that Schaller correctly states the difficulty of Tschirnhausen, but that by leaving out a negative in the sentence in question, he has attributed the doctrine of Prop. v. to Prop. vii., and *vice versâ*.—[TR.]

promised beer, and will requite him, too, in any way that I can. Lastly, I have not yet tried to find out your relation's method, nor do I think that I shall be able to apply my mind to trying it. For the more I think over the thing in itself, the more I am persuaded that you have not made gold, but had not sufficiently eliminated that which was hidden in the antimony. But more of this another time: at present I am prevented by want of leisure. In the meanwhile, if in anything I can assist you, you will always find me, most excellent Sir, your friend and devoted servant,

B. DE SPINOZA.

The Hague, 18 Nov., 1675.

LETTER LXIX. (LXXX.)

* * * * *[1] TO SPINOZA.

[*The writer asks for explanations of some passages in the letter about the infinite* (XXIX.).]

DISTINGUISHED SIR,—In the first place I can with great difficulty conceive, how it can be proved, *à priori*, that bodies exist having motion and figure, seeing that, in extension considered absolutely in itself, nothing of the kind is met with. Secondly, I should like to learn from you, how this passage in your letter on the infinite is to be understood:—"*They do not hence infer that such things elude number by the multitude of their component parts.*" For, as a matter of fact, all mathematicians seem to me always to demonstrate, with regard to such infinities, that the number of the parts is so great, as to elude all expression in terms of number. And in the example you give of the two circles, you do not appear to prove this statement,[2] which was yet what you had undertaken to do. For in this second passage you only show, that they do not draw this conclusion from "*the excessive size of the intervening*

[1] Tschirnhausen.
[2] Viz., "They do not hence infer . . . . component parts."

space," or from the fact that "*we do not know the maximum and the minimum of the said space;*" but you do not demonstrate, as you intended, that the conclusion is not based on the multitude of parts, &c.

2 May, 1676.

LETTER LXX. (LXXXI.)

Spinoza to * * * * *[1]

[*Spinoza explains his view of the infinite.*]

Distinguished Sir,—My statement concerning the infinite, that an infinity of parts cannot be inferred from a multitude of parts, is plain when we consider that, if such a conclusion could be drawn from a multitude of parts, we should not be able to imagine a greater multitude of parts; the first-named multitude, whatever it was, would have to be the greater, which is contrary to fact. For in the whole space between two non-concentric circles we conceive a greater multitude of parts than in half that space, yet the number of parts in the half, as in the whole of the space, exceeds any assignable number. Again, from extension, as Descartes conceives it, to wit, a quiescent mass, it is not only difficult, as you say, but absolutely impossible to prove the existence of bodies. For matter at rest, as it is in itself, will continue at rest, and will only be determined to motion by some more powerful external cause; for this reason I have not hesitated on a former occasion to affirm, that the Cartesian principles of natural things are useless, not to say absurd.

The Hague, 5 May, 1676.

[1] Tschirnhausen.

LETTER LXXI. (LXXXII.)

* * * * *[1] TO SPINOZA.

[*How can the variety of the universe be shown à priori from the Spinozistic conception of extension?*]

MOST LEARNED SIR,—I wish you would gratify me in this matter by pointing out how, from the conception of extension, as you give it, the variety of the universe can be shown *à priori.* You recall the opinion of Descartes, wherein he asserts, that this variety can only be deduced from extension, by supposing that, when motion was started by God, it caused this effect in extension. Now it appears to me, that he does not deduce the existence of bodies from matter at rest, unless, perhaps, you count as nothing the assumption of God as a motive power; you have not shown how such an effect must, *à priori,* necessarily follow from the nature of God. A difficulty which Descartes professed himself unable to solve as being beyond human understanding. I therefore ask you the question, knowing that you have other thoughts on the matter, unless perhaps there be some weighty cause for your unwillingness hitherto to disclose your opinion. If this, as I suppose, be not expedient, give me some hint of your meaning. You may rest assured, that whether you speak openly with me, or whether you employ reserve, my regard for you will remain unchanged.

My special reasons for making the requests are as follows:—I have always observed in mathematics, that from a given thing considered in itself, that is, from the definition of a given thing, we can only deduce a single property; if, however, we require to find several properties, we are obliged to place the thing defined in relation to other things. Then from the conjunction of the definitions of these things new properties result. For instance, if I regard the circumference of a circle by itself, I can only infer that it is everywhere alike or uniform, in which property it differs essentially from all other curves; I shall

[1] Tschirnhausen.

never be able to infer any other properties. But if I place it in relation with other things, such as the radii drawn from the centre, two intersecting lines, or many others, I shall be able hence to deduce many properties; this seems to be in opposition to Prop. xvi. of your Ethics, almost the principal proposition of the first book of your treatise. For it is there assumed as known, that from the given definition of anything several properties can be deduced. This seems to me impossible, unless we bring the thing defined into relation with other things; and further, I am for this reason unable to see, how from any attribute regarded singly, for instance, infinite extension, a variety of bodies can result; if you think that this conclusion cannot be drawn from one attribute considered by itself, but from all taken together, I should like to be instructed by you on the point, and shown how it should be conceived.—Farewell, &c.

Paris, 23 June, 1676.

LETTER LXXII. (LXXXIII.)

SPINOZA TO * * * *[1]

[*Spinoza gives the required explanation. Mentions the treatise of Huet, &c.*]

DISTINGUISHED SIR,—With regard to your question as to whether the variety of the universe can be deduced *à priori* from the conception of extension only, I believe I have shown clearly enough already that it cannot; and that, therefore, matter has been ill-defined by Descartes as extension; it must necessarily be explained through an attribute, which expresses eternal and infinite essence. But perhaps, some day, if my life be prolonged, I may discuss the subject with you more clearly. For hitherto I have not been able to put any of these matters into due order.

As to what you add; namely, that from the definition

[1] Tschirnhausen.

of a given thing considered in itself we can only deduce a single property, this is, perhaps, true in the case of very simple things (among which I count figures), but not in realities. For, from the fact alone, that I define God as a Being to whose essence belongs existence, I infer several of His properties; namely, that He necessarily exists, that He is One, unchangeable, infinite, &c. I could adduce several other examples, which, for the present, I pass over.

In conclusion, I ask you to inquire, whether Huet's treatise (against the "Tractatus Theologico-Politicus") about which I wrote to you before, has yet been published, and whether you could send me a copy. Also, whether you yet know, what are the new discoveries about refraction. And so farewell, dear Sir, and continue to regard yours, &c.

The Hague, 15 July, 1676.

LETTER LXXIII. (LXVII.)

Albert Burgh to Spinoza.

[*Albert Burgh announces his reception into the Romish Church, and exhorts Spinoza to follow his example.*[1]]

I promised to write to you on leaving my country, if anything noteworthy occurred on the journey. I take the opportunity which offers of an event of the utmost importance, to redeem my engagement, by informing you that I have, by God's infinite mercy, been received into the Catholic Church and made a member of the same. You may learn the particulars of the step from a letter which I have sent to the distinguished and accomplished Professor Craanen of Leyden. I will here subjoin a few remarks for your special benefit.

Even as formerly I admired you for the subtlety and keenness of your natural gifts, so now do I bewail and deplore you; inasmuch as being by nature most talented,

[1] The whole of this very long letter is not given here, but only such parts as seemed most characteristic, or are alluded to in Spinoza's reply. —[Tr.]

and adorned by God with extraordinary gifts; being a lover, nay a coveter of the truth, you yet allow yourself to be ensnared and deceived by that most wretched and most proud of beings, the prince of evil spirits. As for all your philosophy, what is it but a mere illusion and chimera? Yet to it you entrust not only your peace of mind in this life, but the salvation of your soul for eternity. See on what a wretched foundation all your doctrines rest. You assume that you have at length discovered the true philosophy. How do you know that your philosophy is the best of all that ever have been taught in the world, are now being taught, or ever shall be taught? Passing over what may be devised in the future, have you examined all the philosophies, ancient as well as modern, which are taught here, and in India, and everywhere throughout the whole world? Even if you have duly examined them, how do you know that you have chosen the best? You will say: "My philosophy is in harmony with right reason; other philosophies are not." But all other philosophers except your own followers disagree with you, and with equal right say of their philosophy what you say of yours, accusing you, as you do them, of falsity and error. It is, therefore, plain, that before the truth of your philosophy can come to light, reasons must be advanced, which are not common to other philosophies, but apply solely to your own; or else you must admit that your philosophy is as uncertain and nugatory as the rest.

However, restricting myself for the present to that book of yours with an impious title,[1] and mingling your philosophy with your theology, as in reality you mingle them yourself, though with diabolic cunning you endeavour to maintain, that each is separate from the other, and has different principles, I thus proceed.

Perhaps you will say: "Others have not read Holy Scripture so often as I have; and it is from Holy Scripture, the acknowledgment of which distinguishes Christians from the rest of the world, that I prove my doctrines. But how? By comparing the clear passages with the more obscure I explain Holy Scripture, and out of my in-

[1] "Tractatus Theologico-Politicus."

terpretations I frame dogmas, or else confirm those which are already concocted in my brain." But, I adjure you, reflect seriously on what you say. How do you know, that you have made a right application of your method, or again that your method is sufficient for the interpretation of Scripture, and that you are thus interpreting Scripture aright, especially as the Catholics say, and most truly, that the universal Word of God is not handed down to us in writing, hence that Holy Scripture cannot be explained through itself, I will not say by one man, but by the Church herself, who is the sole authorized interpreter? The Apostolic traditions must likewise be consulted, as is proved by the testimony of Holy Scripture and the Holy Fathers, and as reason and experience suggest. Thus, as your first principles are most false and lead to destruction, what will become of all your doctrine, built up and supported on so rotten a foundation?

Wherefore, if you believe in Christ crucified, acknowledge your pestilent heresy, reflect on the perverseness of your nature, and be reconciled with the Church.

How do your proofs differ from those of all heretics, who ever have left, are now leaving, or shall in future leave God's Church? All, like yourself, make use of the same principle, to wit, Holy Scripture taken by itself, for the concoction and establishment of their doctrines.

Do not flatter yourself with the thought, that neither the Calvinists, it may be, nor the so-called Reformed Church, nor the Lutherans, nor the Mennonites, nor the Socinians, &c., can refute your doctrines. All these, as I have said, are as wretched as yourself, and like you are dwelling in the shadow of death.

If you do not believe in Christ, you are more wretched than I can express. Yet the remedy is easy. Turn away from your sins, and consider the deadly arrogance of your wretched and insane reasoning. You do not believe in Christ. Why? You will say: "Because the teaching and the life of Christ, and also the Christian teaching concerning Christ are not at all in harmony with my teaching." But again, I say, then you dare to think yourself greater than all those who have ever risen up in the State or Church of God, patriarchs, prophets, apostles, martyrs, doctors, confessors, and holy virgins innumerable, yea, in your blasphemy, than Christ himself. Do you alone surpass all these in doctrine, in manner of life, in every respect? Will you, wretched pigmy, vile worm of the earth, yea, ashes, food of worms, will you in your unspeakable blasphemy, dare to put yourself before the incarnate, infinite wisdom of the Eternal Father? Will you, alone, consider yourself wiser and greater than all those, who from the beginning of the world have been in the Church of God, and have believed, or believe still, that Christ would come or has already come? On what do you base this rash, insane, deplorable, and inexcusable arrogance?

* * * * * *

If you cannot pronounce on what I have just been enumerating (divining rods, alchemy, &c.), why, wretched man, are you so puffed up with diabolical pride, as to pass rash judgment on the awful mysteries of Christ's life and passion, which the Catholics themselves in their teaching declare to be incomprehensible? Why do you commit the further insanity of silly and futile carping at the numberless miracles and signs, which have been wrought through the virtue of Almighty God by the apostles and disciples of Christ, and afterwards by so many thousand saints, in testimony to, and confirmation of the truth of the Catholic faith; yea, which are being wrought in our own time in cases without number throughout the world, by God's almighty goodness and mercy? If you cannot gainsay these, and surely you cannot, why stand aloof any longer? Join hands of fellowship, and repent from your sins: put on humility, and be born again.

[*Albert Burgh requests Spinoza to consider:* (i.) *The large number of believers in the Romish faith.* (ii.) *The uninterrupted succession of the Church.* (iii.) *The fact that a few unlearned men converted the world to Christianity.* (iv.) *The antiquity, the immutability, the infallibility, the incorruption, the unity, and the vast extent of the Catholic Religion; also the fact, that secession from it involves damnation, and that it will itself endure as long as the world.* (v.) *The admirable organization of the Romish Church.* (vi.) *The superior morality of Catholics.* (vii.)

The frequent cases of recantation of opinions among heretics. (viii.) *The miserable life led by atheists, whatever their outward demeanour may be.*] * * * *

I have written this letter to you with intentions truly Christian; first, in order to show the love I bear to you, though you are a heathen; secondly, in order to beg you not to persist in converting others.

I therefore will thus conclude: God is willing to snatch your soul from eternal damnation, if you will allow Him. Do not doubt that the Master, who has called you so often through others, is now calling you for the last time through me, who having obtained grace from the ineffable mercy of God Himself, beg the same for you with my whole heart. Do not deny me. For if you do not now give ear to God who calls you, the wrath of the Lord will be kindled against you, and there is a danger of your being abandoned by His infinite mercy, and becoming a wretched victim of the Divine Justice which consumes all things in wrath. Such a fate may Almighty God avert for the greater glory of His name, and for the salvation of your soul, also for a salutary example for the imitation of your most unfortunate and idolatrous followers, through our Lord and Saviour Jesus Christ, Who with the Eternal Father liveth and reigneth in the Unity of the Holy Spirit, God for all Eternity. Amen.

Florence, III. Non. Sept. CIↃIↃCLXXV. (Sept. 3, 1675.)[1]

LETTER LXXIV. (LXXVI.)

Spinoza to Albert Burgh.

[*Spinoza laments the step taken by his pupil, and answers his arguments. The Hague, end of* 1675.]

That, which I could scarcely believe when told me by others, I learn at last from your own letter; not only have you been made a member of the Romish Church, but you are

[1] There is a kind of affectation very consistent with the letter in the use of the classical calendar and Roman numerals for the date.

become a very keen champion of the same, and have already learned wantonly to insult and rail against your opponents.

At first I resolved to leave your letter unanswered, thinking that time and experience will assuredly be of more avail than reasoning, to restore you to yourself and your friends; not to mention other arguments, which won your approval formerly, when we were discussing the case of Steno,[1] in whose steps you are now following. But some of my friends, who like myself had formed great hopes from your superior talents, strenuously urge me not to fail in the offices of a friend, but to consider what you lately were, rather than what you are, with other arguments of the like nature. I have thus been induced to write you this short reply, which I earnestly beg you will think worthy of calm perusal.

I will not imitate those adversaries of Romanism, who would set forth the vices of priests and popes with a view to kindling your aversion. Such considerations are often put forward from evil and unworthy motives, and tend rather to irritate than to instruct. I will even admit, that more men of learning and of blameless life are found in the Romish Church than in any other Christian body; for, as it contains more members, so will every type of character be more largely represented in it. You cannot possibly deny, unless you have lost your memory as well as your reason, that in every Church there are thoroughly honourable men, who worship God with justice and charity. We have known many such among the Lutherans, the Reformed Church, the Mennonites, and the Enthusiasts. Not to go further, you knew your own relations, who in the time of the Duke of Alva suffered every kind of torture bravely and willingly for the sake of their religion. In fact, you must admit, that personal holiness is not peculiar to the Romish Church, but common to all Churches.

As it is by this, that we know "that we dwell in God and He in us" (1 Ep. John, iv. 13), it follows, that what distinguishes the Romish Church from others must be something entirely superfluous, and therefore founded solely on superstition. For, as John says, justice and

[1] A Danish anatomist, who renounced Lutheranism for Catholicism at Florence in 1669.

charity are the one sure sign of the true Catholic faith, and the true fruits of the Holy Spirit. Wherever they are found, there in truth is Christ; wherever they are absent, Christ is absent also. For only by the Spirit of Christ can we be led to the love of justice and charity. Had you been willing to reflect on these points, you would not have ruined yourself, nor have brought deep affliction on your relations, who are now sorrowfully bewailing your evil case.

But I return to your letter, which you begin, by lamenting that I allow myself to be ensnared by the prince of evil spirits. Pray take heart, and recollect yourself. When you had the use of your faculties, you were wont, if I mistake not, to worship an Infinite God, by Whose efficacy all things absolutely come to pass and are preserved; now you dream of a prince, God's enemy, who against God's will ensnares and deceives very many men (rarely good ones, to be sure), whom God thereupon hands over to this master of wickedness to be tortured eternally. The Divine justice therefore allows the devil to deceive men and remain unpunished; but it by no means allows to remain unpunished the men, who have been by that self-same devil miserably deceived and ensnared.

These absurdities might so far be tolerated, if you worshipped a God infinite and eternal; not one whom Chastillon, in the town which the Dutch call Tienen, gave with impunity to horses to be eaten. And, poor wretch, you bewail me? My philosophy, which you never beheld, you style a chimera? O youth deprived of understanding, who has bewitched you into believing, that the Supreme and Eternal is eaten by you, and held in your intestines?

Yet you seem to wish to employ reason, and ask me, "*How I know that my philosophy is the best among all that have ever been taught in the world, or are being taught, or ever will be taught?*" a question which I might with much greater right ask you; for I do not presume that I have found the best philosophy, I know that I understand the true philosophy. If you ask in what way I know it, I answer: In the same way as you know that the three angles of a triangle are equal to two right angles: that this is sufficient, will be denied by no one whose brain is sound, and who does not go dreaming of evil spirits inspiring us with false ideas like the true. For the truth is the index of itself and of what is false.

But you, who presume that you have at last found the best religion, or rather the best men, on whom you have pinned your credulity, you, "*who know that they are the best among all who have taught, do now teach, or shall in future teach other religions. Have you examined all religions, ancient as well as modern, taught here and in India and everywhere throughout the world?* And, *if you have duly examined them, how do you know that you have chosen the best*" since you can give no reason for the faith that is in you? But you will say, that you acquiesce in the inward testimony of the Spirit of God, while the rest of mankind are ensnared and deceived by the prince of evil spirits. But all those outside the pale of the Romish Church can with equal right proclaim of their own creed what you proclaim of yours.

As to what you add of the common consent of myriads of men and the uninterrupted ecclesiastical succession, this is the very catch-word of the Pharisees. They with no less confidence than the devotees of Rome bring forward their myriad witnesses, who as pertinaciously as the Roman witnesses repeat what they have heard, as though it were their personal experience. Further, they carry back their line to Adam. They boast with equal arrogance, that their Church has continued to this day unmoved and unimpaired in spite of the hatred of Christians and heathen. They more than any other sect are supported by antiquity. They exclaim with one voice, that they have received their traditions from God Himself, and that they alone preserve the Word of God both written and unwritten. That all heresies have issued from them, and that they have remained constant through thousands of years under no constraint of temporal dominion, but by the sole efficacy of their superstition, no one can deny. The miracles they tell of would tire a thousand tongues. But their chief boast is, that they count a far greater number of martyrs than any other nation, a number which is daily increased by those who suffer with singular constancy for the faith they profess; nor is their boasting false. I myself knew among others of a certain Judah called the faithful,[1] who in the midst of the flames, when he was already thought to be dead, lifted his voice to sing the hymn beginning, "To Thee, O God, I offer up my soul," and so singing perished.

The organization of the Roman Church, which you so greatly praise, I confess to be politic, and to many lucrative. I should believe that there was no other more convenient for deceiving the people and keeping men's minds in check, if it were not for the organization of the Mahometan Church, which far surpasses it. For from the time when this superstition arose, there has been no schism in its church.

If, therefore, you had rightly judged, you would have seen that only your third point tells in favour of the Christians, namely, that unlearned and common men should have been able to convert nearly the whole world to a belief in Christ. But this reason militates not only for the Romish Church, but for all those who profess the name of Christ.

But assume that all the reasons you bring forward tell in favour solely of the Romish Church. Do you think that you can thereby prove mathematically the authority of that Church? As the case is far otherwise, why do you wish me to believe that my demonstrations are inspired by the prince of evil spirits, while your own are inspired by God, especially as I see, and as your letter clearly shows, that you have been led to become a devotee of this Church not by your love of God, but by your fear of hell, the single cause of superstition? Is this your humility, that you trust nothing to yourself, but everything to others, who are condemned by many of their fellow men? Do you set it down to pride and arrogance, that I employ reason and acquiesce in this true Word of God, which is in the mind and can never be depraved or corrupted? Cast

[1] "Don Lope de Vera y Alarcon de San Clemente, a Spanish nobleman who was converted to Judaism through the study of Hebrew, and was burnt at Valladolid on the 25th July, 1644."—POLLOCK'S *Spinoza*, chap. ii., last note. Mr. Pollock refutes the inference of Grätz, that Spinoza's childhood must have been spent in Spain, by pointing out that the word used here, "novi," is the same as that used above of Albert Burgh's knowledge of his ancestors' sufferings, of which he was certainly not an eye-witness.

away this deadly superstition, acknowledge the reason which God has given you, and follow that, unless you would be numbered with the brutes. Cease, I say, to call ridiculous errors mysteries, and do not basely confound those things which are unknown to us, or have not yet been discovered, with what is proved to be absurd, like the horrible secrets of this Church of yours, which, in proportion as they are repugnant to right reason, you believe to transcend the understanding.

But the fundamental principle of the "Tractatus Theologico-Politicus," that Scripture should only be expounded through Scripture, which you so wantonly without any reason proclaim to be false, is not merely assumed, but categorically proved to be true or sound; especially in chapter vii., where also the opinions of adversaries are confuted; see also what is proved at the end of chapter xv. If you will reflect on these things, and also examine the history of the Church (of which I see you are completely ignorant), in order to see how false, in many respects, is Papal tradition, and by what course of events and with what cunning the Pope of Rome six hundred years after Christ obtained supremacy over the Church, I do not doubt that you will eventually return to your senses. That this result may come to pass I, for your sake, heartily wish. Farewell, &c.

LETTER LXXV. (LXIX.)

SPINOZA TO LAMBERT VAN VELTHUYSEN (*Doctor of Medicine at Utrecht.*)[1]

[*Of the proposed annotation of the "Tractatus Theologico-Politicus."*

MOST EXCELLENT AND DISTINGUISHED SIR,—I wonder at our friend Neustadt having said, that I am meditating the refutation of the various writings circulated against my

[1] See Letters XLVIII., XLIX.

book,[1] and that among the works for me to refute he places your MS. For I certainly have never entertained the intention of refuting any of my adversaries: they all seem to me utterly unworthy of being answered. I do not remember to have said to Mr. Neustadt anything more, than that I proposed to illustrate some of the obscurer passages in the treatise with notes, and that I should add to these your MS., and my answer, if your consent could be gained, on which last point I begged him to speak to you, adding, that if you refused permission on the ground, that some of the observations in my answer were too harshly put, you should be given full power to modify or expunge them. In the meanwhile, I am by no means angry with Mr. Neustadt, but I wanted to put the matter before you as it stands, that if your permission be not granted, I might show you that I have no wish to publish your MS. against your will. Though I think it might be issued without endangering your reputation, if it appears without your name, I will take no steps in the matter, unless you give me leave. But, to tell the truth, you would do me a far greater kindness, if you would put in writing the arguments with which you think you can impugn my treatise, and add them to your MS. I most earnestly beg you to do this. For there is no one whose arguments I would more willingly consider; knowing, as I do, that you are bound solely by your zeal for truth, and that your mind is singularly candid, I therefore beg you again and again, not to shrink from undertaking this task, and to believe me, Yours most obediently,

B. DE SPINOZA.

[1] The "Tractatus Theologico-Politicus."

A CATALOG OF SELECTED

DOVER BOOKS

IN ALL FIELDS OF INTEREST

A CATALOG OF SELECTED DOVER BOOKS IN ALL FIELDS OF INTEREST

CONCERNING THE SPIRITUAL IN ART, Wassily Kandinsky. Pioneering work by father of abstract art. Thoughts on color theory, nature of art. Analysis of earlier masters. 12 illustrations. 80pp. of text. 5⅜ x 8½. 23411-8 Pa. $4.95

ANIMALS: 1,419 Copyright-Free Illustrations of Mammals, Birds, Fish, Insects, etc., Jim Harter (ed.). Clear wood engravings present, in extremely lifelike poses, over 1,000 species of animals. One of the most extensive pictorial sourcebooks of its kind. Captions. Index. 284pp. 9 x 12. 23766-4 Pa. $14.95

CELTIC ART: The Methods of Construction, George Bain. Simple geometric techniques for making Celtic interlacements, spirals, Kells-type initials, animals, humans, etc. Over 500 illustrations. 160pp. 9 x 12. (USO) 22923-8 Pa. $9.95

AN ATLAS OF ANATOMY FOR ARTISTS, Fritz Schider. Most thorough reference work on art anatomy in the world. Hundreds of illustrations, including selections from works by Vesalius, Leonardo, Goya, Ingres, Michelangelo, others. 593 illustrations. 192pp. 7⅛ x 10¼. 20241-0 Pa. $9.95

CELTIC HAND STROKE-BY-STROKE (Irish Half-Uncial from "The Book of Kells"): An Arthur Baker Calligraphy Manual, Arthur Baker. Complete guide to creating each letter of the alphabet in distinctive Celtic manner. Covers hand position, strokes, pens, inks, paper, more. Illustrated. 48pp. 8¼ x 11. 24336-2 Pa. $3.95

EASY ORIGAMI, John Montroll. Charming collection of 32 projects (hat, cup, pelican, piano, swan, many more) specially designed for the novice origami hobbyist. Clearly illustrated easy-to-follow instructions insure that even beginning papercrafters will achieve successful results. 48pp. 8¼ x 11. 27298-2 Pa. $3.50

THE COMPLETE BOOK OF BIRDHOUSE CONSTRUCTION FOR WOODWORKERS, Scott D. Campbell. Detailed instructions, illustrations, tables. Also data on bird habitat and instinct patterns. Bibliography. 3 tables. 63 illustrations in 15 figures. 48pp. 5¼ x 8½. 24407-5 Pa. $2.50

BLOOMINGDALE'S ILLUSTRATED 1886 CATALOG: Fashions, Dry Goods and Housewares, Bloomingdale Brothers. Famed merchants' extremely rare catalog depicting about 1,700 products: clothing, housewares, firearms, dry goods, jewelry, more. Invaluable for dating, identifying vintage items. Also, copyright-free graphics for artists, designers. Co-published with Henry Ford Museum & Greenfield Village. 160pp. 8¼ x 11. 25780-0 Pa. $10.95

HISTORIC COSTUME IN PICTURES, Braun & Schneider. Over 1,450 costumed figures in clearly detailed engravings–from dawn of civilization to end of 19th century. Captions. Many folk costumes. 256pp. 8⅜ x 11¾. 23150-X Pa. $12.95

STICKLEY CRAFTSMAN FURNITURE CATALOGS, Gustav Stickley and L. & J. G. Stickley. Beautiful, functional furniture in two authentic catalogs from 1910. 594 illustrations, including 277 photos, show settles, rockers, armchairs, reclining chairs, bookcases, desks, tables. 183pp. 6½ x 9¼. 23838-5 Pa. $11.95

AMERICAN LOCOMOTIVES IN HISTORIC PHOTOGRAPHS: 1858 to 1949, Ron Ziel (ed.). A rare collection of 126 meticulously detailed official photographs, called "builder portraits," of American locomotives that majestically chronicle the rise of steam locomotive power in America. Introduction. Detailed captions. xi + 129pp. 9 x 12. 27393-8 Pa. $13.95

AMERICA'S LIGHTHOUSES: An Illustrated History, Francis Ross Holland, Jr. Delightfully written, profusely illustrated fact-filled survey of over 200 American lighthouses since 1716. History, anecdotes, technological advances, more. 240pp. 8 x 10¾. 25576-X Pa. $12.95

TOWARDS A NEW ARCHITECTURE, Le Corbusier. Pioneering manifesto by founder of "International School." Technical and aesthetic theories, views of industry, economics, relation of form to function, "mass-production split" and much more. Profusely illustrated. 320pp. 6⅛ x 9¼. (USO) 25023-7 Pa. $9.95

HOW THE OTHER HALF LIVES, Jacob Riis. Famous journalistic record, exposing poverty and degradation of New York slums around 1900, by major social reformer. 100 striking and influential photographs. 233pp. 10 x 7⅞. 22012-5 Pa. $11.95

FRUIT KEY AND TWIG KEY TO TREES AND SHRUBS, William M. Harlow. One of the handiest and most widely used identification aids. Fruit key covers 120 deciduous and evergreen species; twig key 160 deciduous species. Easily used. Over 300 photographs. 126pp. 5⅜ x 8½. 20511-8 Pa. $3.95

COMMON BIRD SONGS, Dr. Donald J. Borror. Songs of 60 most common U.S. birds: robins, sparrows, cardinals, bluejays, finches, more–arranged in order of increasing complexity. Up to 9 variations of songs of each species. Cassette and manual 99911-4 $8.95

ORCHIDS AS HOUSE PLANTS, Rebecca Tyson Northen. Grow cattleyas and many other kinds of orchids–in a window, in a case, or under artificial light. 63 illustrations. 148pp. 5⅜ x 8½. 23261-1 Pa. $5.95

MONSTER MAZES, Dave Phillips. Masterful mazes at four levels of difficulty. Avoid deadly perils and evil creatures to find magical treasures. Solutions for all 32 exciting illustrated puzzles. 48pp. 8¼ x 11. 26005-4 Pa. $2.95

MOZART'S DON GIOVANNI (DOVER OPERA LIBRETTO SERIES), Wolfgang Amadeus Mozart. Introduced and translated by Ellen H. Bleiler. Standard Italian libretto, with complete English translation. Convenient and thoroughly portable–an ideal companion for reading along with a recording or the performance itself. Introduction. List of characters. Plot summary. 121pp. 5¼ x 8½. 24944-1 Pa. $3.95

TECHNICAL MANUAL AND DICTIONARY OF CLASSICAL BALLET, Gail Grant. Defines, explains, comments on steps, movements, poses and concepts. 15-page pictorial section. Basic book for student, viewer. 127pp. 5⅜ x 8½. 21843-0 Pa. $4.95

BRASS INSTRUMENTS: Their History and Development, Anthony Baines. Authoritative, updated survey of the evolution of trumpets, trombones, bugles, cornets, French horns, tubas and other brass wind instruments. Over 140 illustrations and 48 music examples. Corrected and updated by author. New preface. Bibliography. 320pp. 5⅜ x 8½. 27574-4 Pa. $9.95

HOLLYWOOD GLAMOR PORTRAITS, John Kobal (ed.). 145 photos from 1926-49. Harlow, Gable, Bogart, Bacall; 94 stars in all. Full background on photographers, technical aspects. 160pp. 8⅜ x 11¼. 23352-9 Pa. $12.95

MAX AND MORITZ, Wilhelm Busch. Great humor classic in both German and English. Also 10 other works: "Cat and Mouse," "Plisch and Plumm," etc. 216pp. 5⅜ x 8½. 20181-3 Pa. $6.95

THE RAVEN AND OTHER FAVORITE POEMS, Edgar Allan Poe. Over 40 of the author's most memorable poems: "The Bells," "Ulalume," "Israfel," "To Helen," "The Conqueror Worm," "Eldorado," "Annabel Lee," many more. Alphabetic lists of titles and first lines. 64pp. 5 3/16 x 8¼. 26685-0 Pa. $1.00

PERSONAL MEMOIRS OF U. S. GRANT, Ulysses Simpson Grant. Intelligent, deeply moving firsthand account of Civil War campaigns, considered by many the finest military memoirs ever written. Includes letters, historic photographs, maps and more. 528pp. 6⅛ x 9¼. 28587-1 Pa. $12.95

AMULETS AND SUPERSTITIONS, E. A. Wallis Budge. Comprehensive discourse on origin, powers of amulets in many ancient cultures: Arab, Persian Babylonian, Assyrian, Egyptian, Gnostic, Hebrew, Phoenician, Syriac, etc. Covers cross, swastika, crucifix, seals, rings, stones, etc. 584pp. 5⅜ x 8½. 23573-4 Pa. $12.95

RUSSIAN STORIES/PYCCKNE PACCKA3bl: A Dual-Language Book, edited by Gleb Struve. Twelve tales by such masters as Chekhov, Tolstoy, Dostoevsky, Pushkin, others. Excellent word-for-word English translations on facing pages, plus teaching and study aids, Russian/English vocabulary, biographical/critical introductions, more. 416pp. 5⅜ x 8½. 26244-8 Pa. $9.95

PHILADELPHIA THEN AND NOW: 60 Sites Photographed in the Past and Present, Kenneth Finkel and Susan Oyama. Rare photographs of City Hall, Logan Square, Independence Hall, Betsy Ross House, other landmarks juxtaposed with contemporary views. Captures changing face of historic city. Introduction. Captions. 128pp. 8¼ x 11. 25790-8 Pa. $9.95

AIA ARCHITECTURAL GUIDE TO NASSAU AND SUFFOLK COUNTIES, LONG ISLAND, The American Institute of Architects, Long Island Chapter, and the Society for the Preservation of Long Island Antiquities. Comprehensive, well-researched and generously illustrated volume brings to life over three centuries of Long Island's great architectural heritage. More than 240 photographs with authoritative, extensively detailed captions. 176pp. 8¼ x 11. 26946-9 Pa. $14.95

NORTH AMERICAN INDIAN LIFE: Customs and Traditions of 23 Tribes, Elsie Clews Parsons (ed.). 27 fictionalized essays by noted anthropologists examine religion, customs, government, additional facets of life among the Winnebago, Crow, Zuni, Eskimo, other tribes. 480pp. 6⅛ x 9¼. 27377-6 Pa. $10.95

FRANK LLOYD WRIGHT'S HOLLYHOCK HOUSE, Donald Hoffmann. Lavishly illustrated, carefully documented study of one of Wright's most controversial residential designs. Over 120 photographs, floor plans, elevations, etc. Detailed perceptive text by noted Wright scholar. Index. 128pp. 9¼ x 10¾. 27133-1 Pa. $11.95

THE MALE AND FEMALE FIGURE IN MOTION: 60 Classic Photographic Sequences, Eadweard Muybridge. 60 true-action photographs of men and women walking, running, climbing, bending, turning, etc., reproduced from rare 19th-century masterpiece. vi + 121pp. 9 x 12. 24745-7 Pa. $10.95

1001 QUESTIONS ANSWERED ABOUT THE SEASHORE, N. J. Berrill and Jacquelyn Berrill. Queries answered about dolphins, sea snails, sponges, starfish, fishes, shore birds, many others. Covers appearance, breeding, growth, feeding, much more. 305pp. 5¼ x 8¼. 23366-9 Pa. $8.95

GUIDE TO OWL WATCHING IN NORTH AMERICA, Donald S. Heintzelman. Superb guide offers complete data and descriptions of 19 species: barn owl, screech owl, snowy owl, many more. Expert coverage of owl-watching equipment, conservation, migrations and invasions, etc. Guide to observing sites. 84 illustrations. xiii + 193pp. 5⅜ x 8½. 27344-X Pa. $8.95

MEDICINAL AND OTHER USES OF NORTH AMERICAN PLANTS: A Historical Survey with Special Reference to the Eastern Indian Tribes, Charlotte Erichsen-Brown. Chronological historical citations document 500 years of usage of plants, trees, shrubs native to eastern Canada, northeastern U.S. Also complete identifying information. 343 illustrations. 544pp. 6½ x 9¼. 25951-X Pa. $12.95

STORYBOOK MAZES, Dave Phillips. 23 stories and mazes on two-page spreads: Wizard of Oz, Treasure Island, Robin Hood, etc. Solutions. 64pp. 8¼ x 11. 23628-5 Pa. $2.95

NEGRO FOLK MUSIC, U.S.A., Harold Courlander. Noted folklorist's scholarly yet readable analysis of rich and varied musical tradition. Includes authentic versions of over 40 folk songs. Valuable bibliography and discography. xi + 324pp. 5⅜ x 8½. 27350-4 Pa. $9.95

MOVIE-STAR PORTRAITS OF THE FORTIES, John Kobal (ed.). 163 glamor, studio photos of 106 stars of the 1940s: Rita Hayworth, Ava Gardner, Marlon Brando, Clark Gable, many more. 176pp. 8⅜ x 11¼. 23546-7 Pa. $12.95

BENCHLEY LOST AND FOUND, Robert Benchley. Finest humor from early 30s, about pet peeves, child psychologists, post office and others. Mostly unavailable elsewhere. 73 illustrations by Peter Arno and others. 183pp. 5⅜ x 8½. 22410-4 Pa. $6.95

YEKL and THE IMPORTED BRIDEGROOM AND OTHER STORIES OF YIDDISH NEW YORK, Abraham Cahan. Film Hester Street based on Yekl (1896). Novel, other stories among first about Jewish immigrants on N.Y.'s East Side. 240pp. 5⅜ x 8½. 22427-9 Pa. $6.95

SELECTED POEMS, Walt Whitman. Generous sampling from *Leaves of Grass*. Twenty-four poems include "I Hear America Singing," "Song of the Open Road," "I Sing the Body Electric," "When Lilacs Last in the Dooryard Bloom'd," "O Captain! My Captain!"–all reprinted from an authoritative edition. Lists of titles and first lines. 128pp. 5$\frac{3}{16}$ x 8¼. 26878-0 Pa. $1.00

MY BONDAGE AND MY FREEDOM, Frederick Douglass. Born a slave, Douglass became outspoken force in antislavery movement. The best of Douglass' autobiographies. Graphic description of slave life. 464pp. 5⅜ x 8½. 22457-0 Pa. $8.95

FOLLOWING THE EQUATOR: A Journey Around the World, Mark Twain. Fascinating humorous account of 1897 voyage to Hawaii, Australia, India, New Zealand, etc. Ironic, bemused reports on peoples, customs, climate, flora and fauna, politics, much more. 197 illustrations. 720pp. 5⅜ x 8½. 26113-1 Pa. $15.95

THE PEOPLE CALLED SHAKERS, Edward D. Andrews. Definitive study of Shakers: origins, beliefs, practices, dances, social organization, furniture and crafts, etc. 33 illustrations. 351pp. 5⅜ x 8½. 21081-2 Pa. $8.95

THE MYTHS OF GREECE AND ROME, H. A. Guerber. A classic of mythology, generously illustrated, long prized for its simple, graphic, accurate retelling of the principal myths of Greece and Rome, and for its commentary on their origins and significance. With 64 illustrations by Michelangelo, Raphael, Titian, Rubens, Canova, Bernini and others. 480pp. 5⅜ x 8½. 27584-1 Pa. $9.95

PSYCHOLOGY OF MUSIC, Carl E. Seashore. Classic work discusses music as a medium from psychological viewpoint. Clear treatment of physical acoustics, auditory apparatus, sound perception, development of musical skills, nature of musical feeling, host of other topics. 88 figures. 408pp. 5⅜ x 8½. 21851-1 Pa. $11.95

THE PHILOSOPHY OF HISTORY, Georg W. Hegel. Great classic of Western thought develops concept that history is not chance but rational process, the evolution of freedom. 457pp. 5⅜ x 8½. 20112-0 Pa. $9.95

THE BOOK OF TEA, Kakuzo Okakura. Minor classic of the Orient: entertaining, charming explanation, interpretation of traditional Japanese culture in terms of tea ceremony. 94pp. 5⅜ x 8½. 20070-1 Pa. $3.95

LIFE IN ANCIENT EGYPT, Adolf Erman. Fullest, most thorough, detailed older account with much not in more recent books, domestic life, religion, magic, medicine, commerce, much more. Many illustrations reproduce tomb paintings, carvings, hieroglyphs, etc. 597pp. 5⅜ x 8½. 22632-8 Pa. $12.95

SUNDIALS, Their Theory and Construction, Albert Waugh. Far and away the best, most thorough coverage of ideas, mathematics concerned, types, construction, adjusting anywhere. Simple, nontechnical treatment allows even children to build several of these dials. Over 100 illustrations. 230pp. 5⅜ x 8½. 22947-5 Pa. $8.95

DYNAMICS OF FLUIDS IN POROUS MEDIA, Jacob Bear. For advanced students of ground water hydrology, soil mechanics and physics, drainage and irrigation engineering, and more. 335 illustrations. Exercises, with answers. 784pp. 6⅛ x 9¼. 65675-6 Pa. $19.95

SONGS OF EXPERIENCE: Facsimile Reproduction with 26 Plates in Full Color, William Blake. 26 full-color plates from a rare 1826 edition. Includes "The Tyger," "London," "Holy Thursday," and other poems. Printed text of poems. 48pp. 5¼ x 7. 24636-1 Pa. $4.95

OLD-TIME VIGNETTES IN FULL COLOR, Carol Belanger Grafton (ed.). Over 390 charming, often sentimental illustrations, selected from archives of Victorian graphics–pretty women posing, children playing, food, flowers, kittens and puppies, smiling cherubs, birds and butterflies, much more. All copyright-free. 48pp. 9¼ x 12¼. 27269-9 Pa. $7.95

PERSPECTIVE FOR ARTISTS, Rex Vicat Cole. Depth, perspective of sky and sea, shadows, much more, not usually covered. 391 diagrams, 81 reproductions of drawings and paintings. 279pp. 5⅜ x 8½. 22487-2 Pa. $7.95

DRAWING THE LIVING FIGURE, Joseph Sheppard. Innovative approach to artistic anatomy focuses on specifics of surface anatomy, rather than muscles and bones. Over 170 drawings of live models in front, back and side views, and in widely varying poses. Accompanying diagrams. 177 illustrations. Introduction. Index. 144pp. 8⅜ x11¼. 26723-7 Pa. $8.95

GOTHIC AND OLD ENGLISH ALPHABETS: 100 Complete Fonts, Dan X. Solo. Add power, elegance to posters, signs, other graphics with 100 stunning copyright-free alphabets: Blackstone, Dolbey, Germania, 97 more–including many lower-case, numerals, punctuation marks. 104pp. 8⅛ x 11. 24695-7 Pa. $8.95

HOW TO DO BEADWORK, Mary White. Fundamental book on craft from simple projects to five-bead chains and woven works. 106 illustrations. 142pp. 5⅜ x 8. 20697-1 Pa. $4.95

THE BOOK OF WOOD CARVING, Charles Marshall Sayers. Finest book for beginners discusses fundamentals and offers 34 designs. "Absolutely first rate . . . well thought out and well executed."–E. J. Tangerman. 118pp. 7¾ x 10⅝. 23654-4 Pa. $6.95

ILLUSTRATED CATALOG OF CIVIL WAR MILITARY GOODS: Union Army Weapons, Insignia, Uniform Accessories, and Other Equipment, Schuyler, Hartley, and Graham. Rare, profusely illustrated 1846 catalog includes Union Army uniform and dress regulations, arms and ammunition, coats, insignia, flags, swords, rifles, etc. 226 illustrations. 160pp. 9 x 12. 24939-5 Pa. $10.95

WOMEN'S FASHIONS OF THE EARLY 1900s: An Unabridged Republication of "New York Fashions, 1909," National Cloak & Suit Co. Rare catalog of mail-order fashions documents women's and children's clothing styles shortly after the turn of the century. Captions offer full descriptions, prices. Invaluable resource for fashion, costume historians. Approximately 725 illustrations. 128pp. 8⅜ x 11¼. 27276-1 Pa. $11.95

THE 1912 AND 1915 GUSTAV STICKLEY FURNITURE CATALOGS, Gustav Stickley. With over 200 detailed illustrations and descriptions, these two catalogs are essential reading and reference materials and identification guides for Stickley furniture. Captions cite materials, dimensions and prices. 112pp. 6½ x 9¼. 26676-1 Pa. $9.95

EARLY AMERICAN LOCOMOTIVES, John H. White, Jr. Finest locomotive engravings from early 19th century: historical (1804–74), main-line (after 1870), special, foreign, etc. 147 plates. 142pp. 11⅜ x 8¼. 22772-3 Pa. $10.95

THE TALL SHIPS OF TODAY IN PHOTOGRAPHS, Frank O. Braynard. Lavishly illustrated tribute to nearly 100 majestic contemporary sailing vessels: Amerigo Vespucci, Clearwater, Constitution, Eagle, Mayflower, Sea Cloud, Victory, many more. Authoritative captions provide statistics, background on each ship. 190 black-and-white photographs and illustrations. Introduction. 128pp. 8⅞ x 11¾. 27163-3 Pa. $14.95

EARLY NINETEENTH-CENTURY CRAFTS AND TRADES, Peter Stockham (ed.). Extremely rare 1807 volume describes to youngsters the crafts and trades of the day: brickmaker, weaver, dressmaker, bookbinder, ropemaker, saddler, many more. Quaint prose, charming illustrations for each craft. 20 black-and-white line illustrations. 192pp. 4⅝ x 6. 27293-1 Pa. $4.95

VICTORIAN FASHIONS AND COSTUMES FROM HARPER'S BAZAR, 1867–1898, Stella Blum (ed.). Day costumes, evening wear, sports clothes, shoes, hats, other accessories in over 1,000 detailed engravings. 320pp. 9⅜ x 12¼. 22990-4 Pa. $15.95

GUSTAV STICKLEY, THE CRAFTSMAN, Mary Ann Smith. Superb study surveys broad scope of Stickley's achievement, especially in architecture. Design philosophy, rise and fall of the Craftsman empire, descriptions and floor plans for many Craftsman houses, more. 86 black-and-white halftones. 31 line illustrations. Introduction 208pp. 6½ x 9¼. 27210-9 Pa. $9.95

THE LONG ISLAND RAIL ROAD IN EARLY PHOTOGRAPHS, Ron Ziel. Over 220 rare photos, informative text document origin (1844) and development of rail service on Long Island. Vintage views of early trains, locomotives, stations, passengers, crews, much more. Captions. 8⅞ x 11¾. 26301-0 Pa. $13.95

THE BOOK OF OLD SHIPS: From Egyptian Galleys to Clipper Ships, Henry B. Culver. Superb, authoritative history of sailing vessels, with 80 magnificent line illustrations. Galley, bark, caravel, longship, whaler, many more. Detailed, informative text on each vessel by noted naval historian. Introduction. 256pp. 5⅜ x 8½. 27332-6 Pa. $7.95

TEN BOOKS ON ARCHITECTURE, Vitruvius. The most important book ever written on architecture. Early Roman aesthetics, technology, classical orders, site selection, all other aspects. Morgan translation. 331pp. 5⅜ x 8½. 20645-9 Pa. $8.95

THE HUMAN FIGURE IN MOTION, Eadweard Muybridge. More than 4,500 stopped-action photos, in action series, showing undraped men, women, children jumping, lying down, throwing, sitting, wrestling, carrying, etc. 390pp. 7⅞ x 10⅝. 20204-6 Clothbd. $27.95

TREES OF THE EASTERN AND CENTRAL UNITED STATES AND CANADA, William M. Harlow. Best one-volume guide to 140 trees. Full descriptions, woodlore, range, etc. Over 600 illustrations. Handy size. 288pp. 4½ x 6⅜. 20395-6 Pa. $6.95

SONGS OF WESTERN BIRDS, Dr. Donald J. Borror. Complete song and call repertoire of 60 western species, including flycatchers, juncoes, cactus wrens, many more–includes fully illustrated booklet. Cassette and manual 99913-0 $8.95

GROWING AND USING HERBS AND SPICES, Milo Miloradovich. Versatile handbook provides all the information needed for cultivation and use of all the herbs and spices available in North America. 4 illustrations. Index. Glossary. 236pp. 5⅜ x 8½. 25058-X Pa. $7.95

BIG BOOK OF MAZES AND LABYRINTHS, Walter Shepherd. 50 mazes and labyrinths in all–classical, solid, ripple, and more–in one great volume. Perfect inexpensive puzzler for clever youngsters. Full solutions. 112pp. 8⅛ x 11. 22951-3 Pa. $4.95

PIANO TUNING, J. Cree Fischer. Clearest, best book for beginner, amateur. Simple repairs, raising dropped notes, tuning by easy method of flattened fifths. No previous skills needed. 4 illustrations. 201pp. 5⅜ x 8½. 23267-0 Pa. $6.95

A SOURCE BOOK IN THEATRICAL HISTORY, A. M. Nagler. Contemporary observers on acting, directing, make-up, costuming, stage props, machinery, scene design, from Ancient Greece to Chekhov. 611pp. 5⅜ x 8½. 20515-0 Pa. $12.95

THE COMPLETE NONSENSE OF EDWARD LEAR, Edward Lear. All nonsense limericks, zany alphabets, Owl and Pussycat, songs, nonsense botany, etc., illustrated by Lear. Total of 320pp. 5⅜ x 8½. (USO) 20167-8 Pa. $7.95

VICTORIAN PARLOUR POETRY: An Annotated Anthology, Michael R. Turner. 117 gems by Longfellow, Tennyson, Browning, many lesser-known poets. "The Village Blacksmith," "Curfew Must Not Ring Tonight," "Only a Baby Small," dozens more, often difficult to find elsewhere. Index of poets, titles, first lines. xxiii + 325pp. 5⅝ x 8¼. 27044-0 Pa. $8.95

DUBLINERS, James Joyce. Fifteen stories offer vivid, tightly focused observations of the lives of Dublin's poorer classes. At least one, "The Dead," is considered a masterpiece. Reprinted complete and unabridged from standard edition. 160pp. 5$\frac{3}{16}$ x 8¼. 26870-5 Pa. $1.00

THE HAUNTED MONASTERY and THE CHINESE MAZE MURDERS, Robert van Gulik. Two full novels by van Gulik, set in 7th-century China, continue adventures of Judge Dee and his companions. An evil Taoist monastery, seemingly supernatural events; overgrown topiary maze hides strange crimes. 27 illustrations. 328pp. 5⅜ x 8½. 23502-5 Pa. $8.95

THE BOOK OF THE SACRED MAGIC OF ABRAMELIN THE MAGE, translated by S. MacGregor Mathers. Medieval manuscript of ceremonial magic. Basic document in Aleister Crowley, Golden Dawn groups. 268pp. 5⅜ x 8½. 23211-5 Pa. $9.95

NEW RUSSIAN-ENGLISH AND ENGLISH-RUSSIAN DICTIONARY, M. A. O'Brien. This is a remarkably handy Russian dictionary, containing a surprising amount of information, including over 70,000 entries. 366pp. 4½ x 6⅛. 20208-9 Pa. $9.95

HISTORIC HOMES OF THE AMERICAN PRESIDENTS, Second, Revised Edition, Irvin Haas. A traveler's guide to American Presidential homes, most open to the public, depicting and describing homes occupied by every American President from George Washington to George Bush. With visiting hours, admission charges, travel routes. 175 photographs. Index. 160pp. 8¼ x 11. 26751-2 Pa. $11.95

NEW YORK IN THE FORTIES, Andreas Feininger. 162 brilliant photographs by the well-known photographer, formerly with *Life* magazine. Commuters, shoppers, Times Square at night, much else from city at its peak. Captions by John von Hartz. 181pp. 9¼ x 10¾. 23585-8 Pa. $12.95

INDIAN SIGN LANGUAGE, William Tomkins. Over 525 signs developed by Sioux and other tribes. Written instructions and diagrams. Also 290 pictographs. 111pp. 6⅛ x 9¼. 22029-X Pa. $3.95

ANATOMY: A Complete Guide for Artists, Joseph Sheppard. A master of figure drawing shows artists how to render human anatomy convincingly. Over 460 illustrations. 224pp. 8⅜ x 11¼. 27279-6 Pa. $11.95

MEDIEVAL CALLIGRAPHY: Its History and Technique, Marc Drogin. Spirited history, comprehensive instruction manual covers 13 styles (ca. 4th century thru 15th). Excellent photographs; directions for duplicating medieval techniques with modern tools. 224pp. 8⅜ x 11¼. 26142-5 Pa. $12.95

DRIED FLOWERS: How to Prepare Them, Sarah Whitlock and Martha Rankin. Complete instructions on how to use silica gel, meal and borax, perlite aggregate, sand and borax, glycerine and water to create attractive permanent flower arrangements. 12 illustrations. 32pp. 5⅜ x 8½. 21802-3 Pa. $1.00

EASY-TO-MAKE BIRD FEEDERS FOR WOODWORKERS, Scott D. Campbell. Detailed, simple-to-use guide for designing, constructing, caring for and using feeders. Text, illustrations for 12 classic and contemporary designs. 96pp. 5⅜ x 8½. 25847-5 Pa. $3.95

SCOTTISH WONDER TALES FROM MYTH AND LEGEND, Donald A. Mackenzie. 16 lively tales tell of giants rumbling down mountainsides, of a magic wand that turns stone pillars into warriors, of gods and goddesses, evil hags, powerful forces and more. 240pp. 5⅜ x 8½. 29677-6 Pa. $6.95

THE HISTORY OF UNDERCLOTHES, C. Willett Cunnington and Phyllis Cunnington. Fascinating, well-documented survey covering six centuries of English undergarments, enhanced with over 100 illustrations: 12th-century laced-up bodice, footed long drawers (1795), 19th-century bustles, 19th-century corsets for men, Victorian "bust improvers," much more. 272pp. 5⅜ x 8¼. 27124-2 Pa. $9.95

ARTS AND CRAFTS FURNITURE: The Complete Brooks Catalog of 1912, Brooks Manufacturing Co. Photos and detailed descriptions of more than 150 now very collectible furniture designs from the Arts and Crafts movement depict davenports, settees, buffets, desks, tables, chairs, bedsteads, dressers and more, all built of solid, quarter-sawed oak. Invaluable for students and enthusiasts of antiques, Americana and the decorative arts. 80pp. 6½ x 9¼. 27471-3 Pa. $8.95

HOW WE INVENTED THE AIRPLANE: An Illustrated History, Orville Wright. Fascinating firsthand account covers early experiments, construction of planes and motors, first flights, much more. Introduction and commentary by Fred C. Kelly. 76 photographs. 96pp. 8¼ x 11. 25662-6 Pa. $8.95

THE ARTS OF THE SAILOR: Knotting, Splicing and Ropework, Hervey Garrett Smith. Indispensable shipboard reference covers tools, basic knots and useful hitches; handsewing and canvas work, more. Over 100 illustrations. Delightful reading for sea lovers. 256pp. 5⅜ x 8½. 26440-8 Pa. $7.95

FRANK LLOYD WRIGHT'S FALLINGWATER: The House and Its History, Second, Revised Edition, Donald Hoffmann. A total revision–both in text and illustrations–of the standard document on Fallingwater, the boldest, most personal architectural statement of Wright's mature years, updated with valuable new material from the recently opened Frank Lloyd Wright Archives. "Fascinating"–*The New York Times*. 116 illustrations. 128pp. 9¼ x 10¾. 27430-6 Pa. $12.95

PHOTOGRAPHIC SKETCHBOOK OF THE CIVIL WAR, Alexander Gardner. 100 photos taken on field during the Civil War. Famous shots of Manassas Harper's Ferry, Lincoln, Richmond, slave pens, etc. 244pp. 10⅝ x 8¼. 22731-6 Pa. $9.95

FIVE ACRES AND INDEPENDENCE, Maurice G. Kains. Great back-to-the-land classic explains basics of self-sufficient farming. The one book to get. 95 illustrations. 397pp. 5⅜ x 8½. 20974-1 Pa. $7.95

SONGS OF EASTERN BIRDS, Dr. Donald J. Borror. Songs and calls of 60 species most common to eastern U.S.: warblers, woodpeckers, flycatchers, thrushes, larks, many more in high-quality recording. Cassette and manual 99912-2 $9.95

A MODERN HERBAL, Margaret Grieve. Much the fullest, most exact, most useful compilation of herbal material. Gigantic alphabetical encyclopedia, from aconite to zedoary, gives botanical information, medical properties, folklore, economic uses, much else. Indispensable to serious reader. 161 illustrations. 888pp. 6½ x 9¼. 2-vol. set. (USO) Vol. I: 22798-7 Pa. $9.95
Vol. II: 22799-5 Pa. $9.95

HIDDEN TREASURE MAZE BOOK, Dave Phillips. Solve 34 challenging mazes accompanied by heroic tales of adventure. Evil dragons, people-eating plants, blood-thirsty giants, many more dangerous adversaries lurk at every twist and turn. 34 mazes, stories, solutions. 48pp. 8¼ x 11. 24566-7 Pa. $2.95

LETTERS OF W. A. MOZART, Wolfgang A. Mozart. Remarkable letters show bawdy wit, humor, imagination, musical insights, contemporary musical world; includes some letters from Leopold Mozart. 276pp. 5⅜ x 8½. 22859-2 Pa. $7.95

BASIC PRINCIPLES OF CLASSICAL BALLET, Agrippina Vaganova. Great Russian theoretician, teacher explains methods for teaching classical ballet. 118 illustrations. 175pp. 5⅜ x 8½. 22036-2 Pa. $5.95

THE JUMPING FROG, Mark Twain. Revenge edition. The original story of The Celebrated Jumping Frog of Calaveras County, a hapless French translation, and Twain's hilarious "retranslation" from the French. 12 illustrations. 66pp. 5⅜ x 8½. 22686-7 Pa. $3.95

BEST REMEMBERED POEMS, Martin Gardner (ed.). The 126 poems in this superb collection of 19th- and 20th-century British and American verse range from Shelley's "To a Skylark" to the impassioned "Renascence" of Edna St. Vincent Millay and to Edward Lear's whimsical "The Owl and the Pussycat." 224pp. 5⅜ x 8½. 27165-X Pa. $5.95

COMPLETE SONNETS, William Shakespeare. Over 150 exquisite poems deal with love, friendship, the tyranny of time, beauty's evanescence, death and other themes in language of remarkable power, precision and beauty. Glossary of archaic terms. 80pp. 5³⁄₁₆ x 8¼. 26686-9 Pa. $1.00

BODIES IN A BOOKSHOP, R. T. Campbell. Challenging mystery of blackmail and murder with ingenious plot and superbly drawn characters. In the best tradition of British suspense fiction. 192pp. 5⅜ x 8½. 24720-1 Pa. $6.95

THE WIT AND HUMOR OF OSCAR WILDE, Alvin Redman (ed.). More than 1,000 ripostes, paradoxes, wisecracks: Work is the curse of the drinking classes; I can resist everything except temptation; etc. 258pp. 5⅜ x 8½. 20602-5 Pa. $5.95

SHAKESPEARE LEXICON AND QUOTATION DICTIONARY, Alexander Schmidt. Full definitions, locations, shades of meaning in every word in plays and poems. More than 50,000 exact quotations. 1,485pp. 6½ x 9¼. 2-vol. set.
Vol. 1: 22726-X Pa. $17.95
Vol. 2: 22727-8 Pa. $17.95

SELECTED POEMS, Emily Dickinson. Over 100 best-known, best-loved poems by one of America's foremost poets, reprinted from authoritative early editions. No comparable edition at this price. Index of first lines. 64pp. 5³⁄₁₆ x 8¼.
26466-1 Pa. $1.00

CELEBRATED CASES OF JUDGE DEE (DEE GOONG AN), translated by Robert van Gulik. Authentic 18th-century Chinese detective novel; Dee and associates solve three interlocked cases. Led to van Gulik's own stories with same characters. Extensive introduction. 9 illustrations. 237pp. 5⅜ x 8½. 23337-5 Pa. $7.95

THE MALLEUS MALEFICARUM OF KRAMER AND SPRENGER, translated by Montague Summers. Full text of most important witchhunter's "bible," used by both Catholics and Protestants. 278pp. 6⅝ x 10. 22802-9 Pa. $12.95

SPANISH STORIES/CUENTOS ESPAÑOLES: A Dual-Language Book, Angel Flores (ed.). Unique format offers 13 great stories in Spanish by Cervantes, Borges, others. Faithful English translations on facing pages. 352pp. 5⅜ x 8½.
25399-6 Pa. $8.95

THE CHICAGO WORLD'S FAIR OF 1893: A Photographic Record, Stanley Appelbaum (ed.). 128 rare photos show 200 buildings, Beaux-Arts architecture, Midway, original Ferris Wheel, Edison's kinetoscope, more. Architectural emphasis; full text. 116pp. 8¼ x 11. 23990-X Pa. $9.95

OLD QUEENS, N.Y., IN EARLY PHOTOGRAPHS, Vincent F. Seyfried and William Asadorian. Over 160 rare photographs of Maspeth, Jamaica, Jackson Heights, and other areas. Vintage views of DeWitt Clinton mansion, 1939 World's Fair and more. Captions. 192pp. 8⅞ x 11. 26358-4 Pa. $12.95

CAPTURED BY THE INDIANS: 15 Firsthand Accounts, 1750-1870, Frederick Drimmer. Astounding true historical accounts of grisly torture, bloody conflicts, relentless pursuits, miraculous escapes and more, by people who lived to tell the tale. 384pp. 5⅜ x 8½. 24901-8 Pa. $8.95

THE WORLD'S GREAT SPEECHES, Lewis Copeland and Lawrence W. Lamm (eds.). Vast collection of 278 speeches of Greeks to 1970. Powerful and effective models; unique look at history. 842pp. 5⅜ x 8½. 20468-5 Pa. $14.95

THE BOOK OF THE SWORD, Sir Richard F. Burton. Great Victorian scholar/adventurer's eloquent, erudite history of the "queen of weapons"–from prehistory to early Roman Empire. Evolution and development of early swords, variations (sabre, broadsword, cutlass, scimitar, etc.), much more. 336pp. 6⅛ x 9¼.
25434-8 Pa. $9.95

AUTOBIOGRAPHY: The Story of My Experiments with Truth, Mohandas K. Gandhi. Boyhood, legal studies, purification, the growth of the Satyagraha (nonviolent protest) movement. Critical, inspiring work of the man responsible for the freedom of India. 480pp. 5⅜ x 8½. (USO) 24593-4 Pa. $8.95

CELTIC MYTHS AND LEGENDS, T. W. Rolleston. Masterful retelling of Irish and Welsh stories and tales. Cuchulain, King Arthur, Deirdre, the Grail, many more. First paperback edition. 58 full-page illustrations. 512pp. 5⅜ x 8½. 26507-2 Pa. $9.95

THE PRINCIPLES OF PSYCHOLOGY, William James. Famous long course complete, unabridged. Stream of thought, time perception, memory, experimental methods; great work decades ahead of its time. 94 figures. 1,391pp. 5⅜ x 8½. 2-vol. set.
Vol. I: 20381-6 Pa. $13.95
Vol. II: 20382-4 Pa. $14.95

THE WORLD AS WILL AND REPRESENTATION, Arthur Schopenhauer. Definitive English translation of Schopenhauer's life work, correcting more than 1,000 errors, omissions in earlier translations. Translated by E. F. J. Payne. Total of 1,269pp. 5⅜ x 8½. 2-vol. set. Vol. 1: 21761-2 Pa. $12.95
Vol. 2: 21762-0 Pa. $12.95

MAGIC AND MYSTERY IN TIBET, Madame Alexandra David-Neel. Experiences among lamas, magicians, sages, sorcerers, Bonpa wizards. A true psychic discovery. 32 illustrations. 321pp. 5⅜ x 8½. (USO) 22682-4 Pa. $9.95

THE EGYPTIAN BOOK OF THE DEAD, E. A. Wallis Budge. Complete reproduction of Ani's papyrus, finest ever found. Full hieroglyphic text, interlinear transliteration, word-for-word translation, smooth translation. 533pp. 6½ x 9¼.
21866-X Pa. $11.95

MATHEMATICS FOR THE NONMATHEMATICIAN, Morris Kline. Detailed, college-level treatment of mathematics in cultural and historical context, with numerous exercises. Recommended Reading Lists. Tables. Numerous figures. 641pp. 5⅜ x 8½.
24823-2 Pa. $11.95

THEORY OF WING SECTIONS: Including a Summary of Airfoil Data, Ira H. Abbott and A. E. von Doenhoff. Concise compilation of subsonic aerodynamic characteristics of NACA wing sections, plus description of theory. 350pp. of tables. 693pp. 5⅜ x 8½. 60586-8 Pa. $14.95

THE RIME OF THE ANCIENT MARINER, Gustave Doré, S. T. Coleridge. Doré's finest work; 34 plates capture moods, subtleties of poem. Flawless full-size reproductions printed on facing pages with authoritative text of poem. "Beautiful. Simply beautiful."–*Publisher's Weekly*. 77pp. 9¼ x 12. 22305-1 Pa. $7.95

NORTH AMERICAN INDIAN DESIGNS FOR ARTISTS AND CRAFTSPEOPLE, Eva Wilson. Over 360 authentic copyright-free designs adapted from Navajo blankets, Hopi pottery, Sioux buffalo hides, more. Geometrics, symbolic figures, plant and animal motifs, etc. 128pp. 8⅜ x 11. (EUK) 25341-4 Pa. $8.95

SCULPTURE: Principles and Practice, Louis Slobodkin. Step-by-step approach to clay, plaster, metals, stone; classical and modern. 253 drawings, photos. 255pp. 8⅛ x 11.
22960-2 Pa. $11.95